Proceedings of the
Eighth European Conference on
Computer Supported Cooperative Work

ECSCW 2003

Proceedings of the
Eighth European Conference on
Computer Supported Cooperative Work
14–18 September 2003, Helsinki, Finland

Edited by

Kari Kuutti
University of Oulu, Oulu, Finland

Eija Helena Karsten
University of Turku, Turku, Finland

Geraldine Fitzpatrick
Sapient Ltd., London, United Kingdom &
University of Sussex, Brighton, United Kingdom

Paul Dourish
University of California, Irvine, California, U.S.A.

and

Kjeld Schmidt
IT University of Copenhagen, Copenhagen, Denmark

KLUWER ACADEMIC PUBLISHERS
DORDRECHT / BOSTON / LONDON

Library of Congress Cataloging-in-Publication Data

ISBN 1-4020-1573-9

Published by Kluwer Academic Publishers,
P.O. Box 17, 3300 AA Dordrecht, The Netherlands.

Sold and distributed in North, Central and South America
by Kluwer Academic Publishers,
101 Philip Drive, Norwell, MA 02061, U.S.A.

In all other countries, sold and distributed
by Kluwer Academic Publishers,
P.O. Box 322, 3300 AH Dordrecht, The Netherlands.

Printed on acid-free paper

Preface

This volume gathers together the technical papers presented at the 8th European Conference on Computer Supported Cooperative Work (ECSCW), held in Helsinki Finland.

ECSCW is an international forum for multidisciplinary research covering the technical, empirical, and theoretical aspects of collaboration and computer systems.

The 20 papers presented here have been selected via a rigorous reviewing process from 110 submissions. Both the number of submissions and the quality of the selected papers are testimony to the diversity and energy of the CSCW community. We trust that you will find the papers interesting and that they will serve to stimulate further quality work within the community.

The technical papers are complemented by a wider set of activities at ECSCW 2003, including tutorials, workshops, demonstrations, videos, posters and a doctoral colloquium. Together these provide rich opportunities for discussion, learning and exploration of the more recent and novel issues in the field.

This conference could not have taken place without considerable enthusiasm, support and participation, not to mention the hard work of a number of people. In particular, we would like to thank the following:

- The authors, representing over 17 countries and 97 institutions, who submitted a paper. So many submissions of such high quality are the basis of a good conference.

- The members of the program committee who so diligently reviewed and discussed papers. Their collective decisions result in a good scientific program and their feedback to authors strengthens the work of the community.

- All who participated in workshops, tutorials, colloquium, poster sessions, demonstrations and videos to provide a rich and diverse program beyond the papers track.

- The members of the organising committee and others who have contributed to the planning and execution of this conference, a complex and time consuming task requiring an attention to detail that many of us would find too hard.

- The sponsors and supporters of the conference, including the publisher of the proceedings.

We would also like to acknowledge the organisers of the ACM CSCW conferences for their support and close cooperation. Between both conferences, we have been able to establish an annual focus for the promotion of a strong international CSCW research community. These proceedings represent the ECSCW2003 contribution to that community.

Paul Dourish, Geraldine Fitzpatrick, and Kjeld Schmidt

Table of Contents

ECSCW 2003 Conference Committee

Conference co-chairs:
 Kari Kuutti, *University of Oulu, Finland*
 Eija Helena Karsten, *University of Turku, Finland*
Program Co-chairs:
 Geraldine Fitzpatrick, *Sapient London & University of Sussex, UK*
 Paul Dourish, *University of California Irvine, USA*
Organizing Chair:
 Yrjö Engeström, *University of Helsinki, Finland*
Proceedings chair:
 Kjeld Schmidt, *IT University of Copenhagen, Denmark*
Tutorials chairs:
 Jeanette Blomberg, *IBM Research Almaden, USA, & Blekinge University of Technology, Sweden*
 Helena Karasti, *University of Oulu, Finland*
Workshops chairs:
 Matthew Chalmers, *University of Glasgow, UK*
 Marko Nieminen, *Helsinki University of Technology, Finland*
Demonstrations chairs:
 Mike Fraser, *University of Nottingham, UK*
 Samuli Pekkola, *University of Jyväskylä, Finland*
Video chairs:
 Helge Kahler, *Technical University of Chemnitz, Germany*
 Monica Divitini, *University of Trondheim, Norway*
Posters chairs:
 Susanne Bødker, *University of Aarhus*
 Andy Crabtree, *University of Nottingham, UK*

Doctoral colloquium chairs:
 Rob Procter, *University of Edinburgh, UK*
 Bo Helgeson, *Blekinge University of Technology, Sweden*
 Jaakko Virkkunen, *University of Helsinki, Finland*
Liasons:
 North America: Steve Poltrock, *Boeing Corporation*
 Australia: Toni Robertson, *Sydney University of Technology*
 Japan: Keiichi Nakata, *University of Tokyo*

ECSCW 2003 Program Committee

Mark Ackerman, University of Michigan, USA

Liam Bannon, University of Limerick, Ireland

Michel Beaudouin-Lafon, University of Paris-South, France

Olav Bertelsen, University of Aarhus, Denmark

Tora Bikson, RAND, USA

Tone Bratteteig, University of Oslo, Norway

Peter Carstensen, IT University of Denmark

Matthew Chalmers, University of Glasgow, UK

Elizabeth Churchill, FX-Pal, USA

Prasun Dewan, University of North Carolina, USA

Ludwin Fuchs, Boeing, USA

Antonietta Grasso, XRCE, France

Rebecca Grinter, PARC, USA

Tom Gross, Fraunhofer FIT, Germany

Jonathan Grudin, Microsoft Research, USA

Carl Gutwin, University of Saskatchewan, Canada

Christine Halverson, IBM T.J. Watson & Almaden Research Centers, USA

Vidar Hepso, Statoil Research Center, Norway

Jon Hindmarsh, King's College London, UK

Kristina Hook, SICS, Sweden

Victor Kaptelinin, University of Umea

Eija Helena Karsten, University of Turku

Finn Kensing, IT University, Denmark

Michael Koch, Technical University Munich, Germany

Hideaki Kuzuoka, University of Tsukuba, Japan

Paul Luff, King's College London, UK

Peter Mambrey, Fraunhofer-Institut FIT, Germany

Gloria Mark, UC Irvine, USA

Preben Mogensen, University of Aarhus, Denmark

Anders Mørch, University of Bergen, Norway

Keiichi Nakata, University of Tokyo, Japan

Chris Neuwirth, CMU, USA

Volkmar Pipek, University of Bonn, Germany

Wolfgang Prinz, Fraunhofer-Institut FIT, Germany

Rob Procter, University of Edinburgh, UK

Toni Robertson, UTS, Australia

Tom Rodden, University of Nottingham, UK

Yvonne Rogers, University of Sussex, UK

Mark Rouncefield, University of Lancaster, UK

Kjeld Schmidt, IT University of Copenhagen, Denmark

Carla Simone, University of Milano Bicocca, Italy

Lucy Suchman, University of Lancaster, UK

Yngve Sundblad, Royal Institute of Technology, Sweden

Ina Wagner, Technical University of Vienna, Austria

Steven Viller, University of Queensland, Australia

Jaakko Virkkunen, University of Helsinki, Finland

Volker Wulf, IISI, Germany

K. Kuutti, E.H. Karsten, G. Fitzpatrick, P. Dourish and K. Schmidt (eds.), *ECSCW 2003: Proceedings of the Eighth European Conference on Computer Supported Cooperative Work, 14-18 September 2003, Helsinki, Finland*, pp. 1-20.

Pruning the Answer Garden: Knowledge Sharing in Maintenance Engineering

Volkmar Pipek[*] and Volker Wulf[+]

[*]ProSEC, Inst. for Computer Science III, University of Bonn, Roemerstr. 164, 53117 Bonn, and International Institute for Socio-Informatics (IISI), Heerstr. 148, 53111 Bonn, Germany, volkmar.pipek@iisi.de

[+]Institute for Information Systems, University of Siegen, Hölderlinstr. 3, 57068 Siegen, Germany; and: Fraunhofer Institute for Applied Computer Science (FhG-FIT), Schloß Birlinghoven, 53754 Sankt Augustin, Germany, wulf@fit.fhg.de

Abstract. The Answer Garden supports knowledge sharing in two intertwined ways: by making relevant information retrievable and by mediating access to people with knowledge. We present a case study in which the Answer Garden approach was applied to encourage knowledge sharing in maintenance engineering of a steel mill. The results show that the sheer amount of drawings and the long history of changing classification schemes challenge the Answer Garden approach as well as domain-specific needs for technically mediated communication. Moreover, the given division of labor and organizational micro-politics prevent the Answer Garden approach from encouraging knowledge sharing. Based on these experiences, design directions for knowledge management systems are pointed out. Finally, the results of the study are related to a recent controversy on technology support for expertise location.

Introduction

Knowledge is typically distributed among different actors and embodied in various artifacts (cf. Hutchins 1995; Ackerman and Halverson 1998; Davenport and Prusak 1998). There are mainly two - often interrelated - ways to share knowledge among human actors. In the direct way, human actors with different kinds of expertise can communicate and help each other to construct new knowledge. In the mediated way, a knowledgeable actor can create artifacts which may facilitate knowledge construction processes of others.

People who need to learn face usually the problem of finding either the appropriate material or the right expert. Groupware applications can play an important role in tackling these problems. They can support the locating of experts as well as the communication with them. Moreover, groupware may stimulate joint creation and sharing of artifacts which capture aspects of human knowledge.

Within the field of CSCW, the sharing of knowledge in organizations have been studied both empirically and with regard to the design of information systems (cf. Bannon and Kuutti 1996, Ackerman and Halverson 1998, Trigg et al. 1999, Groth and Bowers 2001, Lutters and Ackerman 2002). Looking at the design-oriented approaches, the Answer Garden (AG) approach by Ackerman (with Malone 1990, 1994, with McDonald 1996, 1998) has been extremely influential and is widely referred to (e.g. Stahl and Herrmann 1999, Fagrell et al. 1999, McDonald 2000). Beyond the author's own realizations, there are several third party implementations available (Smeaton and Neilson 1995).

The AG supports knowledge management in two intertwined ways: by making relevant information retrievable and by making people with knowledge accessible. Ackerman (1994) evaluated the first version of the AG with groups of users who carried out different software engineering projects related to the X-windows system. The results of this study suggest that the basic design assumptions turned out to be supported, while certain design issues had to be reconsidered. Ackerman (1996) provides the results of another evaluation study. However, it focuses on the concept of "organizational memory" rather than on the AG system itself (see Bannon and Kuutti 1996). Due to the evaluations, the AG system was redesigned (cf. Ackerman and McDonald 1996). However, an empirical evaluation of the redesigned system (AG 2) has not yet been published.

The core innovation of the AG is the tighter coupling of information and communication spaces, and their integration into one architecture. Though we concentrate on the AG architecture here, we estimate our results to be relevant for other architectures and tools which aim at supporting knowledge management in a similar way, as well.

In contrasting with earlier success stories, in this paper we report about a failed attempt to introduce the AG approach. We tried to support maintenance engineering of a major German steel mill with the AG architecture. In the following we briefly describe the AG approach, and explain why it seemed promising for our application field. Then we report on problems which the steel mill encountered in knowledge sharing. We present the experiences made when applying the answer garden to the problems of the steel mill. Based on these findings, we evaluate the AG approach and suggest further research directions.

We finally relate our findings to the actual discussion on the nature of expertise sharing and tools for its technical support.

The Answer Garden Approach

The Answer Garden (AG) is an integrated approach which makes recorded knowledge retrievable as well as individuals with knowledge better accessible. Ackerman (1994) does not explicitly mention for which types of knowledge domains the approach fits best. However, the following criterias were relevant for him to select the domain of his field study: software-engineers in need of support in programming with the X-windows system; (cf. Ackerman 1994, p. 246):

- the complex nature of the knowledge domain,
- the interactive nature of the problem solving process,
- sufficient technological infrastructure (computers with network connections and e-mail) at the workplaces,
- lack of a body of commonly accepted knowledge,
- dynamic changes with regard to the relevant knowledge.

For these kinds of knowledge domains, the AG combines an information retrieval system with a communication system in an innovative way (cf. Figure 1). A user who has a problem and seeks information first of all checks in an information retrieval system where relevant artifacts about the knowledge domain are stored. If he can find the necessary information, he will continue working on the problem. If the user can not find the appropriate information, he can ask a question via e-mail to a human expert. By means of a location mechanism, the AG system locates an expert and routes this question to her. The expert may then answer the question (via e-mail) and if she thinks the answer is one of common interest, she can insert it into the knowledge database. In response to a question, the expert may also want to update existing material in the database or change the classification scheme of the database. So the database grows in relevant and retrievable information. Ackerman (1994, p. 245) believes that it pays for the experts to improve the AGs database, because they save time in answering frequently asked questions.

As a result of the first evaluation study, a second version of the AG system was developed. Besides a modularized technical infrastructure, the location mechanism to route the mails to the appropriate experts was improved. Moreover, the expert's publishing process to the database received increased support.

In the first version of the AG system, the location mechanism was based on the idea that there was a fixed list of external experts to whom the questions could be routed. Indeed this group was divided into two subgroups: first and second level experts. All questions were first routed to the first level experts, who forwarded them to the second level experts whenever they felt that they were unable to answer the questions appropriately (cf. Ackerman 1994, p. 246). Such a location mechanism is based on the assumption that the group of experts is different from the other users. In the second version of the AG this assumption was abandoned and the collaborative help among all users became the design rationale of the location mechanism. An "Escalation Agent" was implemented which incorporated a hierarchy of different user groups or media (e.g. local chat system, bulletin board, human experts). Whenever a user cannot find the relevant information in the database, his question is routed to the first level of the hierarchy (e.g. chat system). After a certain period of time the escalation agent asks the user whether his question was answered. In case it is not, the agent sends the question to the next level in the support hierarchy. The escalation agent can be used to navigate through different levels of locality, assuming that this way the information seeker is investigating appropriate contexts first. (Ackerman and McDonald 1996, pp. 101 ff.).

Concerning the publishing process, in the first version of the AG it was assumed that the (edited) answers given by the experts would also be helpful to others. They were published to the shared database. In the second version of the AG, additional functions to support the authoring process of the experts were developed. These functions allow collecting, culling, and classifying, and finally distilling cooperatively those materials which have been authored to answer questions from support seekers (cf. Ackerman and McDonald 1996, pp. 102).

Figure 1 gives an overview of the AG approach for sharing knowledge within an organization. In the following we look at the case of knowledge sharing in maintenance engineering to find out whether the AG approach is applicable in that domain.

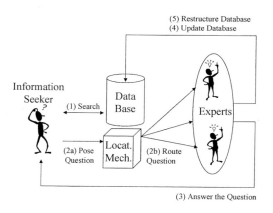

Figure 1: The Answer Garden Approach

Maintenance Engineering – Setting and Research Approach

We have investigated knowledge sharing in maintenance engineering processes of a Major German steel mill in the Ruhr area. The investigations took place in the context of the ORGTECH project (Wulf et al. 1999). The project's goal was to support cooperative work processes within the steel mill as well as between the steel mill and two engineering offices. The two engineering offices take on subcontractual work from the steel mill in the field of maintenance engineering, e.g. the construction and documentation of steel furnace components. A construction department inside the steel mill coordinates the planning, construction and documentation processes, and manages the contracts with the external offices.

Research Method

The OrgTech project follows an action research approach, the Integrated Organization and Technology Development (OTD) framework (Wulf and Rohde 1995). The OTD process is characterized by: a parallel development of workplace, organizational and technical systems; the management of (existing) conflicts by discourse and negotiation; and the immediate participation of the organization members affected.

The project started with on-site visits, semi-structured interviews, a market overview of relevant applications, and participative workshops to build a shared understanding (project establishment phase). The project proceeded in an evolutionary way, i. e. completing cycles of problem analysis, interventions and their evaluation (cf. Wulf et al. 1999). Within this change process, the question of how to support the sharing of knowledge among the different experts involved in the maintenance of the steel mill became a focus of concern.

Our decision to apply the AG approach was motivated by several issues. First, our application field carried the properties that have been recommended in the literature for the application of the AG approach (see section above). Second, the engineers basically showed a culture of cooperation at a personal level that made it likely that technological support for knowledge sharing would be appreciated. So we developed an architecture for an AG system for the steel mill that involved and extended the existing technological infrastructures, and demonstrated prototypical implementations of some of its

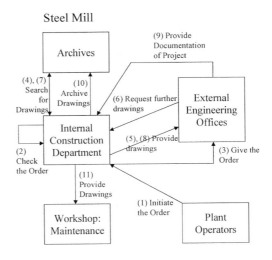

Figure 2: The Process of Maintenance Engineering

functionality in workshops. In the discussions following these presentations and workshops, it became clear that the AG architecture was rejected. These discussions and observations in that context helped us to reassess the AG approach as well as to broaden our understanding of organizational dynamics of knowledge sharing.

The results presented in this paper stem from a variety of different sources:

Analysis of the work practice: By means of about 25 semi-structured interviews, further workplace observations and additional open-ended interviews, the given work practice was examined.

Analysis of the documents available: By looking at the documents relevant for the maintenance engineering process, especially the drawings and the system descriptions (user handbooks), the relevant artifacts were investigated.

System evaluation: On the basis of task-oriented examinations like usability tests and expert reviews, the given database system was examined, especially with regard to its suitability for the maintenance engineering tasks.

Project workshops: During different workshops, organizational and technological interventions were presented and discussed to improve the maintenance engineering processes.

Field of Application

The Maintenance Engineering Department of the steel mill deals with repairing and improving the plant. Maintenance Engineering is a distributed process in which different organizational units of the steel mill and the external engineering offices are involved. Figure 2 gives a schematic overview of the maintenance engineering process.

In general, the starting point for a maintenance order is the plant operator. The steel mill consists of several organizationally independent plants, e.g. coke chambers, blast-furnace. The operators of each plant control the production equipment and machinery in their plant. Maintaining the plant also involves the repair, replacement or even redesign of outdated or deteriorated parts of the machinery, pipelines or buildings. When this kind of maintenance is necessary, the maintenance department of the plant operator asks the internal construction department for further processing. Depending on the type of order and the measures required, the transaction is handled internally or passed on to the external engineering offices. An external order will be prepared and surveyed by the responsible contact person in the internal construction department. For this reason, the necessary drawings and documents are compiled from the archives and passed on to the engineering office for further processing. Usually, the order specifications contain errors and need further clarification right from the very beginning. So discussions among the different actors and extensive re-ordering of drawings often become necessary. The additional requirements for documents are to be expressed in a comprehensive way and have to be returned to the construction department of the steel mill. Once again drawings and documents have to be found, coordination work has to be done and contacts with other departments have to be initiated. This process of renegotiating the order and reordering additional drawings requires a high level of work and expenditure of time for all participants involved.

After the external offices finish their engineering task, the internal construction department has to check it, to include the modified drawings and new ones into the archives, and to initiate the production process of the required spare parts. After being either produced by the internal workshop or ordered externally, the spare parts are assembled into the plant. While this is the general process schema of maintenance engineering, various sorts of informal communication and self-organized variations of the process can be found and add to the complexity of the problems we will describe now.

The Current State of a Plant – A Problem of Knowledge Sharing

In the following we will investigate the problem of knowledge sharing concerning one specific aspect of the process of maintenance engineering. In this case, the problem to be solved is to find out the "actual state" of those parts of a plant that are relevant for a maintenance engineering problem. "State" addresses e.g. details of the assembly of a machinery, the materials it consists of and their age, or the production process it is involved in. But it also addresses information on its location and related conditions that might interfere with necessary maintenance construction efforts, e.g. strength of the ground or where old pipelines run in the walls. This information should be available in the official technical drawings referring to that machine or location, but as we describe further below, the state described in the drawings is not necessarily the actual state of the plant.

The steel mill has a history of more than 100 years. During that time the different plants of the steel mill have been continuously modified, destroyed and replaced with other plants. The knowledge about this process is distributed among different actors in the plant and several archives containing drawings of the plant. These drawings are stored on various media. The central drawing archives contain about 300,000 technical drawings, about 2,500 files with technical descriptions, part lists, statics information and calculations, and about 500 files with plans of electronic and hydraulic devices.

A large part of these documents is filed in conventional paper form and saved on microfilm. The electronic drawing data consists of scanned drawings, which are saved in raster format and specific CAD formats. The electronically archived document stock contains about 5,000 CAD-drawings, about 20,000 raster format drawings and 30,000 scanned drawings on microfilm files, and about 90,000 documents describing the plant, maintenance processes and drawings.

In order to be able to handle the large number of drawings and documents, in 1995 an electronic archiving system was implemented to archive and provide the technical documentation. This system allows one to find drawings by numbers or keywords. Drawings are identified by two types of numbers. The first type is the drawing number which is given in a rather chronological order to all newly created drawings. It is specified by the filing clerk and does not contain any semantic information concerning the content of the drawing. For classification reasons the drawings get a second number, the so-called basic number. These basic numbers classify the drawings according to the plants and plant components they refer to. This classification scheme stems from accounting and controlling demands. It classifies the components of the plants in a way which does not fit well with the concepts and needs of engineers.

The electronic documentation is stored on a data jukebox, which is equipped with magneto-optical disks. Descriptions of the documents are stored on an Oracle data base and may be retrieved via the archiving system (called ADOS) programmed in Microsoft Access. At present, conventional and electronic archiving methods are being used in parallel, since the conversion from conventional to electronic archives is expensive and takes a long period of time to be implemented. A continuous conversion of all relevant data is aimed for. The central archives suffer from a couple of problems (cf. Hinrichs 2000):

- Approximately 20% of the drawings stored in the archives do not have any classification; a direct assignment to plants or their location is not stated. Their categorization can only be processed with in-depth system knowledge.
- A large number of drawings is old, of bad quality or has to be reconstructed in order to provide the information.
- Approximately 25% of the drawings are saved in the archive system without the correct basic or drawing number or are stored without keywords. Such drawings can only be found by the description used in the ADOS system or are accessible by search via indirect paths only (e.g. asking colleagues).
- The existing archive system does not offer extended search functions. Only drawing numbers and basic numbers (both of which are not self-explanatory) can be used as search attributes.

Due to the problems of the central archives there exist a couple of local archives maintained by the different actors involved in plant maintenance.

- Additional drawings are distributed among individuals in the maintenance department of the different plants. These individuals often have built up their private paper-based archives of those aspects of the plant they are responsible for. These archives contain up to 500 sketches and often occupy several shelves in their offices.

- Individuals of the internal construction department store documents relevant for construction, such as plant specific compiled drawing lists, in a decentralized way. They are typically filed in local paper-based archives. Some of the engineers prefer using these documents instead of the "official" ones when searching for drawings, since they contain important information in a compact form. Such documents are not within the range of electronic search functions and electronic access.

Further aspects add to the complexity of the problem to find out about the actual state of a plant in the steel mill. While already the handling of the different types of documents and archives requires some knowledge of the actors involved, certain modifications of the state of the plant cannot be found in the drawings at all. When handling accidents, plants may be modified instantly without prior planning and documentation by means of drawings. At the end of a budget year, certain work is carried out instantly to use still available funds of the respective plants. This work is typically not documented in drawings. Finally, even well planned and documented modifications of the plant may have been finally realized in a slightly different way than they are documented in the drawings. This can be caused by inadequate plans, which have to be adapted to the given environment. Sometimes the realization is carried out completely disregarding the given plans. So the knowledge about the actual state of the steel mill is distributed between different drawing archives and human actors. The workers of the maintenance departments of the different plants within the mill typically kept the best record about the actual state of their plant.

So, the problem of finding out the actual state of a plant has similar properties to the problem discussed in Ackerman's study (1994). As a reason for choosing his approach to support knowledge management for programmers of the X windows system he described specific attributes of the problem to be solved (cf. section 2). In our these attributes also apply:

- The knowledge domain is typically complex because the individual plants of the steel mill typically consist of a big variety of different components, which are interrelated in different ways. Moreover a huge variety of physical constraints has to be taken into account to understand the state of a plant.
- Like in the software engineering case, there is a lack of a body of commonly accepted knowledge. In the case of the steel mill, actors in the different organizational units maintain different drawing archives which again may document different states of the plant.
- The state of the plant changes dynamically. Maintenance activities are typically triggered by accidents, technological progress, capacity adjustments, or market changes. Some of these modifications of the plants

are not documented in drawings, because they had to be carried out instantly. This prevents actors in the steel mill from acquiring a lasting expertise.

- Maintenance engineering is often an interactive process because ideas to improve a plant have to be discussed and reversed several times.

So, the AG approach should be well applicable to the problem of finding out about the actual state of a plant.

Applying the Answer Garden Approach to Maintenance Engineering

Finding out about the actual state of a certain plant in the steel mill is a central problem in maintenance engineering. We investigated how the different elements of the AG approach could be applied to this problem.

The Steps of the Answer Garden Approach

We will discuss our experiences along the different steps of the AG approach and describe underlying organizational problems.

Search the database: The first element of the approach is the provision of electronic artifacts about the knowledge domain in a retrievable form. These artifacts exist in the case of the steel mill; the central archives contain different types of technical documents in three different media. The internal construction department and the plant operators maintain their own local paper archives. The paper artifacts are not easily retrievable as they are distributed among various locations of the steel mill. Their owners regard them as their „private" property. By contrary, the central electronic archives are easily accessible by any engineer. But the artifacts are not easily retrievable in the database. The common way to retrieve documents is via their basic number. The classification scheme according to basic numbers is not very intuitive to engineers because it was set up by the accounting department to allocate costs. Additionally, many documents are not included in the database or are not classified by basic numbers. Finally, the specification of queries to the archives is not very intuitive. So, retrieving documents in the archive database already requires quite some experience.

We have discussed different approaches to improve the electronic support for the retrieval of drawings with the engineers. First, all the drawings could be included into the database and could be classified correctly according to the basic numbers. However such an approach would require a huge amount of time of human experts. Due to the high costs and the fact hat the long-term future of the steel mill is unclear, this option is not viable from the point of view of the steel mill's management. Another approach could be to make more attributes of the drawings available for retrieval. For instance, one could apply pattern recognition or optical character recognition (OCR) algorithms on the scanned drawings to make the legend on each of the drawings available for key word search. The information given in drawing lists could be used to find drawings of artifacts which have been created or modified within the same project. All these extensions of the database scheme would require considerable input of labor because it cannot be implemented automatically. Due to the high costs involved it was not acceptable for the management, either. A similar scenario and the related problems have been described by Trigg et al. (1999).

Finally, the user interface of the drawing database could be improved. For instance, users could document and share successful search inquiries to help each other in finding relevant search results. This approach was agreed upon and is currently implemented in a prototype.

In conclusion one can say that the retrieval of the drawings is a complex problem in databases which have a long history of usage. As classification schemes change over time, information retrieval requires considerable expertise. In these cases information retrieval in the database can not be seen as an isolated first step as Ackerman (1994) describes it. Only if the required expertise to retrieve the information is available, can the drawing database serve as a primary source of information.

Pose a Question: If the database retrieval does not lead to the desired information, the AG offers the chance to formulate a corresponding question in textual form. In our case, the textual explication of a question is not always a viable way. The engineers typically ask specific questions, which may be further refined in an ongoing discussion with each other and the plant operators. Within such a discussion, artifacts like drawings, sketches or even the parts of the plants help to improve the mutual understanding.

Route the Question: Next, in the AG system the questions are routed to human experts. The system incorporates location mechanisms to find the appropriate expert. Such a location mechanism requires explicit algorithms for how to locate human experts. Indeed, such an algorithm is given in the case of the steel mill. If the information seeker is able to refer to a certain part of a plant by means of the two leading figures of the basic number, the relevant experts in the internal construction department as well as in the maintenance departments of the plant operators can be located. Additionally, the members of the archives have gained relevant experience since they have always been responsible when drawings of the plant had to be found. So, the guidance to find appropriate experts could also be provided by the information systems.

We discussed an extension of the database, which would give hints to the users whom to ask concerning certain aspects of a plant. This was assessed by the plant staff as an improvement which was mainly relevant for newcomers. Engineers who work for a longer time in maintaining the plant would typically know whom to ask.

Answer the Question and Update the Database: As a next step, in the AG approach the experts answer the questions of the information seekers and they incorporate this answer into the database with little extra effort. By updating the database they benefit from being less often asked by information seekers lateron. As already mentioned, in our case it may be difficult to share knowledge by one-way text-based communication channels. Typically an artifact-supported discussion is required. To document a given advice, multimedia recording and editing tools need to be applied. The complexity in handling these tools may well exceed the technological abilities of the experts.

Moreover, the efforts being made to help the information seeker can not always be represented within the database. The database offers a structure to store drawings. Indeed some of the advice given to information seekers will lead to either an update or a better categorization of certain drawings. However most advice will just be given verbally. The current structure of the database does not allow this type of content to be represented.

Organizational Issues

Even if these problems could be overcome, the existing division of labor within the steel mill would prevent the AG approach from being applied. The maintenance of the drawing archives and especially of the database is the responsibility of the archives group. This group is, like the internal construction department, a part of the central support division of the steel mill. Between the central support division and the different plant operating divisions there is an ongoing rivalry for power and resources (despite good relations among the engineers at a personal level). The competition for resources has led to a strict division of labor between these organizational units. Only the archives group has the right to modify the central database. The construction department has to send the drawings to the archives group after their job is finished. Afterwards, they have only read access to the central database. They cannot modify missing or incorrect classifications or update documents. On the other side, they don't have a strong interest in the material stored in the central archives. The workers in the local maintenance departments, who have built up their own local archives based on paper drawings, do not use the electronic drawing database very much. This is also due to the poor user interface for searching (Hinrichs 2000).

The restrictive access rights make it difficult to gain the benefits of the AG approach in our case. Most of the persons responsible for the inquiries of external engineers concerning the current state of a plant, cannot document their answers or at most parts of them in the shared database. While the given technological equipment at the workplaces does not allow for multimedia explanations, the reclassification and the update of certain parts of the drawings would be possible.

In case of a more flexible division of labor and corresponding access rights, the maintenance departments of the plant operators and the internal construction department could both update and improve the content of the database. When we discuss this issue with the workers of the different plants, they were not willing to improve a database they have been neither responsible for nor using much. The given division of labor and the existing conflicts between the organizational units prevented the actors from activities which would have improved the quality of the central database.

Discussion

We discuss our experiences along two lines. First, we abstract from our concrete experiences and comment on possible future directions of the AG approach and similar functionality. Second, we add to a recent discussion on the usefulness of expertise location algorithms.

Growing an Answer Garden

Our experiences showed several obstacles for realizing the AG approach. We believe that the AG is based on the following implicit assumption which were not all given in our case:
- The information seekers know exactly what their problem is.
- The categorization scheme of the database is understandable by information seekers. Moreover, they are able to handle the retrieval mechanism of the database in an appropriate way.
- Information seekers are able to use computer mediated communication (CMC) and are able express their questions in plain text.
- The location mechanism incorporates appropriate assumptions about the location of human expertise within the organization.
- If an expert is found, she is able to understand the question and give an understandable answer by means of written language.
- The experts (group of persons) have an interest in investing additional work in updating the common database.
- The experts are able to understand the given categorization scheme of the database.

Given these assumptions underlying the AG approach, we now can explicate criteria for settings in which the AG is especially applicable:

Settings in which CMC is a usual way for organizational communication: In distributed settings, like virtual organizations, there is a chance that members have built a culture of organization- and work-related CMC, which also eases the communication between expert and information seeker.

Settings with a complex expertise structure: The basic problem the AG approach addresses is: "What do I do when expertise is not at hand?". In some situation this relates to the fact that it is hard to get an overview on the competences and expertise available in complex organizational settings. Again, that problem is more likely to occur in distributed settings, when there is less opportunity for a peripheral awareness of others' expertise. The AG helps to find knowledgeable people in these settings (cf. Groth and Bowers 2001).

Settings with a strong tradition in using digital storage and collaboration media: Obviously, the problems surrounding digital artifacts made the application of the AG difficult in our case. However, one has to realize that the AG approach relies on algorithms which use metadata (e.g. who worked on what project?) to operate. This data has to be available. So the reality the data represents needs to be formalized appropriately, and that there should be cost-effective ways to maintain the metadata and the associated models. This was surely given in the AG's first application domain, i. e. the work group of programmers of the "X windows" system.

Settings with an open help culture: Several aspects related to the organizational culture may lead to restrictive practices of passing knowledge to others. Our example showed - despite good relations at a personal level - a conflict between two departments, but knowledge ownership might also be a relevant issue for individual experts. Establishing and maintaining an open help culture is important for many approaches to support knowledge transfer, but to systems like the AG it is crucial.

Referring to our experiences, we can also comment on some ways to improve the approach:

Opening up personal acres for the Answer Garden: We saw in our examples, that the engineers created private archives with own information artifacts. These often manifest a personal perspective on a problem, item or project, and often represent information which is only interpretable with the background of the private archive's creator. Yet, private archives are the first information experts refer to when explaining things to others, and they support the experts' re-contextualization process related to a problem they solved maybe years ago. Relating this personal information landscape to the public information base (e.g. as retrievable, contextualized "second opinion" on information available in public artifacts, or as a secondary stage for information retrieval before asking the expert), and supporting the use of this material in expertise communication seem to be an important direction of future work.

Growing answers using representations as seed: In the context we described, the drawings are not purely information "containers", but also focal points for given explanations. They represent an abstraction of the reality which is, when related to a specific problem, usually enriched by further information from other sources (bookkeeping information, project descriptions, co-workers) to complete the picture accordingly. These kind of representation can be valuable to clarify the communication between an expert and the information seeker, and to use representation in these communications should be supported. Using representations from the database would add the opportunity to collaboratively improve the information stored there (Buckingham Shum 1997, Pipek and Won 2002).

Harvesting in the neighbor's garden: Not being able to retrieve the information needed from own resources, the employees of the steel mill sometimes ask external engineering offices involved in related projects for material (drawings and other information) to approach a problem. This practice shows that networking AG systems could also improve the overall quality of the information infrastructure. "Distributed AGs" have been part of the original concept, but our case would also call for a concept of interconnectivity for different implementations of the AG concept which works across organizational boundaries.

On technological support for expert finding

A recent controversy on a specific part of the AG approach again posed the question, to what extent technology support may be appropriate for knowledge management. McDonald and Ackerman (2000) described an architecture (ER-Arch) which used concepts from the field of recommender systems for the problem of expertise location. In this architecture they used metadata derivable from information artifacts or other sources (groupware, email clients, browsers, organization models) to support the identification and the selection of experts.

Groth and Bowers (2001) challenged the architecture and the relevance of these algorithms with a study on expert finding in a consultancy company. Consultants there showed patterns of behavior (i.e. choosing accessibility and availability for prioritizing which expert to contact) when searching expertise which were seemingly not covered by the ER-Arch (the ER-Arch prioritizes according to heuristics which are based on data concerning expertise and concerning personal/organizational relations between the information seeker and potential experts). The study's authors further claim that, since expert location in practice is always situated, an architecture for building expertise locators would pose undesired restrictions on the information seeker. Rather than supporting expertise location they suggest to increase the awareness of experts' activities and availability.

We will now revisit our case study and provide further empirical evidence to that debate. Expertise location follows very explicit heuristics in our case. After the identification of a problem in maintenance engineering, the experts are rather easy to be found when asking concerning the current state of (one part of) the plant. Many of the workers are very confident with the machines and plants they work with, and they are experts for the functioning and current state for them. But the process of maintenance engineering is a specialized activity in which only few actors (plant operators, maintenance staff) are involved. So, the choice among the experts is rather limited. A heuristic can be easily explicated and implemented. Often the given organizational micro-politics determine whom to ask in which order (see section 5).

Contrary to Groth and Bower's (2001) observation, the current availability or a notion for activity/workload patterns is not a key factor in selecting somebody to ask in our case. Although steel mill workers devote a considerable part of their time to meetings, contact with them is not the major problem. But even in case it would become a major problem, there is little chance to ask somebody else. Awareness mechanisms may facilitate the interaction between information seeker and expert here.

Our case study suggests that history data concerning artifacts which represent knowledge may be a source for further heuristics for expertise location. In case more external service provider supports the maintenance engineering process, the relevant knowledge will be distributed among more actors. The simple matching algorithm between the experts and plants would not apply anymore. Due to the incomplete documentation provided by the drawings up to now, such a heuristic may just partially solve the problem.

A closer examination of McDonald's work sheds new light on the controversy discussed here. In his dissertation in which the ER-Arch is worked out, McDonald (2000, p. 176) describes a use scenario where he explicitly describes how recommendations brought up by the system are discarded because the user has additional information about the recommended experts' availability. The realizations of the architecture obviously are open to users' choices on how to proceed in the overall expert contacting process. So, it is possible (and potentially helpful) to work with heuristics which seem to cover a significant amount of strategies encountered in an organization. However, one should allow the choice among different strategies (e.g. with the "escalating" functionality by McDonald, or with different or no technological support). On the other hand, even from the case given by Groth and Bowers (2001) it is not credible that information seekers do not consider the competences and knowledge of their colleagues before thinking about their availability. The steps of the ER architecture reflect these considerations and give the interactive choices to navigate in recommendations.They do not restrict the strategies and options users choose from.

This controversy shows a common discussion pattern among the disciplines involved in CSCW. Designers of technology are criticized for working with inappropriate abstractions of the reality. But there is an inherent need to abstract when computer support is implemented. We have to remember that technological artifacts always face the challenge of practice some day, and that their appropriation in practice decides merciless on the quality of these abstractions.

Given McDonald's (2000) design approach which is grounded in a profound field study, the complete inappropriateness of the resulting artifacts is rather implausible. However, his work does not reflect the "total cost of modeling" (meaning model generation as well as model maintenance) to which his approach leads. In his approach, huge amounts of metadata have to be generated and frequently updated to make the expertise identification and expertise selection algorithms work. Whether the benefit of the concept justifies its costs is still to be evaluated, and repositioning the concept with regard to appropriate organizational contexts might be required.

Conclusion

The understanding of the dynamics between technical tools and organizational aspects is still a challenge for knowledge management in organizations (cf. Ackerman, Pipek, and Wulf 2003). In this contribution we discussed the failure of an introduction of the Answer Garden (AG) architecture in a steel mill.

We mentioned reasons for the introduction of the AG when describing the application field (see above). We now want to briefly comment on traditional approaches from the field of knowledge management we considered and rejected. Looking back at the experiences presented in the section "Search the Data Base", it becomes clear that the traditional approach of repository-based support for knowledge management would have failed in this field of application. Approaches such as improving the interoperability of the distributed databases, imposing a general categorization scheme or establishing a universal access point (e.g. a web portal) to all documents could have helped improving the knowledge exchange processes. However, inaccurate and incomplete data, a complex classification problem, cost considerations, and organizational rivalries made such options unviable.

Extending traditional repository-based approaches by combining information and communication spaces into one architecture, the Answer Garden offered an innovative architecture. Therefore we applied it to a knowledge management problem which could not have been solved by traditional repository-based approaches: retrieving the current state of the plant within the general maintenance engineering process. However, our proposal has been rejected by the different actors although the scenario in the application field seems to fulfill the preconditions of the AG. So the case study adds to the discussion of appropriate organizational settings and possible improvements of the AG, or similar architectures. From revealing some implicit assumptions of the AG, we derive four conditions for organizational settings where the AG approach might be especially appropriate to use. These relate to the acceptance of computer-mediated communication, to the complexity of the expertise structure, to the tradition of digital collaboration media, and to the organization's culture.

Extensions of the concept our experiences suggest are
- the consideration of the experts' strategies to maintain private archives with information artifacts they can use for re-contextualization and explanation processes connected to a request,
- the use of representation in communication, the option to collaboratively improve representations from the database,
- and the idea to connect available archives and databases to improve the quality of the overall information infrastructure.

We also showed that in our case the given division of labor and intra-organizational rivalries also hindered an AG implementation, processes of organizational development may be required. Additionally, actors which provide information to others may need some additional qualification in documenting their knowledge (e.g. in editing the corresponding documents) and indexing their input appropriately. If knowledge cannot be easily expressed via electronic media or if the size of the knowledge domain requires sophisticated classification schemes, it is questionable whether experts are willing to take the additional efforts required. All our experiences stress the importance of an integrated perspective on technical tools and organizational issues in the context of knowledge management support.

Along the second line of argumentation, we referred to a recent discussion on the appropriateness of heuristics generated for expert finding support. This is a problem which is also central to the AG approach. Groth and Bowers (2001) challenged McDonald's and Ackerman's (2000) proposal questioning the usefulness of their heuristics. According to them, the situatedness of expertise finding strategies prevents implemented heuristics for expertise location from being effective. Due to the distribution of expertise in our field study, appropriate heuristics could easily be generated. However, they were not regarded to be useful.

We believe that the ER Arch approach (like the AG and other expertise management systems) may be problematic due to the high costs involved in building and maintaining appropriate computer models on expertise location. So the "total costs of modeling" have to be considered carefully.

Like our study with the AG, we need more in depth evaluations of expertise management systems in different organizational settings. So insights about the match between technical artifacts and organizational settings can be gained. Inappropriate design assumptions become obvious and directions for future research can be derived.

This controversy around the ER-Arch shares some aspects with the one between Suchman and Winograd concerning the Coordinator (Flores et al. 1988, Winograd 1988, Suchman 1993, JCSCW 1995). In both cases, the technological system (there: Winograd's "Coordinator") which derived design aspects from technically manifesting empirical concepts and results (there: speech acts used to coordinate work) was challenged because the resulting artifacts imposed major restrictions on users' ability to act. We do believe that it is important to observe these design trajectories carefully and critically, but we want to point out that there is a difference whether or not an architecture or technological concept is meant to replace other practices in the work setting it addresses. "Replacement architectures" (like the "Coordinator" since its concepts address a task – coordination – which inherently affects all work group members) have to be challenged much harder than "Supplement Architectures". With regard to Supplement Architectures, practice will show whether or not the ideas of the designers work out. The AG approach and McDonald's ER-Arch were never meant to replace other knowledge finding strategies. So other choices are still available to work group members.

Acknowledgements

We would like to thank Gerry Stahl for inspiring and valuable discussions on earlier versions of this paper. We would also like to thank our colleagues Joachim Hinrichs, Markus Klann, Matthias Krings, Bernhard Nett, Tim Reichling, Markus Rohde, Gunnar Stevens, and Markus Won for their comments and contributions to the field work.

References

Ackerman, M.S.; Malone, T.W. (1990): *Answer Garden: A tool for growing Organizational Memory*; in: Proc. of the ACM Conference on Office Information Systems, pp. 31 - 39

Ackerman, M.S. (1994): *Augmenting the organizational memory: a field study of Answer Garden*, in: Proc. of the CSCW'94 Conference, ACM Press, pp. 243 - 252

Ackerman, M. S. (1996): *Definitional and Contextual Issues in Organizational and Group Memories*, in: Technology and People, Vol. 9, No. 1, pp. 10 - 24

Ackerman, M.S.; McDonald, D.W. (1996): *Answer Garden 2: Merging Organizational Memory with Collaborative Help*, in: Int. Conf. on CSCW'96, ACM Press, pp. 97 - 105

Ackerman, M.S. (1998): *Augmenting Organizational Memory: A Field Study of Answer Garden*, in: ACM Transactions on Information Systems (TOIS), 16 (3). pp. 203 - 224

Ackerman, M. S.; Halverson, C. (1998). *Considering an Organization's Memory*. Int. Conf. on CSCW'98, Seattle, WA, ACM Press, New York, pp. 39 – 48

Ackerman, M. S.; Pipek, V.; Wulf, V. (eds) (2003): Sharing Expertise: Beyond Knowledge Management, MIT Press, Cambridge MA

Bannon, L.; Kuutti, K. (1996): *Shifting Perspectives on Organizational Memory: From Storage to Active Remembering*, in: Proceedings of HICSS-29, pp. 156 - 167

Buckingham Shum, S. (1997): *Negotiating the Construction and Reconstruction of Organisational Memories*; in: Journal of Universal Computer Science (Special Issue on IT for Knowledge Management), 3 (8), 899-928, http://www.jucs.org/

Davenport, T.H. and Prusak, L. (1998): *Working Knowledge: How Organizations Manage What They Know*. Harvard Business School Press, Boston, MA, USA.

Ehrlich, K. (2003): *Locating Expertise: Design Issues for an Expertise Locator System*, in: Ackerman, M.; Pipek, V.; Wulf, V. (eds): Expertise Sharing: Beyond Knowledge Management, MIT-Press, Cambridge MA, pp. 137 - 158

Fagrell, H., Ljungberg, F. and Kristofferson, S. (1999): *Exploring support for knowledge management in mobile work*. in: Proceedings of the 6th European Conference on CSCW (Copenhagen, Denmark, 1999), Kluwer, Dordrecht, The Netherlands, pp. 259 - 276

Flores, F., Graves. M., Hartfield, B., Winograd, T. (1988). *Computer Systems and the Design of Organizational Interaction*. Tran. on Office Information Systems. 6(2), pp.153-172.

Groth, K.; Bowers, J. (2001): *On Finding things out: Situated organizational knowledge in CSCW*, in: Proceedings of the 7th ECSCW, Kluwer, Dordrecht, pp. 279 - 298

Hinrichs, J. (2000): *Telecooperation in Engineering Offices - The problem of archiving*. in: Designing Cooperative Systems (COOP 2000), IOS Press, Amsterdam, pp. 259 - 274

Hutchins, E. (1995): Cognition in the Wild. MIT Press, Cambridge MA

JCSCW (1995), Several contributions in the Commentary Section, Int. Journal on CSCW 3(1), Kluwer, pp. 29-95

Lutters, W. G.; Ackerman, M. S. (2002): Archiving Safety : A Field Study of Boundary Objects in Aircraft Technical Support, in: Int. Conf. on CSCW'02, New Orleans, LO, ACM Press, New York, pp. 266 – 275

McDonald, D. W. (2000): *Supporting Nuance in Groupware Design: Moving from Naturalistic Expertise Location to Expertise Recommendation*, PhD-thesis, University of California, Irvine 2000

McDonald, D. W.; Ackerman; M. (2000): *Expertise Recommender: A Flexible Recommendation System and Architecture*, in: Int. Conf. On CSCW, ACM Press, New York, pp. 231-240

Pipek, V.; and Won, M. (2002). *Communication-oriented Computer Support for Knowledge Management*. Informatik/Informatique - Magazine of the Swiss Informatics Societies 2002(1): pp. 39-43.

Smeaton, C.; Neilson, I. (1995). *The Answer Web*. Fourth International World Wide Web Conference 1995, Boston, MA, USA, available upon request from *http://www.orbitalsw.com.*

Stahl, G.; Herrmann, T. (1999): *Intertwining Perspectives and Negotiation*; in: Int. Conference on Supporting Group Work (GROUP'99), ACM Press, New York, pp. 316-325

Suchman, L. (1993). *Do Categories Have Politics? The Language/Action Perspective reconsidered*. Europ. Conf. on Computer Supported Cooperative Work (ECSCW'93), Milan, Italy, pp. 1-14.

Trigg, R.H., Blomberg, J. and Suchman, L. (1999): *Moving document collections online: The evolution of a shared repository*. In: 6th European Conference, Kluwer, Dordrecht, NL, pp. 331-350.

Winograd, T. (1988): *A language/action perspective on the design of cooperative work*. In: Greif, I. (ed.), CSCW - A book of readings, Morgan Kaufman, San Mateo, CA, pp. 623-656.

Wulf, V.; Krings, M.; Stiemerling, O.; Iacucci, G.; Maidhof, M.; Peters, R.; Fuchs-Fronhofen, P.; Nett, B.; Hinrichs, J. (1999): *Improving Inter-Organizational Processes with Integrated Organization and Technology Development*, in: JUCS, Vol. 5, No. 6, 1999, pp. 339 - 365

Wulf, V.; Rohde, M. (1995): *Towards an Integrated Organization and Technology Development*. in: Symposium on Designing Interactive Systems (DIS'95), (Ann Arbor, MI, USA, 1995), ACM Press, New York, pp. 55 – 64

K. Kuutti, E.H. Karsten, G. Fitzpatrick, P. Dourish and K. Schmidt (eds.), *ECSCW 2003: Proceedings of the Eighth European Conference on Computer Supported Cooperative Work, 14-18 September 2003, Helsinki, Finland*, pp. 21-40.

Discovery of implicit and explicit connections between people using email utterance

Robert McArthur and Peter Bruza

Distributed Systems Technology Centre, Brisbane, Australia

{mcarthur,bruza}@dstc.edu.au

Abstract. This paper is about finding explicit and implicit connections between people by mining semantic associations from their email communications. Following from a socio-cognitive stance, we propose a model called HALe which automatically derives dimensional representations of words in a high dimensional context space from an email corpus. These dimensional representations are used to discover a network of people based on a seed contextual description. Such a network represents useful connections between people not easily achievable by 'normal' retrieval means. Implicit connections are "lifted" by applying latent semantic analysis to the high dimensional context space. The discovery techniques are applied to a substantial corpus of real-life email utterance drawn from a small-to-medium size information technology organization. The techniques are computationally tractable, and evidence is presented that suggests appropriate explicit connections are being brought to light, as well as interesting, and perhaps serendipitous implicit connections. The ultimate goal of such techniques is to bring to light context-sensitive, ephemeral, and often hidden relationships between people, and between people and information, which pervade the enterprise.

Introduction

Our information environment becomes ever more complex, but our ability to comprehend it does not keep pace. As a consequence, the connections between individuals, groups and information become lost, or forgotten, and individuals and groups become ever more isolated. The cost to the individual, and the enterprise, is a lack of awareness. The broad goal of the research reported in this paper is to discover appropriate and perhaps serendipitous connections within a given context thereby promoting the awareness of individuals to their environment: other individuals, groups and information.

It seems established organisational units often consist of informal social networks as much as of permanent formal teams. Like Nardi *et al.* (2000), we feel that "One of the most important resources we share with each other is access to those in our social networks". Appropriately discovering and sharing context-specific personal networks is an important part of the life of people and knowledge in an organisation. More specifically, this paper is about finding useful and sometimes serendipitous connections between people by mining semantic associations from their email communications. Since using an individual's email, and therefore their social networks, raises important issues of consent and privacy, these are separately discussed at the end of the paper.

A feature of current email use is its ubiquity: Ducheneaut and Bellotti (2002) commented that "while this [people spending a lot of time on email] may not be surprising for those who collaborate over distance, we have observed that even colleagues having offices next to each other, or sitting *in plain sight* of each other, still use email as a principal communication medium." "Work objects are easily accessible while communicating over email in a way that they cannot be in most face-to-face encounters." Their studies show how email exhibits characteristics as "a preferred medium for talking about work...[and] a valuable product of communication: email conversations, often standing as or evolving into work objects themselves."

While email itself is a vitally important office communications medium that has a history of research (a very useful map of research in email is presented in Ducheneaut (2002)), studies using semantic information are few. Semantic knowledge is important for, as Kimble *et al.* (1998) note, "Linguistic and philosophical research has suggested that the interpretation of utterances depends not on isolated sentences but on the context....Wittgenstein, for example, asserts that we can only make sense of utterances and actions by seeing them within the contexts in which they were uttered or undertaken". Their work examines a large organisation's email overload problem, and their conclusions reiterate the importance of context, especially to the perceptions of users about the information which email (and other computer-mediated communication systems) provides.

Previous work on finding people in organisations has used a variety of methods. PeCo (Ogata and Yano, 1998) used email From & To headers to collect acquaintances and relationships between people, and collected 'expertise' by keywords extracted from the message text by morphological analysis. A similarity-based matching system completes their expertise management tool. However, those methods cannot use information in the email, such as may occur from person A to person B: "C said that D is too slow". These references may be to other, unquoted, email messages, or to a discussion held outside the electronic realm, and are not represented in the Subject, From or To lines of the email message.

Schwartz and Wood (1993) mined 1.2M email headers to detect shared interests between people using graph theory. Specialised subgraphs for a person were aggregated to cover all their interests; specific interests could be determined only by starting with a specific set of people known to have that interest. The methods have the advantage that no processing, or even knowledge of, the message text (including Subject) is needed. However, it suffers from a lack of specificity, as does PeCo above, purely because it ignores the text – the context of the message. It also requires a known starting set for any specific interest area.

Kautz *et al.* (1997) used the co-occurrence of names in close proximity in Web pages as evidence of a direct relationship. They state "Searching for a piece of information...thus becomes a matter of searching the social network for an expert on the topic together with a *chain* of personal referrals from the searcher to the expert." Importantly, we agree that

> ...manually searching for a referral chain can be a frustrating and time consuming task. One is faced with the trade-off of contacting a large number of individuals at each step, and thus straining both the time and good will of possible respondents, or of contacting a smaller, more focussed set, and thus being more likely to fail to locate an appropriate expert.

However, as Ogata and Yano (1998) respond, "...it may be difficult to find real private networks." Within a small-medium enterprise, the sources are less likely to provide evidence for a social network. For example, internal web pages are more likely to indicate organisational grouping rather than task- or interest-based relationships.

Ackerman and McDonald (1996) sought a surrogate for hallway talk for people seeking help: "Normally, one attempts to examine the documentation or other help sources, and then wanders out into a hallway in search of friendly colleagues." They collected databases of commonly asked questions that grew "organically" – collecting "organisational memory". This type of questioning and seeking is but part of a larger set; by itself it cannot find an answer, or person to answer, a question that is (probably) going to be asked only once and is possibly time-dependent as well. Unfortunately, these harder questions are all too prevalent. Instead of searching for an explicit answer, it often is necessary to search for someone who could answer, or direct to someone else who can.

This paper is about making people's work easier by finding who has the information, knowledge or expertise that will directly help. Other people in the organisation benefit from the sharing, and the person engaged in informing and being informed about the people in an extra-organisational network increasingly need tools to do that important work (Nardi *et al.*, 2000). Following from a socio-cognitive perspective, we propose a model called HALe which automatically derives dimensional representations of words within a high dimensional context space from an email corpus. These dimensional representations are used to discover a network of people based on a seed contextual description. Connections, perhaps explicit, sometimes serendipitous, are made by analysis of the explicit and tacit knowledge captured and represented in the high dimensional space.

The next section describes relevant theories of knowledge and of communicability of knowledge. Techniques for extracting and representing knowledge from email messages are then presented. These are then applied in an experiment with significant real-world data, showing one way of producing links between people based on semantic analysis. A brief discussion of privacy issues and further work concludes the paper.

Knowledge and Information

Nonaka and Takeuchi (1995) wrote a seminal book on organisational knowledge creation. Their knowledge creation spiral is often cited in the literature. They made a clear distinction between tacit knowledge (personal, context-specific, hard to formalise and communicate) and explicit knowledge (transmittable in a formal, systematic language), and their thesis is that "...the key to knowledge creation lies in the mobilization and conversion of tacit knowledge."

Four modes of knowledge conversion are created when tacit and explicit knowledge interact – socialisation, externalisation, combination and internalisation. "These modes are what the individual experiences. They are also the mechanisms by which individual knowledge get articulated and 'amplified' into and throughout the organisation." In this paper our interest is in externalisation, in which the tacit knowledge in the communications of the members of an organisation is made explicit. It is vital for an organisation as "Among the four modes...externalization holds the key to knowledge creation".

To make tacit knowledge explicit, it must first be identified, then represented. The final, full, step of externalisation is one that, as yet, is still squarely in the realm of the human. Computer systems such as the one described in this paper can assist the final step, but it is the human who accomplishes it and internalises it. Electronically, both the identification and representation is very difficult: it is hard enough for people to attempt to identify and articulate tacit knowledge.

We would like to note, in passing, that the relatively recent focus on "knowledge management" (KM) is not achievable without tacit knowledge and externalisation: "Organizational knowledge creation is a continuous and dynamic interaction between tacit and explicit knowledge" (Ibid, p70). While KM is important, it is how knowledge can assist individuals, who in turn create more knowledge, which is the focus of this work.

There exists a shared background in email messages. "Persistent talk [in email] provides the context for the solitary activity of viewing the content to which it relates....However, during our interviews we, in fact, saw many more examples of imprecise references that were immediately understood than long, drawn-out, explicit and literal descriptions or references." "...email conversations are grounded in sufficient mutual understanding to allow very brief, sketchy and implicit references to succeed without posing significant problems in interpretation." (Ducheneaut and Bellotti, 2002).

We agree with Nonaka and Takeuchi in that "The semantic aspect of information [as against the syntactic] is more important for knowledge creation, as it focuses on conveyed meaning." Freyd (1983) provides a socio-cognitive frame for a viable communal (i.e., shared or conveyed) knowledge representation:

"what seems common to most of the main approaches to semantics is an assumption that values of semantics components, or features, are critical to word meaning. What is relevant to shareability theory is that a smaller number of features seem to be used than number of words." (pp195-6)

"I am arguing that a dimensional structure for representing knowledge is efficient for communicating meaning between individuals. That is, a small dimensional structure with a small number of values on each dimension is argued to be especially shareable, which might explain why such structures are observed." (pp198-9)

Freyd's suppositions on the dimensional nature of shared knowledge are compatible with a recent, three-level model of cognition by Gärdenfors (2000). How information is represented in this model varies greatly across three different levels. It is the conceptual level that is of relevance to this work.

Gärdenfors argues that the meanings of words come from conceptual (i.e. dimensional) structures in people's heads. In addition, he adopts a socio-cognitive position that the meanings emerge from the conceptual structures harboured by individual cognition together with the linguistic power structure within the community. Of significant note is his adoption of Freyd's supposition: social interactions will constrain these conceptual structures. This has implications for computer-based representations because it may mean that relevant dimensions are not represented, or the value in a dimension may not be weighted sufficiently.

This constriction of the dimensional structure by the individual for social interaction is important. We tend to economise our utterances, for example, by use of anaphora and liberal use of abbreviations made permissible by shared background.

Techniques for extracting knowledge from utterances

Representation

To bridge the gap between cognitive dimensional structures and actual computational representations, we propose using a variant of Hyperspace Analogue to Language (HAL) (Burgess et al., 1998). HAL produces vectorial representations of words in a high dimensional space that seem to correlate with the equivalent human representations. For example, word associations computed on the basis of HAL vectors seem to mimic human word association judgments. HAL is "a model that acquires representations of meaning by capitalizing on large-scale co-occurrence information inherent in the input stream of language". It "...correlated with lexical decision latencies from a word priming task" and "...simulations using HAL accounted for a variety of semantic and associative word priming effects that can be found in the literature...and shed light on the nature of the word relations found in human word-association norm data." In short, HAL vectors seem to be promising computational representations of word meanings from a semiotic-cognitive perspective.

Utterances must be represented for computation so they can be mined. In light of the works of Perry (1997, 1998) and Gärdenfors (2000), and in accord with our semiotic-cognitive stance, we advocate representing words in utterances as dimensional structures. These are the basic carriers of the meaning of the word in question, but in addition, the dimensional structures have pre-semantic (i.e. what is needed to render a syntactic evaluation to an utterance) information embedded.

Prior work (McArthur and Bruza, 2003a and 2003b) has shown benefits of using these structures: pre-semantic information, in the form of part-of-speech, and LSA (see below) for generating post-semantic information by inference. An updated model for the automatic derivation of the dimensional structures from utterances is briefly explained below.

Vector creation

The basic carriers of meaning are the vectorial representations of words in an utterance. These vectors, created by our modified HAL, are input into the mining process.

Part-of-speech (POS)

POS (Part of Speech) tagging is a computationally efficient means of mapping arbitrary tokens into syntactic classes, determining basic linguistic information from a corpus. It is the means by which pre-semantic context can be automatically gleaned from utterances. The technology has matured to achieve high levels of precision. It is gathered by various methods (rule-based, probability-based, and memory-based being most common) all of which add part of speech tags—noun, verb, pronoun etc.—to the original text. LTCHUNK's (Mikheev, 2000; LTCHUNK) POS tagger was used.

Basic anaphora resolution

Anaphora is the co-reference of one expression with an antecedent (*cataphora* is co-reference with a following expression). The antecedent provides the information necessary for interpreting the expression. An example is between the two sentences: "A well-dressed man was speaking. He had a foreign accent." The term "He" in the second sentence is an anaphoric reference to the "well-dressed man" in the first sentence.

Anaphora is common in utterances and in email in particular. We do not attempt full anaphora resolution but implement an extremely basic algorithm: replace references to 'I', 'my' or 'me' with the first name of the sender of the email, and references to 'you' or 'your' with the first name of the receiver (if there is only one; the 'Cc:' metadata was ignored); these elements are part of the email metadata and easily accessible. No other anaphoric references are as easily determined, so terms such as 'he', 'we', 'they', 'it' etc. are left unchanged. We adopt this conservative approach as imprecise anaphora resolution would pollute the vector representations of some words with spurious dimensions.

HAL

Thus far, the exposition of information representation has centred largely upon aspects of Perry's (1998) pre-semantic context. The second level of Perry's three levels, semantic context, will now be addressed. This involves attaching meaning to syntactic structures.

A human encountering a new concept derives the meaning via an accumulation of experience of the contexts in which the concept appears. This opens the door to "learn" the meaning of a concept through how it appears within the context of other concepts. Following this idea, Burgess *et al.* (1998) developed a representational model of semantic memory called Hyperspace Analogue to Language (HAL), which automatically constructs a dimensional semantic space from a corpus of text. The space comprises high dimensional vector representations for each term in the vocabulary. Briefly, given an n-word vocabulary, the HAL space is a n x n matrix constructed by moving a window of length l over the corpus by one word increments ignoring punctuation, sentence and paragraph boundaries. All words within the window are considered as co-occurring with each other with strengths inversely proportional to the distance between them. After traversing the corpus, an accumulated co-occurrence matrix for all the words in a target vocabulary is produced. Note that word pairs in HAL are direction sensitive – the co-occurrence information for words preceding every word and co-occurrence information for words following it are recorded separately by its row and column vectors. By way of illustration, the HAL matrix for the example text *"The effects of spreading pollution on the population of atlantic salmon"* is depicted in Table 1 using a 5 word moving window (l=5). An example of reading the matrix would be that the word *spreading* occurs before *on* (is related to) with strength 4 (5 - 1 intervening word in the window).

Our pilot studies revealed that it was not useful to preserve order information, so, for our purposes, the HAL vector of a word is represented by the addition of its row and column vectors. The quality of HAL vectors is influenced by the window size; the longer the window, the higher the chance of representing spurious associations between terms. Burgess *et al.* used a size of ten in their studies (Ibid). In addition, it is sometimes useful to identify the so-called *quality properties* of a HAL-vector. Quality properties are identified as those dimensions in the HAL vector which are above a certain threshold (e.g., above the average weight within that vector).

	the	eff	of	spr	poll	On	pop	Atl	sal
The		1	2	3	4	5			
eff	5								
of	8	5		1	2	3	5		
spr	3	4	5						
poll	2	3	4	5					
on	1	2	3	4	5				
pop	5		1	2	3	4			
atl	3		5		1	2	4		
sal	2		4			1	3	5	

Table 1: Example of a HAL matrix

Developing dimensional representations of words in emails involves unique challenges, so we modified HAL accordingly. To distinguish Burgess *et al.*'s HAL and our model, we describe our model as HALe (for *e*mail) from this point.

The differences between HAL and HALe are:

1. HAL slides a fixed window across the text with all terms used: semantic information is not used. We use a smaller window (8 versus 10), and only terms tagged by POS as nouns ('NN*'). This is based on earlier trials using verbs ('VB*') and adjectives ('JJ') as well as nouns. Also, nouns are of most interest as all people were tagged as nouns. A simple stop-word removal would not have the same effect, hence our use of POS tagging.

2. The strength of the association between terms is inversely related to their direct distance apart in HAL. Since HALe effectively ignores some terms (see above), it also ignores them as far as strength of association is concerned. So a noun followed by determiner followed by a noun would have the noun-noun association as though the determiner was invisible.

3. The sender and receiver (if there is only one) of the message is weakly associated with every word in the email. The rationale is that the author and receiver of the message should be associated with the communication. Often, no mention of their names occurs in the message itself (ignoring the signature), even with our anaphora resolution, so HAL on the message itself would not associate the people correctly.

In previous work (McArthur and Bruza, 2003a) a non-linear weighting function was used based on identifying syntactic structures (trees) using a shallow natural language parsing technique. We did not make use of such structures in this work since email messages tend to produce trees lacking branches, hence a loss of expressivity.

LSA

Until now, the creation of a high dimensional space, while interesting, is not necessarily better for the discovery of useful associations between people given a certain contextual description. A simple search using, for example, Microsoft Outlook®, could search for authors in the 'From' field and some text in the main body of the email. While the recall and precision of such searches may not be optimal, it is possible to retrieve 'information' and, with more work on the part of the user scanning many messages, perhaps even the same 'knowledge'. Latent Semantic Analaysis (LSA) (Landauer *et al.*, 1998) is a technique through which implicit associations between words that did not exist can be brought to light. Therefore, it is an interesting candidate for uncovering serendipitous associations between the names of people mentioned in emails in relation to a given contextual description (normally expressed by a few keywords). LSA represents the meaning of words as vectors in a dimensional space reduced by singular value decomposition (SVD). The meaning can be considered "as a kind of average of the meaning of all the passages in which it appears and the meaning of a passage as a kind of average of the meaning of all the words it contains" (p261).

The role of SVD is fundamental to LSA. The general claim is that similarities between words can be more reliably estimated in the reduced dimensional space than in the original one. The rationale is that contexts which share frequently co-occurring terms will have a similar representation in the reduced dimensional space, even if they have no terms in common.

For our purposes, the input to the LSA process is the n x n matrix produced by HALe. We did not normalize the values in the matrix as advocated in (Landauer, *et al.*, 1998) because pilot studies revealed a 6-9% improvement using un-normalized values. This is perhaps due to the smaller data set, but may also be due to the pre-semantic and semantic processing before HALe.

After dimensional reduction, the weight (i,j) may be non-zero, whereas it was zero before dimensional reduction. Where positive, it suggests that word i is implied within context j. In other words, LSA can discover implicit associations, or strengthen/weaken existing associations. Such behaviour is relevant for the mining of useful or serendipitous associations: those associations that appear after dimensional reduction, or are strengthened by it, may be suggestive of post-semantic context. Due to space constraints, the dimensional reduction process will not be described further; the details can be found in (Landauer *et al.*, 1998).

Connections: an Example System

Consider the situation in which Naomi is writing a company's annual report. She's interested in the highlights of the year for the 'Guidebeam' product. Guidebeam, created and developed by Peter, has been worked on by many people including Robert. For example, Rupert does all the business-development. Although Naomi works at the desk next to Rupert, and often socialises in the coffee room, she has forgotten that Rupert is involved. She emails Peter asking him to describe the highlights of Guidebeam's year. In truth, Naomi is more immediately interested in the business highlights than the development highlights, so it would be better to ask Rupert rather than Peter.

Naomi, like most people, is blessed with the ability to forget what she perceives to be unimportant, or at least to forget that she knows it. This is a feature of what some have termed "cognitive economy" (Gabbay and Woods, 2000). It may be behind the change in discourse structure brought about by information overload (Jones *et al.*, 2001). Having forgotten Rupert's involvement, the information need Naomi has is primarily "tell me the highlights of Guidebeam in 2002". However, there is no-one or no system to ask such a question of, so her next question is "tell me who I can contact *now* to satisfy my original question."

The remainder of this paper describes a system that was built so that Naomi could answer such a question should, say, Rupert and Peter not be available (on holiday, perhaps not with the organisation anymore, or even deceased). These situations tax both the asker and receiver of questions: Peter would need to spend some time and effort determining the reason behind Naomi's request, and then answering it as best he could. It is a high cost solution.

Tacit knowledge extracted from the email utterances of Rupert, Peter and Robert assists Naomi to answer the 'who' question. It also shows the rich detail of explicit and implicit relationships that can support Naomi becoming more informed about Guidebeam and promote the internalising of the tacit knowledge from the relevant associations.

Data

The base data used for these experiments came from 14,424 email messages from the 'sent' and work-related folders of three individuals at our small-medium organisation: Peter, Robert and Rupert (see Table 2). Only messages from 2001 and 2002 were used since in our scenario, Naomi's need is for recent information. No attempt to separate private and work communications was made on the sent messages. Categories used by the individuals to store their email were not used: data was simply concatenated together into a single large email folder for each person. Not all messages relating to work have been kept by any of the three people. This is reflective of the usual state of practice in the real-world of email.

No standard test set of electronic mail exists (to our knowledge), since organisations, groups and individuals are reluctant to have private email made public. It behoves us to note, therefore, that the experiments cannot be independently verified as we also cannot make available the raw data. We strongly believe that any similar data will generate results that do not differ substantially from those shown here.

	Peter	Robert	Rupert	Total
2001 messages	710	1775	521	3006
2002 messages	1713	1190	1691	4594
2001 and 2002	2423	2965	2212	7600
	(528)	(602)	(430)	(1560)

Table 2: Email data statistics

Numbers in brackets are "Usable" messages: those not from mailing lists (ignoring messages in the 'sent' folder where the receiver was the originator of the email), and where the unquoted section of the body of the message had less than 150 lines. The latter condition being used to eliminate large text documents as the primary focus was the direct communication as originally authored in the email.

Method

The email messages were manipulated in the following ways and order:
- Text pre-processing
  - Messages from mailing lists were discarded, as the focus was messages internal to the organisation
  - URI's were replaced with the term 'URL' otherwise the POS tagger erroneously separated out the components and tried to tag them
  - Shorthand words using quotes were expanded for the POS tagger: 'll (will), 've (have), I'm (I am), 're (are), and some words ending in 's (is)
  - Parts of messages whose MIME tag was not 'text/plain' were discarded
  - The identifying name of the sender and receiver of the message was made consistent where the change was unambiguous over the whole set of messages. For example, some messages to Robert were sent to '<xxx@yyy>' or 'Rob <xxxx@yyy>', while a large majority were sent to 'Robert <xxx@yyy>'; all messages of the first two kinds were modified to be the same as the latter in such cases.
  - Quotations of other messages were deleted since they usually occurred within the email collection already. Again, the focus was in the words the author was using for that particular message, rather than the context surrounding the message. Lewis and Knowles (1997) demonstrated that, in finding parents of messages to be threaded, words in the quoted

part of emails are reiterated enough in the non-quoted section(s) to provide a useful level of similarity between the messages. We anticipate examining whether incorporating quotations between messages leads to any improvements.
- Signatures and other trailing 'garbage' were deleted
- POS tagging
  - POS tagging was applied to all remaining message parts
- Anaphora resolution
  - Simple anaphora resolution changed words 'I', 'my', 'me', 'you', 'your' and 'yourself' in the POS'ed text. In some cases no first name of author and/or receiver could be determined so the term was left unchanged so as not to pollute the vector space. For example, in Robert's total usable email, the count of anaphoric references by the 'PRP' POS tag is shown in Table 3 (bold indicates terms we resolved). Almost 50% of PRP-tagged anaphora was resolvable.

Word	Frequency	%
I	**1299**	**18.1**
you	**1270**	**17.7**
It	1137	15.8
we	1047	14.6
your	**557**	**7.8**
they	272	3.8
our	263	3.7
Me	**245**	**3.4**
My	**198**	**2.8**
their	177	2.5
...	709	9.8
Total	7174	100

Table 3: Anaphora references (Robert's email, all usable messages)

- HALe
  - HALe was performed on the tagged messages and used to uncover explicit connections between people
- LSA
  - LSA was performed on the set of vectors produced by HALe to uncover tacit or implicit connections by creating new associations, or strengthening and weakening existing ones

Results

Table 4 shows some statistics of the email corpus used as input to HALe.

	Robert	Peter	Rupert	Total
Total words in the POS-tagged messages	49035	91788	37315	178138
Total HALe unique words	2623	1818	3010	5052
Total HALe unique words accepted by Unix spell	1750 (67%)	1203 (66%)	1898 (63%)	3043 (60%)

Table 4: Number of vectors produced by HALe

As a sample of the type of associations and explicit knowledge that HALe produces, Table 5 shows a single (un-normalised) vector for "guidebeam" from the combined emails of Peter, Rupert and Robert. People's names are in boldface.

peter:199, guidebeam:148, search:126, **rupert:114**, technology:114, installation:87, url:62, us:61, **robert:61**, com:60, government:59, query:55, management:54, categories:53, dstc:53, www.:51, engine:51, meeting:46, component:45, information:45, boeing:44, tool:42, catch-up:42, kernel:42, system:41, philosophy:39, p:39, knowledge:39, abc:37, chic:35, people:34, yp:33, panoptic:32, user:31, zen:30, **paul:31**, re:29, think:28, need:28, licence:28, **naomi:28**, partners:27, minutes:25, words:24, package:24, terms:23, project:23, gbst:23, ability:23, specs:23, citr:23, media:23, **justin:23**, @noptic:22, **yvonne:22**, **rob:22**, term:22, examiners:21, we:21, base:21, pb:21, agencies:21, acquiring:21, use:21, actions:21, team:21, +panoptic:21, google:21, and:21, data:21, way:21, web-based:21, libraries:20, time:20, feedback:20, review:20,site:20, recommendations:20, awards:20, article:20, keyword:19, development:19, yahoo:19, intranet:19, week:18, reformulation:18, anything:18, presentation:18, dll:18, proposal:18, **dave:17**, queries:17, results:17, capex:16, cheers:16, test:16,tuesday:16, box:15, **simon:15**, health:15, portal:15, doc:15, fee:15, niche:15, business:15, hib:14, ideas:14, context:14,web:14, file:14, website:14, work:14, idea:14, problem:14, organisation:14, advantage:14, view:14, access:14, talking:14, title:14, log-files:14, reason:14, …

Table 5: "guidebeam" vector produced by HALe

Observe that not all of the associations embedded in the above vector make sense to a wide audience, nor should they, as they are associations relevant within a certain context[1]. Nevertheless, some associations are clearly understandable to anyone (from Table 5: guidebeam is probably a search technology, with some relationship with government, and does queries or management using categories – all true); some relationships require general or specific domain knowledge ('abc', 'gbst' and 'citr' are organisations, p@noptic is a search engine); while some such as "dll" require specific knowledge probably only available to the owner of the email. Finally, serendipitous associations, one of the rationales behind our techniques, can be uncovered (see the discussion of "yukio" in the next section).

---

[1] For this reason, the developers of HAL refer to the matrix produced by HAL as a "high dimensional context space" (Burgess *et al.* 1998)

As Naomi is specifically interested in people associated with Guidebeam, Tables 6 describes the highest weighted associations for "guidebeam" from each person's email, and the combination of all three email sets, along with the same vectors after applying LSA. Table 7 shows more detail of the changes wrought by LSA in uncovering implicit associations for "guidebeam".

Analysis and Discussion

Let us return to the scenario where Naomi wishes to find out who are the major people involved in the Guidebeam product for her marketing report. Figure 1 is a network representation of some of the data from Table 6 (for clarity, the weights of the connections are not shown). It depicts a network of people surrounding the context description "Guidebeam". The people who are most highly connected to the context – Peter (199), Rupert (114) and Robert (61) – are identified from the combined HALe vector for "guidebeam". They are the highest weighted people, and they are also internal to the organisation and fortuitously have their email available. It is to this full organisational information space that Naomi would initially come, and the results could be immediately presented.

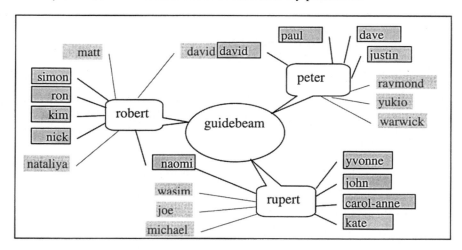

Figure 1: Context-sensitive network of people (Context = "guidebeam")

Radiating from these three key people are others associated with "guidebeam". Those shown with a dark-grey enclosed box [   ] are derived in the same way as the key people, except they are taken from the "guidebeam" vectors of the respective person's email: that is, from a localised space not from the global (combined) email space. For example, "naomi" can be seen in the HALe "guidebeam" vectors of both Robert (16) and Rupert (12).

Table 6: "guidebeam" vector (people's names only)

	Rupert		Peter		Robert		Combined	
	HALe	LSA (6)	HALe	LSA (6)	HALe	LSA (6)	HALe	LSA (6)
	peter 105	rupert 75	robert 77	Peter 76	robert 28	robert 30	peter 199	peter 202
	rupert 66	wasim 26	rupert 17	Bruza 31	rupert 25	peter 28	rupert 114	rupert 95
	robert 33	peter 25	peter 12	raymond 22	peter 17	matt 10	robert 61	robert 70
	yvonne 22	carol-anne 17	naomi 8	robert 17	naomi 16	rupert 7	paul 31	bruza 39
	rob 15	robert 15	simon 6	yukio 13	simon 15	lee 7	naomi 28	julia 39
	naomi 12	lee 15	ron 5	sweeney 9	ron 12	bruza 6	justin 23	lee 20
	mcarthur 9	joe 9	kim 4	warwick	kim 11	rob 6	yvonne 22	wasim 18
	bruza 9	michael 9	justin 4	mark	mcarthur 10	mcarthur 5	rob 22	raymond 17
	john 9	charley 6	nick 3	dawei	kim 7	kim 5	dave 17	yukio 15
	carol-anne 8	kevin 6	rob 3	dave	davies 7	davies 3	simon 15	keith 11
	kate 7	jacqui 5	andry 3	andry	ron 3	ron 2	nick 14	joe 11
	⋯	⋯	⋯	⋯	⋯	⋯	⋯	⋯
Avg	0.9	11	11	0.7	9	0.7	14	1.4
Stdd	3.2	11	11	2.6	6	2	18	6

Table 7: Change in "guidebeam" vector between pre and post LSA (people's names only)

	Rupert		Peter		Robert		Combined	
	Additions	Largest change	Additions	Largest change	Additions	Largest change	Additions	Largest change
	wasim 26	peter -80	bruza 17	paul -20	rupert 10	matt -30	julia 39	paul -28
	lee 15	yvonne -20	raymond 12	rupert -20	naomi 6	bruza -20	wasim 18	naomi -26
	joe 9	robert -18	robert 8	dave -18	simon 5	mcarthur -15	raymond 17	rupert -19
	michael 9	rob -12	yukio 6	justin -12	ron 2	davies -12	yukio 15	justin -18
	charley 9	⋯	sweeney 5	⋯	david 2	david 1	keith 11	⋯
	kevin 8	kate 2	warwick 4	peter 4	nataliya 1	lee 2	joe 11	robert 10
	jacqui 7	warwick 9	mark 9	warwick 9	ross	robert 1	jacqui 8	lee 15
	teresa 7	dawei 11	dawei 3	mark 11	philippe	peter 11	mark 8	bruza 30

Naomi can see several details immediately: firstly, Robert, Peter and/or Rupert are the most likely people she needs to contact; secondly, she is aided to recall, by the connection between herself and Rupert and Robert, that she has had emails before about Guidebeam from these two people.

Figure 2 presents a similar view of the data to Figure 1[2], except the focus is no longer on the second tier of people, but on non-people elements. Naomi can see that Rupert's work with Guidebeam has been with "chic" and "boeing" (organisations), and "management", "installation", "licence" and "meeting".

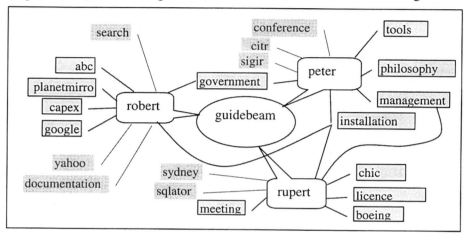

Figure 2: Context-sensitive network of topics (Context = "guidebeam")

In both figures, further important information is available. Thus far, what has been available to Naomi has been explicit knowledge: that which HALe has captured and made available. However, there is implicit or tacit knowledge also available. This is uncovered by techniques such as LSA. Table 7 displayed the changes in people's names, and these are reflected in Figure 1 by light-grey un-enclosed boxes .

The implicit connection between Robert and David, shown in Figure 1, links Peter and Robert by some association to David (again, without going into detail, there is a strong association between the three people). Similarly in Figure 2 Naomi can see that there is an implicit association from Rupert with Guidebeam and SQLator (they are both products that Rupert is associated with; being products many associated terms are in common – installation, licence, etc.).

Naomi is reasonably satisfied – she has identified the key players for Guidebeam within the organisation; been assisted to recall that Rupert, sitting next to her, is someone she should talk with; and been made aware of connections

---

[2] Space precludes the presentation of the base data from which this diagram is drawn

between people and topics associated with Guidebeam. However, two further examples can demonstrate serendipitous flows of information.

Peter has an association with Justin in connection with Guidebeam (Fig.1). The "Justin" connection in Peter's email provides connections with Robert and Rupert. In turn, Justin in Rupert's email and Robert's email show strong associations with Nick. Again, the strong associations of Nick, in these two email sets, both agree on a connection with Kate. Thus a network of explicit and implicit connections can be formed, and Naomi can become informed that an association of some form exists between Justin, Nick and her colleague Kate. Note that no attempt to disambiguate the nature of the association is necessary, although it may be assisted by examining the vectors.

The second example shows how, if access is available to the original email messages, associations can be disambiguated and explained. From Fig.1., the LSA vectors offer the (possibly) implicit connections to "Warwick", "Raymond" and "Yukio". Naomi is curious about "Yukio", so she sends an expanded query to a text retrieval system storing the emails, based on the LSA vector for Yukio. From the emails retrieved, Naomi learns that years before, Peter and Yukio were performing joint research on the "Hyperindex browser", a forerunner of the Guidebeam product.

The last example used the LSA (or HALe) vector as the basis of an expanded query to a text retrieval system serving the email collection. The vector contains weighted associations to terms which the retrieval system can use to boost precision. Recent large-scale experiments using HAL vectors for query expansion in text retrieval has produced encouraging results with respect to precision (Bruza & Song, 2002). In practice, high precision can equate to lower cognitive load on the user as they are not confronted by large amounts of irrelevant material (in this case emails). Compare this to a "normal" search system which would process the 14000+ email messages and find that 1020 mention the word 'guidebeam' in the message body. Even a browsing system which measured, for example, how many messages mentioned "guidebeam" for each sender, would not uncover particularly useful associations (the rankings would be Peter >> Kevin > Rupert > Justin > Robert > Ron, Carol-Anne, Craig > ... among a total of 34 unique senders evenly spread through the three personal email data sets).

Although all the three people whose email is being used have an organisational association with Guidebeam, it is not necessarily their major concern: only 1,020 of the 14,424 messages mentioned Guidebeam somewhere in the message body. The vectors with the largest dimensions in the combined messages of the three people, i.e. the words with the largest number of associations and thus used in the largest number of contexts, were peter (1275), robert (968), url (729), rupert (619), information (494), guidebeam (422), time (305), etc. We do not believe that the choice of only three email contributors, and their associations to Guidebeam, has hade any negative impact on the experiment.

The use of private email[3] is a difficult issue for privacy reasons. For this work, the use of the unmodified email was required as the purpose was to identify useful and interesting people. It would be feasible to produce the dimensional spaces from the original email messages, and allow people access to the spaces without providing access to the original text: an expertise management assistant could send an email to the 'owners' of particular emails that match an external search for specific expertise; it would then be the decision of the individuals concerned to answer the query. While fraught with dangers, we use the reasoning implied by Nardi *et al.* (2000), and believe that the various ends are worth the troubles.

Conclusions & Future Work

This paper is about finding useful and sometimes serendipitous connections between people by mining semantic associations from their email communications. To this end, the HALe model has been detailed which produces high dimensional representations of words within a context space defined by a collection, or sub-collection of emails. HALe can be used as the basis of a discovery mechanism to extract explicit associations between people given a seed contextual description (e.g., the name of a product, a particular person etc.). Latent Semantic Analysis (LSA) is applied to the high dimensional context space produced by HALe to "lift" implicit associations between people.

By means of a substantial email corpus, the discovery techniques have been shown to be feasible. We believe the techniques would scale to larger corpora, and probably be applicable to other utterance-based data sets such as mailing lists. The dimensional reduction aspect inherent to LSA has the potential to become a computational bottleneck for larger collections of email, but recent research from the knowledge discovery and data mining community has uncovered approximations of LSA, which seem to outperform LSA as well as being computationally tractable (e.g. Karypis & Han, 2000).

The scenarios presented in this paper are drawn from real-life experience in a small-to-medium information technology company. Anecdotal evidence suggests that useful, appropriate and at times serendipitous associations between people are being brought to light modulo the given context. Future experiments with larger datasets will feature more detailed user feedback. Our results show that the range of associations to people are very sensitive to the context space being used; for example, the network of people surrounding Guidebeam from Rupert's email is different to the network computed from Peter's email. Therefore we conclude that discovery of networks should not be restricted to a global email corpus, but should involve a mixture of information gleaned from the global corpus to

---

[3] or email considered private; some country's laws make the use of email conducted using an account supplied by the organisation the property of the organisation. There is still resistance to this.

investigate associations within particular sub-corpora. In this paper, the sub-corpora were static, but there is no reason not to employ dynamic corpora, like a set of emails retrieved from an intranet search engine based around a certain contextual description.

We feel that the techniques presented here form part of a solution to allow informal, ephemeral and mostly hidden networks of people to be discovered. Such "social networks" are integral to fostering collaboration in the enterprise, making use of all the resources possible. In short, we claim to have made a step to help enhance the awareness of individuals to their environment: other individuals, groups and information.

Acknowledgments

The work reported in this paper has been funded in part by the Co-operative Research Centre for Enterprise Distributed Systems Technology (DSTC) through the Australian Federal Government's CRC Programme (Department of Industry, Science & Resources). We are also immensely grateful to Rupert for allowing us access to his email repository.

References

Ackerman, M. and McDonald, D. (1996): 'Answer Garden 2: merging organizational memory with collaborative help'. In *Proceedings of the ACM Conference on Computer-Supported Cooperative Work* (CSCW), 1996

Bruza, P.D and Song, D. (2002): 'Inferring query models by computing information flow'. In *Proceedings of the 11th International Conference on Information and Knowledge Management (CIKM 2002)* ACM Press, pp.260-269.

Burgess, C., Livesay, K. and Lund, K. (1998): "Explorations in context space: words, sentences, discourse". *Discourse Processes*, v25, pp.211-257

Ducheneaut, N.B. (2002): 'The social impacts of electronic mail in organizations: a case study of electronic power games using communication genres'. *Information, Communication and Society*, v5, n2, pp.153-188

Ducheneaut, N.B. and Bellotti, V. (2002): 'Ceci n'est pas un objet? Talking about things in email', forthcoming in a special issue of the *Journal of Human-Computer Interaction*

Freyd, J. (1983): "Shareability: the social psychology of epistemology", *Cognitive Science*, v7, pp.191-210

Gabbay, D. and Woods, J. (2000): 'Abduction', Lecture notes from *ESSLLI 2000 (European Summer School on Logic, Language and Information)*. Online: http://www.cs.bham.ac.uk/~esslli/notes/gabbay.html

Gärdenfors, P. (2000): *Conceptual Spaces: the Geometry of Thought.* MIT Press, London, 2000

Jones, Q., Ravid, G. and Refaeli, S. (2001): 'Information overload and virtual public discourse boundaries'. In *INTERACT, Eighth IFIP TC.13 Conference on Human-Computer Interaction,* Japan IOS Press

Karypis, G. and Han, E-H. (2000): 'Concept indexing: a fast dimensionality reduction algorithm with applications to document retrieval & categorization'. University of Minnesota, Department of Computer Science, Technical Report #00-016

Kautz, H., Selman, B. and Shah, M. (1997): 'ReferralWeb: combining social networks with collaborative filtering'. In *Communications of the ACM*, v40 n3, March 1997

Kimble, C., Hildreth, P. and Grimshaw, D. (1998): 'The role of contextual clues in the creation of information overload'. In *Proceedings of the 3rd UKAIS Conference*. April 1998, Lincoln University, McGraw Hill, pp.405-412

Landauer, T.K., Foltz, P.W., and Latham, D. (1998): 'Introduction to Latent Semantic Analysis'. *Discourse Processes*, v25, pp.259-284

Lewis, D. and Knowles, K. (1997): 'Threading electronic mail: a preliminary study'. *Information, Processing and Management*, v33 n2, pp.209-217

LTCHUNK (software): online (6 May 2003) http://www.ltg.ed.ac.uk/software/index.html

Lund, K. and Burgess, C. (1996): "Producing high-dimensional semantic spaces from lexical co-occurrence". *Behavior Research Methods, Instruments & Computers*, v28(2), pp.203-208

Mikheev, A. (2000): 'Document centered approach to text normalization'. In *Proceedings of SIGIR'2000*, pp. 136--143.

McArthur, R. and Bruza, P.D. (2003a): 'Dimensional representations of knowledge in online community', in Ohsawa, Y. (ed.) (2003, in press) *Chance Discovery*, Springer-Verlag

McArthur, R. and Bruza, P.D. (2003b): 'Discovery of tacit knowledge and topical ebbs and flows within utterances of online community', in Ohsawa, Y. (ed.) (2003, in press) *Chance Discovery*, Springer-Verlag

Nardi, B. and Engström, Y. (1999): 'A web on the wind: the structure of invisible work'. In Nardi, B. and Engström, Y. (eds) *Computer-Supported Cooperative Work*, v8 n1-2

Nardi, B., Whittaker, S., and Schwarz, H. (2000): 'It's not what you know, it's who you know: work in the information age'. *First Monday*, v5, n5, May 2000. Online: http://firstmonday.org/issues/issue5_5/nardi/index.html

Nonaka, I. and Takeuchi, H. (1995): *The Knowledge-Creating Company*, OUP, New York

Ogata, H. and Yano, Y. (1998): 'Collecting oganisational memory based on social networks in collaborative learning'. In *WebNet*, pp.822-827

Perry, J. (1997): 'Indexicals and demonstratives,' in *A companion to the philosophy of language*, Hales, B. and Wright, C. Eds. Oxford: Blackwell, 1997, pp.593-595.

Perry, J. (1998) 'Indexicals, contexts, and unarticulated constituents', in *Proceedings of the 1995 CSLI-Amsterdam Logic, Language and Computation Conference*. Stanford: CSLI Publications, 1998

Schwartz, M. and Wood, D. (1993): 'Discovering shared interests among people using graph analysis of global electronic mail traffic'. In *Communication of the ACM*, v36, n8, 1993

K. Kuutti, E.H. Karsten, G. Fitzpatrick, P. Dourish and K. Schmidt (eds.), *ECSCW 2003: Proceedings of the Eighth European Conference on Computer Supported Cooperative Work, 14-18 September 2003, Helsinki, Finland*, pp. 41-60.

Applying Cyber-Archaeology

Quentin Jones
New Jersey Institute of Technology, USA
qgjones@acm.org

Abstract. Online spaces that enable public shared inter-personal communications are of significant social and economic importance. This paper outlines a theoretical model and methodology, labeled cyber-archaeology, for researching the relationship between such spaces and the behaviors they contain. The methodology utilizes large-scale field studies into user behavior in online spaces to identify technology-associated user constraints to sustainable patterns of online large-scale shared social interactions.

Empirical research was conducted to assess the validity of both the theoretical model and methodology. It was based on the analysis of 2.65 million messages posted to 600 Usenet newsgroups over a six month period, and 478,240 email messages sent to 487 email lists managed by Listserv software over a 5-month period. Overall, our findings support a key aspect of the model, namely that individual 'information overload' coping strategies have an observable impact on mass-interaction discourse dynamics. Further, that it is possible to demonstrate a link between technology type and information overload impacts through field studies of online behavior.

Cyber-archaeology is discussed in terms of its ability to offer insight into aspects of CMC-tool usability, technology design, and to guide future empirical research.

Introduction

It is widely accepted that the online spaces that enable public shared inter-personal communications are of significant social and economic importance (e.g. Wellman 2001). To date, a very large proportion of research into the behavior of users of online spaces such as interactive email lists, Usenet newsgroups, and bulletin board systems have been in terms of "virtual community" (e.g. Rheingold 1993; Cherny 1999). Researchers have typically utilized one form of social theory or another to guide analysis and paid little attention to the impact on user-behavior of the virtual spaces where shared public online interactions occur. The result is that we have a limited understanding of how the virtual spaces created by different technologies differ in their impact on user interactions. However, it is in the design of these online spaces, rather than user's social networks, where we can often exert the greatest level of control. Therefore, there is a need for CSCW researchers to examine the nature of the relationship between the virtual spaces typically used for shared public online-interactions, their technological platforms, and the behaviors such systems contain. This alternate focus, which is adopted in this paper, shifts the emphasis away from notions of community, and its attention to people and their relations, to the nature of the virtual spaces where shared public interpersonal interactions occur, and the constraints such places impose on online behavior.

To understand the impact of online public interpersonal interaction spaces on behavior an appropriate methodology is needed that is not culture or time specific. Unfortunately, the fact that this question is under-researched means that no clear analytical technique leaps to mind as a preferred or even obvious method of choice. The difficulty in choosing an appropriate methodology is exacerbated by the demand for measures that are relatively culture and time independent, as this means we cannot rely on the in-depth examinations of a small number of unique spaces and associated users' online behavior. This suggests that virtual ethnography in its various forms is not a preferred methodology. At the same time, we cannot use normative statistics to predict in a deterministic fashion the relationship between a technology and user-behavior (Jones 1997). This is because social context determines social outcomes (Spears and Lea 1992), not the enabling technology. For the same reasons it is extremely difficult to design laboratory studies with the necessary ecological validity.

In the sections that follow the cyber-archaeology approach is outlined as a means to understanding and comparing types of computer mediated shared interpersonal interactions spaces. The approach described utilizes large-scale field studies into user behavior in online spaces to identify technology-associated constraints to large-scale interaction dynamics. After outlining the theoretical foundations of the method, a description is given of the empirical research undertaken to assess its validity. This empirical research is based on the analysis of 2.65 million messages posted to 600 Usenet newsgroups over a six month period, and 478,240 email messages sent to 487 email lists managed by Listserv software over a 5-month period.

Theoretical Model

Mobilizing Archaeological Theory for CSCW

Scientists frequently seek to understand new phenomena by using analogies (Steinfeld and Fulk 1987) thereby mobilizing an existing body of knowledge to help explain new phenomena and new situations. Labeling a new phenomenon such as online social structures with a familiar name, such as 'community' or 'social group', and others listed in Table I, is useful because it allows authors to effectively communicate and generalize their findings by presenting results in a larger context. Each of the authors listed in Table I is struggling to find terminology to depict the sense of identity and connectedness, which is a feature of cyber-society. While on the surface a number of these metaphors may seem to be interchangeable, each is associated with a different set of assumptions about the significance of various social processes. However, the degree of interchangeability suggests a lack of specificity and a tension between social understanding and research strategy. Further, these analogies are not sufficient for an examination of the impact of the relationship between various computer mediated communication (CMC) technologies and the interactions they support.

Table I. Examples of Metaphors Used for Group-CMC Based Social Structures

Social Structure	Examples of Authors
Community	Rheingold 1993
Small Social Group	Sproull and Farj 1997
Social Networks	Wellman 2000
Forum / Discussion Groups	Rojo 1997
Voluntary Network	Butler 2001

The discussion above leads us to distinguish computer mediated social structures from the spaces and places where users gather and perhaps interact online. In Table II metaphors for interaction spaces are listed. Most of these suggest something about underling social processes. However, if the aim is to investigate the relationship between an interaction space and interaction dynamics, as it is here, then we do not want to prejudice research by using terms with connotations about particular social processes. Jones and Rafaeli (2000a) proposed the use of the term virtual public in part, because the label conveys a neutral picture of the social processes that occur within such spaces.

Table II. Examples of Metaphors Used for Places and Spaces

Place	Examples of Authors
Chat Rooms	Reid 1991
Team Rooms / Workrooms	Roseman and Greenberg 1996
Conference	Hiltz 1985
Virtual Airport Bar	Doheny-Farina 1996
Cyber-Inns	Coate 1992
Virtual Settlement	Jones 1997
Commons	Kollock and Smith 1996
Virtual Public	Jones 2000a
Information Super highway	Jones 1995

Virtual publics are symbolically delineated computer mediated spaces such as email lists, newsgroup, Internet Relay Chat (IRC) channels etc., whose existence is relatively transparent and open, that allow groups of individuals to attend and contribute to a similar set of computer-mediated interpersonal interactions. The term 'virtual public' is adopted here, primarily, for two reasons. Firstly, for our purposes it is important that we distinguish between cybersociety (Jones 1995), virtual communities (Jones 1997), and open public interactions spaces (Jones and Rafaeli 2000a). Secondly, as will become apparent below, we need a simple label to describe online, shared, interpersonal interaction spaces, whose membership and existence is fairly open for both observation and user participation. However, the development of the term of virtual public does not immediately bring to mind any particular research approach.

To arrive at a broad understanding of various aspects of human social behavior typically requires examination of findings from a number of research approaches, with the value of each depending upon the issue under investigation. In this case, where an examination is being made of the link between mediated-space and online behavior, a number of other established disciplines that attempt to come to terms with human environments stand out as being of potential value. These include geography, human or bio ecology, architecture, urban design, and archaeology. Each of these disciplines shares and uses techniques and methods originally developed in other fields, including physics and mathematics.

In Jones (1997), and Jones and Rafaeli (2000b), various reasons were listed as to why CSCW researchers might find theories from archaeology of potential value. These include a mutual interest in artifacts, for the archaeologist items like pottery and arrow heads, for HCI researchers items like listserv postings, web site structures, Usenet content, user logs etc. Second, differences between duration of social action and material remains both online and offline. Archeology has had to deal directly with the problem of explanatory scale when examining the relationship between artifacts and society. An understanding of how to deal with this issue is of crucial importance to the construction of valid theories of online behavior. By examining explanatory scale, archaeological theory has been able to produce explanations of the connection between technology and society without recourse to simple technological determinism. Third, although social theory dominates archaeology as it does in CMC research, a significant body of relevant theory exists regarding phenomena that operate over a range of analytical levels. Finally, archaeological theory exists that guides research into the impact of material on human settlements, namely that of Fletcher (1995), that can be adapted to guide CSCW researchers.

Fletchers' (1995) model shows how the material components of settlements play a substantial and essential role in many large-scale transformations of human community life. Material becomes recognizable as an actor without intent, whose operations occur at a scale beyond the limited perceptions of daily community life. Using Fletcher's methodology, cybersociety can also be examined one step removed from social theory, where human intent is not of particular importance and larger-scale relationships between technology and behavior can be observed. Fletcher argues that the starting point for modeling the impact of technology on social structures is to recognize the degree to which material entities can effectively control or aid social life.

Fletcher (1995) mapped various settlement types over the last fifteen thousand years by geographic size and population. What he discovered was a relationship between the upper boundaries of a ratio of community size to residential density, and a society's available technology. Figure 1 below provides a simplified graphical illustration of the results of mapping this relationship. It summarizes the proposed behavioral constraints on the growth of various types of human settlements. The boundaries represent zones rather than rigid, deterministic, instantaneous halt lines. They are indicators of an uncertain range of likelihood within which the behavioral limitations become severe.

Figure 1. Settlement Interaction-Communication Stress Model
Simplified from Fletcher 1995

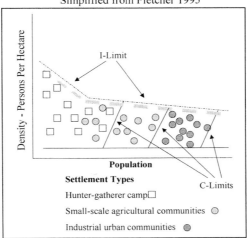

The I-Limit in the Figure 1 refers to the interaction limits individuals can cope with and which place a limit on the maximum density of a settlement. For example, hunter-gatherer communities are able to support a higher level of average residential density than industrial urban communities, although their populations are much smaller. The recognition of this relationship has a significant and important impact on our understanding of the growth of human settlement size and population. The C-Limits represent the constraints imposed on population expansion by the maximum extent to which a given assemblage of communication technologies can function adequately. Thus, for example, city populations were able to dramatically increase because of the industrial revolution. Fletcher's approach provides a modeling technique to explore the boundaries of virtual publics.

In a similar fashion to Fletcher's notion of constrained human settlement, and despite technological advances and popular thinking about the limitlessness of cyberspace, it is taken as axiomatic here that each CMC technology acts to enable only a limited range of social interactions. Further, that the range of social interactions enabled and constrained by different CMC technologies will vary. It follows from these assumptions that if we could take the appropriate measures of interactions occurring in different computer mediated shared interpersonal interaction spaces, then we would be able see the ways in which these spaces enable and constrain interactions, and how various types of spaces differ. By applying Fletcher's approach, which is, not time-line or historically focused we hope to mobilize one archaeological theory for CSCW, which we have labeled cyber-archaeology. This will be achieved by first examining the main human constraints to CMC discussed in the literature as limiting online public shared interpersonal interactions, information overload. Second, by outlining a constraints-model of virtual public interaction dynamics and a methodology for testing various associated hypotheses.

Information Overload

The amount of information available to people is growing rapidly so it not surprising that many of us have experienced what is commonly referred to as "information overload", with the associated sensation of being swamped (Shenk 1997). This occurs because the degree to which we can effectively process information is limited by the finite capacity of human cognition. Information overload is defined here as "the state of an individual or system in which excessive communication inputs cannot be processed and utilized, leading to breakdown" (Rogers and Agarwala-Rogers 1975). In the field of psychology where most empirical research into information overload has been conducted, information overload has traditionally been operationalized as information presented at a rate too fast for a person to process (e.g. Gopher and Donchin 1986). In the context of CMC research, information overload has been interpreted in the light of two additional interrelated concepts. First, the delivery of too many communications, that results in individuals receiving more communications than they can respond to. This type of information overload is referred to as 'conversational overload' (Whittaker et. al. 1998). The second, which is termed 'information entropy' (Hiltz and Turoff 1985), is when incoming messages are insufficiently organized by topic or content to be easily recognized as significant or as part of a conversation's history.

Psychologists have recognized for many years that humans have a limited-capacity to store current information in memory (e.g. William James in the 19th century). The analysis of this information overload producing limitation led in the 1950's to foundational work in cognitive psychology. Technologists also recognized early on the need to address the limited ability of people to cope with the vast amounts of information produced in the modern world. Vannevar Bush's landmark paper "As We May Think" (1945) which led to the windows computer interface and the World Wide Web, can in fact be seen as a paper proposing that we need to build better tools for coping with information overload (Simpson et. al. 1996). However, while technologies have helped individuals process more information, and through technologies such as email, to increase the size of their personal social networks (Whittaker, Jones, Terveen 2002), it is shown in this paper that information-processing limits still impact on social interactions observed online.

One of the first scientists to notice the negative social effects of information overload was the sociologist Georg Simmel (1950) who wrote of the overload of sensations in the modern urban world that caused city dwellers to become jaded and develop an incapacity to react to new situations with the appropriate energy. This was followed by the writings of the social psychologist Stanley Milgram who used the concept of information overload to explain bystander behavior (1969). Milgram hypothesized that the bystanders' often disregard events and depersonalize others in their environment as a means of coping with information overload. Since early research into the connection between information overload and city life, researchers have linked information overload to human evolution (Dunbar 1996), settlement size (Fletcher 1995), and as shown below, patterns of inter-personal interaction on the Internet.

As noted in the discussion above, the maximum density and geographic spread of a culture's settlements is also linked to the management of information overload (Fletcher 1995). It is reasoned here that in a similar fashion to interactions in real settlements, sustainable interaction dynamics that occur using virtual publics (Jones and Rafaeli 2000a), such as open interactive email lists, open Internet Relay Chat channels, Usenet newsgroups etc., are constrained by information overload. This occurs because it logically follows that if limitations exist to an individual's ability to effectively process certain virtual public message patterns, then this will impact on the sustainability of such patterns of group-CMC. That is, beyond a particular level of average user communication processing-load, behavioral stress will make existing patterns of public interactive group communication unsustainable. Communication load is the processing effort required to deal with a set of communications.

Individuals can take a range of actions to reduce the impact of information overload resulting from group-CMC. Actions include: making an increased effort; learning new information management techniques to reduce the information overload; failing to respond or attend to certain messages, thereby lowering the growth in communication load; producing simpler responses; storing inputs and responding to them as time permits; making more erroneous responses; and ending all participation in the group communication. It is possible to reduce these seven responses to two primary options for a population of experienced users. The first option is simply to end participation. The second option is to change ongoing communicative behavior. It is hypothesized below that these seven individual responses to overloaded group-CMC can lead to observable impacts of virtual public interaction dynamics.

Although we do not have an exact measure of communication-processing load, we do know that it relates to a number of message system characteristics. Users generally have to make more of an effort to reply coherently to a thread (a chain of messages) than to a single message (Lewis et al. 1997). Higher message interactivity correlates with higher communication-processing load. Similarly, a dense pattern of messages (high frequency of postings) will require quicker and more sustained processing by group members. Therefore, message density will also co-vary with communication-processing load. It is also likely that an increase in interactional-incoherence (e.g. fragmented sentences, disrupted turn adjacency, reversed sequencing, communication lags, agrammatical language, and interactionally disjointed messages) will also increase communication-processing load (Herring 1999).

Abstracting the notion of individual responses to information overload, to impacts on virtual public interaction dynamics, requires a systemic approach to virtual public discourse. This can be achieved by the recognition of virtual public discourse, which is produced by members who are free to vocally participate, lurk, or unsubscribe, as the output of a complex social system (Jones and Rafaeli 2000a, and Jones 2001). Analysis of the systemic nature of social relations can be achieved through a focus on feedback-loops (Forrester 1969).

Figure 3. Virtual Public System Dynamics

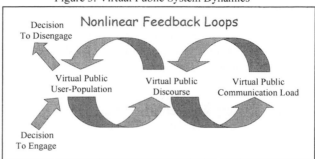

Figure 3 illustrates how the constraints acting on virtual public discourse result in non-linear feedback-loops. It works as follows: An increase in the membership of a virtual public will probably result in an increase in virtual public communication and communication load. However, it will not be possible for individuals to expand their involvement in virtual public communication indefinitely because of limits to the resources available to them to process group communication. Once virtual public communication becomes unmanageable or incoherent to individuals, then, the pattern of their involvement will alter, which in turn will impact on subsequent discourse dynamics.

A Method for Comparing Virtual Publics

This section contains an outline of a method for observing empirically some of the impacts of the "Average Maximum Communication Load" [AvMaxCL] individuals are prepared to invest in processing the interaction dynamics of virtual publics. The method is centered on the large-scale observations of "mass interaction", the shared discourse between hundreds, thousands or more individuals (Whittaker 1996). It is hypothesized that when the structure of group-CMC discourse is close to AvMaxCL, then a further increase in any one part of the communication load function will result in an increased preference by individuals to engage in communicative actions that require less cognitive effort, this will in-turn change the dynamics of the group-CMC in question. For example, at AvMaxCL an increase in the number of interactive users may result in two of the seven individual responses to information overload listed above, shorter reply messages and or a higher turnover of users. In this case, both the proportion of users maintaining an active involvement, and message length, are 'free variables' as they are not constrained by the number of active users. Mass interaction, which in many cases is likely to be fairly overloaded, provides a unique opportunity to observe and explore such relationships. This is because the large number of both messages, and users involved in mass interaction should enable observations that may otherwise be hidden by differences between individuals and the social contexts of communication. Not only is it hypothesized that the analysis of mass interaction AvMaxCL effects can lead to an increased understanding of various behavioral implications of a particular type of virtual public technology, but it can also be used for comparative purposes. This is because different CMC-tools are likely to enable different discourse dynamics, so that the way AvMaxCL associated non-linear feedback loops impact on mass interaction should also relate to the CMC-tool type. The theoretical foundations of this aspect of the research are discussed in detail in Jones (2001).

Figure 4 aims to illustrate how the large-scale mapping of virtual public discourse should enable the modeling of the relationship between CMC-technologies and communication load. In so doing it hints at how a research methodology could be developed based on the analysis of virtual public mass interaction. The Figure plots for a number of virtual publics the hypothesized relationships between their user population and various free variables such as average message complexity. This is done in order to graphically display the argument that the stress zones caused by overloaded interactive communication can be identified empirically by mapping active participation in different virtual publics against various components of the communication load function. The plots of the different virtual publics vary widely because of differences in their social context. The hypothetical synchronous virtual publics are plotted as relatively close to the left-axis because they require user co-presence for message exchange, which occurs quickly, and limits group size. On the other hand, the hypothetical plots of asynchronous virtual publics have larger user populations because users can take time to digest and respond to messages. Thus, the Figure displays differences between virtual public technologies.

The approach / model outlined in Figure 4 does not assume that the technology per se will not determine its use. Further, it does not suggest anything about the content of virtual public discourse within the boundaries imposed by technology, nor who will use one virtual public or another. To say something meaningful about the content of discourse, social theory and a focus on context is required. It may also be the case that different types of social aims and social structures for online discourse (e.g. empathetic as opposed to technical; moderated or facilitated, as opposed to unmoderated) may be associated with different stress boundaries. The model does not deal with this issue, although it provides a means for addressing it empirically. The model does not attempt to explain individual variations in the discourse patterns observed; rather it focuses on stress-boundaries, as these provide a key link between technology and discourse structures.

Figure 4. Virtual Public Technology
and Message Processing Capacity

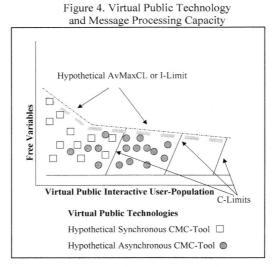

Hypotheses and Research Methodology

Hypotheses

To test the validity of the theory and method outlined above three hypothesized impacts of individual information overload on virtual public mass interaction dynamics were examined through a study of Usenet Newsgroup postings. A fourth hypothesis was also examined, that the approach can be used to differentiate virtual public technologies, specifically email list and Usenet newsgroup interaction dynamics.

Hypothesis 1: As volume and complexity increase and group-CMC becomes overloaded there will be a decrease in the average complexity of response messages, although this will approach asymptote. The reason for this hypothesized reduction in message complexity is due to the increased effort required by authors to create such messages.

Hypothesis 2: Simple group-CMC messages will be more likely to generate responses than complex messages. When users are confronted with overloaded mass interaction it is hypothesized that they are more likely to fail to respond and / or attend to the messages that are more onerous to process.

Hypothesis 3: As volume and complexity increase and group-CMC becomes overloaded there will be an increased tendency for individuals to end or reduce active participation. Figure 3 above describes this hypothesis, that disengagement is a strategy users will often adopt to cope with overloaded discourse. It follows, then, that on average at average maximum communication load the larger the number of individuals involved in discourse the less stable the participant population.

Hypothesis 4: The collective impact on virtual public mass interaction dynamics of individuals' responses to overloaded group-CMC will relate to virtual public technology type. This hypothesis is explored empirically by examining if the tendency to end or reduce active participation as group-CMC overload increases is linked to virtual public technology type. This measure was chosen because it is a metric that can be easily computed for a wide variety of virtual public technologies.

Methodology

From the above theoretical analysis, it is clear that the method of choice is field research involving the mapping and analysis on a large-scale of naturally occurring patterns of sustained interactive online communication. To implement such field studies and assess the hypotheses outlined we need to: choose appropriate virtual public technologies; collect large data samples; and analyze virtual public interaction dynamics.

Virtual Public Technologies

A number of practical considerations make Usenet Newsgroups a good virtual public technology with which to assess the first three hypotheses. These are: (1) the collection of hundreds to thousands of newsgroup user interactions is relatively straightforward. This is important as prior to this research it was not apparent how large a sample size was required to demonstrate the hypothesized effects. (2) The capture and chaining of inter-user-interactivity data, in this case discussion threads, is straight forward (Liu 1999 outlines why this is not the case with synchronous technologies such as IRC). (3) Anecdotal evidence suggests that a large percentage of Usenet newsgroups are overloaded (Smith 1999, Smith and Fiore 2001). The importance of this third requirement is linked to the need to include in the sample discourse operating at Average Maximum Communication Load (AvMaxCL).

In order to assess the hypothesis that the collective impact of user responses to information overload relates to virtual public technology type, Usenet newsgroups and email list data are compared. This choice was made because of the greater complexities involved in comparing synchronous and asynchronous interactions, and the comparative simplicity of collecting and analyzing email messages.

Data collection

Representative sampling of Usenet discourse is difficult; Whittaker et al's (1998) solution was to produce a randomly stratified sample, of 500 English text based Usenet newsgroups. For this project, 600 newsgroups, using Whittaker et. al.'s approach, 100 of which were moderated, were studied. The full content of 3,293,995 postings were collected over eight months and stored in an Oracle database. The 2,652,552 messages collected over the 6-months from 1st August 1999 to 29th February 2000, were used to conduct this study.

A wide variety of email list management software exists which vary in the ways they deal with subscriptions, postings and user information. Therefore, to reduce potentially unwanted variability, this study focuses on email lists maintained by Listserv. Listserv was the first mailing list management software package. Lsoft, the company that produces Listserv, maintains a database of public Listserv lists called Catalist (www.lsoft.com). On July 28, 1999 there were 24,696 lists contained in Catalist. The lists detailed in Catalist account for approximately 20% of the total number of Listserv lists known to Lsoft. In theory, the provision of Catalist to selected academic researchers makes it possible for researchers to construct a random sample of public Listserv based email discussion lists that are open to the public. For this study 1800 lists were initially extracted from the Catalist database using a stratified random sampling technique, and then a smaller sample was produced through the removal of lists using an iterative process. Lists removed were: non English language based; had a default digest mode of operation; were not active during the entire 5 month period; and did not receive at least 10 messages. This was achieved by subscribing to these lists over a number of weeks. At the end of this process, 478,240 email messages from 487-Listserv email-lists were collected for this study, over 5 months (December 1999 to April 2001). This sample was deemed adequate for the task, although we recognize that ideally the email list sample should exactly parallel the Usenet sample (this difference was the result of the research server being hacked).

Results

Analysis published elsewhere (Jones, Ravid, and Rafaeli 2002) showed that it was possible to correctly identify Usenet replies in over 99% of cases. Further, that within the data of the Usenet study it was possible to identify approximately 87% of the parent messages of replies. These percentages were deemed adequate for thread reconstruction and the analytical task at hand.

Hypothesis 1: As volume and complexity increase and group-CMC becomes overloaded there will be a decrease in the average complexity of response messages, although this will approach asymptote. This was operationalized as: There will be a decrease in surrogate measures of complexity (e.g. message length) as interactive message communication increases, and or the number of discussion threads increases, although this will approach asymptote.

Figure 5 is a scatter plot of the average number of words in threaded messages (replies) by the number of posters of such messages. The shapes of the curve of this scatter plot, and all the others derived from the various measures of message complexity by various measures of the size of the interactive discussion groups, looked similar. The plot in Figure 5, as do all the other related plots not shown in this paper, displayed the expected relationship between the size of the interactive newsgroup and various surrogate measures of complexity.

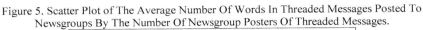

Figure 5. Scatter Plot of The Average Number Of Words In Threaded Messages Posted To Newsgroups By The Number Of Newsgroup Posters Of Threaded Messages.

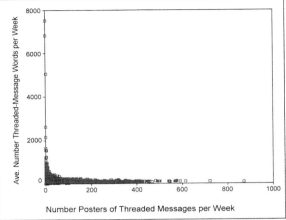

Standard linear regression cannot be used to describe the untransformed relationship between the measures observed because of the Zipf (Zipf 1949, Gunther et. al. 1996) like shape of the curve, with a clearly nonlinear relationship. Further, the curve cannot be tested as a standard Zipf / Power curve because the points on the plot represent means rather than frequencies. Multiple transformations of the variables under study did not succeed in enabling regression modeling using weekly averages for newsgroups. Instead, to perform regression modeling the 1.5 million threaded messages were ranked according to various measures of comparative message complexity. Variables were then computed and matched to individual messages regarding the newsgroup activity during the study week messages were posted. Using these new variables it is possible to see if the number of posters, and or number of interactive threads, is at all predictive of message complexity without the concern of 'regression to the mean'. This approach also allowed for factors such as newsgroup type (e.g. "Comp.", "Misc.", etc.) and message crossposting to be taken into account. Unfortunately, while the ranking and variable matching enabled regression modeling, this approach results in a loss of variance and predictive / explanatory power. As a result, the aim was not to understand the strength of the relationship between newsgroup activity and message size, but rather to simply to see if further support could be found for the notion that group activity related to message complexity. The regression modeling suggested that the newsgroup size (number of threaded messages posted or number of threaded posters) did predict message length (shorter messages being posted to more active groups). Of the five measures of message complexity, each used in different regression models as the dependent variable, the one most strongly predicted by group size was the average number of message lines calculated by the posters client newsreader ($F=14836.24$, $df= 1499124$, $p < 0.0000$). Other influences on message length included the type of newsgroup messages were posted to, the extent of crossposting (messages that were crossposted were longer on average), and the messages' position / depth in a discussion thread (deeper messages were longer overall).

Hypothesis 2: Simple group-CMC messages will be more likely to generate responses than complex messages. There were 593,019 messages that could be considered true unambiguous broadcast or one-way messages. From this sample of one-way messages, 255,697 were found to have initiated (seeded) discussion within their newsgroup during the study period.

As predicted, on average, broadcast messages that seed discourse were significantly smaller/shorter than those that fail to seed discourse. This was consistently the case, no matter how message length was measured. For example, using message header information the mean number of message lines for those that seed discourse was 24.50 lines and for those that did not 62.29 lines.

The outcome of regression modeling was that the following factors are all predictors of a one-way message seeding new discourse: The overall activity of the newsgroup (measured by the number of messages posted per week); All the measures of message complexity such as number of words (examined separately to avoid multi-colinearity); Newsgroup type (e.g. 'talk', 'misc.', etc.); and Moderation status (using a variety of approaches including newsgroup name and newsgroup information center descriptions).

As one would expect, one-way messages posted to larger groups that are more active were more likely to receive a response. Further, all measures of message complexity were found to negatively correlate with seeding discourse (i.e. smaller messages were more likely to seed discourse) and the client header calculation of message length, which is influenced by attachment lengths, was found to be the best predictor. Posting a one-way message to the 'comp' or 'sci' newsgroups resulted in a greater chance of receiving a reply than posting to the other newsgroups, and finally moderation reduced the chances of receiving a reply. The logistic model that appears to best describe the dynamics of discourse seeding was able to predict 63.57% of the cases with a Wald χ^2 of 56559.408, p > 0.0001. The findings of the logistic regression modeling argue strongly for the conclusion that smaller messages are more likely to generate ongoing discourse.

Hypothesis 3: As volume and complexity increase and group-CMC becomes overloaded there will be an increased tendency for individuals to end or reduce active participation. For the purposes of this study, poster stability is the percent of posters in a month that also posted in the previous study month. This allowed for the examination of user stability over a 5-month period. Figure 6 displays the number of messages posted to the 578 newsgroups that were active during the first 5 months of the study.

On average only 11.5% of posters sent messages 2 months in a row. Because of the constraints imposed by the proportionality of the stability measure (zero to one hundred) it seems reasonable in this case to also plot on Figure 6 a regression line to highlight the reduction in stability as newsgroup activity increases. The drop in the proportion of individuals involved in sustained discourse is quite strong, with a Spearman's rank correlation coefficient of -.43 (p < .000, n=565). When the outliers are removed by only examining the top third of the sample (newsgroup months with more than 2957 messages posted to them, accounting for 1,943,343 of the studies messages) the Spearman's rank correlation coefficient was -0.47 (p < .000, n=192). Linear regression modeling showed the number of posters to be the best predictor of proportional stability, followed by average newsgroup message crossposting (more crossposts results in greater stability), and then newsgroup type (R^2=.43, F=17.7, df=183, P < .001).

Figure 6. Proportional Newsgroup Poster Stability

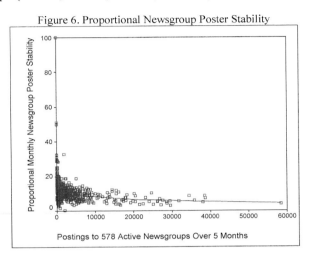

Figure 7. Proportional Listserv List Poster Stability

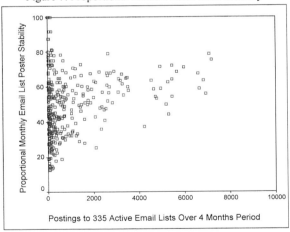

Hypothesis 4: The collective impact on virtual public mass interaction dynamics of individuals' responses to overloaded group-CMC will relate to virtual public technology type. Of the three hypotheses examined above the easiest both to compute and to compare with other technologies is Hypothesis 3 of ending or reducing active participation as group-CMC overload increases. After an examination of the Listserv list data it was determined that for 335 lists, active data was collected for at least 5 months on a continuous basis, enabling an

aggregation of 4-months of poster stability data. This subset of Listserv lists was then used to create Figure 7, a monthly poster stability plot of Listserv lists. It is equivalent to the Usenet plot except it is over a shorter time-period and has a smaller but sufficient sample size.

The comparison of Figure 7 to Figure 6 highlights just how much more stable the activities of posters are for Listserv email lists than for Usenet newsgroups. This is the case even if we adjust for the shorter time-period used to produce the email list plots of 4 as opposed to 5 months. Note that a number of lists have over 50% of users posting two months in a row, even when over 5000 messages were posted in a 4-month period. Further, unlike the Usenet plot with its -.43 ($p < .000$, $n=565$) Spearman's correlation, no significant Spearman's correlation was found for the data presented in Figure 7.

Discussion and Conclusions

This paper examines the nature of the relationship between the virtual spaces typically used for public online behavior, their technological platforms, and the behaviors such systems contain. A theoretical model and methodology labeled cyber-archaeology was described which utilizes large-scale field studies into user behavior in online spaces to identify technology-associated constraints to sustainable patterns of virtual public interaction dynamics. Applying the label cyber-archaeology was not meant to imply an historical, timeline-orientated perspective, which is just one of many approaches adopted by archaeologists. Rather, the label was given because the approach is based on archaeological theory and focuses on differences between the duration of impacts of social action and material remains (in this case CMC).

Empirical research was undertaken to assess the validity of both the theoretical model and methodology. Overall, the empirical findings support the assertion that individual 'information overload' coping strategies have an observable impact on mass-interaction discourse dynamics. Evidence was also found for the hypothesized link between virtual public technology type and constraints to sustainable patterns of large-scale virtual public interaction dynamics.

While our results are in line with the theoretical model, the findings raise a number of issues. First, our failure to find a decrease in proportional email list poster stability as interactive user populations increased, raises questions as to the validity of the model, which should be addressed. Two possibilities are: 1) Our sample did not contain email lists with a large enough active user population to enable the observation of the hypothesized effect; and 2) That for push technologies such as email lists, to some degree user subscription is akin to posting activity. Whatever the case, it is clear that email lists are typically able to support a much higher level of proportional active poster stability than Usenet newsgroups.

The second and perhaps most important objection that can be raised with regards to this research is the validity of the interpretation of our empirical findings in terms of the collective impact of individual information overload on virtual public interaction dynamics. While collectively the results are supportive of our overload model, obviously it is possible to propose a number of alternative explanations for each of the findings. For example, higher poster turnover in larger groups could relate to the impact of size on social network node structure rather than individual information overload. Although such possibilities are more than reasonable, what is more important is the utility of the method and theory outlined to:

(1) Compare virtual publics and virtual public types;
(2) Make novel predictions that can be examined empirically (good scientific puzzle solving); and
(3) Suggest a further research as outlined by Jones (2002; Chapter 6), Liu (1999), and Ekeblad (1999).

Therefore, while the validity of explanatory model is debatable, it is clear that the significance of the results and method is of greater importance.

The emergence of mass interaction has presented new opportunities to learn about and understand human communication, and information technologies. The availability and persistence of such communications, and the scale at which it operates allows us to explore various system effects on group discourse. To date empirical research into the *systemic* nature of the patterning of social relationships in cyberspace has been relatively rare. Research based on a systems approach to examine internet group communication, such as: the modeling of free riding using the Napster like Gnutella network (Adar and Huberman 2000); modeling the inter-relationship between homepages (Adamic and Adar 2000); exploring the self-organizing nature of email lists (Ekeblad 1999); and showing the World Wide Web to be structured like a small world network (Adamic 1999); have all been undertaken in the last five years. The work described in this paper is the first to explore empirically the impact of systems effects in Usenet discourse.

The recognition of the systemic nature of virtual public discourse allows for the examination of CMC technologies in terms of group-level usability. Currently, it is widely accepted that "reliable measures of overall usability can only be obtained by assessing the effectiveness, efficiency and satisfaction with which representative users carry out representative tasks in representative environments" (Bevan and Macleod 1994). This view supports the use of usability laboratories, and ethnographic methods, which can put user behavior in context. While, not discounting the value of these approaches, using the methodology presented in this paper for comparative purposes represents an alternative approach. This is because it potentially allows us to see and compare the normal range of user interaction dynamics for different types of CMC-technologies.

Not only do the techniques outlined offer insight into aspects of CMC-tool usability, but they also provide insight into technology design. For example, research is currently being undertaken to utilize an understanding of the discourse dynamics of real-time chat channels on IRC in order to build a smart real-time chat channel recommender system (see Terveen and Hill 2001 for a review of recommender systems). The smart recommender system aims to take into account conventional issues such as content as well as notions of group critical mass and overload. Other researchers are also examining how the approach outlined in this paper can be used to inform moderators of online discussion boards.

This research can progress in a number of different directions through:

(1) The large-scale comparative analysis of virtual-public discourse dynamics for a variety of other technologies (IRC, Web based bulletin board systems, Etc.).

(2) A thorough empirical examination of the impact of the various ways in individuals can respond to overloaded virtual public discourse.

(3) The formal proposing of and empirical research into alternative explanations for the underlying causes of consistent patterns of virtual public mass interaction.

(4) Various methodological and theoretical refinements that would result from an examination of related issues such as time scaling, and longitudinal impacts (e.g. Schoberth et. al. 2003); and

(5) The utilization of the knowledge gained into group-level usability to design better CMC-technologies.

The findings of the empirical research suggest that the cyber-archaeology approach is of value. It made verifiable predictions as to the nature of online behavior, specifically that the impact of individual cognitive processing limits are observable in the interaction dynamics of online spaces, and that these impacts differ between technologies. Overall, our theoretical model, methodology, and empirical results suggest a new way of understanding how classes of CMC-technology impact on the discourse they support.

References

Adamic, L. A. 1999. The Small World Web. *Proceedings of the 3rd European Conf on Digital Libraries*. Lecture notes in Computer Science, 443-452. New York: Springer.

Adamic, L., and E. Adar 2000. Friends and neighbors on the Web. PARC Xerox Manuscript, 1501 Page Mill Rd. MS 1U-19, Palo Alto, CA 94304, available online at: http://www.hpl.hp.com/shl/people/eytan/fandn.html

Adar, E., and B. Huberman 2000. Free Riding on Gnutella. *First Monday* 10(5), available online at: http://www/firstmonday.dk

Bevan, N., and M. Macleod, 1999. Usability assessment and measurement. In: *The Management and Measurement of Software Quality,* M. Kelly, ed. Ashgate Technical/Gower Press.

Bush, V. (1945) "As We May Think," The Atlantic Monthly, July 1945.

Butler, B., 2001. Membership size, communication activity, and sustainability: A resource-based model of online social structures. *Inform Systems Research.* 13(4).

Cherny, L., 1999. *Conversation and Community: Chat in a Virtual World,* Center for the Study of Language and Information, Stanford.

Coate, John., 1992. Innkeeping in Cyberspace, In: *Directions and Implications of Advanced Computing (DIAC-92)*, Computer Professionals for Social Responsibility, Palo Alto, CA., Berkeley, CA, . http://gopher.well.sf.ca.us:70/0/Community/innkeeping.

Doheny-Farina, Stephen, 1996. *The wired neighborhood*, Yale University Press, London.

Dunbar, R., 1996. *Grooming, gossip and the evolution of language*, Harvard University Press, Cambridge, Mas.

Ekeblad, E. 1999. The emergence and decay of multilogue: Self regulation of a scholarly mailnglist. *European Association for Research on Learning and Instruction (EARLI)*, Sweden.

Fletcher, R., 1995. *The limits of settlement growth: A theoretical outline*, Cambridge University Press.

Forrester, J. (1969) *Urban Dynamics*. The M.I.T. Press. Cambridge, Mass.

Gopher, D. and E. Donchin, 1986. Handbook of perception and human performance. In: *Cognitive processes and performance*, Vol. 2 (Eds. K. R.B, L. K. and J. P.T.), John Wiley & Sons, New York, pp. 1-49.

Gunther, R., L. Shapiro, P. Wagner. 1996. Zipf's law and the effect of ranking on probability distributions. *International J of Theoretical Physics* 35(2) 395-417.

Herring, S. C. 1999. Interactional coherence in CMC. *Proceedings of the 32nd Hawaii International Conference on System Sciences*, IEEE, Hawaii.

Hiltz, S. R., and M. Turoff 1985. Structuring computer-mediated communication systems to avoid information overload. *Communications of the ACM* 28.

Hiltz, S.R. and M. Turoff, 1978. *The network nation: Human communication via computer*, Addison-Wesley Publishing Company, Inc, London.

Jones Q. 1997. Virtual-communities, virtual-settlements & cyber-archaeology: A theoretical outline. *J of Comp Mediated Communication* 3(3).

Jones Q., and S. Rafaeli 2000a. Time to Split, Virtually: 'Discourse Architecture' and 'Community Building' as means to Creating Vibrant Virtual Publics. *Electronic Markets: The International Journal of Electronic Commerce and Business Media*. 10(4) 214-223.

Jones Q., and S., Rafaeli. 2000b. What do virtual 'Tells' tell? Placing cybersociety research into a hierarchy of social explanation. *33rd Hawaii International Conference on System Sciences, (Hawaii 2000), Hawaii*, IEEE Press.

Jones Q. 2001. The boundaries of virtual communities: From virtual settlements to the discourse dynamics of virtual publics. PhD Thesis, Graduate School of Business, University of Haifa, Israel.

Jones Q., Ravid G., and Rafaeli S. (2002). "An Empirical Exploration of Mass Interaction System Dynamics: Individual Information Overload and Usenet Discourse." In: *Proceedings of the 35rd Annual Hawaii International Conference on System Sciences*, IEEE, Big Island, Hawaii.

Jones, S., 1995. Cybersociety: Computer-mediated communication and community. In: *Understanding Community in the Information Age*, Sage, Thousand Oaks, CA, pp. 10-35.

Kollock, P. and M. Smith, 1994. Managing the virtual commons: Cooperation and conflict in computer communities. In: *Computer-Mediated Communication*, (Ed. S. Herring), John Benjamins, Amsterdam.

Lewis, D., and K. Knowles 1997. Threading electronic mail: A preliminary study. *Inform Processing and Management* 33(2) 209-217.

Liu, G.Z., 1999. Virtual community presence in Internet relay chatting, *Journal of Computer-Mediated Communication [online]*, 5 (1). http://www.ascusc.org/jcmc/vol5/issue1/liu.html.

Milgram, S. (1969). Experience in Living in Cities. *Science*, 167: 1461-8.

Reid, E. M., 1991. *Electropolis: Communications and community on Internet Relay Chat*, Honors, History, University of Melbourne. http://www.ee.mu.oz.au/papers/emr/work.html.

Rheingold, H. 1993. *The virtual community: Homesteading on the electronic frontier*. Addison-Wesley, Reading, MA.

Rogers, E. M., & Agarwala-Rogers, R. (1975). Organizational communication. In G. J. Hanneman & W. J. McEwen (Eds.), *Communication and behaviour* (pp. 218-236). Reading, MA: Addison Wesley.

Rojo, Alejandra and Ronald G. Ragsdale, 1997b. Participation in electronic forums: Implications for the design, *Telematics and Informatics,* 14 (1): 83-96.

Roseman, M. and S. Greenberg, 1996. Teamrooms: Network places for collaboration, In: *Computer Supported Collabrative Work*, ACM Inc, Cambridge MA pp. 325-333.

Schmitz, J. and J. Fulk, 1991. Organizational colleagues, media richness, and electronic mail: A test of the social influence model, *Communication Research,* 18: 487-523.

Schoberth, T., Preece J., Armin H., (2003) Online Communities Longitudinal Analysis of Communication Activities Thomas. The Proceedings of the *36th Hawaii International Conference on System Sciences, (HICSS), Hawaii*, IEEE Press.

Shenk, D., 1997. *Data smog - Surviving the information glut*, HarperCollins, New York.

Simpson, R., Renear A., Mylonas E., & van Dam A. (1996) 50 years after *"As we may think"*: the Brown/MIT Vannevar Bush symposium. *Interactions*, ACM Press, March 1996 Volume 3 Issue 2.

Smith, M. "Invisible Crowds in Cyberspace: Measuring and Mapping the Social Structure of USENET" in Communities in Cyberspace, edited by Marc Smith and Peter Kollock. London, Routledge Press, 1999.

Smith, M. and A. Fiore. "Visualization Components for Persistent Conversations," *Proceedings of ACM Computer-Human Interaction 2001.*

Spears, R. and M. Lea, 1992. Social influence and the influence of the 'social' in computer-mediated communication. In: *Contexts of computer-mediated communication,* (Ed. M. Lea), Harvester Wheatsheaf, New York, pp. 30-65.

Sproull, L., and S. Faraj 1997. Atheism, sex and databases: The Net as a social technology. Culture of the Internet. S. Kiesler, ed. Lawrence Erlbaum Assoc, Inc., Mahwah, NJ,

Steinfield, C. and Fulk. J., On the role of theory in research on information technologies in organizations. *Communication Research*. 14, 5, 1987, 479-490.

Terveen, L.G and Hill, W. Human-Computer Collaboration in Recommender Systems, in Carroll, J. (ed.), *HCI in the New Millennium* (2001), Addison Wesley.

Wellman, B., 2001. Computer networks as social networks, www.sciencemag.org 293.

Whittaker, S., 1996. Talking to strangers: An evaluation of the factors affecting electronic collaboration, In: *CSCW '96*, ACM, Cambridge, MA pp. 409-418.

Whittaker, S., and C. Sidner, 1996. Email overload: exploring personal information management of email., In: *CHI'96 Conference on Computer Human Interaction*, ACM Press, NY pp. 276-283.

Whittaker, S., Jones, Q., and Terveen, L. (2002). Managing Long Term Conversations: Conversation and Contact Management. In: *Proceedings of the 35th Annual Hawaii International Conference on System Sciences*, IEEE, Big Island, Hawaii.

Whittaker, S., L. Terveen, W. Hill, L. Cherny. (1998). The dynamics of mass interaction. *CSCW 98*, ACM Press, Seattle,

Zipf, G. K. 1949. *Human behaviour and the principle of least effort*. Cambridge, MA.

K. Kuutti, E.H. Karsten, G. Fitzpatrick, P. Dourish and K. Schmidt (eds.), *ECSCW 2003: Proceedings of the Eighth European Conference on Computer Supported Cooperative Work, 14-18 September 2003, Helsinki, Finland,* pp. 61-80.

Dependable Red Hot Action

Karen Clarke, John Hughes, Dave Martin, Mark Rouncefield, Ian Sommerville

Departments of Computing and Sociology, University of Lancaster

{k.m.clarke\j.hughes\d.b.martin\m.rouncefield\i.sommerville}@lancs.ac.uk

Corin Gurr, Mark Hartswood, Rob Procter, Roger Slack, Alex Voss

School of Informatics, University of Edinburgh

{corin\mjh\rnp\rslack\av}@inf.ed.ac.uk

Abstract. We present a brief observational, 'ethnographic', study of the Roughing Mill in a steel plant and use material from recorded activities to provide 'illustrative vignettes' of some aspects of the accomplishment and problems of everyday work. The account provides a 'bottom up' method for developing a more sophisticated and situated view of the problems of dependability. The paper documents the social organisation of work in the Roughing Mill, the interaction between the computer scheduler and the skill of the mill operator in accomplishing 'dependable' production of steel plates from slabs.

Introduction: dependability and socio-technical systems

"Dependability is defined as that property of a computer system such that reliance can justifiably be placed on the service it delivers." (Randell, 2000)

As computer-based systems – embracing humans, computers and engineered systems- become more complex and organisationally embedded, so the challenges of dependability – of building systems involving complex interactions amongst computers and humans – increase. In these systems, failure, lack of dependability, can result in financial or human loss and, consequently, improved means of specifying, designing, assessing, deploying and maintaining complex computer-based systems would seem of crucial importance. Much of the work on dependability has necessarily, and naturally, focused on massive, extraordinary, public failures such as the London Ambulance Service failure of 1992, the space shuttle catastrophe of 1986, or the Ladbroke Grove train disaster of 1999. This paper is, however, concerned with rather more ordinary, everyday instances of dependability and failure. Instances of undependability in many settings are not normally catastrophic, but are rather mundane events that occasion situated practical (as opposed to legal) inquiry and repair. Dependability can then be seen as being the outcome of people's *everyday, coordinated, practical actions*. Workers draw on more or less dependable artefacts and structures as a resource for their work of achieving overall dependable results in the work they are doing (Voß et al., 2002; Clarke et al., 2002).

In this paper, we wish to explicate how overall dependability is practically achieved in the operations of a steel rolling mill, a rather different setting than most studies of dependability in IT systems have looked at. Here, the research is not situated in bright, clean offices of the services industries or the technologically advanced and safety critical sectors of the nuclear industry or aircraft safety, but in the noisy, dirty and dangerous world of steel manufacture. Although the focus of activity is transforming a slab of red hot steel into steel plate rather than, for example, the provision and control of information, similar dependability issues of timeliness, responsibility, security etc can arise, and need to be resolved, in the interaction between computer systems and human skills. Our research consists of a brief observational, 'ethnographic', study (Hughes et al., 1992; 1994) of the Roughing Mill in a steel plant. Although 'quick and dirty', the fieldwork covered all three daily working shifts and a number of roughing mill operators of varying levels of skill and experience. In the paper we offer 'illustrative vignettes' of aspects of this particular work in the Roughing Mill as an example of a more 'bottom up' method for developing a richer situated view of the practical problems of dependability (Suchman, 1995).

The paper provides us with an opportunity to respecify the problem of dependability, and hence the lessons for IT systems design, by documenting 'real world, real time' practices whereby dependability is rooted within the practical ongoing social organisation of work. Our argument is hardly radical in emphasising the point that any abstract 'rules for dependability' – such as procedures, models, proscriptions, prescriptions, etc. – have to be applied within the context of some socially organised work setting in which those who have to apply such rules have to deal with all the contingencies and other demands on their attention and effort. What is perhaps more radical is the intention to treat this observation seriously as both a research endeavour and as an input to system design. Our interest in the social organisation of work is in how the work activities (which are often glossed and idealised) are actually carried out and accomplished as day-to-day activities with whatever resources, including technological, are to hand and facing up to whatever contingencies arise. As far as system design is concerned – and as we have said elsewhere – such an interest seeks to understand the work as a first priority so that any innovation in system design better resonates with the work as actually done. This point of view is based on two suppositions: first, that most systems fail because they do not resonate with the work as it is actually done as a 'real world, real time' phenomenon; second, that even when the intention is to change the work (to make it more efficient, reliable, etc.), it is always best to have a good idea of what may be lost in doing so to put against any putative gains.

Image 1: Problems – getting 'turn-up'.

The research reported upon in this paper was motivated by several observed 'problems' in the Roughing Mill, some of which may be viewed as relevant to issues of dependability. The dependability issues were manifested in the complex interrelationship of skill, teamworking and awareness that could result, for example, in a range of 'troubles'. These included:

- 'Cobbles' or 'turn-up' of the part rolled slab that makes it difficult, and sometimes impossible, to manipulate the slab through the Mill (see Images 1 and 2).
- Badly shaped slabs coming into the Mill that produce, for example, 'fishtails' or other defects in the finished slab.

- Slab defects produced by the furnace, for example, 'thermic shock' requiring the Mill operator to make adjustments in how the slab is rolled and that may mean the final rolled plate will not yield all the ordered plates.
- Various kinds of marking etc. on the slab produced by difficulties in rolling that may influence the quality of the final plate.
- A variety of computer problems related to the identification, measurement and sequencing of the slabs.

Image 2: A 'cobble' being lifted from the line.

As in any tightly structured sequence of interdependent activities, such 'troubles', even though they are often regular and routine, are 'troubles' which detract from the dependability of the system by producing waste, slowing production, creating frustration and increasing overall costs. However, and again as with most systems of high interdependency, achieving 'smooth' operation day in and day out is extremely difficult and requires a great deal of experienced skill on the part of the operators of the technology.

The analysis that follows uses a framework of 'sensitising' concepts (Blumer, 1954; Blythin et al., 1997) that have been developed over the years in doing ethnography as a contribution to system design. It provides a means of bringing out the grounding of dependability on the social organised skill and competences of those involved in the work setting. As Popitz et al. remark in their much earlier study:

"It is not sufficient to remark that the individual work activities are embedded within a larger work context. One must be more concrete and with each individual work activity demonstrate how and to what extent cooperation with other work activities is a requirement." (Popitz et al. 1957, in Schmidt, 1994)

There are, of course, some important differences from the steel rolling mill studied by Popitz et al.; ours is predominantly computer controlled; operators have far greater overview of the whole process and facilities for communicating and coordinating work. It certainly is no longer the case that "operators simply take their cues from the state of the field of work and infer the actions and intentions of their colleagues from that." While it remains the case that "a strip is just a strip, and whatever is done to it is done with the single purpose of transforming it the proper way" (Schmidt 1994: 27), we wish to provide some important insights into just how this is done. The concepts we employ are distributed coordination, the situated orientation to plans and procedures, and the achievement of various forms of awareness of work. To begin, we describe the work of the Rolling Mill and the rolling process in a rather idealised fashion. In this way we can begin to bring out the situated actual activities done by the operators as routines of their daily work.

The roughing process

Like many unfamiliar work activities, the process of rolling a slab of steel appears complicated beyond belief. Ideally, however, it is simple enough. Slabs, or blocks of steel, are rolled into steel plates of varying thickness. The process begins with the available steel slabs being assembled in the slabyard and moved to furnaces. Usually more than one steel plate will be made from each rolled slab so 'as rolled' plated will be cut on one of the shear lines. 'Build rules' are used to determine how many plates of required sizes can be made from standard slab sizes with minimum wastage.

There are two furnaces each with two 'strands' of slabs passing through them. The temperature for each slab is calculated and passed to the furnace controller. The slabs are heated to around 1250°C. Each slab's temperature is repeatedly calculated as it is heated and when it has reached the required value is flagged as ready to roll. A another slab is then pushed into the furnace so moving the strand one along with the slab ready to be rolled dropping out of the discharge end. The mill – really the Roughing and the Finishing Mill – use reversing mills or rollers. The incoming slab will have already been specified, and displayed to the operator, as to be rolled in one of two orientations: length to width or length to length. However, this requirement is not imperative and is sometimes overridden, if, for example, there are flaws in the slab that make it difficult to follow the requirement.

The slab is reduced in thickness by a series of 'passes' back and forth through the mill until the desired thickness is reached. The Roughing Mill 'stand' (where our observations were concentrated) is a large structure that supports two steel rollers turned by two large electric motors. The distance between the rolls – the 'roll gap' – is adjusted by the 'screws'. Slabs are transported on roller tables that are controlled in sections to give more delicate control over the movement of the slab. The slab can be turned on the 'turning table' which consists of alternate rolles, thinned on alternate sides, and which can rotate in opposite directions. Moving side guides are used to square up and centralise the slab for passage through the rollers. The thickness of the slab can at any stage be inferred from the screw position the last time the slab passed through the roll gap. This process is typically fraught with problems since the whole mill is significantly elastic under the forces generated by rolling along with the fact that the rolls expand as they heat and wear as more steel is rolled. The process of 'zeroing' the mill – adjusting it so that the unloaded roll gap is actually zero when the indicator says it is – is difficult to carry out and often poorly understood. The length and width of the slan can be measured by an optical gauge known as the 'Kelk' or 'Accuplan' but only when it is held still on the turning table. At this stage it is important to achieve the final plate width and the keep the slab – by now almost a plate – as close to the ideal rectangle as possible.

The computer calculates the sequence of screw settings and turns. The screws are reset automatically after each pass. The computer requires a width reading when necessary and corrects to achieve an acceptable width and keeps track of what has been rolled. The operator is responsible for manipulating the slab to turn it and enter it through the rollers centrally and squarely after the screws have been automatically set. This involves hand and foot controls. If necessary the operator can also take control of the screws. At each 'pass' through the mill the steel is reduced in thickness by the 'draft'. As the volume remains the same, the other dimensions must increase. Most of this increase appears as extra length in the rolling direction and is quite easy to predict. (There is also some 'spread' outwards as it passes through the rollers. This may be large in terms of product tolerances but is always small in relation to the elongation of the slab. However, it is difficult to predict.) The first target is to elongate one of the slab's dimensions until it reaches the width of the final product. It may be rolled in both orientations until this is achieved. It is then turned through 900 and rolled in the same orientation from then on. The drafts from then on will, ideally, be the maximum possible in order to reduce rolling time and minimise heat loss. Different limits apply at different parts of the process.

Although there are variations according to the composition and quality of the slab, the general procedure in the Roughing Mill is as follows. The slab is pushed from the furnace, through the wash boxes to remove scale and then aligned and centred on the rollers. Information on the monitor in the 'pulpit' – the control room where the operator works – tells the operator the slab quality, its present width and length, the width and length required, the orientation, the 'turning point' (the measured point at which the operator should turn the slab to roll for final length), and the 'finish point' (the point at which the operator should send the slab through to the Finishing Mill).

The rolling operation itself begins with 'pre-broadside passes' through the Mill and the slab is sprayed to remove scale. The operator then 'goes for width' by rolling the slab to produce the desired width up to the 'turning point'. Measurement of the slab through the Accuplan is displayed in the 'pulpit'.

Image 3: Aligning the Slab — the mill lights are green.

One red light indicates that measuring is taking place, two that the slab has achieved width. Green lights are displayed for the operator to turn the slab to roll for length. As the operator puts the slab through the mill he turns and aligns it (see Image 3). The scheduler reduces the gauge at each pass – displayed on the overhead monitor and the 'clock') until finish point is achieved. The final pass is a reverse pass. The rollers are then lifted and the plate sprayed on its way to the Finishing Mill.

Of course, in actuality the process rarely goes as smoothly as this. 'Troubles' of various kinds are a regular feature. One prominent trouble is when the part rolled slab 'turns up' to form a U or W shape that makes it impossible to manipulate. There are a number of techniques, all involving heavy manual labour, to recover from such events, but they cause delays and do not always succeed. Although the process is not fully understood, the cure is straightforward. The screw settings should ensure heavy drafting at critical points in the process but this requires considerable experience on the part of the controller. Indeed, many of the more experienced operators will go into manual mode for the last few passes. A related problem is when the plan view of the plate is not the ideal rectangle. If the problem is severe the final rolled plate will not yield all the plates required. The operator does have a degree of control over this but the automatic controller gives no help. Sometimes the length or the width does not turn out as planned and further action is necessary.

In the pulpit, the operator has various monitors and controls. On his left is the furnace monitor (in this case misaligned after a mishap with a crane), load measures, mill light, screw inject (this can also be done through the central control pad) and levers for screwing the rollers up and down. To the right of the monitor is the main control pad, the main monitor, rack lever, amp meter, the monitor for sprays, and temperature gauges (see Image 4). To the front of the operator are a number of foot pedals for turning the lab on the rollers and sending it through to the Finishing Mill. There is also a head level display that provides the reference points for the slab currently being rolled. Outside, on the Mill itself, the mill 'clock' and measuring lights provide further information. Indeed, the mill 'clock' – the way in which the 'hands' alter to reflect the changing of the screws – was a clear and persistent focus as the operator worked.

Image 4: Pulpit Controls: Right Side

Some concepts for analysis

We now want to move onto some analysis of the fieldwork materials using the presentation framework developed out of previous ethnographic studies in a variety of domains. It is important to stress that the framework of concepts is in no way a theory of work, organisation or whatever. The rationale for this insistence on the framework not being a theory would take us too far afield, but, briefly, is connected to Garfinkel's critique of constructivist sociology. It is in an important part a heuristic and practical device for bringing out the generic everyday features of socially organised work settings and, at the same time, presenting these in a form useful for designers. In this particular instance we are interested in whether the heuristic of the framework facilitates the identification of dependability issues. The features we want to illustrate in this paper are as follows: 'distributed coordination', 'plans and procedures' and 'awareness of work'.

Distributed coordination

This points to how work tasks are performed as coordinated activities, that is, as activities that have interdependence with activities done by others who may not be co-located. It is clearly a notion closely tied to the idea of a division of labour but goes further in emphasising the ubiquity of the day-to-day need to achieve coordination within a division of labour. Depending on the work setting and the activities concerned, distributed coordination can take many forms, involve varied technologies and operate at different periodicities. As with the other concepts, 'distributed coordination' is a methodological injunction to treat work settings, persons and activities as embedded in an organised ensemble. The activities and the persons who perform them are interconnected as part of some organisation of activities and persons which has to be coordinated in order to 'get the work done'.

Plans and procedures

'Plans and procedures' refers to one of the more obvious means by which distributed coordination is achieved and supported. Project plans and schedules, manuals of instructions, procedures, workflow diagrams are all ways of enabling persons to use as resources for coordinating work activities. There is no implication here that any particular set of plans, etc., is successful at coordination, or conforms to some ideal standard. The explicit point of plans is to coordinate the work of different persons so that separate work activities, either in parallel or serially, have a coherence and, typically, through this meet other goals such as efficiency, meeting time constraints, beating the enemy, growing the company, and so on (Schmidt, 1997). Although 'plans and procedures' are, of course, about coordination – and often an important resource in its achievement – 'plans' are abstract construction that require implementation within the specifics of the circumstances in which it is to be followed (Suchman, 1987; Dant and Francis, 1998). The accomplishment of a 'plan' is dependent upon the practical understanding of what the plan specifies in *these* circumstances, using *these* resources, and facing up to *these* contingencies. In many cases of 'real time, real world work', accomplishing the plan often involves using local knowledge, 'cutting corners', 'bending the rules', even revising the plan in order to meet its overall objective.

Awareness of work

'Awareness of Work' refers to the way in which work tasks are made available to others and constitutes a major aspect of the means through which co-ordination of work tasks is achieved as a practical matter. As Popitz argues:

> "An operator only operates the system rationally and effectively if each operation is carried out with a view to the necessary cooperation with others ... he has to take into account the preceding, concurrent and immediately ensuing operations." (Schmidt 1994: 26)

The various ways in which 'awareness' is developed, in which work is made public are of interest as essential ingredients in 'doing the work' as part of a socially distributed division of labour. It is intended to encompass a range of informal as well as formal phenomena for indicating the 'state of the work thus far'. It is also, as with plans and procedures, intimately connected to distributed coordination in that making others aware of the state of the work is an important resource for making distinct aspects of a division of labour work together. 'Awareness of work' does not point to some psychological property but, rather, to those visible features of the work and its setting by which those involved can make judgements about the 'state of the work'.

Before filling these concepts out using 'vignettes' from the fieldwork on the Rolling Mill, it is important to stress that these concepts direct attention to different features of the work process, features which are not necessarily discrete in the sense that one might see 'distributed coordination' and then 'awareness of work' and then 'plans and procedures'. The same work activity can, that is, often be seen from the perspective of any of these concepts. We want now to move on to illustrate the above concepts using fieldwork material from the Rolling Mill.

Everyday work in the Roughing Mill

Distributed coordination

It can be no surprise that the rolling process involves coordination. It is a process designed from the outset (no doubt based on less technologically sophisticated predecessors) to coordinate the various activities of men and machines involved in turning a slab of steel into a plate. The Roughing Mill is part of a series of work activities beginning with the Furnace, the Roughing Mill itself, the Finishing Mill and the Shear Lines where the 'mother plate' is cut into the various 'daughter plates' ordered by customers. (This series could, of course, be linked to other aspects of the organisation – producing the slab itself, loading, invoicing the customers, etc., etc. Our concern, however, is with the Roughing Mill.) Further, the process of reducing a slab of hot metal to a plate has to be done in 'real time'. The slab cannot be parked for any time until the Roughing or the Finishing Mill are ready for it otherwise it loses heat and becomes unworkable. Moreover, it is a dangerous place, noisy, full of steam and pieces of molten metal. Accordingly, communication and coordinating between the various stages of the process has to be dependable, reliable and unequivocal. Further, processing the slabs into plate is subject to various and not always controllable inconsistencies in the quality of the material being worked with: slabs are not always the right size or shape, not always at a workable temperature, cannot always be 'roughed' satisfactorily, and so on. Yet contingencies such as these need to be dealt with by the operators and in a way which keeps the process running as smoothly as it can be under the circumstances. Accordingly, communication and coordination between the processes needs to be as simple and as quick as possible.

For the Roughing Mill operator, coordination with the Finishing Mill (the next stage in the production process) is important and was achieved in a number of ways. For example, the lights on the Finishing Mill enabled the Roughing Mill operator to see when the Finishing Mill had done with the current plate and therefore ready for the next, as this short extract from the fieldwork illustrates:

"(points to Finishing Mill) two lights … a red one and a white one … the white one means its finished … so that's a guide to us … if we can see through the steam."

However, as the comment suggests, it is not always possible to see the lights so 'at a glance' information about the state of the Finishing Mill was not always available. Hence, recourse was often made to the RT link (a microphone) in the Pulpit that was also used to alert the Finishing Mill to any problems with the roughed plate. This two-way link also functioned to alert the Roughing Mill operator to anything – such as particularly long slabs or the imminence of 'turn-up' – that might affect his work.

"he was letting me know that the front end was up … so he was bringing it back just to knock it down … That's another thing we look for … this (slab) finished length is 12 metres long … I notice that (pointing at one in Finishing Mill) was 24 metres (that's) why I'm waiting for him to finish."

The process is not always smooth and, accordingly, coordination in this case between two closely connected processes is essential to regulating the pace of the process in 'real time'.

Coordination with the Furnace was done mainly through the microphone, a monitor and the Mill 'light', the latter being used to control the supply of slabs to the Roughing Mill.

"I've put the Mill light off … or they might push another one before I start that one."

"I turned my light off because … if I'd had problems with it I'd have had another one standing there getting cold and I'd have the same problems again."

However, the monitor and RT were mainly used. The monitor is especially important in checking which furnace a slab came from in case its size was incorrect.

"looking at monitor to see where slab is coming from (*which furnace*) … so if I get another wrong size again I know where its come from. (*Speaking into microphone to Furnace controller*) That's a bad shaped slab, Pete … cut short on one side … I've got to send that one back, mate … it's stuck under the washbox … it's got a dirty great black line through it."

There were innumerable instances in which communication using the RT was used between all sections of the process trying to make the process as smooth as possible. Of course, it sometimes this fell short of the ideal – slabs the incorrect size, taking longer over a process than expected, roughed plates not sufficiently rectangular, etc., – and which have to be communicated to others up and down the process. What we see in these exchanges – and they are but an exceedingly small set of examples that could have been used – is the everyday work that goes into achieving coordination dependably in the process of changes slabs into plates. In this sense coordination is part and parcel of the working division of labour itself, using the resources to hand.

Plans and procedures

As the idealised description of the process suggests, transforming a slab of hot metal into a plate is designed as a linear, step-by-step process moving from the Furnace to the Roughing Mill, to the Finishing Mill and, finally, to the Shear Mill where the plate is cut into sizes for the eventual customer. Of course, much more goes on within these stages, however, the point is that being a step-by-step process certain conditions have to be met before moving onto the next stage. That is, key to the whole process is scheduling and pacing.

As we have already noted, scheduling and pacing were not always straightforwardly achievable. As one, highly experienced, operator wryly remarked about the 'them' who had designed the system: '... for them to design scheduling ... is a bit like me trying to design a plane because I've flown in one." (A common enough sentiment, in many settings, that we simply note.) A number of problems inevitably arose when the computer and automatic systems went awry. In one case, for example, computer problems in the Finishing Mill produced wrong readings for number of passes and wrong measures on every pass. In another instance, the computer lost its reference point and the operator had to take over manually. In another case an operator noticed that the computer was failing to update:

> "it's not been giving us first draft reference ... it's brought up the plate draft but kept it at whatever we sent the last plate at ... it's not updating on the screen at all...for some reason it's not updating ...so there's obviously a fault somewhere ... that's why I'm in manual ... I don't trust it now because I don't know what it's doing ... and the computer hasn't pushed now (provided another slab) because it thinks I'm still at 230 (the initial draft of the plate - 230)."

In this case, the pacing of the mill has been compromised by the computer failure and the operator is waiting for a slab from the Furnace.

The successful accomplishment of a 'plan' or a 'procedure' is dependent on the practical understandings about what the plan specifies in *these* circumstances, using *these* resources, and so on, not least when things 'do not go according to plan'. In such cases it means adapting to the situation at hand as in the following example.

> "... if a slab comes down and its all got thermal cracking ... then we'd roll it the other way ... tell them ... make a note ... they'll say ... why did you roll it that way".

That is, if a slab appears with a thermal crack on one side, rather than following the computer's instructions and rolling the slab so that the crack appears at the side of the plate and effectively ruins the quality of all the 'daughter' plates that are cut from it, the operator will override the computer and roll the slab so that the crack appears at the end of the plate and may be discarded in the waste. Indeed, there were a number of occasions where operators used their own judgements rather than the computer in order to realise the aims of the procedure. For example, the work of the Roughing Mill critically depends upon slab quality, that is, the metallic composition of the slab and the relative proneness to 'turn up'.

"I shan't give this a lot of water as it's 269 quality and liable to turn up … with 269 quality a lot of drivers drive with barrel water off to keep the heat in the slab."

"going for manganese … real hard stuff … we don't use any water … you just have to work real fast."

The operators were aware that different slab qualities are liable to various defects, such as 'fishtails' and 'tongues' (see Figure 1) and the work was adjusted accordingly.

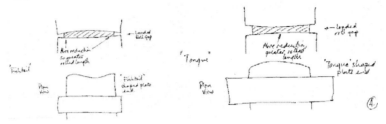

Figure 1: 'Fishtail' and 'Tongue' defects.

However, scheduling and pacing are not simply about doing one's job in isolation from how it might impact on others further down the process. The Roughing Mill operator concludes his task when the slab has been 'finished at measure', that is, rolled to a specified thickness, length and width. Occasionally operators were observed to ignore their 'finish at' measure – instigating an alarm – in order to send the plate through to the Finishing Mill in an adequate state.

"If I send that at 49 … it's going to shoot up *(turn up in the Finishing Mill)*…it's 233 quality which is the worst one for turn-up … you need a minimum of 3 metres in length … because if you get less than that there's a good chance it could turn-up in the Finishing Mill."

"instead of finishing at 35 I'll drive it down and put a bit more length on it … less chance of it turning-up then."

This clearly involves knowledge of the work of the Finishing Mill on the part of the Roughing Mill operator as well as knowledge of the Finishing Mill (that plates need to be over 3 metres to roll easily) and the relative capacities of the two mills:

"… it wants to send it at 60 … but it's a bit short … so I take over manually and knock it down a bit (alarm) … gone to manual … it wanted to send it away at 50 … it makes it difficult for the other (FM) drivers … it'll take him 2-3 passes to get it down to that."

As these examples suggest, 'real time, real world' work often involves the utilisation of 'local knowledge' and 'local logics', commonly interpreted as 'cutting corners' or 'bending the rules', to support the overall objectives of the plan. In the Roughing Mill this was perhaps most obvious when things began to go wrong and operators were faced with slabs 'turning up'. As Rognin and Bannon (1997) suggest:

> "Despite our attempts to automate an ever larger set of control functions, and to build-in forms of automated reasoning and intelligence into these computerised control systems, there is still a crucial need for human agency to monitor and, if necessary, to over-ride computerised systems under special circumstances or unusual conditions." (Rognin and Bannon 1997)

Awareness of Work

> "... horrible plates these are ... they've been turning up all night."

One aspect of 'awareness' that seems of particular importance in the Roughing Mill, concerns having an awareness of what happens to a slab once it has been through the Mill – that is an awareness of what happens to a plate once the Roughing Mill operator has effectively 'done his job'. This involves some knowledge of how the end product is arrived at, what happens when the slab leaves the Roughing Mill and how what happens to a slab in the Roughing Mill may impact on the work done elsewhere in producing the finished product. That is, having such knowledge that not only can the Roughing Mill operator 'do his job' but also he accomplishes it in such a way as to enable others to do their work – by providing a plate with appropriate qualities. Observations revealed a number of successes and failures in this respect – the most obvious failure being lack of much immediate feedback on the quality of the plates produced.

Awareness: Professional Vision

> "... sometimes you can sit here and look at it and think, 'that one's going to be a bastard'."

One way of understanding and analysing awareness issues for operators in the Roughing Mill is in terms of Goodwin's (1994) notion of 'professional vision':

> "... a community of competent practitioners ... expect each other to be able to see and categorize the world in ways that are relevant to the work, tools and artifacts that constitute their profession."

There are a range of subtleties to this notion but in many ways it involves being able to see, at a glance, whether something is right or wrong, is going to be easy or difficult and having the knowledge to do something about it. Sometimes – as the phrase 'professional vision suggests – it does involve just looking:

> "Can you see around the edges of that plate ... how its cold (darker) ... that's when it starts turning up and you've got problems."

> "... turn the water off on this one ... it's not very bright ... turn the water off to keep the heat there."

> "... a lot of slab defects you see as you roll lines from the furnace ... gauge variation ... sometimes we send back because of worry about overload."

This vision is based around an idea of achieving the appropriate 'ideal' shape, the 'dog bone', whilst recognising that this perfect shape is predicated on *"a 2600 slab and a nice set of rollers"*. When this is not the case, adjustments need to be made and professional vision deployed, for example:

"It's Wednesday ... I'm thinking of the state of the rollers (changed every Thursday) ... they'll be hollow in the middle now." Sometimes, for example, this involves altering the transfer references: "this one will want to turn at 120 ... I'll do it at 118 ... that will offset the roller."

The other important aspect of 'professional vision' is the coordination between what the operator sees happening in the mill and on the rollers, and the foot and hand various actions performed in the pulpit. This is where professional vision links with 'skill', where to ensure adequate throughput the operator needs to get a rhythm going that requires anticipating what is happening with the slab on the rollers.

Professional Vision: Interacting with the computer

"We're stopping for a while ... Houston's got a problem."

A good part of the observed 'professional vision' in the Roughing Mill involved some kind of comparison between what the computer 'said' and the operator's experience and skill. This was most obvious where the operator went into manual or over rode the scheduler in some way. So, for example, it was common for the most experienced operators to go into manual for the last few passes – because their experience was that *"... because the computer at less than 45 pisses about ... does 4-5 passes ... that's what causes turn-up."* and *"because it says 45 the computer tries to do it in 3-4 passes when you can do it in 2 ... it's to do with the pacing of the mill ... we're rolling plates quicker than the computer thinks we are.."* In some ways the end product of this was – at least in the case of the most experienced operators though less so in the case of newer operators – a healthy suspicion of what the computer was 'telling them' or asking them to do. This was heightened by cases of the computer providing wrong slab sizes or instructions:

(Concerned about wrong slab sizes being given by computer) "I've just had a look at that (the slab waiting) and it looks about right ... if the size here (monitor) said 30 metres I'd know straight away that was wrong." or (reference number gone) "it's not updating on the screen at all ... for some reason its not updating ... so there's obviously a fault somewhere ... that's why I'm in manual .. I don't trust it now because I don't know what its doing."

It also generally involves a reliance on the (inaccurate) Mill 'clock' rather than the head display for an understanding of what the Mill is doing:

(watching the clock) "the clock is out but only by about 3mm ... we use the clock because its easier to read ... we can anticipate the speed of the screw ... (compared with head display) ... if it's going down in a pattern ... and it suddenly puts 15 on you know something's wrong."

Discussion: dependable red hot action

"... how important it is to accept the reality of human fallibility and frailty, both in the design and the use of computer systems ... all too often, the latest information technology research and development ideas and plans are described in a style which would not seem out of place in an advertisement for hair restorer." (Randell, 2000)

When defined as "The ability to deliver service that can justifiably be trusted" – dependability has a number of attributes – many of which apply in this particular case. These include: availability (readiness for correct service); reliability (continuity of correct service); safety (absence of catastrophic consequences); integrity (absence of improper system state alterations); maintainability (ability to undergo repairs) and more. But as we consider broader, socio-technical, notions of "system", the ability to achieve a clear and documented understanding of the intended service of the system – and hence some view of dependability – becomes increasingly difficult. Once we start taking into account the actual practice of a socio-technical system rather than any idealisation of it, it seems increasingly difficult to determine with sufficient precision what is meant by the "service" the system offers. Thus it also becomes difficult to determine what is meant by a "failure" of that service, and thus what is meant by "dependability" in this broader context. In these circumstances, we may need to broaden our understanding of what dependability means beyond the simple "absence of failure", particularly if we consider 'quality of service'. In this case this would, for example, include the quality of the eventual 'daughter' plates that could be cut from the plate; the amount of waste; the timeliness with which the plate is presented to the next stage in the rolling process and so on. Moreover, in this instance many of the 'failures' observed are 'low consequence' that may not directly cause dependability-critical problems. However, they can contribute to a reduction in quality of service, and also give rise to a more fragile operating environment in which dependability-critical problems may become more likely.

To improve system dependability, we can reduce the number of human errors made, include system facilities that recognise and correct erroneous states, and so on. But, when we start considering people using a computer-based system, the notion of failure becomes rather more complex. In a situation where computer-based systems are used by groups or teams of people, usually in conjunction with other systems then recognising failure becomes even more difficult because different users may have (in this case did have) different models of how the system is supposed to behave. Unexpected behaviour to one user – such as the novice mill operator – is normal behaviour to another. Some users – the experienced mill operators – may have learned how to work-round problems in the system, others may not have.

One of the most obvious dependability issues to have emerged from this research concerns various forms of awareness and its impact on dependability – in particular a lack of awareness in several, perhaps crucial instances. So, for example, while the computer system is configured to ensure the manager knows the composition of the slabs in the furnace and the order in which they may appear, none of this information is conveyed to the Roughing Mill. Here operators simply respond to whatever slab appears in front of them. Such an awareness – of what's coming out of the furnace – may prove useful both for pacing and teamwork in the Roughing Mill. This applies both in the sense of developing a rhythm of work but also to ensure either that the more experienced operators roll the more difficult slabs or are available for assisting the less experienced operators. At the same time, there appears to be little in the way of form of 'reverse awareness' – from the Shear Lines to the Roughing Mill, for instance, in terms of information about the quality of finished plates. This might, for example, enable a mill operator to decide that a plate should be scrapped before it goes through the Finishing Mill because the defects in it – such as lines – make it worthless. At the moment there appears to be a touching faith that any such defects will be remedied somewhere else in the production process. At present there appears to be no real, useful feedback to ensure that poor quality plates are taken off early in the production process ensuring that production time and resources are not wasted.

Another aspect of improving dependable production relates to the setting of the controls and the information provided (Andersen, 1999). To some this may appear to be an essentially ergonomic problem in terms of the best positioning of the available controls. The issue of modifying the pulpit controls raised a number of interesting, though different, opinions. Some operators would prefer the measurement gauges to be on or nearer the monitor (so that they did not need to turn their head), others appeared to have incorporated the head turning seamlessly into their work. Others felt that the mill load gauges should be more easily visible to the operator. The head display was dismissed by many as 'going too fast' to be of much use in the work of rolling but a useful indicator for when the computer goes down. As for the monitors, apart from the main display monitor, the other displays appeared to be rarely used, especially by the less skilled drivers. This links with some of the points made above and highlights the issue of generating displays that are appropriate to the right people at the right time and in the right place. This may also be related to dependability issues of 'diversity' – of providing a range of measures by which operators can obtain relevant information. In practice this issue of diversity rarely arose as an everyday concern but it became important when things began to go wrong, when the computer started giving the wrong measure or the wrong slab or the wrong dimensions.

In terms of problems with the plates in the form of cobbles, or faults, or quality the observations revealed an interesting tension and trade-off in terms of dependable production between human skill and computer scheduling. The problem of cobbles was seen by the operators as a product of particular steel features – such as high manganese, no washes, poor sizing etc that were exacerbated by scheduler problems. This meant that the more experienced operators routinely and regularly over rode the scheduler and went into manual to drive down faster and prevent turn-up. At the same time problems with the pacing system seemed to result in reduced productivity with slabs not being pushed through fast enough; alongside poor combinations of steels and sizes and bad slab planning such as too much rolling in one direction. Finally, a number of teamwork and more general 'human factors' issues appear relevant to issues of dependability. Clearly the observations revealed remarkably different levels of operator skill. Of particular interest was the different working 'tactics' adopted by the differently skilled workers with the less skilled (and often younger) operators rigidly following the schedule – which may cause problems in the Finishing Mill in terms of the length and gauge of the plates. Skilled (and generally older) operators were far more likely to go into manual to prevent or reverse turn up, and to over ride the turning and finishing measures in order to reduce the problems elsewhere. In some ways the most problematic were the 'intermediate' skilled who were prepared to override the computer but occasionally lacked the requisite skills or experience.

Various incidents observed highlight the issue of dependability and trust that arose in everyday work – whether it was trusting the technology, trusting the process or trusting others in the working division of labour. While there are a number of different theoretical approaches to the study of trust (Axelrod, 1997; Kipnis, 1996; Luhmann, 1979; 1990), Luhmann points to the problem of conceptualising trust, suggesting that most approaches fail to pay attention to the *social process of trust production*, i.e., they leave unspecified "the social mechanisms which generate trust" (1990:95). Our study accommodates Luhmann's recommendation to look at trust accomplishment as a social process, and rather than emphasising theoretical accounts of trust, our investigation is concerned with how trust is achieved, how it can be seen in action. Our interest is in how trust is woven into the fabric of everyday organisational life – the workaday world – as part of the 'taken for granted' moral order (Garfinkel, 1967) and the impact this might have on 'dependable' production. As Fogg and Tseng (1999) suggest, "trust indicates a positive belief about the perceived reliability of, dependability of, and confidence in a person, object or process." (Fogg and Tseng 1999) Of particular interest is the inter-relationship between trust and technology. Although based on a relatively small number of observations in a short period of time, a number of conclusions concerning 'dependability' and the everyday working of the Roughing Mill are readily apparent. Considered in terms of improving dependability, while there are clearly things that need to be maintained – such as the levels of skill, and aspects of awareness in the Mill team; others may need to be done differently or supported differently – such as pacing and the scheduler or more general awareness in the plant as a whole. However, any changes need to be carefully considered in terms of their interactional effect - for example changes in the scheduler may make greater demands on the operators skill and may thereby impact on the quality of the finished product.

Observations suggest that problems were an everyday, commonplace feature of work – mundane, generally low consequence failures. When we consider problems or 'failure' as an everyday fact of life, we shift our ideas of problems, failure and dependability. We are, perhaps, drawn away from thinking about creating *failsafe* systems for such complex environments. Indeed it may be, as Law (2000) suggests (though in a rather different context) that imperfection is *necessary* to effective system functioning. Instead, the problem becomes one of *dynamically responding in the best way* to problems as they arise; and providing support for this response. This suggests that achieving or accomplishing dependable production involves far more than simply reconfiguring the scheduler or pacing system – even if this can be done – but needs to attend to the complexities of collaborative working and the classic CSCW problem – what to automate and what to leave to human skill and ingenuity.

Acknowledgements

This work was funded by the ESRC/EPSRC Dependability Interdisciplinary Research Initiative. We particularly thank the Roughing Mill operators for their tolerance of the 'professional stranger' amongst them and Roy Nicholls for facilitating access. Thanks also to Kjeld Schmidt for some insightful comments and references.

References

Andersen, P.B. (1999): 'Elastic Interfaces: Maritime instrumentation as an example', in *proceedings of CSAPC'99*, Valenciennes, France, pp. 35-41.

Axelrod, R. (1997): *Complexity of Co-operation: agent based models of competition and collaboration*. Princeton. NJ. Princeton University Press.

Blumer, H (1954): 'What Is Wrong with Social Theory?', *American Sociological Review*, vol. 19, pp. 3-10 (reprinted on line at: http://www.calvin.edu/academic/crijus/courses/blumer.htm

Blythin, S., Hughes, J., O'Brien, J., Rodden, T. and Rouncefield.M. (1997): 'Designing with Ethnography: A presentation Framework for Design', in *Proceedings of Designing Interactive Systems '97*, ACM Press, Amsterdam.

Clarke, K., Hartswood, M., Procter, R., Rouncefield, M. and Slack, R. (2002): 'Minus nine beds: some practical problems of integrating and interpreting information technology in a hospital trust' in *Proceedings of the BCS Conference on Healthcare Computing*, Harrogate, March 18-20.

Dant T. and Francis, D. (1998): 'Planning in organisations: Rational control or contingent activity?', *Sociological Research Online*, vol. 3, no. 2.

Fogg, B. J. and Tseng, H. (1999): 'The elements of computer credibility', *Proceedings of CHI 99*, New York, NY: ACM, pp. 80-87.

Garfinkel, H. (1967): *Studies in Ethnomethodology*, Englewood Cliffs, New Jersey, Prentice Hall.

Goodwin, C. (1994): 'Professional Vision', *American Anthropologist*, vol. 96, no. 3, pp. 606-633

Hughes, J., King, V., Rodden, T. and Andersen, H. (1994): 'Moving out of the control room: ethnography in system design', *Proceedings of the Conference on Computer-Supported Cooperative Work (CSCW'94)*, Chapel Hill, ACM Press, pp. 429-438.

Hughes, J., Randall, D. and Shapiro, D. (1992): 'Faltering from Ethnography to Design', *Proceedings of CSCW'92*, North Carolina, ACM Press.

Hughes, J,. King, V., Rodden. T. and Andersen, H. (1994): 'Moving out of the control room: ethnography in systems design', *Proc. CSCW '94*, North Carolina, ACM Press, pp. 429-438.

Kipnis, D. (1996): 'Trust and Technology', in R. M. Kramer and T. R. Tyler (eds.): *Trust in Organizations: Frontiers of Theory and Research*, London: Sage, pp. 39-50.

Laprie, J-C. (1995): 'Dependable Computing, Concepts, Limits, Challenges', Invited paper to *FTCS-25 25th IEEE International Symposium on Fault-Tolerant Computing*, Pasedena, USA.

Law, J (2000): 'Ladbroke Grove, or How To Think about Failing Systems', Centre for Science Studies and the Department of Sociology, Lancaster University at http://www.comp.lancs.ac.uk/sociology/soc055jl.html

Luhmann, N (1990): 'Familiarity, Confidence, Trust: Problems and Alternatives', in Gambetta, D, (ed.): *Trust: Making and Breaking Cooperative Relations*, Oxford. Basil Blackwell. Available online at www.sociology.ox.ac.uk/trustbook.html

Luhmann, N. (1979): *Trust and Power*, Chichester Wiley.

Popitz, H., Bahrdt, H., Jures, E. and Kesting, H. (1957): 'Technic und Industriearbeit', *Soziologische Untersuchungen in der Huttenindistrie*, J.C.B. Mohr, Tubingen.

Randell, B. (2000): 'Facing Up to Faults', Turing Lecture, January 31st.

Rogers, W.F. (1986): *Report of the Presidential Commission on the Space Shuttle Challenger Accident*. http://science.ksc.nasa.gov/shuttle/missions/51-l/docs/rogers-commission/table-of-contents.html

Rognin, L. and Bannon, L. (1997): 'Sharing Information: The Role of Teams in contributing to Systems Dependability Constructing Shared Workspaces through Interpersonal Communication', *Proceedings of Allocation of Functions (ALLFN'97)*, October 1-3, Galway, Ireland.

Schmidt, K. (1994): 'Modes and Mechanisms of Interaction in Cooperative Work: Outline of a Conceptual Framework'. Riso National Laboratory.

Schmidt, K. (1997): 'Of maps and scripts: the status of formal constructs in cooperative work', *Proceedings of GROUP'97*, ACM Press.

Suchman, L. (1995): 'Making Work Visible', *CACM*, vol. 38, no. 9, pp. 56-64.

Suchman, L. A. (1987): *Plans and Situated Actions: The Problem of Human-Machine Communication.*, Cambridge, Cambridge University Press.

The Ladbroke Grove Train Inquiry http://www.hse.gov.uk/railway/paddrail/lgri1.pdf

Voß, A., Slack, R., Procter, R., Williams, R., Hartswood, M. and Rouncefield, M. (2002): 'Dependability as Ordinary Action', *Computer Safety, Reliability and Security: Proceedings of the 21st International Conference, SAFECOMP 2002*, Catania, Italy, September. Reprinted in S. Anderson, S, Bologna, M. Felici (eds.): *Lecture Notes in Computer Science* vol. 2434, Springer Verlag, pp. 32-43.

K. Kuutti, E.H. Karsten, G. Fitzpatrick, P. Dourish and K. Schmidt (eds.), *ECSCW 2003: Proceedings of the Eighth European Conference on Computer Supported Cooperative Work, 14-18 September 2003, Helsinki, Finland*, pp. 81-98.

Reconsidering Common Ground:
Examining Clark's Contribution Theory in the OR

Timothy Koschmann
Southern Illinois University
tkoschmann@siumed.edu

Curtis D. LeBaron
Brigham Young University
lebaron@byu.edu

Abstract. The constructs of "common ground" and "grounding" are frequently invoked in the CSCW literature as a mechanism by which participants engaged in joint activity coordinate their respective understandings of matters at hand. These constructs arise from a model of conversation developed by Herbert Clark and sometimes referred to as "contribution theory." We describe here the basic features of this theory and attempt to apply it in analyzing a fragment of enacted interaction. The interaction was recorded during an abdominal surgery performed with the aid of an endoscopic camera. We encountered difficulties, however, in applying contribution theory as an analytic framework within this concrete setting. We found further that the notion of common ground represents a confusing metaphor rather than a useful explanatory mechanism. We conclude with a suggestion that researchers in the future seek ways of constructing descriptions of joint activity that do not rely on the troublesome notions of grounding and common ground.

Such words insert a name in place of a problem, and let it go at that; they pull out no plums, and only say, "What a big boy am I!"

Dewey and Bentley (1991)

Introduction

How collaborators make sense of their unfolding interaction has been a recurring topic within the CSCW literature, as well it should. Collaborators' meaning-making practices serve as the foundation upon which all cooperative work depends. The construct of "common ground" is frequently invoked as a mechanism by which joint understanding is achieved. McCarthy, Miles, and Monk (1991) described common ground as "the mutual knowledge, beliefs, and assumptions of the participants in a conversation" (p. 209). *Grounding*, then, is thought to be a process whereby "common ground is updated in an orderly way, by each participant trying to establish that the others have understood their utterances well enough for the current purposes" (p. 209).

The present paper reconsiders the notion of common ground and associated concepts. First, we review prior work in CSCW that builds on Clark's notion of common ground and revisit Herbert Clark's seminal writings on common ground (e.g., Clark & Brennan, 1991; Chark & Schaefer, 1989). We examine an actual fragment of interaction, an exchange that occurred in the operating room (OR) of a teaching hospital, and ask how does Clark's contribution theory and his notion of common ground help us explain what has transpired. We conclude by raising some concerns about employing grounding as an explanatory mechanism in CSCW research.

Common Ground in CSCW Research

The effects of various media on grounding has been an important focus of research in CSCW. McCarthy et al., for example, compared two forms of textually mediated communication—pure on-line chat and on-line chat augmented with a shared "report space." Basing their predictions on Clark's contribution theory of discourse (Clark & Brennan, 1991; Chark & Schaefer, 1989), they hypothesized that the introduction of the shared report space window would facilitate grounding by constraining potential meanings through visibility and co-presence. In their study, pairs of subjects were asked to solve a design problem communicating only through the synchronous, text-based interface. For half of the dyads, the participants had a chat window and a private report space; the other half had chat windows and a shared report space. All subjects were asked to record their arguments and possible solutions. The groups were compared in terms of the number of solutions and arguments recorded in each pair by only one participant. This "degree of disagreement" measure was assumed to be inversely related to the development of common ground within the dyads.

A more recent experiment reported by Veinott, Olson, Olson, and Fu (1999) examined grounding in pairs of native English speakers (NS) and pairs of non-native English speakers (NNS) communicating either in an audio-only condition or an audio supplemented with 'talking-head' video. The researchers hypothesized that the introduction of video would more dramatically improve grounding for the non-native speakers who presumably start the conversation with less common ground. Pairs were asked to perform a joint map tracing exercise. The maps given to the two participants were similar, but not identical. Each speaking turn was coded using a pre-established set of categories. NS subjects had more turns coded as "giving instructions," defined as "first offering of new information to the partner" (p. 306), than the NNS pairs. Pairs were compared for time and accuracy of task completion. NS pairs performed better than NNS pairs, but NNS pairs showed more improvement through the introduction of video. Grounding was assumed to be directly related to task performance and the augmented communication medium was theorized to compensate for differences across groups of subjects in initial common ground.

Jackson, Anderson, McEwan, and Mullin (2000) reported on the effect of video frame rate on grounding. They had their subjects perform a variant on a "referential communication task" while communicating via a video channel. Two team sizes were employed: 2-member teams with each member working at different workstations and 4-member teams with two members working at each workstation. In addition to standard measures of communication and task performance, Jackson et al. examined the length of referential expressions. An established finding in psycholinguistics is that the length of referring expressions declines with repeated references to the same object. The experimenters found longer expressions of definite reference in pairs (but not foursomes) operating in the low-frame rate condition. In this case, the longer referring expressions can be interpreted as representative of greater effort toward grounding.

Fussell, Kraut, and Siegel (2000) also studied the effects of communicative medium on grounding. In their study, unskilled workers were paired with either an expert or novice helper and asked to perform manual repair tasks on a bicycle. A repeated measures design was used in which each dyad did one repair in each of three media conditions: (1) side-by-side, (2) partners separated but able to communicate via full-duplex audio, and (3) audio supplemented with video. In the video condition, the worker viewed a miniature monitor positioned directly in front of her/his right eye, while the helper was seated in front of a conventional desktop monitor. Both saw the same display consisting of pages from a repair manual along with two video windows. One video window displayed a head shot of the helper, while the other display captured video from a camera mounted on the worker's head. The experimenters hypothesized that "ease of conversational grounding, as indicated by message length, number of conversational turns, and use of deictic expressions, should be easiest in the side-by-side condition and hardest in the audio condition" (p. 24). Their findings were consistent with this prediction and in agreement with Clark's contribution theory. Participant utterances were coded and special attention given to referential statements. They observed that deictic references were always possible in the side-by-side condition, but were only possible in the video condition when the worker's head-mounted camera was directed toward the object of reference. They also observed that in the video condition, only the worker could perform acts of ostensive reference, not the helper. This was consistent with the predicted finding that performance in the video condition approached that of the side-by-side condition only to "the extent to which the collaborators are able to use the video technology to facilitate grounding" (p. 24).

Clark's Contribution Theory

The body of work summarized in the previous section orients to the question of how the media through which communication is conducted affect the ability of cooperating agents to accomplish a shared task. These affects are theorized in terms of differences in common ground and in the processes of grounding afforded by the media. The notion of common ground arises from a model of conversation advanced by Herbert Clark and his students. Clark's contribution theory extended the traditional sender/receiver model of communication by enlarging the frame of analysis from the single message unit (utterance) to an interactionally-developed "contribution." Clark and Schaefer (1989) described the model in this way:

> In most traditional views, the speaker's job is to issue understandable utterances, and the listener's is to understand them. Conversations proceed utterance by utterance. In the collaborative view, the speaker and addressees try to do something more at the same time; establish the mutual belief that the addressees have understood what is uttered, to establish what the speaker meant as common ground. The process of contributing to a conversation consists of both specifying some content and grounding it, and the products are units we will call *contributions*. Conversations proceed, in this view, not utterance by utterance, but contribution by contribution. (p. 124)

Clark and Brennan (1991) stipulated that contributions to common ground have two phases:

> *Presentation phase:* A presents utterance *u* for B to consider. He does so on the assumption that, if B gives evidence *e* or stronger, he can believe that she understands what he means by *u*.

> *Acceptance phase:* B accepts utterance *u* by giving evidence *e* that she believes she understands what A means by *u*. She does so on the assumption that, once A registers that evidence, he will also believe that she understands. (p. 130)

After presentation, they described the recipient as being in one of four possible states:

> State 0: B didn't notice that A uttered any u.
> State 1: B noticed that A uttered some u (but
>   wasn't in state 2).
> State 2: B correctly heard u (but wasn't in state 3).
> State 3: B understood what A meant by u.
>   (p. 130)

If B achieves State 3 with regard to u, then A is justified in placing it in common ground. Contributions to conversation, therefore, are contributions to common ground.

Clark and Brennan (1991) described how different media change the constraints on grounding in conversation. They list (p. 141) eight features of interaction: co-presence, visibility, audibility, co-temporality, simultaneity, sequentiality, reviewability, and revisability. They pointed out that face-to-face communication does not constrain interaction with regard to the first six features, but does not afford the last two. Electronic mail, on the other hand, offers *only* the last two features. Co-presence and visibility—the capability "to see and hear what each other is doing and looking at" and the capability to "see each other," respectively—are the most important for the discussion that follows.

In the corpus of directory assistance inquiries analyzed by Clark and Schaefer (1989), they found that conversational partners employed three methods of accomplishing acceptance: the partner presumes acceptance by making a new contribution, the partner asserts acceptance through some form of acknowledgment or continuer (e.g., *yes, uh hah, okay*), or the partner requests clarification of some or all of the contributor's presentation. The need for grounding may vary in different situations. Clark and Schaefer postulated that those engaged in conversation apply a *grounding criterion*, i.e. "the contributor and his or her partners mutually believe that the partners have understood what the contributor meant to a criterion sufficient for current purposes" (p. 129). This seems reasonable enough, as far as it goes, but it leaves open how such a criterion is established and satisfied in actual practice. To explore these matters in greater depth and to make this discussion a bit more concrete, we turn now to an instance of interaction in which a complex series of contributions are made.

Contributing to Conversation in the OR

The setting within which we have chosen to study conversational "contributions" is the operating room (OR) of a busy teaching hospital. In the fragment analyzed here, there are three participants: one ("Attending") is a highly-experienced surgeon who reportedly has performed 1200-1300 surgeries of the type described here; another surgeon

("Resident") is in the final year of his residency, having participated in 80 to 90 of these surgeries; a third ("Clerk") is a medical student enrolled in a clerkship rotation. This operation was Clerk's first surgical experience. Attending, therefore, is providing guidance and supervision to Resident, while both Attending and Resident are responsible for giving instruction to Clerk.

The participants are performing a surgery known as a cholecystectomy—dissection and removal of the gallbladder. The gallbladder is a small, sack-like organ located near the liver. It receives and releases bile through the cystic duct and is supplied with blood by the cystic artery. To perform a cholecystectomy, therefore, a surgeon must isolate both the cystic duct and cystic artery, and then sever both vessels. This may sound straightforward enough, but the relevant body parts vary considerably from patient to patient. Furthermore, these body parts come swaddled in layers of connective and fatty tissue. So it is often difficult, even to the trained eye, to visually distinguish fine structures such as the cystic artery. Way finding within the abdominal cavity, consequently, is never a trivial matter and can challenge the skills of the most experienced surgeons.

Cholesysectomies are often performed endoscopically, a technique sometimes referred to as "keyhole surgery." Rather than make a single large incision, the surgeon inserts a fiber optic camera lens and special tools through small openings or "ports" in the patient's abdominal wall. Endoscopic surgeries interest us because of the manifold challenges to perception and coordination they pose to participants.[1] The use of video in endoscopic surgery differs from traditional video-mediated communication. The endoscopic camera enables co-located participants to jointly view a visual field not otherwise accessible to them—i.e., the interior of the patient's body. By revealing the potential referents of their conversation, the view afforded by the endoscopic camera represents an example of what Nardi et al. (1997) referred to as "video-as-data."

Here we analyze a videotaped fragment of interaction less than one minute in duration.[2] Our approach is microethnographic (see LeBaron, in press; Streeck & Mehus, in preparation). We account for human experience through careful descriptions of participants' vocal (Sacks, 1992) and visible (Kendon, 1990) behaviors, occurring naturally within unfolding strips of interaction, altogether situated within a social and material environment. Our emphasis on naturally occurring behaviors diverges from other research traditions that rely on invented examples, which propose how people might behave; surveys or journals, which depend on people's ability to recollect and account for their behavior; and data generated through experimental methods where

---

[1] See Koschmann, LeBaron, Goodwin, and Feltovich (2001) for further discussion of these challenges.

[2] A full transcript is provided in Appendix B. The transcription conventions, which are summarized in Appendix A, were developed by Gail Jefferson (see Atkinson & Heritage, 1984; Ochs, Schegloff, & Thompson, 1996).

subjects behave within laboratory conditions, removed from the people and things associated with their everyday lives. Microethnography adheres to principles of empirical social science: A particular phenomenon is taken to exist, to the extent that data, analyses, and conclusions are verifiable by others. Although participant observations, field notes, and interviews are acceptable data for microethnographic work, videotaped data have become a mainstay because they capture subtle details of interaction that analysts can review and others can verify. With ethnomethodological roots, microethnography privileges subjects' perspectives: Researchers avoid imposing their own theorized views on the social phenomena they examine by attending to the orientations and relevancies that the research subjects display (e.g., Potter, 1998).

Microethnographic research has consistently shown that "human action is built through the simultaneous deployment of a range of quite different kinds of semiotic resources" (Goodwin, 2000, p. 2); that "talk in interaction shares billing with space, with artifacts, with work, and with the visible palpable body" (Moerman, 1990, p. 182). The physical arrangement of the operating room is shown in Figure 1. By maneuvering their bodies, participants oriented toward each other and the object of their collective work. Resident is located on the right side of the table and is primarily responsible for dissecting and removing the gallbladder. Attending assists (and supervises) from the left side of the table. Clerk stands adjacent to Resident and operates the rod lens of the endoscopic camera with close guidance from Resident. Looking within the endoscopic space is a team effort: Clerk steadies and directs the fiber-optic lens, Attending holds aside obstructing organs using a retractor tool, while Resident isolates relevant structure from surrounding connective tissue. One challenge is to correctly—and jointly—identify the cystic artery, as serious post-operative complications might arise if the wrong vessel were inadvertently ligated. The many ways in which the participants coordinate their activity, through understandings visibly displayed, seems beyond the reach of contribution theory, which is presently preoccupied with vocal pairs of presentation and acceptance.

As the transcribed moment begins, Attending (Lines 1 and 2) continues with a description of the surgical procedure for the benefit of Clerk, while Resident (Line 3) demonstrates the location of some abdominal feature.

Excerpt 1

```
1    Attending: Yeah (.) the other [thing to do:: is make sure
2               you have your cystic (.) artery out too.
3    Resident:                     [(Right there)
4    Clerk:     Uh huh
```

Lines 1 and 2 appear as an example of "presentation" within a conversational contribution, as described by Clark and Schaefer (1989). Notice that Clerk's acceptance (line 4), the reduced continuer "Uh huh," is ambiguous in this situation because it is unclear whether it serves to accept Attending's statement concerning the cystic artery, Resident's demonstration, or both. Thus, we immediately encounter complexity not seen within the Clark and Schaefer report. Their examples consist exclusively of dyadic exchanges within telephone conversations. Here we have a moment of multi-party interaction with overlapping utterances in quick succession, making the relationship between presentations and acceptances ambiguous for participants and analysts alike.

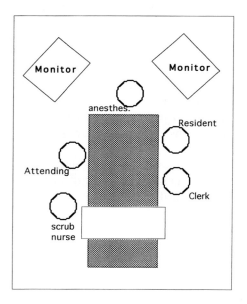

Figure 1: Organization of the workspace.

Throughout our videotaped fragment, Resident is performing a blunt dissection to expose the cystic duct and the cystic artery using a tool in his right hand (a "black grasper"). His dissection is performed by burrowing the tip of the grasper into a bundle of connective tissue binding the bottom edge of the gallbladder to the common bile duct and then gently spreading apart the jaws of the instrument. He performs this continuously without performing any visible action that might be construed as a point. However, he occasionally provides a demonstrative reference, such as "Which is right back in here" (Line 5).

Excerpt 2

```
5   Resident:   [Which is right back in here]
6   Attending:  [That way there is nuthin ] else before you
7               h- (.) hit the edge of the liver
8               (1.6)
```

Spatial deictics such as "here" were probably not common in the corpus examined by Clark and Schaefer, because the telephone participants were not co-present. Within the OR, however, spatial deixis is an integral part of the ongoing teaching work, as the experts orient themselves and their student within the uncharted spaces of this particular patient. Moreover, notice that Clerk does not respond to Resident's demonstrative reference at Line 5. In the conversational space in which Clerk might be expected to provide evidence of acceptance (Line 8), we have instead silence. What does silence mean? By remaining silent, does Clerk perform a kind of acceptance, showing Resident's demonstrative reference to be unproblematic and, therefore, not needing comment? Or does Clerk's silence represent a withholding of acceptance? To the extent that ambiguities of this sort are a pervasive feature of social life (and we think they are), Clark's contribution model is inadequate.

Ambiguities compound when Clerk eventually speaks at Line 10: "Can you see the cystic artery yet?"

Excerpt 3

```
9   Attending: That (kinda) guarantees you're safe too.
10  Clerk:     Can you see the cystic artery yet? I:'d=
```

How should we categorize Clerk's query in terms of Clark's contribution theory? Who is Clerk addressing? In relation to Resident's prior talk (specifically the demonstrative reference at Line 5), Clerk's query may be regarded as an ongoing withholding of acceptance—that is, Clerk questions the location of what Resident says is "here." In relation to Attending's prior talk (lines 1, 2, 6, 7, 9), Clerk's query may be regarded as a presentation (i.e., moving the conversation forward through introduction of a new issue) and hence an implied acceptance of what Attending has been saying. Within ongoing streams of multi-party interaction, the distinction between presentation and acceptance may be complicated as an utterance may connect forward or backward to various other utterances.

From Lines 11 to 25, Resident provides no less than five demonstrative references to the cystic artery's location.

Excerpt 4

```
11  Resident:  =It's ↑r::ight back in the:re
12             (2.1)
13  Attending: (We'll)  get it out here in a minute.
14             (0.2)
15  Resident:  See it right there?
16             (0.2)
17  Clerk:     U::mmmmm=
18  Resident:  =Right (0.2)  [there
19  Clerk:                   ⌊Okay yeah (.) yeah
20             (0.2)
21  Resident:  That looks like the (0.2) where the money's a:t
22  Clerk:     Uhkay
23             (0.2)
24  Resident:  En yih can see it's hanging out in that
25             ⌈tract.
```

Resident's behavior speaks to the environmental uncertainty of the current activity. The surgeons are literally moving through unfamiliar territory, changing (through dissection) the very scene that they are working to identify. This changing environment is at odds with Clark's contribution theory in that the theory would seem to require that contributions to common ground aggregate over time and remain relevant. The patient's abdominal cavity is not self-explicating: What objects are (and how they should be regarded) is something that the participants discuss and decide—not something they take for granted (see also Koschmann, et al., 2001). In this way, our data contrast with Clark and Brennan's (1991) discussion of "constraints" on grounding, which depicts the physical environment as fixed and readily accessible to co-present interlocutors. Our data shows how the component parts of the sender-receiver model (e.g., environment) may be brought into being through human interaction within and upon it.

When a physical environment is uncertain and unfolding, the relationship between presentation and acceptance may be muddled. After the first of Resident's five demonstrations, Clerk provides no response (Line 12). After the second demonstration, Clerk's response is delayed (Line 16) and non-committal (Line 17). Resident's third demonstration is more than a vocal aside: He interrupts his dissecting work and uses the grasper tool as a prosthetic pointer in conjunction with his utterance (Line 18). It is then, and only then, that Clerk offers evidence of acceptance (Line 19). Nonetheless, Resident's demonstrations continue: He says "That looks like the (0.2) where the money's a:t" (Line 21); and "En yih can see it's hanging out in that tract" (Lines 24 and 25). With reference to Clark's contribution theory, the purpose of Resident's presentations in lines 21 and 24 is unclear. Since Clerk has already signaled acceptance at Line 19, why make two additional presentations? Resident's subsequent presentations would suggest a rejection of Clerk's acceptance, both in Line 19 and later in Line 22. Thus, our data show how the boundaries of a contribution may be ambiguous when conversation is tied to an ongoing activity.

In overlap with the end of Resident's last demonstration (Line 26), Attending makes a few critical presentations of his own.

Excerpt 5

```
24   Resident: En yih can see it's hanging out in that
25             ⌈tract.
26   Attending: ⌊ (That's) actually big.
27   Attending: That's pretty bi:g.
28   Attending: That may be ri:ght,
29             (0.4)
30   Resident: That's right hepatic?
```

Attending says, "That's actually big" (Line 26); he repeats, "That's pretty big" (Line 27); and then he says, "That may be right" (Line 28). In this way, Attending invites more discussion of Resident's demonstrations, providing evidence that he does not accept Resident's presentation, raising the possibility that Resident has misidentified the cystic artery[3]. In turn, Resident provides evidence that he accepts Attending's non-acceptance (see Line 30). This exchange between Attending and Resident arguably constitutes a failure to achieve common ground, which highlights a gap in Clark and Schaefer's (1989) description: Although they describe methods by which participants in a conversation may achieve acceptance, they are silent regarding methods that contributors and their partners may employ to withhold acceptance. Additional questions remain. Does Clerk ever achieve state 3 with respect to identifying the cystic artery? Like Resident and Attending, we have no privileged access to Clerk's mental state at the time

---

[3] On the written page it might appear that the utterance "That may be right" (Line 28) is affirming. However, the prosodic cues and other features of Attending's delivery, along with his intent stare at the monitor, suggest another reading. Indeed, when he replied "That's right hepatic?" (Line 30), Resident's treated Attending's presentation as an incompletely formed utterance or question.

that this conversation occurred. We can only attempt to assess his understanding based on the accountable ways it is manifest within the observed interaction.

In the remainder of the fragment (Lines 31 through 41), Resident and Attending jointly decide to keep searching for the cystic artery.

Excerpt 6

```
31                (1.2)
32  (Attending):  ⌈(Comin' up)
33  Resident:     ⌊The cystic may be up a little higher?=
34  (Attending): =(Yup)
35  Resident: You can see how easy that is to do we were
36            just talking about that.
37  Clerk:    So you jus' dissect until you'r:e absolutely sure
38  Attending: Ah ⌈hah
39  Resident:     ⌊Yeah=
40  Clerk:    =Till you see both the right hepatic and the cystic and then
41                (4.6)
```

Resident treats the possible misidentification of the cystic artery as an instructable moment for the Clerk (Lines 35-36), who in turn formulates what may be learned from this exchange (Lines 37-40). Alternatively, if we chose to treat the series of demonstrative references (Line 11-30) as a side sequence, Clerk's extended utterance (Lines 37-40) could be seen as an acceptance of Attending's earlier description (Lines 1-9) of the surgical procedure. For participants and analysts alike, the relevancies of any utterance within an ongoing conversation are open to inference, question, and negotiation.

Did the Clerk ever learn to see and recognize the cystic artery? Although he participated in its surgical removal, and although he talked as one who understood (e.g., Lines 37-40), the Clerk's understanding remains an open question. Before the surgery, Attending asked Clerk to explain the "triangle of Calot" which is a region of the body that includes the cystic artery. The Clerk responded quickly and competently by naming abdominal features and their relative locations, including the cystic artery. However, he was evidently uncertain as to the location of these same anatomical features during the surgical procedure, suggesting that his textbook understanding did not translate into surgical practice. Moreover, we conducted interviews with Attending, Resident, and Clerk after the cholecystectomy. During our interviews, we played a video recording of their surgical procedure and asked each of them to identify (circle with a pen) the cystic artery when it appeared. The Clerk identified and circled something different than the others. According to our microethnographic study, the participants pursued share understandings that had no obvious arrival. The tenuous nature of mutual understanding within this practical setting contrasts with contribution theory's description of human interaction as an accumulation of contributions achieved.

By our reading, this sample of naturally occurring interaction poses certain challenges for Clark's theory. Commonplace ambiguities of everyday conversation (e.g., silence) frustrate applications of this theory to naturally occurring interaction. Within ongoing streams of interaction, the distinction between presentation and acceptance may be complicated as an utterance may connect forward or backward to various other utterances. Contributions, therefore, may seldom occur in tidy, recognizable packages. Complications associated with multi-party interaction (e.g., overlapping utterances) may make the relationship between presentations and acceptances ambiguous for participants and analysts alike. Contribution theory is, in the final analysis, a psycholinguistic account of a form of situated meaning making. Left out of this account are the embodied phenomena (e.g., gesture, gaze, facial expression, posture) that may play such an important role in human interaction. Also neglected are all the features of the material and social environment that participants draw upon in making sense of their own and others' utterances. These features are not static. When a physical environment is uncertain and unfolding, the relationship between presentation and acceptance may be muddled because relevancies for participants are constantly in flux.

The Troubles with Common Ground

What is this thing called common ground? The research reports cited earlier from the CSCW literature would seem to suggest that it can be employed as an explanatory mechanism subject to experimental measurement, albeit indirectly. Our attempt to locate it in within naturally occurring discourse, however, would suggest that its status is considerably more ephemeral. It is at best a metaphor for a contingently-achieved and endlessly-defeasible state of alignment, independently inferred by each participant for every other participant to a conversation. The problem with the metaphor, however, is that, by its very nature, it tends to foster certain misconceptions about the phenomena it describes.

Clark (1996), in his more recent writings on common ground discusses it as a distributed form of mental representation. It is the superset of all of the sets of inferred understandings of *each* participant in a conversation independently maintained with respect to *every* other participant to the conversation. The superset is an abstraction, however, only observable by a god-like, omniscient outsider with privileged access to the participants' representational inventories. Serious problems arise when one begins to treat common ground as if it were a singularity, a possession of the participants, a place, an arrived at state, in short, as a noun instead of as a verb. McCarthy et al., (1991) spoke of common ground as a singularity that is updated in an "orderly fashion." The single entity, the superset, however, is only available to the omniscient outside observer, so what value does it hold for the participants themselves? Veinott et al. (1999) described achieving common ground as a negotiated process, but also spoke of it as possession of conversational partners ("when these pairs are provided with a video connection their performance improves to the point of being equal to those who *have* more basic common ground," p. 308). Conversational partners who share a common language or cultural heritage would presumably have more inferred common understandings, but who possesses the common ground? Is it the individual participants? The pair? The conversation? In Jackson et al. (2000) the length of referring expressions is assumed to be a function of what has been placed in common ground. Fussell et al. (2000) studied "the ways in which the presence of visual information facilitates *grounding*" which they defined as "the development of mutual understanding between conversational participants." In both cases, the researchers were attempting to measure changes in common ground as it was updated by the participants. Common ground cannot and should not be treated as an empirical fact. It is not a thing that can be measured, either directly or indirectly. Clark (1996), himself, makes this clear in more recent writings on the topic. There is a problem, however, with the notion of common ground even when it is understood in the more strict sense employed by Clark.

In prior writing (Koschmann et al., 2001) we have argued that Clark and Marshall's (1981) model of reference repair dissects common ground in a way that obscures, but does not dispose of, the problem of intersubjectivity. Here we apply a similar critique to the notion of common ground itself. By its name it would seem to index a place, a place where things can be stored or recorded, but this is a profoundly misleading connotation. Common ground is, after all, a place with no place. It is a cooperatively constructed mental abstraction, available to no one. To paraphrase Dewey and Bentley, it inserts a name where the problem should be. Left out is an account of how participants in conversation routinely and unproblematically coordinate their understandings of matters at hand. Suggesting that they do so by placing propositions in common ground would seem to offer little in terms of conceptual understanding or descriptive power. What it provides instead is fertile ground for confusion. Perhaps it is time that we set this terminology aside and seek new ways to describe how people come to understand each other.

Acknowledgements

We thank Herb Clark and four anonymous reviewers for numerous helpful suggestions. We also thank our collaborators on this project, Paul Feltovich, Chuck Goodwin, and Alan Zemel. Support came from a grant from the National Science Foundation.

References

Atkinson, J.M. and Heritage, J. (1984). Transcription Notation. In J.M. Atkinson & J. Heritage (eds.), *Structures of Social Action*. Cambridge University Press, New York.

Dewey, J. and Bentley, A. (1991). Knowing and the Known. In J. A. Boydston (ed.), *John Dewey: The Later Works, 1949–1952, Vol. 16*. SIU Press, Carbondale, IL.

Clark, H. (1996). *Using Language*. NY: Cambridge University Press.

Clark, H. and Brennan, S. (1991). Grounding in Communication. In L.B. Resnick, J.M. Levine, and S.D. Teasley (eds.), *Perspectives on Socially-Shared Cognition*. APA, Washington, D.C.

Clark, H. & Marshall, C. (1981). Definite reference and mutual knowledge. In A.K. Joshi, B.L. Webber, and I.A. Sag (Eds.), *Elements of discourse understanding* (pp. 10-63). NY: Cambridge University Press.

Clark, H. & Schaefer, E. (1989). Collaborating on Contributions to Conversations. In R. Dietrich and C.F. Graumann (eds.), *Language Processing in Social Context*, Elsevier Science Publishers, North-Holland.

Fussell, S., Kraut, R., & Siegel, J. (2000). Coordination of Communication: Effects of Shared Visual Context on Collaborative Work. In *Proceedings of CSCW 2000*, pp. 21-30.

Goodwin, C. (2000). Action and embodiment within situated human interaction. *Journal of Pragmatics, 32*, 1489-1522.

Jackson, M., Anderson, A., McEwan, R., & Mullin, J. (2000). Impact of Video Frame Rate on Communicative Behavior in Two and Four Party Groups. In *Proceedings of CSCW 2000*, pp. 11-20.

Kendon, A. (1990). *Conducting interaction: Patterns of behavior in focused interaction*. Cambridge: Cambridge University Press.

Koschmann, T., LeBaron, C., Goodwin, C., & Feltovich, P. (2001, August). Dissecting common ground: Examining an instance of reference repair. In J. D. Moore & K. Stenning (Eds.), *Proceedings of the Twenty-Third Annual Conference of the Cognitive Science Society* (pp. 516–521). Mahwah, NJ: Lawrence Erlbaum Associates

LeBaron, C. (in press). Considering the social and material surround: Toward microethnographic understandings of nonverbal behavior. In V. Manusov (Ed.), *The Sourcebook of Nonverbal Measures: Going Beyond Words*. Mahwah, NJ: Erlbaum.

McCarthy, J., Miles, V., & Monk, A. (1991). An Experimental Study of Common Ground in Text-Based Communication. In *Proceedings of the ACM Conference on Human Factors in Computing Systems*, pp. 209-215.

Moerman, M. (1990). Exploring talk and interaction. *Research on Language and Social Interaction, 24*, 173-187.

Nardi, B., Kuchinsky, A., Whittaker, S., Leichner, R., & Schwarz, H. (1997). Video-as-Data: Technical and Social Aspects of a Collaborative Multimedia Application. In K. Finn, A. Sellen, S. Wilbur (eds.), *Video-Mediated Communication*, Lawrence Erlbaum, Mahwah, NJ.

Potter, J. (1998). Cognition as context (Whose cognition?). *Research on Language and Social Interaction, 31*, 29-44.

Sacks, H. (1992). *Lectures on conversation*. Oxford: Blackwell.

Streeck, J., & Mehus, S. (in prep). Microethnography: The study of practices. In K. Fitch & R. Sanders (Eds.), *Handbook of Language and Social Interaction*. Mahwah, NJ: Erlbaum.

Veinott, E., Olson, J., Olson, G., & Fu, X. (1999). Video Helps Remote Work: Speakers Who Need to Negotiate Common Ground Benefit from Seeing Each Other. In *Proceedings of CHI '99*, pp. 302-309.

Appendix A: Transcription conventions

Timing		
Brackets	[ ]	Marks the beginning and end of temporal overlap among utterances produced by two or more speakers.
Equal sign	=	Indicates the end and beginning of two sequential 'latched' utterances that continue without an intervening gap. In some cases, the symbol is used in combination with brackets.
Timed silence	(1.8)	Measured in seconds, a number enclosed in parentheses represents intervals of silence occurring within (i.e. pauses) and between (i.e. gaps) speakers' turns at talk.
Micropause	(.)	A timed pause of less than 0.2 sec.
Delivery		
Comma	,	Indicates a continuing intonation with slight upward or downward contour that may or may not occur at the end of a turn constructional unit (TCU) as in the enunciation of an item in a not yet completed list.
Period	.	Indicates a falling pitch or intonational contour at the conclusion of a TCU.
Question mark	?	Rising vocal pitch or intonational contour at the conclusion of a TCU. An inverted mark represents a half rise.
Exclamation point	!	Marks the conclusion of a TCU delivered with emphatic and animated tone.
Hyphen	-	An abrupt (glottal) halt occurring within or at the conclusion of a TCU.
Colon(s)	:	A colon indicates sustained enunciation of a syllable vowel, or consonant. Longer enunciation can be marked using two or more colons.
Greater than/ Less than signs	> < < >	Portions of an utterance delivered at a noticeably quicker (> <) or slower (< >) pace than surrounding talk.
Degree signs		Marks speech produced softly or at a lower volume than surrounding talk.
Capitalization		Represents speech delivered more loudly than surrounding talk.
Underscored text		Underscoring indicates stress on a word, syllable or sound.
Arrows	↑ ↓	Marks a rise or fall in intonation.
Other		
	hhh	Audible expulsion of breath (linguistic aspiration) as in laughter, sighing, etc. When aspiration occurs within a word, it is set off with parentheses.
	•hh	Audible inhalation is marked with a preceding dot.
Parentheses	( )	Text enclosed in parentheses represents transcribed talk for which doubt exists. Empty parentheses represent untranscribed talk or unknown speaker.
Double parentheses	(( ))	Transcript annotations (text italicized).

```
1   Attending: Yeah (.) the other ⌈thing to do:: is make sure
2                      you have your cystic (.) artery out too.
3   Resident:                    ⌊(Right there)
4   Clerk:        Uh huh
5   Resident: ⌈Which is right back in here⌉
6   Attending:⌊ That way there is nuthin ⌋ else before you
7                    h- (.) hit the edge of the liver
8                    (1.6)
9   Attending: That (kinda) guarantees you're safe too.
10  Clerk:     Can you see the cystic artery yet? I:'d=
11  Resident: =It's ↑r::ight back in the:re
12                   (2.1)
13  Attending: (We'll)  get it out here in a minute.
14                   (0.2)
15  Resident:    See it right there?
16                   (0.2)
17  Clerk:     U::mmmm=
18  Resident: =Right (0.2) ⌈there
19  Clerk:                 ⌊Okay yeah (.) yeah
20                   (0.2)
21  Resident: That looks like the (0.2) where the money's a:t
22  Clerk:     Uhkay
23                   (0.2)
24  Resident: En yih can see it's hanging out in that
25                ⌈tract.
26  Attending:⌊ (That's) actually big.
27  Attending:    That's pretty bi:g.
28  Attending:    That may be ri:ght,
29                   (0.4)
30  Resident: That's right hepatic?
31                   (1.2)
32  (Attending): ⌈(Comin' up)
33  Resident:    ⌊The cystic may be up a little higher?=
34  (Attending): =(Yup)
35  Resident:    You can see how easy that is to do we were
36                just talking about that.
37  Clerk:     So you jus' dissect until you'r:e absolutely sure
38  Attending: Ah ⌈hah
39  Resident:    ⌊Yeah=
40  Clerk:        =Till you see both the right hepatic and the cystic and then
41                   (4.6)
```

K. Kuutti, E.H. Karsten, G. Fitzpatrick, P. Dourish and K. Schmidt (eds.), *ECSCW 2003: Proceedings of the Eighth European Conference on Computer Supported Cooperative Work, 14-18 September 2003, Helsinki, Finland*, pp. 99-118.

Group-to-Group Distance Collaboration: Examining the "Space Between"

Gloria Mark, Steve Abrams, Nayla Nassif
University of California Irvine, Irvine, California, USA
{gmark,sabrams,nayla}@ics.uci.edu

Organizations are moving towards a new type of work: group-to-group collaboration across distance, supported by technologies that connect rooms across distance into large collaboration spaces. In this study we report on distributed group-to-group collaboration in the domain of space mission design. We use the metaphor of the "space between" distant groups to describe the connections, interdependencies, and gaps that exist. To the extent that the "space between" remains wide, the risk for design errors increases. We found that different teams, who had different processes and methodologies, were able to form hybrid solutions. However, their hybrid solutions addressed mostly terms and results, and did not address the deeper methodologies that created the results. We also found that some individuals acted as information bridges across sites, representing the teams in articulation. To a large extent small groups were used for reconciling perspectives, but the majority of results were not communicated and integrated back into the larger team. We discuss the challenges that group-to-group collaboration designers face in meeting requirements for supporting these new technologies.

Introduction

Over the last decade in CSCW, a number of empirical studies have described the difficulties people face when collaborating at a distance. These studies have mostly highlighted the constraints that exist when people communicate over media channels that limit social information. These studies have typically examined individuals interacting in teams and they span a range of technologies such as an audio media space (Ackerman et al., 1997), desktop conferencing (Mark et al., 1999), a virtual work environment (Fitzpatrick et al., 1996), video (Ruhleder and Jordan, 1999), chat (Bradner et al., 1999), and instant messaging (Nardi et al., 2000) across many domains (Olson and Olson, 2000).

However, in response to demands of combining whole team expertise, organizations are now moving toward a new collaborative configuration: group-to-group collaboration. As opposed to an individual at each site, entire teams are now collaborating across distance in real time. This enables organizations to benefit from larger bodies of increased specialization at distant sites.

To support such large group-to-group collaboration, new technologies are being developed using larger interfaces and multiple wall-sized displays to convey larger views of people and data. Access Grid technologies (2002) and HDTV video conferencing (Mark and Deflorio, 2001) are two examples. Access Grid technologies use interactive multi-media technologies with multicasting, showing multiple views from different sites. There are currently large numbers of site nodes, and these are increasing. The high resolution of HDTV video shown on a wall-sized display is designed to overcome the tradeoff experienced by ISDN video of showing clear talking heads versus the entire room. Despite these exciting technology advances, the study of problems and experiences with group-to-group collaboration still needs more attention. The study of collaboratories (e.g. Finholt, 2003) has been an important step in this direction.

In this paper, we report on distributed group-to-group collaboration in the domain of space mission design. The nature of the task—conceptual space mission design—is highly complex. Design has been characterized as an ill-defined problem (e.g. Carroll 2000). As a result, it requires much negotiation and articulation as design tradeoffs are discussed. Collocated environments are advantageous for designers not only because they provide awareness of the state of the design (Robertson, 1997) but they also enable designers to have immediate access to others, e.g. to question the relevancy of a requirement, to negotiate design tradeoffs, to collectively "walk through" the design and discuss discrepancies. A distributed environment makes these activities more difficult. Furthermore, in an arena with multiple teams and sites, the difficulty of accessing another designer is even more compounded.

Group-to-group and individual distance collaboration are significantly distinct in several ways. First, in group-to-group collaboration there are multiple actors at most nodes, generally teams, whereas in individual distance collaboration, there are mostly individuals at each node, though some nodes may have small groups. Second, group-to-group interaction can be characterized as information being communicated through many different networks, primarily within and across sites. The entire group at each site may participate in information exchange, but also subgroups may interact in parallel. Last, group-to-group technologies to support such collaboration are generally room-sized environments with large data and video displays. These distinctions are not perfect, as for example, in some individual distributed interactions, communication also occurs through multiple networks in parallel.

We envision a new class of interaction problems that exist with group-to-group collaboration compared to distance collaboration with individuals. First, as articulation is a central activity in design, we expect inter-site articulation to be difficult as it involves articulation of entire team perspectives. To add to the difficulty, each team needs to engage in articulation at their own site. Next, we expect that it will be difficult for individual team members to contribute to the discussion simply because of the large number of actors and distance between them. Last, we also expect that information from different actors will be difficult to integrate into the larger team. For example, design tradeoffs may be discussed at one site or across distance by a few individuals, and the results may not get communicated and integrated back into the larger team's design.

The "space between" in group-to-group collaboration

Weick and Sutcliffe (2001) write that high reliability organizations attempt to accomplish on a large scale what people do well on a small scale. A distributed group-to-group space mission design team attempts the same: performing the activities that smaller groups do at one site, but on a larger scale. The coordination increases to manage collaboration not only within, but also between sites. We adopt a relational orientation (Bradbury and Lichtenstein, 2000) which focuses on the relations between individuals and groups in the organization as opposed to focusing solely on the properties of individuals or entities. With this approach, we view a collaborating network as a configuration of relationships and see the space of interaction between team members as where the actual teamwork occurs. A relational orientation enables us to shine the spotlight on the "space between" (Bradbury and Lichtenstein, 2001; Roberts and Yu, 2003), i.e. the connections, interdependencies, and gaps that exist between groups across organizational sites. It is through these gaps where common meaning is lost or misconstrued, and conversely the connections where the potential exists for constructing and/or restoring meaning. We feel that a focus on the "space between" distributed groups enables us to understand where groups are aligned in their perspectives and where they are not. The extent to which coordination and articulation can bridge the gaps determines how much meaning can be transported and aligned across group borders.

The relations among actors have often been focused on in the field of CSCW, using perspectives such as articulation work (e.g. Gerson and Star, 1986), activity theory (Nardi, 1996), and distributed cognition (Hutchins, 1995). We believe our focus on the "space between" distributed groups can inform us of where gaps and connections lie in group-to-group collaboration.

We maintain that, to the extent that the "space between" remains large in collaborating groups, then risk increases for errors in the group product. An example of human and organizational risk in space mission design occurred in the space shuttle Challenger disaster. Vaughan (1997) writes about the "normalization of deviance" in the NASA organization as an explanation for events that led to the disaster. Vaughan's argument points out that human and organizational factors interacted with technology problems to expand the boundaries of acceptable risk. Vaughan showed that the errors occurred in what we call the "space between" distributed groups with different organizational cultures.

We expect the "space between" distributed groups to impact design in different ways. First, articulation has been discussed for some time in CSCW and other fields, e.g. with respect to how people of different social worlds use different terminologies (e.g. Gerson and Star, 1986; Schmidt and Bannon, 1992). However, in group-to-group collaboration, articulation is a much more difficult task than within a single group, as it must reconcile perspectives from entire teams. Teams from various organizational sites can use different terms and even the same terms can be interpreted distinctly in different organizational contexts (Bechky, forthcoming). We expect that team processes are well-known and visible within a team but much less visible outside of a team. Distance impedes the visibility. Second, though current group-to-group collaboration technologies enable a many-to-many information network, we expect that some individuals will act as "bridges" connecting the team sites. In social network theory, information bridges are individuals who have a significant degree of influence on interaction within a network and how information diffuses throughout the network (Freeman, 1991; Bavelas, 1950). The process by which information is conveyed in the large group-to-group configuration can impact the expertise that is communicated from a site. Last, in large groups with semi-formal or informal interaction, it is natural for the team to break up into smaller "sidebar" conversations (i.e. smaller group conversations that are conducted by telephone across sites or by clustering together within a site). Negotiations and decisions reached in some sidebars are important and should be communicated to the larger group. We would expect that multiple sites have difficulties in accessing and integrating the results of sidebar decisions. Though we can focus on many aspects of group-to-group collaboration, as a first step, we examine interaction: articulation, information networks, and information integration.

Research Setting and Methodology

The study took place at a large distributed aerospace organization whose main mission is to research, invent, and develop new technologies to enable (mainly) space-based scientific research. This study examines primarily four engineering teams distributed around the U.S. who synchronously designed an actual conceptual space mission design. Team 1 (Site 1) on the west coast had 24 contributors, Team 2 (Site 2) in the midwest had 12, Team 3 (Site 3) in the south had 9, and a single participant was in the southwest (Site 4). The majority of the people at Site 1 had worked together as a team for several years, and most people at Sites 2 and 3 had years of experience working together within their teams. Site 1 had two facilitators, and Sites 2 and 3 each had one. The purpose of collaboration was to combine different team specializations. Site 1 was responsible for science and mission coordination, and Sites 2 and 3 were responsible for propulsion and power. Sites 3 and 4 shared responsibility for the power supply of the overall system. We refer to all teams together as the entire Design Team.

A combination of technologies was used to support the large-scale interaction. For all distributed design sessions, a shared application, Microsoft NetMeeting, was used on a public display to show linked spreadsheets and graphics that were imported into a software presentation tool. For our primary data set, all four sites were linked by a video-teleconferencing (VTC) service that automatically switched views available to each local site for a short duration. It displayed the video stream from the non-local site that had the greatest average volume. This maximized bandwidth utilization by displaying to one site the most vocally active of the other sites. People were thus subjected to changing views of remote sites that occasionally did not match the locale of the current speaker (i.e. due to delays in volume sampling). Site 1 had three large public displays each 12 x 6 feet (one showed the video and the other two showed NetMeeting), Site 2 had two public displays of 6 x 5 feet showing video and NetMeeting, and Site 3 had one public display of 6 x 5 feet showing NetMeeting and a TV monitor showing the video. Other technologies used were *ICEMaker* (LSMD), which provided the linking between workstations and the shared spreadsheet. It enabled the members of the Design Team to publish specifications and parameters relevant to a particular subsystem. Voice conferencing software managed small group sessions by providing a single point of access for sharing multiple voice streams by telephone.

We examined several sets of data. We focused mainly on a space mission design that lasted nine hours over a week-long period, three hours on three separate days. Three different researchers traveled to Sites 1–3 during this period to observe, videotape, and interview team members. We thus had videotapes to compare the different team perspectives. Individuals at Site 1 wore wireless microphones and their voices were recorded on separate audio channels. Fourteen semi-structured interviews were conducted with team members at Sites 2 and 3 ranging from 30 to 60 minutes each. In addition, we used data from two other design collaborations. In one of them, three members of the research team observed Site 1 who collaborated on a conceptual design for a real space mission with two other teams at distributed sites around the U.S. These sessions lasted 18 hours and interaction at Site 1 was videotaped. Video data from a third collaboration involved only Site 1, so that we could get a better understanding of the team process and how it differed when the team collaborated across distance.

The videotapes from the nine-hour session were transcribed and coded. The coding scheme was identified through an iterative process of watching videotapes and discussing interaction. The design process was also parsed into different aspects based on field observations and a review of the design literature.

Coding was done for each actor's conversation turn in the transcript. Short utterances were not coded. We coded for factors affecting gaps and alignment in groups: human-human communication, technology used, the role of external representations, and organizational factors. We also coded design processes relating to design requirements, mutual construction of methods and terms, design rationale, information loss, and design coordination. We used grounded theory (Strauss and Corbin, 1998) to relate concepts.

Narrowing and extending the "space between" groups

Design-oriented discussion is inherently wide-ranging, complex and iterative, and not an orderly progression from initial idea to final design. The overall design process was semi-structured around a system of networked spreadsheets (shown on public displays) where design information was recorded. Though the teams used the spreadsheet to guide the topics and order in which they would be addressed, the Design Team often departed from this "agenda" when an issue emerged that evoked more in-depth discussion. When the issue had been resolved, or deferred pending future discussion, the Design Team returned to the spreadsheets to guide them to the next topic of discussion.

Different group methodologies used in design

Articulation is a necessary component to close the gap of the "space between" interacting groups. Team differences, however, can extend quite deep. Inter-organizational teams not only use different concepts and terms, but unique methodologies and processes for designing that are not readily visible to other teams. In collaborative design, often just the "point result" of a calculation is communicated and other teams are not aware of the methodology used to achieve the result. Thus, although results and terms are visible during the interaction, the deeper processes and methodologies used to create results can be invisible to other teams. They must be explicitly communicated.

Figure 1 illustrates how different teams in the same engineering disciplines employed different methodologies involving a fairly "standard" computation. Two sites had proposed different values for a mass contingency factor, each with a different rationale (Site 1 used guidelines and Site 2 used a subsystem model), and each led to different consequences for mission duration. The line numbers in

Figure 1 indicate the order in which the various points are made/proposed, demonstrating that the order of their emergence in the design process is clearly different than their relationships, in terms of rationales and consequences.

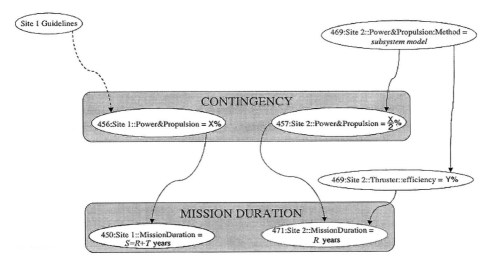

Figure 1. Different methodologies employed by two teams for the same design concept.

This figure illustrates a small part of a broad design space which can be further partitioned into two domains, defined by who actually makes the choices. Choices made by the Design Team are part of the "internal" design space; otherwise it is "external" made for example by the physics of a situation, (e.g. Mars cannot be moved closer to Earth to shorten the trip time), requirements imposed on the design space by external organizations (e.g. the customer), or by discipline-specific best practices. Internal choices are subject to change by the design team; external choices are not. In Figure 1, the "Site 1 Guidelines" used to support a factor of $X\%$ for contingent mass in the power and propulsion system is an example of a requirement from the external design space that can only be over-ridden with difficulty (such as with a waiver) or not at all (such as might be expected for human safety requirements).

The multidisciplinary aspect of the Design Team's process is not emphasized in the simple illustration in Figure 1. To reconcile the different approaches, in order to converge to a mutually-acceptable solution, each site must articulate their own methodologies and rationales and adopt the common solution.

We discuss four situations that illuminate how articulation is done across sites. In each case, different approaches to the same task emerged that reflected differing interpretations by the unique social worlds. As each site learned of the others' approaches, the sites constructed new methods, with new terminology, to apply in an emergent hybrid solution that satisfied each of their different needs.

However, although hybrid terms were agreed upon, the deeper methodologies and processes failed to be adopted, which led to consequences.

Contingent mass: hybrid methods that are not accepted

Though two successive hybrid solutions cooperatively emerged to reconcile different spacecraft masses, neither solution was accepted by the Design Team.

Key drivers of any space mission design are the masses of the various components of the technological system. These masses are initially estimated and iteratively refined as the design evolves. To allow for unanticipated growth of mass values at later stages of development, mass estimates are increased by a "contingency factor."

Sites 1 and 2 each had responsibility to design a trajectory for this mission (see next example) and to do so, needed to develop a mass estimate for the spacecraft, including "contingent mass." Site 1 employed a *top-down* approach by applying a single, default scaling factor of $X\%$ (defined by their site's design guidelines) to the entire spacecraft. Site 2 used a *bottom-up* approach by estimating contingent mass for each subsystem, as a percentage of that subsystem's mass, and then averaging the results over the entire craft. This resulted in a scaling factor of approximately $X/2\%$. These highly discrepant values had significant impact on the mission duration and cost.

A sidebar, with representatives from Sites 1–3, met and converged on a hybrid approach that applied Site 1's default scaling factor to some of the subsystems (but not all) in Site 2's model and which yielded an intermediate value of approximately $2/3X\%$. This also corresponded with an organization-wide default value. To determine to which subsystems different factors would apply, a new term "*validity*" was created based on prior experience with subsystems.

However, a facilitator at Site 1 continued to push for their default value, arguing that experience had shown them that $X\%$ was necessary to "sell" a proposal to those who make funding decisions. Articulation resulted in the emergence, and tentative adoption, of a second hybrid solution, in which Sites 1 and 2 would each use their own methods for design aspects for which they were responsible. At the end, the actual decision was deferred, by the Site 1 facilitator, until a sidebar with other facilitators could re-consider the issue. Site 2 was surprised by this resistance, considering the common agreement during the sidebar, and by Site 1's conservative approach. Site 2 expressed apprehension that such a policy-based approach would defeat their more mathematical approach.

Thus, in spite of considerable effort to cooperatively resolve such a key driver, articulation failed to deliver a solution, perpetuating the "space between" sites.

Trajectory design: decontextualized values that are not accepted

One of the most important consequences of mass determination is the range of viable trajectories that result. In this example, the sites' unique methodologies resulted in different trajectories that impacted the duration of the mission. Articulation revealed that sites used differing definitions of "trajectory." This led to the emergence of new terminology but it failed to be accepted.

The importance of the trajectory in the design was to accomplish the mission goals in a window of time bracketed, in the near term, by programmatic limits on how quickly the spacecraft could be built and, in the far term, by changing physical conditions at the destination that would impede mission goals. In general, a deep space trajectory consists of several distinct stages: launch from Earth to orbit, spiraling out from this orbit, transit to the destination, spiraling into orbit at the destination, and then performing operations in orbit to achieve the mission's goals. The time to complete all stages determines the length of the mission, which must fit into the specified window of time.

Sites 1 and 2 had primary and secondary responsibilities for the design of a trajectory for this mission, which had an unusual mass/power-ratio. Each site had different definitions of trajectory. In a top down manner, Site 1 began with the mass of a previous mission design and linearly scaling up from that mission's mass/power-ratio, it proposed a *"flight time"* of S years for a trajectory. In contrast, using a bottom-up approach, Site 2 developed a mass estimate for each subsystem that yielded a *"trip time"* of R years. Site 1's proposal combined the spiral-out and transit stages; Site 2's estimate also included the spiral-in stage.

Following Site 2's proposal, Site 1 adopted Site 2's term *"trip time,"* though no value changed to indicate an expanded definition of "trajectory." No decision was immediately reached between the two proposals, as the discussion identified "contingent mass" as the critical distinction between the two proposals and this issue was deferred to a sidebar held between Days 1 and 2.

Towards the end of Day 1, the operational stage was included with flight/trip times and the hybrid term *"mission duration"* was inaugurated by Site 1. Site 2, however, never adopted this new hybrid term, preferring to use their term *"trip time"* to include this additional, operational stage. Later on Day 1, Site 1 reverted back to its term *"flight time"* to characterize its trajectory proposal. Thus, the hybrid term was never fully adopted by the Design Team.

These difficulties in articulating the different terms were increased by similarities in their related numerical values during subsequent discussion. In addition to the "S year" and "R year" values introduced, some discussion included the operational stage (required to be T years to achieve the science goals, where $S=R+T$). This led to some confusion at Site 1, as different people interpreted "S years" as referring to both the initial flight time and to the expanded "mission duration" ($R+T$ years). In the articulation, the confusion over the decontextualized values surfaced and agreement on common terminology failed to be adopted.

Power mode: new terminology that is not adopted

The power available to a spacecraft is also a key driver of space mission design. In this example, new terminology was developed to reconcile different power mode views, yet it was not adopted.

Power is a critical spacecraft subsystem. The provision of power can interfere with the ambient electromagnetic environment that the science instruments are measuring. It can also interfere with the operational instrumentation supporting navigation, telecommunications, and command and control of the craft. To work around this, different power modes are considered for different stages of the mission, to interleave the operational and science activities. These modes range from "no power" (0%) to "full power" (100%). Full power is usually defined as only a little more than is necessary to do the job because superfluous power generally has penalties of increased mass and higher costs. A 0% power mode has risks of loss of control and the freezing of critical systems. In this mission design, Sites 2–4 had the primary and secondary responsibilities for various aspects of the design's power system, providing expertise that Site 1 lacked.

The initial discussion of power modes, initiated by Site 1, used the term *"power down"* to refer to a 0% power mode. When discussion concerned engineering safety, led by the Site 3 facilitator mid-Day 1, the term *"shut down"* was used to refer to this same 0% power mode. When this discussion led to other aspects, at the end of Day 1 by Site 2, the preferred term reverted to *"power down."* This pattern of using two different terms to refer to the same design concept, in the context of engineering safety and in other contexts, was generally repeated on Day 2 when Site 2 reported on a sidebar that used the two terms according to their different contexts.

The two contexts had different impacts on the overall mission. There was no science requirement for a 0% power mode, but engineering safety did require one. Midway through Day 2, a hybrid solution emerged in which there would be no 0% power mode planned during science operations, but such a mode would be planned for all other phases of the mission. In addition to the persistent use of two different terms to refer to the same concept, a facilitator at Site 1 also introduced a third term, *"safing,"* to refer to the same 0% power mode in the engineering safety context. Failure to converge on specific terminology at least reflected, and perhaps contributed to, the failure of the team to adopt this hybrid solution.

These multiple terms persisted through Day 3 and, to complicate matters further, Site 4 proposed new terms to refer to five distinct power modes ranging from "no power" to "full power". At the end of this discussion, at nearly the end of the overall design session, the team finally converged on the definitions of two terms, although not in time to incorporate them into other aspects of the design developed earlier in the session. *"Shut down"* was defined as the 0% power mode and *"power down"* was defined as referring to a value between 0% and 100%.

Multiple terms, representing similar aspects of design, increase the opportunity for confusion. Though attempts to construct consistent terminology were articulated, the entire Design Team did not consistently adopt these terms.

Rotational deviation margin: neglecting to address deeper rationales

This example shows how different sites, using distinct rationales, specified conflicting values of a significant design parameter.

Rotational Deviation (RD) results from the dynamics of the engine (produced by Site 4) and from spacecraft factors. Each RD (of the engine, spacecraft, or both) can be expressed by either its raw value, or a padded value (the raw value multiplied by a precautionary margin called RDM). RD is a significant design value because it negatively impacts the precision of on-board instruments (designed by Site 1). Therefore, the Design Team must specify tolerable values of RD and adopt a value of RDM based on organizational safety requirements and historical standards, to design the engine and instruments accordingly.

On Day 2, Sites 1 and 4 initially converged on an RD value of 5°. The Site 1 facilitator asked about the spacecraft RD and its RDM. Coincidentally, this RD also happened to be 5° with RDM of 2. A question from Site 4 revealed that team members were using the number 5° liberally without explicit reference to whether it was the raw engine RD or the padded spacecraft RD, both equal to 5°. Later, both sites referred to total RD. It was clear to the observers that "total" for Site 1 meant both RDs, whereas "total" for the Site 4 participant meant engine RD, for which he was responsible. Each site was thinking about its own component.

The team then focused on specifying protection for instruments. This revealed a difference of design methodology between sites. The Site 1 methodology began with 5°, multiplied it by RDM, and designed instruments to withstand 10°. The Site 4 methodology instead began with 5°, divided it by the margin, and designed the engine for the resulting number, namely 2.5°, while expecting the instruments to withstand 10°. This suggested that the Site 4 participant still did not use the term "*margin*" with the same understanding as that of Site 1.

The customer then asked Site 4 to explore a more desirable engine RD, namely, by cutting the value in half so that the total RD is 5°. Exchanges, clarifications, and repetitions of numbers ensued, further complicated by the fact that there was a different significance to the factor 2, and to the value 5°. So when someone used the number 5°, without explicit clarification (which was frequently done), it could have meant raw engine RD, desirable padded engine RD, padded spacecraft RD, or desirable raw total (engine and spacecraft) RD.

In conclusion, the team recorded the decision to use engine RD as 5° with no RDM, and spacecraft RD as 5° with RDM of 2. This decision did not explore the deeper rationales for selecting this choice of numbers. Though the numbers were settled on, the deeper methodologies underlying how the numbers were generated were still not resolved.

Surface and deep articulation

These four cases are complex (space mission design is very complex) but they all illustrate the same idea: hybrid terms and even simple processes were agreed on, but the deeper differences of the different team approaches were not sufficiently articulated. When an issue came to the attention of the Design Team, to some extent each site supported their proposed solutions—their design rationales—by explaining on the public channel "where they were coming from." New terminology was constructed to distinguish it from site-specific terminology. The hybrid solutions were accepted by the Design Team, but in language only. Though the facilitators initially believed that a hybrid solution was achieved and would therefore be adopted, in fact it was not.

In group-to-group collaboration, a "group-centric" view of the design can occur. The processes and methodologies at one's own site are visible and known. Articulation is triggered when results—in the Design Team's case, calculations or point estimates—are incommensurate, or seem questionable to another site. The deeper processes and methodologies used to calculate those results are not visible. Though the Design Team successfully created new hybrid terms, they neglected to reconcile the deeper methodologies and processes that lay "underneath" the terms. Although on the surface the term was agreed upon (at least initially), the many layers of methodologies and meaning that the term represented were not similarly reconstructed for the entire Design Team.

Insufficient translation is a problem endemic to different specialist groups because of their development of different languages, cultures, and approaches (Heath and Staudenmayer, 2000). It is not surprising that teams approach design differently (though they are all in the aerospace engineering domain in the same organization[1]) because through long term team relationships, methodologies and processes become embedded within team cultures. Even though hybrid solutions were formed to achieve consensus, translation of the deeper processes did not occur. As a result, the "space between" groups remains wide leaving much potential for error in design.

Information bridges across sites

We propose that in large networks people can be information bridges that affect the "space between" distributed teams. These information bridges may not only function to pass on content from the local site, but they may also represent the site in articulation. This is exactly what we found.

The VTC was a major part of the synchronous collaboration though information was also communicated through sidebars with telephone and by entering results into publicly displayed spreadsheets. The data suggested to us that

---

[1] Site 4 was in a different organization though also in the engineering domain.

the VTC was important to focus on for information transmission. In all four of the cases described earlier, most discrepancies between methods were discovered through conversation over the VTC channel. We should note that discrepant values were also identified in the shared spreadsheet.

Group-to-group collaboration technologies enable anyone at any site to freely participate. For example, anyone can speak through the VTC or enter their results into the networked spreadsheet that is publicly displayed. On the other hand, if everyone speaks freely without social protocols, chaos can possibly ensue. We were interested in exploring the social mechanism by which information was conveyed across sites using the VTC channel. In particular, we were interested in the role of information bridges in communicating information.

To explore this, we transcribed the VTC communication into conversational "exchanges." Such exchanges are contiguous streams of one speaker's speech and should not be confused with conversational "turns." In this transcript, a classic conversational turn may be split over several exchanges as people speak over and interrupt one another. We felt this approach was closer to the actual conversation and might afford opportunities to explore the impact of such conversational missteps on the design process. We coded each conversational exchange to determine whether it involved articulation or design content[2]. Using Gerson and Star's (1986) definition of articulation, we coded for any exchange that concerned *"all the tasks needed to coordinate a particular task, including scheduling subtasks, recovering from errors, and assembling resources"* (p. 258). This also included any discussions to reconcile different perspectives. We also coded for any exchange in which design content was discussed. Extraneous discussion not fitting into these other categories (e.g. jokes) was coded as "other."

Figure 2 shows the proportion of time the Design Team spent in articulation. There are several interesting aspects of this data. First, note that articulation occurred fairly regularly over the entire design session. One exception shows articulation increasing in frequency at the beginning of Day 3, when the designers know they have a limited time left. By correlating this with the transcript, we propose that the articulation provides a frame for the next design activity. The Team articulates their plans, designs in depth, and then coordinates to "recover" from the depth. The Team then moves on to the next topic.

We found that people whose roles involved coordinating the design process at their site tended to act as "bridges," speaking as representatives of their site to the entire Design Team. This is not a typical role for facilitators whose primary responsibility was to keep the team at their own site on track. The facilitators evolved their roles into becoming information bridges across sites.

---

[2] One member of the research team was a domain expert in space mission design.

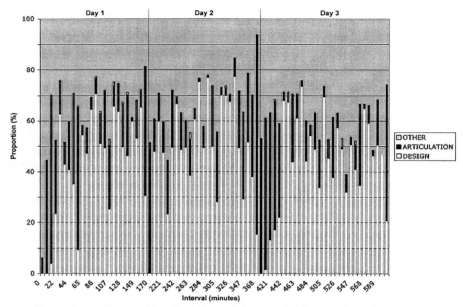

Figure 2. Proportion of time spent in articulation and design activities over the entire session.

The engineers who were more directly engaged in designing spoke less. Facilitators accounted for 61% of the public conversation (Table 1). Site 1's dominance of the common communication channel is also reflected, accounting for 70% of the shared conversation. Moreover, after agreeing on using voice protocols to identify themselves, Site 1 provided only 13% of self-identifications over the entire three-day period. Site 2 provided 58% of the self-identifications and Site 3 provided 29% though it contributed only 12% of the public conversation. This suggests that Site 1 did not make the extra effort to adapt their normal procedures to this new Design Team environment, as the other sites had done.

	Site 1	Site 2	Site 3	Site 4	TOTAL
Facilitators	45%	7%	9%	n/a	61%
Other team members	25%	6%	3%	5%	39%
TOTAL	70%	13%	12%	5%	100%

Table 1. Proportions of VTC-communicated content.

Second, we examined how much of the time was spent on articulation activities versus working on design content (e.g. calculations, meeting requirements). We discovered that about 70% of the discussion was spent discussing design content, and about 30% was spent on articulation (Table 2). Thirty percent is perhaps not so high considering the great amount of articulation needed, as the four earlier examples illustrated. Furthermore, the information bridges spent three times as much of their discussion time on articulation discussion (21.4%) as the rest of the team members, who spent only 7.0%. Thus, it appears that information bridges represented their local team in articulation. They also spent slightly more time on design discussion (39.4%) compared to the other team members (31.7%) which suggests that they also served as bridges for their teams in public discussion about design.

Thus, in this group-to-group collaborative setting, most of the discussion over the public VTC channel was done by "information bridges" representing their sites. To what extent can this result be generalized to other group-to-group collaborative settings? It seems reasonable that most information would pass publicly across sites through information bridges simply due to the large number of actors at multiple sites. The implications for design are that much of the articulation is dependent on these bridges. Not only is the quality and depth of articulation governed by such bridges but also the amount of articulation. Even if the facilitators agree on a hybrid solution (as in the four cases in the last section), this is far different than reconciling team methodologies. The fact that the rest of the team engaged in public articulation only 7% of the time may have hindered the Design Team from converging toward common methodologies and processes.

Conversation	Facilitators	Other team members	TOTAL
Design	39.4%	31.7%	70.5%
Articulation	21.4%	7.0%	28.4%
Other discussion	.2%	.3%	.5%

Table 2. Proportion of time spent on design and coordination/articulation conversation over the three-day mission design.

Lost information within and across sites

In the last section we discussed "public articulation," i.e. what occurs over the public VTC channel, that is available to the entire team. In this section we report how sidebars (subgroup conversations) are an important part of the articulation process in group-to-group distance collaboration. In the cases described earlier, in articulating mass contingency, a facilitator sidebar was formed to reconcile the approaches. Similarly, a sidebar was formed to articulate the design of power modes. It is critical in the articulation process that the results of the sidebar be communicated back to the team. Yet we discovered this was not the case. When critical information from sidebars are lost to the larger team, this further expands the "space between" distributed groups.

During the design, many sidebars occurred in parallel to the main VTC channel discussion. These sidebars occurred to gather information or to work on a small segment of the design, but mostly they convened for articulation purposes, i.e. to reconcile different team perspectives. In short, if a problem could be solved by relegating it to a sidebar, then it was. Sidebars were formed either by the team members, or they were assigned by a facilitator. They occurred both within a site and across sites, using telephones and the voice conferencing technology.

In fact, the different teams entered the collaboration with different practices of conducting articulation. It was normal practice at Site 1 to defer to a sidebar any topic in disagreement or requiring specialized expertise. These sidebars involved either the parties in disagreement or expertise from multiple sites and/or disciplines. Our data confirm how multiple perspectives are reconciled in sidebars to yield a commonly accepted solution. In the earlier contingent mass example, there was strong resistance from Sites 2 and 3 (noted in two instances) to defer topics to sidebars when there was disagreement among the sites. As the Site 3 facilitator expressed: *"if we don't have consensus on it, I think it should be brought out."* These sites expected contentious issues to be resolved publicly, instead of being deferred to sidebar discussions.

Coding the sidebars over the three-day session revealed that the coordination of all sidebar discussions fell into four categories: suggestions to convene a sidebar discussion and actual set-up, public reference to sidebars (after their suggestion and before their reports), the report of results, and the resolution of technical difficulties[3]. The public references to sidebars suggests that the entire Design Team was made aware that a sidebar was in progress, and with it, the expectation that the results would be communicated back to the team. Thus, the Design Team knew that people in a sidebar were articulating an issue.

	Site 1	Site 2	Site 3	Site 4	TOTAL
Suggestion/Setup	50	2	3	3	58
Reference	28	6	4	1	39
Report	4	2	1	0	7
Resolution	4	1	1	0	6
TOTAL	86	11	9	4	110

Table 3. Coded numbers of specific phases of sidebar processes, for 22 distinct topics, identified by Site.

The most surprising observation is the asymmetry between the number of references suggesting to convene and set up sidebar discussions and the relatively few reports back to the entire Team (Table 3). Though 58 sidebars were set up, in only seven cases (6%) were they publicly reported back to the team. Even though

---

[3] Codes included both collocated and distributed sidebars.

it is likely that the results of the sidebar discussions were implicitly communicated back to those interested, e.g. via changes made to the shared spreadsheets, their public call for, and subsequent public coordination, created an *expectation* that the information would be forthcoming via a public channel as well. Sites 2 and 3 made at least four references to such expectations. Thus, when sidebar results, especially those concerning articulation, are reported back to either one site only or not reported at all, then this is a way for common meaning to be lost in group-to-group collaboration.

Discussion

Designing for group-to-group distance collaboration presents a great challenge to CSCW. Currently the development of new room-size technologies that take advantage of large bandwidth is proceeding at an astounding pace, as with Access Grid Technologies. In this study we have attempted to understand problems in working with this new type of collaborative configuration. The extent to which technologies, communication, translation and articulation can close the gap of the "space between" is a challenge for distributed large-scale group-to-group meetings to be able to engage in meaningful and effective collaboration.

First, it is difficult for teams to achieve common aligned methods. Bechky (forthcoming) describes that knowledge is contextual in different organizational communities. Decontextualization occurs as different groups use different words and concepts to refer to the same concept. Recontextualization occurs when individuals use methods (e.g. providing a tangible definition) to arrive at a common understanding. We found that the team differences extended deeper than different terms/concepts. Design methodologies and processes were developed in different organizational contexts resulting in deep differences between the teams.

These methodologies are not readily visible to other teams across distance. Though hybrid solutions were achieved as a result of articulation, the local teams failed to adopt them. Team processes are deeply embedded (e.g. they may be local site design guidelines) and may not readily change even though a common solution is nominally agreed upon. Group-centric views, found in intergroup collaboration (Ancona and Caldwell, 1992), can inhibit the adoption of methods from outside the group. Early on, Gerson and Star (1986) proposed that a conceptual basis for the design of computer systems must be based on an understanding of articulation. The design of large-scale group-to-group collaborative technologies must enable not only point results but also the *visibility of team methodologies and processes* so that they can be articulated. For example, algorithms and formulae used by teams could be easily linked to the point result in the shared spreadsheet so that they are visible to the entire distributed set of teams. Increasing visibility is one small step, however. Adopting new methodologies is another large leap. Research needs to focus on how different teams can overcome group-centric views to adopt methodologies common to a larger-scale collaboration.

The use of information bridges was a major part of this design effort. We expect that such bridges are common in group-to-group collaboration efforts. A technology requirement is for a tool that can track team progress at a local site to enable the person serving as an information bridge to better represent the team. One possibility is to display a spreadsheet publicly to all sites that presents each sites' progress. This enables multiple "eyes" to detect discrepancies and nonalignment. This also can trigger opportunities for articulation.

We discovered that results of small group discussions that concern articulation (and other topics) rarely get reported publicly and integrated back into the larger distributed team. An important value of publicly conveying the results is that it documents the design rationale which can be later accessed. No mechanism existed in the collaborative technology for sharing the results of sidebar discussions with the entire team. A requirement for large-scale group-to-group systems is to provide a mechanism for tracking sidebars, their topics, and for channeling their results back to the larger team.

Technology can serve to close the gap of the "space between" actors and groups, but it can also function to widen the gap. We found examples with the sampling approach of the VTC and with the networked spreadsheets on the public display. As described earlier, to maximize bandwidth utilization, the video-teleconferencing service switches each site's local display between the remote sites, depending upon their most recently sampled volumes. This approach enabled people at a local site to get a video image of who was speaking currently or recently. But this has two drawbacks for supporting multiple site collaboration. First, during the volume sampling period, viewers see the site that was most vocally active before the sampling period, not the site currently speaking. This discrepancy was noticed at Site 2 and mistakenly identified as both a problem of temporal synchronization between the audio and video streams and as an effect of transmission delays.

The second drawback is more subtle. As designed, the system should work as intended if all sites vocalize in equal amounts and volumes. However, if one site dominates the discussion (e.g. Site 1), the video stream may tend to reinforce that dominance relationship. Since the VTC system will not display the dominant site to itself, viewers at the "speaking" site will primarily see video streams of people from the other sites listening to them (more or less equally) and not talking. Conversely, the less vocal sites will be presented with video streams primarily from the dominant site. Some research suggests that people evaluate persons in visual images who speak much more than listen as being "more in control" than if persons in the image seem to be primarily listening (Dovidio and Ellyson 1982). Conversely, visual imagery of a person listening more than speaking will be evaluated as "less in control." We suggest that the VTC sampling could have reinforced the verbal dominance of Site 1 by making them seem more in control to the other sites while making the other sites seem less in control to Site 1.

Conclusion

To the extent that the "space between" remains wide between entire teams at a distance, the risk for errors increases. With time, congruent agreed-upon practices and methodologies could likely be reached to narrow the "space between" collaborating groups. Currently ad hoc collaborations appear to be common in group-to-group collaborative situations, i.e. when groups convene across distance for specific discussions. Long-standing group-to-group collaborations are still rare, though as technology improves they may become more common. Providing large interfaces, e.g. to display video images or large data sets, are a first step, but may provide only a "quick fix" to enable such large-scale collaboration. An understanding of the adaptation and alignment of local team practices in different organizational contexts is not keeping pace with the development of group-to-group collaborative technologies.

Acknowledgements

We would like to thank Rebecca Wheeler, Paul DeFlorio, Steve Prusha, and members of the Design Team. This material is based upon work supported by JPL/NASA Grant No. 1240133 and the National Science Foundation Grant No. 0093496.

References

Access Grid (2002): http://www-fp.mcs.anl.gov/fl/accessgrid/default.htm

Ackerman, M. S., Hindus, D., Mainwaring, S. D., and Starr, B. (1997): 'Hanging on the wire: A field study of an audio-only media space', *ACM Trans. on Computer-Human Interaction*, vol. 4, no. 1, pp. 39-66.

Ancona, D. G. and Caldwell, D. F. (1992): 'Bridging the boundary: External activity and performance in organizational teams', *Admin. Science Quarterly*, vol. 37, no. 4, pp. 634-665.

Bavelas, A. (1950): 'Communication patterns in task-oriented groups', *Journal of the Acoustical Society of America*, vol. 22, pp. 271-282.

Bechky, B. (forthcoming): 'Sharing meaning across occupational communities: The transformation of understanding on a production floor', *Organization Science*.

Bradbury, H. and Lichtenstein, B. (2000): 'Relationality in organizational research: Exploring the space between', *Organization Science*, vol. 11, pp. 551-564.

Bradner, E., Kellogg, W., and Erickson, T. (1999): 'The adoption and use of 'Babble': A field study of chat in the workplace', *Proceedings of the ECSCW'99*, Copenhagen, pp. 139-158.

Carroll, J. M. (2000): *Making Use: Scenario-based Design of Human-Computer Interactions*, The MIT Press, Cambridge, MA.

Dovidio, J. F. and Ellyson, S. L. (1982): 'Decoding Visual Dominance: Attributions of Power based on Relative Percentages of Looking-while-Speaking and Looking-while-Listening', *Social Psychology Quarterly*, vol. 45, no. 2, pp. 106-113.

Finholt, T.A. (2003): 'Collaboratories as a new form of scientific organization', *Economics of Innovation and New Technologies*, vol. 12, pp. 5-25.

Fitzpatrick, G., Kaplan, S., and Mansfield, T. (1996): 'Physical spaces, virtual places and social worlds: A study of work in the virtual', *Proceedings of CSCW'96*, pp. 334-343.

Freeman, Linton C. (1991): 'Centrality in valued graphs: A measure of betweenness based on network flow', *Social Networks*, vol. 13, pp. 141-154.

Gerson, E. M. and Star, S. L. (1986): 'Analyzing due process in the workplace', *ACM Transactions on Office Information Systems*, vol. 4, no. 3, pp. 257-270.

Heath, C. and Staudenmayer, N. (2000): 'Coordination neglect: How lay theories of organizing complication coordination in organizations, in B. M. Stay and R. I. Sutton (eds.): *Research in Organizational Behavior*, Elsevier, Oxford: pp. 153-191.

Hutchins, E. (2000): *Cognition in the Wild*, The MIT Press, Cambridge, MA.

LSMD (Laboratory for Spacecraft and Mission Design): ICEMaker, http://www.lsmd.caltech.edu/tools/icemaker/icemaker.php

Mark, G. and DeFlorio, P. (2001): 'An experiment using life-size HDTV', *Proceedings of the IEEE Workshop on Advanced Collaborative Environments*, San Francisco, CA.

Mark, G., Grudin, J. and Poltrock, S. (1999): 'Meeting at the desktop: An empirical study of virtually collocated teams', *Proceedings of ECSCW'99*, Copenhagen, pp. 159-178.

Nardi, B., Whittaker, S., and Bradner, E. (2000): 'Interaction and outeraction: Instant messaging in action', *Proceedings of CSCW2000*, pp. 79-88.

Nardi, B., (ed.) (1996): *Context and Consciousness: Activity Theory and Human-Computer Interaction*, The MIT Press, Cambridge, MA.

Olson, G. M., & Olson, J. S. (2000): 'Distance Matters', *Human-Computer Interaction*, vol. 15, no. 2/3, pp. 139-178.

Roberts, K. and Yu, K. (2003). 'The space between: Partitioning and component focus as sources of error in healthcare.' *Unpublished manuscript.*

Robertson, T. (1997): 'Cooperative work and lived cognition: A taxonomy of embodied actions', *Proceedings of ECSCW'97*, Lancaster, UK, pp. 205-220.

Ruhleder, K. and Jordan, B. (1999): 'Meaning-making across remote sites: How delays in transmission affect interaction', *Proceedings ECSCW'99*, Copenhagen, pp. 411-429.

Schmidt, K. and Bannon, L. (1992): 'Taking CSCW Seriously: Supporting Articulation Work', *Computer Supported Cooperative Work*, vol. 1, no. 1-2, pp. 7-40.

Strauss, A. L. and Corbin, J. M. (1998): *Basics of Qualitative Research: Techniques and Procedures for Developing Grounded Theory*, Sage Publications, Thousand Oaks, CA.

Vaughan, D. (1997): *The Challenger Launch Decision: Risky Technology, Culture, and Deviance at NASA*, University of Chicago Press, Chicago, IL.

Weick, K. E. and Sutcliffe, K. M. (2001): *Managing the Unexpected: Assuring High Performance in an Age of Complexity*, Jossey-Bass, San Francisco, CA.

K. Kuutti, E.H. Karsten, G. Fitzpatrick, P. Dourish and K. Schmidt (eds.), *ECSCW 2003: Proceedings of the Eighth European Conference on Computer Supported Cooperative Work, 14-18 September 2003, Helsinki, Finland,* pp. 119-138.

Informing the Development of Calendar Systems for Domestic Use

Andy Crabtree, Terry Hemmings and Tom Rodden

The School of Computer Science & IT, The University of Nottingham, Jubilee Campus, Wollaton Road, Nottingham NG8 1BB, UK.
{axc, tah, tar}@cs.nott.ac.uk

John Mariani

Computing Department, Lancaster University, Lancaster LA1 4YR, UK.
jam@comp.lancs.ac.uk

Abstract. This paper contributes to the design of Groupware Calendar Systems (GCSs) for use in domestic life. We consider a number of ethnographic studies of calendar use in domestic circumstances to illuminate the design space and inform design reasoning. GCSs have been employed in the workplace for sometime and have been informed by studies of 'calendar work'. As design moves out of the workplace and into the home, the unique demands of domestic use now need to be considered. Existing insights into calendar work are restricted to the workplace however, and are constrained by analytic taxonomies. In the absence of first-hand knowledge of calendar use in domestic settings, we suspend the use of taxonomies and describe the 'interpretive work' implicated in calendar work in order to explicate real world practices of calendar use in domestic life. These novel studies draw attention to a corpus of accountable work-practices that impact directly on design. In particular, they emphasize the need for design to consider how the physical and the digital may be merged to support collaboration 'anywhere, anytime'; the necessity of devising negotiation protocols supporting computer-mediated communication; and the development of collaborative access models and interaction techniques to support data sharing.

The Social Character of Calendars

Electronic versions of the mundane calendar are one of the most successful kinds of collaboration technology to be adopted by end-users to date (Palen and Grudin 2002). Calendars are ubiquitous tools in office work, where it has long been recognised that they play an important role in the coordination of organizational affairs (Kincaid and Dupont 1985). Calendars are also prominent coordinational devices in the domestic environment - a setting not characterised by the organization of action for purposes of production and efficiency, but an organized setting nonetheless (Venkatesh 1996). The manufacturers of integrated office systems have included electronic versions of the calendar in almost every system they offer. As the computer moves out of the workplace and into the home we might expect to see the continued development of electronic calendars and other Personal Information Management technologies for home use. This is not simply a matter of technology transfer, however. The home is a distinct environment and it has already been recognised that there is a need for design to be sensitive and responsive to the unique demands of domestic life (Gaver 2001).

The development of calendars supporting office work was initially informed by empirical studies of paper-based calendar use (Kelly and Chapanis 1982) and the same strategy might be usefully employed as design moves into the domestic space. Empirical studies of calendar use in the workplace have identified a wide range of properties implicated in calendar use. In addition to their ubiquity, it is noted that calendars are both personal and social objects, providing a means for individuals to organize their affairs and a visible resource making others aware of the individual's schedule. This observation has led to the development of open, restricted, and closed models of calendar use in design, where the availability of personal information may be constrained by users according to the social circumstances of use (Palen 1999). Recognition that calendars are information-management tools (Bellotti and Smith 2000) complements the observation that calendars are also communication devices that provide for awareness in their visibility (Ehrlich 1987). To this we may add that the visible character of calendars gives them a mnemonic function in 'marking out' and so reminding users of important events that they must attend to (Zerubavel 1981).

The various complementary properties of calendars (information management, communication and mnemonic functions) coupled with that essential property – time – provides a rationalized representation of the user's actual schedule of real time activities (Lauer 1981). This is not to say that the calendar actually matches the user's activities but rather, to draw attention to the planful character of calendars in their real world employment. Calendars are temporal plans of coordinate action situated in social space and may be characterised as temporal maps constructed by users to coordinate events with others. In the *in vivo* course of their construction, calendars come to assume the character of workspaces consisting of a discrete body of 'calendar work' (Palen 1998). This work has been accounted for in terms of a taxonomy that is intended to "identify the basic components of calendar work and illustrate the richness of calendar interaction" (ibid.). Accordingly, the taxonomy highlights how calendar work 1) 'orients' users to the temporal order of events, and enables users to 2) 'record', 3) 'remind', 4) 'schedule', 5) 'track', and 6) 'recall' events within and over that temporal order. Coupled with appropriate access and privacy protocols, it is suggested that awareness of these essential features of calendar work may inform the continued development of shared workspaces – i.e., Groupware Calendar Systems (GCSs) that may by shared either synchronously or asynchronously and in either a co-located or distributed manner by more than one party.

Moving from the Workplace to the Domestic

As noted above, moving design into the domestic is not simply a matter of technology transfer. GCSs will need to be responsive to the unique organizational demands placed on calendars and other personal information tools in the home. In the first instance, it might be noted that domestic calendars – and by that is meant calendars that are situated in the physical environment of the home - are not employed to support groupwork as they are in the workplace. Domestic calendars are not shared as they are at work to coordinate meetings with members of the organizational team or to schedule resources, for example. Nor are they open or closed but, as a result of their physical placement in the home (often in the kitchen), they are 'proximally' available to co-located members of the household. Further contrasts could be made, but the point to appreciate here is that the assumptions and insights developed in the design of GCSs for the workplace are not readily or straightforwardly transportable to the domestic. The workplace and the home are different and while it might reasonably be expected that the essential character of 'calendar work' will persist, this too is problematic.

The problem is not that household members do not use calendars to 'orient' themselves to the temporal order of events, and to 'record', 'remind', 'schedule', 'track', and 'recall' events within and over that temporal order. Rather, calendar work is problematic because it has not yet been explicated and described. To provide a taxonomy of calendar work – i.e., a scheme of classification – is not to make that work visible and available to design reasoning, it is only to classify a discrete ensemble of real world activities. What do those activities look like? What does 'orienting' to the temporal order of events consist of as a recognizable calendar-based activity? How is that activity and the other basic components of calendar work put together or constructed in interaction? Taxonomies don't answer questions like these because they do not show the work involved in the real world, real time accomplishment of discrete activities. Taxonomies make reference to real world activities – they talk *about* them – but they do not display the activities referenced in actual details *of* their accomplishment. The taxonomy is offered as a proxy for the work, then, and so stands as a gloss that remains to be explicated (Garfinkel 1967). This is not to criticise taxonomies in general – obviously they have important uses, especially in the natural sciences – but to draw attention to their limitations when used to describe and represent human interaction. It is, however, to recognise that as we do not know what calendar work consists of as an accomplished ensemble or corpus of real world activities in the home – do not know what the 'basic components' look like as it were – then it is difficult for us to determine what appropriate design solutions might consist of concretely.

One solution to the problem is to complement taxonomies of interaction with a consideration of the 'interpretive work' that is observably and reportably implicated in calendar work (Dourish et al. 1993). The notion of interpretive work draws our attention to the ways in which members make sense of calendars in the actual course of using them. As Dourish et al. put it, "interpretation is guided by a context which many electronic systems do not acknowledge ... [but which is important] for the design, deployment and evaluation of shared information systems" (ibid.). While there are many notions of 'context' at work in computer science today, Dourish employs the following when invoking the word: "context is managed moment-by-moment, achieved by those carrying out some activity together, and relative to that activity and the forms of action and engagement [with artefacts] that it entails" (Dourish 2002). This notion of context provides us with a firm orientation to the interpretative work implicated in calendar work in the home and elsewhere, drawing our attention to the moment-by-moment nature of that work and, more specifically, to the observable forms of collaborative action and engagement-with-artefacts made visible in and across an unfolding series of moments that make up the work. Studying the interpretative work of calendar work will consist, then, of making the embodied arrangements of interaction and collaboration implicated in domestic calendar use visible and available to design reasoning (Dourish 2001).

This paper provides a provisional explication of the interpretative work implicated in domestic calendar work in order to inform the design of GCSs that are responsive to the unique demands of domestic use. The study is provisional in the sense that it is not exhaustive – more will undoubtedly be uncovered through further inquiry and, as in the workplace, this course of inquiry is likely to take some time. Specifically, we present a number of concrete empirical instances of interpretive work gathered through ethnographic inquiry. These instances make family members of a corpus of work-practices visible and available to design reasoning. These practices show us that the domestic calendar is an accountable social object whose use is organized in terms of its availability to collaboration, through members compliance with discrete coordination protocols, through the making of distinct annotations and notations, and through practices governing collaborative access and control. This corpus of practices suggests that design needs to consider how the digital and physical may be merged to support collaborative use 'anywhere, anytime', how the making of annotations and notations is organized so as make entries accountable to members who use electronic versions of the calendar, and how data sharing is managed through the development of collaborative access models enabling members to specify a variety of access, read, and write privileges.

Studying Interpretive Work (Methodology)

As design moves out from the workplace and into the home it is widely recognised that new methods are required to support the development of appropriate technologies. Ethnography has been of considerable utility to work-oriented design, providing rich insights into the social circumstances of systems usage, and has promised to do so in a domestic context for some time (Venkatesh 1985). When considering the potential role of ethnography in supporting design in domestic settings it needs to be appreciated that, strictly speaking, ethnography is not actually a method, but a gloss on various competing analytic frameworks. As Shapiro (1994) has had occasion to put it in the past,

> While 'ethnography' as a term strikes a useful contrast to traditional methods of requirements capture, within sociology and anthropology themselves it denotes rather little. It marks a distinction between quantitative and qualitative approaches to social science and carries with it a commitment to a period and degree of immersion in the social setting being studied that is sufficient to reach a qualitative understanding of what happens there. These are important matters, but beyond this, ethnography can be put to the service of virtually any theoretical school: there are, for example, functionalist, structuralist, interactionist, Weberian and Marxist ethnographies.

As ethnography is not a method but a gloss on a veritable host of analytic perspectives on social life and social activity it does not need to be adapted to support design in a domestic context: ethnography is not a tool that needs reconfiguring, but an analytic sensibility and way of accounting for social action. Indeed, ethnography has already provided valuable insights into domestic life and the role of technology in the milieu of domestic activities (Mateas et al. 1996, O'Brien and Rodden 1997, Venkatesh et al. 2001).

One particular analytic perspective that has been widely employed in CSCW and workplace design more generally, and which continues to inform systems development as design moves into the domestic (O'Brien et al. 1999), has been that of the ethnomethodological mode of analysis (Crabtree et al. 2000). Ethnomethodology (Garfinkel 2002) replaces a concern to account for human interaction through the use of theories, models, taxonomies, and other formal analytic and representational devices for a concern with the 'thick description' (Sharrock and Button 1991, Ryle 1971) of the work manifest in members' observable and reportable interactions. The ethnomethodological notion of 'work' does not refer to either paid or (as one might find in the home) unpaid labour. Rather, 'work' refers to the discrete courses of practical action whereby persons construct, organize and reflexively coordinate their mutual activities in their interactions together. Making these recurrent real world, real time courses of action or 'work-practices' visible and available to reflection in design is the primary concern of the ethnomethodological analytic (Button and Harper 1996). It is an analytic point of view that supports Dourish's notion of context, and indeed, a point of view from which that notion is derived. Thus, when accounting for the interpretive work of calendar work, the ethnomethodological analytic will do so in terms of the observable and reportable work-practices made visible by the embodied arrangements of interaction and collaboration whereby calendars come to be embedded in home-life.

Interpretive Work Implicated in Real World Calendar Use

This section presents and considers a number of concrete empirical instances of the interpretive work implicated in calendar work in the home, both as a means of elaborating ethnomethodological study and as a resource informing the development of future technologies supporting Personal Information Management within domestic settings. The empirical instances presented are not representative in a numerical sense, but are instead concerned to examine actual empirical events in details of their actual collaborative construction so that we may learn what we can of the ways in which calendars are used in the home and so inform the design of appropriate forms of Groupware Calendar Systems for domestic use. The instances were gathered as part of a wider, long-term and ongoing study of 22 homes in the UK covering a wide range of domestic media usages some findings of which have been published elsewhere (e.g. Crabtree et al. 2002a; Crabtree et al. 2002b; Crabtree et al. 2003a; Crabtree et al. 2003b; Crabtree 2003).

Instance 1) The Calendar is an Accountable Social Object

The following sequence of interaction takes place between Alex and Sam in the kitchen, where their calendar is situated on the door. Alex and Sam both have jobs which often require them to travel to different places across the country. They have recently had their first child, Jake, and need to coordinate their busy schedules so as to ensure that one of them is available to pick Jake up from the nursery at the end of each working day. Alex has decided to use a calendar as a solution to the problem of coordination, which provides an economical way of displaying their schedules to one another 'at-a-glance' (Kincaid and Dupont 1985). The sequence of interaction emerges in the course of their evening routine: Jake has been fed and put to bed and Alex and Sam are preparing their evening meal; they are having a glass of wine and discussing the day's events and what's on tomorrow's agenda; Alex reminds Sam of tomorrow's work commitments, which means that Sam will have to pick Jake up. At this point in the conversation Sam also remembers a work commitment, one that has not been recorded on the calendar because it only arose two days ago as a result of a conversation with Sam's boss, Jane:

Alex: It's always the bloody same - you leave it to the last minute every time!

Sam: No I don't. Sometimes I don't get enough notice to

Alex: Doesn't Jane understand about Jake?

Sam: It's not her problem is it.

Alex: Oh come on, she's not that bad - and besides, you could have phoned me at work.

Sam: I was busy, then I forgot all about it. It was only when you said what you were doing tomorrow that it reminded me of

Alex: You, you can see - *look* (Alex points to the row of arrows on the calendar)

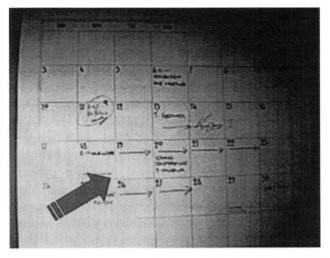

Figure 1. The arrows → → → indicate and display Alex's schedule.

Alex: I'm really pushed and Stuart [Alex's boss] will expect

Sam: I know and "Kinda Like" [a nickname for one of Alex's colleagues] can't drive yet, so it's down to you again. And *that* [causing a conflict in their schedule's] is my fault, *again!* It's my Alzheimer's coming on.

Alex: That's not f...ing funny anymore!

Sam: It's not that I do it on purpose. You're more organized. I just don't always remember until it's too late.

The outcome of this conversation was that Alex had to reorganize the following day's work so as to be able to pick Jake up. It is a grossly observable feature of Alex and Sam's conversation that, in details of real world, real time human praxis, the calendar is an 'accountable' social object – i.e., a discourseable object oriented to and employed to negotiate schedules and to coordinate practical action. 'Negotiate' is a gloss on an unfolding course of interpretive work in which the calendar is recurrently implicated. Over its unfolding course, that work is observably and reportably concerned to elicit reasonable grounds for the negotiation in hand: for Sam failing to notifying Alex of recent contingencies that effect Alex's schedule.

What makes the calendar an accountable object, one that is employed, invoked, appealed to, and in other ways skillfully and artfully implicated in the co-construction of a reasoned and reasonable familial discourse providing for the reorganization of scheduled commitments and the coordination of practical action (picking Jake up from nursery), is an ensemble of accountable work-practices that provide the calendar with its recognizable and discourseable features and give it life and meaning. By 'life and meaning' we wish to draw attention to the fact that although calendars consist of certain abstract and generalisable attributes such as various representations of time which lend calendars their planful character, such attributes are meaningless in themselves. Naturally, regardless of whatever attributes calendars may be said to possess, calendars are dead objects in the absence of use. Use transforms the object into a living thing that has meaning, purpose, utility, and demonstrable sense and reference. Use breathes life into the object and that life consists of everything that the accountable work-practices comprising its use could be. We do not claim to identify all the members of the discrete corpus or family of work-practices implicated in calendar use in the home. We do offer the following observations, however.

The accountable character of calendars - and with that, their real world, real time collaborative uses - relies on their availability to collaboration. This issue is currently addressed by household members in practice by placing the calendar in a location where it can be shared, such as on the kitchen door. Shared use relies on members' compliance with coordination protocols. The protocols state, in this case, that members should update the calendar to reflect their schedules and to 'articulate' (i.e., identify, avoid, point out, negotiate their way around, etc.) potential conflicts. Coordination protocols are embodied and expressed in terms of visibly distinct annotations. In Figure 1, for example, Alex indicates and displays her schedule by making visibly distinct annotations to those made by Sam: Sam employs arrows → to mark out and make visible his schedule, whereas Alex employs circles ○. Visibly distinct annotations are accompanied where necessary with explicatory notations. These textual notations 'tell' members who use the calendar what some particular annotation is about, what event it refers to and marks out. Notations do not necessarily accompany annotations and may stand on their own. Visibly distinct annotations and explicatory notations provide for the at-a-glance intelligibility of the calendar for the members who use it. They provide for the accountable character of the calendar, giving it life and meaning, and merit consideration in their own right.

Instance 2) Calendar Use Relies On Essential Accountable Work-Practices

The at-a-glance intelligibility of the calendar for members who use it is demonstrably provided through the annotations and notations that give it sense and reference. Annotations and notations are essential features in the negotiation of schedules and coordination of practical action. We have already seen how annotations and notations are implicated in Alex and Sam's occasioned use of the calendar. Figure 2 shows a range of annotations employed by Veronica and Julian to coordinate and organize their actions around important events in their lives. Here the calendar shows us that Veronica and Julian employ annotations and notations for a variety of purposes.

- Vertical lines on the margin of the calendar are used to mark out holidays;
- Capped lines inside the calendar mark out particular holiday arrangements (such as going to a friend's for a couple of days);
- Notations in the margins mark out the unfolding order of Veronica's work schedule;
- Red notations accompanied by a name mark out birthdays;
- Red notations elsewhere mark important events (like going to the doctor's);
- And a plethora of contingent notations otherwise populate the calendar.

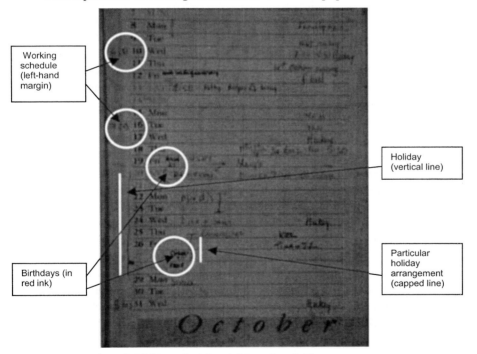

Figure 2. Making schedules visible and available to account

Annotations and notations on paper calendars may be thought of as idiosyncratic, marking the calendar out as a 'private' and 'personal' object and, if supported in design, as limiting the collaborative value of moving calendars online (Palen and Grudin 2002). As Palen (1999) puts it,

> Conventional paper calendars support people in idiosyncratic, personally customised ways. GCSs replace conventional calendars, requiring that they be used both for personal and social coordination.

As noted above, the home is a very different environment to the workplace. For one thing it is not characterised by a large working division of labour or the need to use calendars to coordinate activities on an hourly basis. This, in turn, means that the intelligibility of the calendar does not rely on standardised arrangements of use. Any array of annotations and notations will do for members as long as that array allows them to mark out and display the things they need to mark out and display for one another. In the home, the personal and the social are, already and through local agreement, thoroughly intertwined. Rather than ignore the idiosyncratic, design will need to appreciate its importance when it comes to the domestic and support 'personal customisation' because that is what calendar use in homes is all about and that is the great utility of existing calendars: that they can be easily and readily appropriated to support the very personal coordinational needs of household members. Demonstrably, Veronica and Julian's use of lines and coloured notations along with Alex's circles O and Sam's arrows → show us that the personal and idiosyncratic does not exclude or inhibit or limit coordination but provides for it, and provides for it at-a-glance (even where just what it provides is the re-negotiation of coordinate action). Providing members with means of making visibly distinct annotations and explicatory notations is not all that the negotiation of schedules consists of as work-practice, however, as the following instance shows.

Instance 3) Collaborative Access Underpins Negotiation

The following sequence of interaction takes place between Sarah and Helen in Helen's living room. Sarah is the partner of Adrian, Helen's son. Helen has asked Sarah and Adrian when they are going to visit her again? Having agreed that it will be sometime soon, "sometime in half-term", Helen goes and gets her calendar off the kitchen door. She brings it back into the living room where Helen and Sarah orient themselves to the calendar to negotiate just when in half-term the visit might occur, which they then relay to Adrian.

> Sarah: I've got two weeks, Ian [Helen's grandson] has got six.
> Helen: I've got Ian at half-term, the week before Sarah's off (points to area marked out on the calendar; Sarah looks at area pointed out).
> Sarah: Because we have different term dates in Derbyshire from what they do here.
> Helen: So I'll have Ian on the Monday and the Tuesday, all day I would think, and the half-day (points to a day on the calendar). But also, Lyn [Ian's mother] has started on maternity cover so that means both he and Rachel [Ian's sister] will be here (points to a day on the calendar) on *those* mornings [of the second week] I would think (points to first date then second date and re-emphasises by repeating the action)
> Adrian: When's Sarah, when do you want to come down?

Sarah: Next week, after Ian.
Helen: (Circles the date on the calendar that follows the two she has previously highlighted).
Helen: That's the day when you're coming.

Figure 3. Shared orientation provides for negotiation.

The sequence makes it visible and available to design reasoning that the negotiation of schedules is made possible by collaborative access situating the calendar between the negotiating parties and so enabling a shared orientation. It is worth noting that collaborative access is permitted by the calendar owner following provisional agreement to schedule an event and, for the practical purposes to hand, access is restricted to the time frame in question (which is to say that access to the entire calendar of events is not occasioned). Shared orientation to the calendar is not a given thing but an achieved phenomenon, which is to say that the users mutual orientation is worked up and maintained moment-by-moment over the unfolding course of the accompanying negotiation. Noticeably, the work is done through 'ostensive definition' – i.e., by pointing, gesturing, drawing imaginary lines across dates with a pen or finger and similar transient actions which provide specific reference, direction and emphasis to the conversationalist's talk. Through situated practices of ostensive definition, the negotiation proceeds. Thus, and for example, Helen points out that on these days marked here on the calendar her grand children are coming. Here, the work of negotiation employs previous annotations and notations to identify a possible date for scheduling the event to hand. This is achieved by highlighting those days that are ruled out of play. Reflexively, and in light of Sarah announcing the days on which she is free (the week after Ian breaks up for half-term), this action articulates these unmarked days as candidates. Over an unfolding course of ostensively defined work appealing to and manipulating previous annotations and notations a definite date is mutually identified and fixed.

A Corpus of Accountable Work-Practices

The instances of calendar use we have presented allow us to identify a number of discrete real world, real time work-practices belonging to the corpus of practices implicated in calendar use in the home and which provide for negotiation and the coordination of practical action. The corpus includes:

- **Situating Calendars so that they are Available to Collaboration:** Negotiation and the coordination of practical action rely on situating the calendar in a location where it is readily available to household members and from where it may found, moved and accessed when needed.
- **Complying with Coordination Protocols:** Effective collaborative use requires compliance with discrete protocols for sharing personal information that affects the members' schedules. These protocols are characterised by updating the calendar with personal information that directly relates to schedules.
- **Making Visibly Distinct Annotations:** Compliance with collaboration protocols is embodied in a wide range of distinct annotations that display particular member's schedules and which serve as a resource articulating conflicts. Annotations take a wide variety of forms as they are used to express a range of different and contingent events.
- **Adding Explicatory Notations:** Annotations are often accompanied by textual notations that give particular annotations their sense and reference. Notations may stand alone however, they do not necessarily accompany annotations.
- **Accomplishing Collaborative Access:** Where calendars are shared with non-household members access is restricted to the time frame in question. Annotations and notations are available to collaborative action however, their use being embedded in situated practices of ostensive definition that enable members to establish a shared orientation and provide for negotiation and the coordination of practical action.

This is not an exhaustive listing of the essential practices implicated in collaborative calendar use in the home, only a provisional one. No doubt that there is still more to be uncovered, just as our current studies have shown that there is more to the design of GCSs as design moves from the workplace and into the home. The listing does give us a definite or concrete starting point for reasoning about the design of GCSs for domestic use, however.

Moving GCSs from the Workplace into the Home

The accountable character of calendar use in the home moves design beyond automation to consider how the collaborative and artful uses of calendars might be supported. Previous work on calendar use has identified a taxonomy of 'calendar work' involved in the collaborative construction of 'shared workspaces' or, more specifically, of GCSs. In our ethnographic studies of calendar use in home settings we have paid deliberate attention to the interpretive work involved in calendar work, which consists of an orientation to and careful description of the 'missing interactional what' of organizational studies (Garfinkel 1986). Explication of the missing interactional what of calendar work specifies in real world, real time detail just what such abstract taxonomic categories as 'orienting', 'recording', 'reminding', 'scheduling', 'tracking', and 'recalling' events within and over the temporal order of calendar work look like concretely; what 'orienting', 'recording', and 'reminding' consist of as recognisable 'jobs' of cooperative work; how 'scheduling', 'tracking', and 'recalling' get done in members collaborations. Furthermore, paying attention to the missing interactional what serves to respecify abstract taxonomic categories in terms of a distinct corpus of accountable work-practices that observably and reportably make up or constitute 'calendar work' in the real world. That corpus of practices is ignored by formal analytic accounts of calendar work, replaced by abstract taxonomic categories that describe work-practice generically and in terms of definitions. Real world work-practice is, as such, rendered unavailable to design reasoning.

Moving from Home Studies to Inform Design Reasoning

Explication of corpus members serves to highlight a number of essential issues as the design of GCSs moves from the workplace into the home. In the first instance, it is grossly apparent that the availability of calendars to collaboration is currently constrained. Paper-based calendars are situated in the home and, as such, are not available to collaboration outside of the home. This may seem like a trivial point to make. If we consider the occasion of Alex and Sam's dispute, however, or the interaction between Sarah and Helen, it soon becomes clear that this is not so. Where Sarah and Helen are concerned, it is plainly visible that only one party has access to a calendar. The other party must remember the date scheduled for meeting and update her own calendar at some later point when access is achievable. Personal schedules are often arranged on-the-fly and human memory is notoriously faulty – we can and often do forget to update our schedules. It is just such an occurrence that occasions Alex and Sam's dispute – Sam "didn't get enough notice", he was "busy", he "forgot" and, because he forgot to update Alex as to the change in schedule at the time the change arose, he didn't broach the issue until it was "too late" to do anything about it. So the first design issue that arises is that of making calendars available to collaboration outside the home; of transcending existing constraints of paper by 'getting the calendar off the wall' and making it 'transportable' through design so that it is available to collaboration 'anytime, anywhere', a demand long recognised in studies of workplace calendar use (Ehrlich 1987).1

Supporting off-site calendar use anytime, anywhere raises a number of issues that we think it important for design to consider:

1) Merging the Digital with the Physical

It might be argued that there is no challenge for design here, that solutions are already at hand in the form of PDAs which include electronic calendars. This would be to miss one of the central points of domestic calendar use: namely, that they are situated in the home in order to provide for collaboration and awareness. Making the calendar disappear from the home is not the solution to off-site access. Rather, it is important for design to maintain the calendar's visible presence in the physical space of the home and, at the same time, to devise support providing off-site access. Design needs to merge the digital with the physical then, enabling members to situate electronic calendars in the physical space of the home - to locate the electronic in a physical and visible place - and to provide access to the physically situated electronic calendar outside the home via mobile devices. An example of one such arrangement is provided by Tullio et al. (2002):

> The Augur system is comprised of a number of components that process, store, and serve calendar information located in a central relational database ... To harvest calendar information, we have implemented PalmOS conduit software that automatically sends calendar information via FTP to our parsing module upon synchronisation with a networked computer. The parsing module reads the PalmOS calendar and updates a table of events in the database whose fields are designed to match the VCalendar specification. A user ID number is associated with each event to identify its owner. A second table lists the system's users and their IDs.

While the Augur system is designed for workplace use, it nevertheless articulates one way in which designers might think about configuring technical solutions for home use, exploiting networked displays with relational databases and mobile devices to support calendar use inside and outside the home. Such configurations may serve to make personal schedules available to account anywhere, anytime, not only supporting Sarah in her work with Helen, or Alex and Sam's scheduling arrangements, for example, but also, making Sam's schedule available to account in his conversation with his boss, which might see different outcomes in the first place. Where Tullio et al. concentrate on making members schedules available to account in terms of predicting event attendance and co-scheduled participants when considering support for 'interpersonal communication', we would suggest that the design of GCSs needs to consider

---

1 As Erhlich put it, "interviews revealed that managers maintain off-site contact with their calendars ... [this] suggests that direct phone access to the calendar may in fact be very valuable". Today, with the emergence of the mobile phone and PDAs, design can easily configure new ways of supporting direct access to the calendar off-site.

supporting the negotiation of schedules when moving from the workplace to the home. This is not to criticize Tullio et al., it is only to recognise that the needs of the home are different to the needs of the workplace: predicting event attendance and making members aware of who else is attending a scheduled event is not a pronounced feature of calendar use in the home, whereas negotiating schedules evidently is.

2) Devising Negotiation Protocols

The ethnographic instances we have provided instruct us that calendars are employed in domestic settings as temporally projected plans. It is observable too, especially in Alex and Sam's case, that these plans are not fixed but subject to contingency and change. Schedules are continuously negotiated and updated then, and it is important that design support this central aspect of calendar use. What we have in mind here is the augmentation of coordination protocols through the design of negotiation protocols. The instances show us that coordination protocols are embodied in and expressed through a contingent range of visibly distinct annotations that enable the members who use the calendar to see at-a-glance who has made an entry to the calendar, and explicatory notations that 'tell' members what particular entries are about, what they refer to. While it is important to support these accountable practices, we believe that design also needs to consider how the making of annotations and notations is provided for and organized in the electronic workspace? In other words, we believe that design needs to consider the development of a range of negotiation protocols that make data transactions transparent to the members who use the calendar to coordinate their actions and so support the accountable computer-based scheduling and re-scheduling of events.

By 'negotiation protocols' we refer, then, to computer-mediated methods of interaction and communication that allow the users who own and share the calendar to make one another aware of and respond to data transactions, such as annotating a particular date on the calendar and adding a notation (Greif and Sarin 1987). Thus, and for example, when a member makes an entry, or updates an entry, others sharing the calendar are made aware of the making of that entry or update and may, in turn, enter into negotiation. The question is how?

- Are data transactions reflected in the physically situated calendar, by the use of colour highlights for example, and for how long?
- What about situations in which members are distributed, is some form of alert required via SMS when an entry is made?
- How are the conditional statuses of data entries to be represented on the calendar and conveyed to distributed users: is a 'candidate' entry being scheduled, is a 'conflict' caused by the entry, is a 'change' to the schedule being occasioned?

- How are users sharing the calendar to respond to data transactions, how are they to 'query' an entry, 'put it on hold', or 'approve' a new data entry or change to an existing entry?
- And how do these issues combine with annotation and notation to provide a coherent range of functionality across a network of static and mobile devices?

While there are undoubtedly a variety of ways in which these core issues may be addressed technically, the point here is not to sketch out a design solution but to inform design reasoning by recognising the need to devise negotiation protocols to support the collaborative and distributed use of domestic calendars.

3) Supporting Collaborative Access

It is observable in our studies that the collaborative use of domestic calendars extends beyond the home and the parties who own them. 'Outsiders', including members of the wider family, are often party to the use of domestic calendars. This raises the issue of access rights, as it is observable in our studies that access is occasioned: outsiders only have access to calendars when they are directly involved in the scheduling of events, and even then they do not appear to have write permissions. Supporting access control is an important matter when we think about making calendars available to collaboration online. Unlike many GCSs designed for the workplace, open models of collaboration cannot and indeed should not be assumed. The domestic calendar is a personal object, not in the sense that it belongs to one individual, but in the sense that it belongs to a very small collection of individuals to organize and coordinate what can only be described as their intimate affairs. Respecting the intimate character of the domestic calendar is important as design moves into the home, which means that designers will have to consider the development of collaborative access models that enable members to control distributed access and use.

At a gross level, distributed access and control will rely on the definition of roles enabling members to specify certain categories of user such as 'owner', 'friend', and 'guest' to which gradations of access, read and write privileges are assigned. Thus, 'owners' might have full access, read and write privileges; 'friends' might have partial read access where the details of the owners' full monthly schedule is made visible; and 'guests' might have limited read access where the details of the owners' full monthly schedule are concealed, for example. Many of these techniques are already available in workplace GCSs. The challenge for design here is one of devising an appropriate and intelligible collaborative access model that enables members to manipulate existing techniques and so control and manage distributed access to the domestic calendar through the specification of roles determining access to the available range of calendar operations (Grief and Sarin 1987). A further challenge is presented by the possibility of distributed real time collaboration, in contrast to co-located collaboration, where members simultaneously interact with the calendar from different locations. This will require the development of a further set of computer-mediated interaction techniques that enable members accessing the calendar and collaborating from distributed locations to establish, work up and maintain a shared orientation to the calendar and so conduct their negotiations. These 'tele-pointing' protocols will support the moment-by-moment making of the transient physical gestures that allow members to highlight, point out, and draw connections between calendar items, which successful negotiations observably and reportably turn upon.

Supporting Accountable Work-Practices

Consideration of the technical implications of members' accountable calendar-based work-practices has led us to reason about the essential nature of technical support and suggest a number of important factors that we believe design should take into consideration when moving GCSs from the workplace to the home. These include but are not limited to the following.

- **Anywhere, Anytime:** Considering the nature of technological configurations to move calendar use beyond existing constraints while, at the same time, respecting and supporting existing configurations. In short, electronic calendars should be made available to collaboration in the physical space of the home and off-site, anywhere, anytime as occasion demands.
- **Computer-Mediated Communication and Interaction:** Considering how compliance with coordination protocols through the making of annotations and notations is organized. This requires design to devise negotiation protocols that support computer-mediated communication and interaction and so enable members to negotiate their schedules through the active use of the technology.
- **Data Sharing and Distributed Collaboration:** Considering the development of distributed collaborative access models that enable users to control and manage data sharing through the specification of roles and other appropriate criteria. It is also important to consider the design of computer-mediated interaction techniques supporting the production of shared orientations that underpin negotiation.

Again, this listing is not exhaustive but provisional – undoubtedly, as with the development of GCSs in the workplace, there is more to be articulated at this early stage in design's progression into the home, particularly regarding just how these concerns might be addressed as a technical job of work in design. As ethnographers we do not possess the technological competence to construct particular design solutions – that is a matter for a technical staff to work out (Rouncefield et al. 1994). The utility of our work lies in the elaboration of the design space and our articulation of the ways in which that might be achieved methodologically as design moves out of the workplace and into the home. Specifically, in this case, our studies provide first-hand knowledge of the accountable work-practices implicated in domestic calendar use; practices that are missed by formal analytic accounts. Our studies make real world uses of domestic calendars visible and inform design reasoning as to the real time arrangements of collaboration that provide for and constrain calendar use in domestic life. We would suggest that developing such an appreciation of domestic media more generally will open up new possibilities for design (Anderson 1994).

Conclusion

This paper contributes to the design of Groupware Calendar Systems (GCSs) for use in domestic life. Through ethnographic studies of domestic calendar use, family members of a corpus of accountable work-practices illuminating the design space and informing design reasoning have been unearthed. In particular, the corpus emphasizes the need for design to consider how the physical and the digital may be merged to support collaboration 'anywhere, anytime'; the necessity of devising negotiation protocols supporting computer-mediated communication; and the development of collaborative access models and interaction techniques to support data sharing. At a more general level, this paper contributes to the continued development of CSCW as design moves out of the workplace and into the home through the articulation of a distinct methodological approach to ethnographic study. That approach instructs us to attend to the 'interpretive work' involved in the use of artefacts to coordinate practical action – i.e., instructs us to attend to the ways in which members make sense of artefacts, make them meaningful, intelligible and accountable and so effect coordination through the use of artefacts in the home. This focus requires that we suspend the use of formal analytic and representational devices such as theories, models, and taxonomies of interaction and instead attend to the missing interactional what of such organizational studies. This, in turn, draws our attention to the family members of distinct corpus' of accountable work-practices – embodied work-practices which observably and reportably give life, purpose and utility to particular artefacts. Through these real world practices, artefacts come to find a place in the home and members collaborative activities. Their explication through careful description serves to sensitise design to important factors influencing the ways in which future technologies may be appropriated by members and so be made to fit into and resonate with the requirements of domestic life.

Acknowledgement

This research was funded by the Equator IRC (EPSRC GR/N15986/01), www.equator.ac.uk, and the EU Disappearing Computer Initiative ACCORD (IST-2000-26364), www.sics.se/accord

References

Anderson, R. J. (1994) "Representations and requirements: the value of ethnography in system design", *Human-Computer Interaction*, vol. 9, pp. 151-182.

Bellotti, V. and Smith, I. (2000) "Informing the design of an information management system with iterative fieldwork", *Proceedings of the 2000 Symposium on Designing Interactive Systems*, pp. 227-237, New York: ACM Press.

Button, G. and Harper, R. (1996) "The relevance of 'work-practice' for design", *Computer Supported Cooperative Work: The Journal of Collaborative Computing*, vol. 4 (4), pp. 263-280.

Crabtree, A., O'Brien, J., Nichols, D., Rouncefield, M., and Twidale, M. (2000) "Ethnomethodologically informed ethnography and information systems design", *Journal of the American Society for Information Science and Technology*, vol. 51 (7), pp. 666-682.

Crabtree, A., Hemmings, T. and Rodden, T. (2002a) "Pattern-based support for interactive design in domestic settings", *Proceedings of the 2002 Symposium on Designing Interactive Systems*, London: ACM Press.

Crabtree, A., Hemmings, T. and Rodden, T. (2002b) "Coordinate displays in the home", CSCW Workshop on Public, Community and Situated Displays, *Proceedings of the 2002 ACM Conference on Computer Supported Cooperative Work*, New Orleans: ACM Press.

Crabtree, A., Hemmings, T. and Rodden, T. (2003a) "Supporting communication within domestic settings", Proceedings of the 2003 Home Oriented Informatics and Telematics Conference, Newport, California: International Federation for Information Processing.

Crabtree, A., Hemmings, T. and Rodden, T. (2003b) "The social construction of displays: coordinate displays and ecologically distributed networks", to appear in *Public, Community and Situated Displays* (eds. O'Hara, K. et al.), Dordrecht: Kluwer Academic Publishers.

Crabtree, A. (2003) "The social organization of communication in domestic settings", to appear in *Proceedings of the 2003 Conference of the International Institute of Ethnomethodology and Conversation Analysis*, 2nd –4th July, Manchester: IIEMCA

Dourish, P., Bellotti, V., Mackay, W. and Ma, C-Y. (1993) "Information and context", *Proceedings of the 1993 ACM Conference on Organizational Computing Systems*, pp. 42-51, Milpitas, California: ACM Press.

Dourish. P (2001) "Seeking a foundation for context-aware computing", *Human-Computer Interaction*, vol. 16, pp. 2-3.

Dourish, P. (2002) *What We Talk About When We Talk About Context?* University of California, Irvine: Department of Information and Computer Science. www.ics.uci.edu/~jpd/

Ehrlich, S.F. (1987) "Social and psychological factors influencing the design of office communication systems", *Proceedings of the 1987 CHI Conference on Human Factors in Computing Systems and Graphical Interface*, pp. 323-329, Toronto: ACM Press.

Garfinkel, H. (1967) Studies in Ethnomethodology, Englewood Cliffs, New Jersey: Prentice-Hall.

Garfinkel, H. (1986) "Introduction", *Ethnomethodological Studies of Work*, vii-viii, London: Routledge and Kegan Paul.

Garfinkel, H. (2002) *Ethnomethodology's Program*, Lanham: Rowman & Littlefield.

Greif, I. and Sarin, S. (1987) "Data sharing in group work", *ACM Transactions on Information Systems*, vol. 5 (2), pp. 187-211.

Kelley, J.F. and Chapanis, A. (1982) "How professional persons keep their calendars: implications for computerization", *Journal of Occupational Psychology*, vol. 55, pp. 241-256.

Kincaid, C.M. and Dupont, P.B. (1985) "Electronic calendars in the office", *ACM Transactions on Information Systems*, vol. 3 (1), pp. 89-102.

Lauer, R.H. (1981) *Temporal Man: The Meaning and Uses of Social Time*, New York: Praegger Publishers.

Mateas, M., Salvador, T., Scholtz, J. and Sorensen, D. (1996) "Engineering ethnography in the home", *Proceedings of the 1996 CHI Conference on Human Factors in Computing Systems*, pp. 283-284, Vancouver: ACM Press.

O'Brien, J. and Rodden, T. (1997) "Interactive systems in domestic environments", *Proceedings of the 1997 Symposium on Designing Interactive Systems*, pp. 247-259, Amsterdam: ACM Press.

O'Brien, J., Rodden, T., Rouncefield, M. and Hughes, J.A., (1999) "At home with the technology", *ACM Transactions on Computer-Human Interaction*, vol. 6 (3), pp. 282-308.

Palen, L. (1998) *Calendars on the New Frontier*, Ph.D. Dissertation, University of California, Irvine. www.cs.colorado.edu/%7Epalen/dissertation/

Palen, L. (1999) "Social, individual and technological issues for groupware calendar systems", *Proceedings of the 1999 CHI Conference on Human Factors in Computing Systems*, pp. 17-24, Pittsburgh, Pennsylvania: ACM Press.

Palen, L. and Grudin, J. (2002) *Discretionary Adoption of Group Support Software*, www.research.microsoft.com /research/coet/Grudin/DiscChoice/paper.doc

Rouncefield, M. et al. (1994) "Working with 'constant interruption'", *Proceedings of the 1994 ACM Conference on Computer Supported Cooperative Work*, pp. 275-286, Chapel Hill, North Carolina: ACM Press.

Ryle, G. (1971) "The thinking of thoughts", *University Lectures No. 18*, Canada: University of Saskatchewan.

Shapiro, D. (1994) "The limits of ethnography", *Proceedings of the 1994 ACM Conference on Computer Supported Cooperative Work*, pp. 417- 428, Chapel Hill, North Carolina: ACM Press.

Sharrock, W.W. and Button, G. (1991) "The social actor: social action in real time", *Ethnomethodology and the Human Sciences* (ed. Button, G.), pp. 137-175, Cambridge: Cambridge University Press.

Tullio, J., Goecks, J., Mynatt, E.D. and Nguyen, D.H. (2002) "Augmenting shared personal calendars", *Proceedings of the 15th Annual Symposium on User Interface Software and Technology*, pp. 11-20, Paris, France: ACM Press.

Venkatesh, A. (1985) "A conceptualization of the household/technology interaction", *Advances in Consumer Research*, vol. 12, pp. 189-194.

Venkatesh, A. (1996) "Computers and other interactive technologies for the home", *Communications of the ACM*, vol. 39 (12), pp. 47-54.

Venkatesh, A., Stolzoff, N., Shih, E. and Mazumdar, S. (2001) "The home of the future: an ethnographic study of new information technologies in the home", *Advances in Consumer Research*, vol. 28, pp. 88-96.

Zerubavel, E. (1981) *Hidden Rhythms: Schedules and Calendars in Social Life*, Chicago: University of Chicago Press.

K. Kuutti, E.H. Karsten, G. Fitzpatrick, P. Dourish and K. Schmidt (eds.), *ECSCW 2003: Proceedings of the Eighth European Conference on Computer Supported Cooperative Work, 14-18 September 2003, Helsinki, Finland*, pp. 139-158.

Supporting Collaboration Ubiquitously: An augmented learning environment for architecture students

Giulio Iacucci and Ina Wagner

Department of Information Processing Science, University of Oulu, Finland; Institute for Technology Assessment & Design, Vienna University of Technology, Austria

Abstract. While CSCW research has mostly been focusing on desktop applications there is a growing interest on ubiquitous and tangible computing. We present ethnographic fieldwork and prototypes to address how tangible computing can support collaboration and learning. The student projects at the Academy of Fine Arts in Vienna is a relevant case to study, for the variety and distributed character of the cooperative arrangements, and for the richness of interactions with heterogeneous physical artefacts. After describing current practices, we propose qualities of the environment that support collaboration and learning: creative density, multiple travels in materials and representations, re-programming (seeing things differently), and configurability. We then describe several prototypes that address in various ways these qualities. Finally we discuss how tangible and ubiquitous computing supports collaboration in our case by providing *intermediary spaces*, and *dynamic objectifications*.

Introduction

This paper uses fieldwork in a specific learning environment – an architectural master class at the Academy of Fine Arts in Vienna[1] – for exploring the relevance

---

1   The fieldwork was carried out as part of the IST Project ATELIER (http://atelier.k3.mah.se/).

of a ubiquitous computing environment for collaborative work. We use ubiquitous computing[2] as an umbrella term for describing an environment, which reaches beyond the desktop, integrating the physical environment of space, objects, and people. As collaboration takes many different forms inside and outside the Academy, and students, teachers, and design representations are in continuous movement, we are interested in an environment that allows creating layers of and connections between spaces, objects, events, and people with ease. As part of this we focus on prototyped technologies as well as spatial arrangements that are simple and easy to use.

While most of the work in CSCW focuses on desktop applications, attention has been given recently to some aspects of such an environment, namely: the importance of physical objects and embodied interactions (e.g. Luff and Heath 1998, Heath et al 2002); the possibilities of connecting physical objects with digital objects and media (e.g. tangible bits; Brave, Ishii, Dahley 1998); boundaries between realities (e.g. the physical world and 3D environments) and how to manage them (Koleva, Benford, and Greenhalgh 1999); mobility (Orr 1996, Bellotti/Bly 1996, Luff/Heath 1998) and mobile devices (e.g. Berqvist et al. 1999). Dourish (2001) refers to tangible computing, which "expands the ubiquitous computing vision by concentrating on the physical environment as the primary site of interaction with computation". He proposes a new framework for HCI introducing embodied interaction, which he defines as "the creation, manipulation, and sharing of meaning through engaged interaction with artefacts" (p. 126). Embodied interaction as a paradigm for HCI and CSCW requires to free computing from the desktop and to take account of the social embedding of people's interactions with artefacts in systems of meaning.

We position our contribution in this debate on how to better integrate the computational into the physical world, focusing on people's embodied interactions with it, and contextualize it in a particular case. The architectural master class is particularly relevant for ubiquitous and tangible computing, as it is rich of interactions with heterogeneous artifacts in different media, with the physical space as an important resource. The variety and distributedness of cooperative arrangements makes it an interesting place for studying cooperation.

Important for understanding the learning practices at the Academy was previous ethnographic work studying architects' work practices (e.g. Büscher et al. 1999, Lainer/Wagner 1998, Schmidt/Wagner 2002). This helped us see students' work as an enculturation in professional design practices. It drew our attention to issues such as the conceptual nature of design, the role of design representations in a process, which is non-linear, informal, and highly cooperative, and the need to transform and re-program. Working with architects

---

2   Ubiquitous or more recently pervasive computing is connected to the vision of "a physical world richly and invisibly interwoven with sensors, actuators, displays, and computational elements, embedded seamlessly in the everyday objects of our lives and connected through a continuous network." (Weiser, Gold, Brown 1999).

also helped understand the relevance of the physical space for collaborative work – the students use the space for exhibiting their work and maintaining it visible but also for physically exploring qualities such as scale, dimensionality, and ambience.

After an initial phase of intense field work, we started exploring the idea of a ubiquitous computing environment in a hands-on way, using simple technical solutions and early prototypes with an emphasis on concept-creation and exploration, asking ourselves what such an environment could possibly be and offer. We also approached this question through describing the environment in terms of particular atmospheric, material and spatial *qualities* that should be created. For this we analysed examples of inspirational environments from architecture and the arts. Finally, we produced a series of scenarios of use and set up a space with materials and technologies for students' ongoing work. In all phases we drew upon the creative potential of the students and their teachers.

In this paper, we will report on these quite intense experiences in several steps: We will illustrate learning practices at the Academy, using some examples from the field work; we will propose current and desirable *qualities* of the environment in our specific case to support learning and collaboration; we will briefly describe some prototypes we developed that in different ways integrate computing and interactivity in the environment. Finally we will discuss how our case is relevant for CSCW research, by showing how including the physical environment of artefacts and spaces in design thinking gives rise to new forms of support for learning and collaboration.

Observations of learning as cooperative work

Learning at the Academy takes place in the 'master class' - a universal, complexly linked didactic concept. The master class is the place where students carry out their manifold activities, most of them project based. Here they learn how to mobilize a diversity of resources – art work, concepts, metaphors, analogies, fieldwork experiences, project examples, samples of materials, technologies, etc. – for generating project ideas. Here they get to know the techniques and standards of their field that help them translate their ideas into architectural designs. They do this through engaging in different forms of individual and cooperative activities. Teachers at the Academy do not lecture (or not primarily so). They define the requirements, they introduce topics, roles and observational techniques that direct and facilitate students' learning. They give continuous feedback, commenting on students' work and suggesting different ways of viewing, and they through their interventions communicate and represent the historically grown and culturally mediated practices of the field.

Paraphrasing Kjeld Schmidt's statement 'taking serious work seriously' (Schmidt 2002) we might want to ask if this kind of learning is cooperative work.

It is, in several ways. Students' work is distributed, in time and space, conceptually, and in terms of control. There is a common field of work, which evolves in the design process and is pre-defined by the semester programme and student projects. Architectural work is different from many other types of work insofar as the field of work does not exist in advance but is constructed in and through the process of design which "proceeds through the architects' producing successive objectivations of the design and interacting with them in a variety of ways" (Schmidt/Wagner 2002). Much of the students' interactions with each other and their teachers is mediated through the diversity of design representations they produce. Another peculiarity of architectural work is the relevance of physical artefacts for the development of a design and the extensive use of space as a resource.

The following paragraphs describe the practice of learning at the Academy, using episodes from a variety of student projects. The first round of fieldwork at the Academy was carried out in the first half of 2002. The methods used were observation and informal interviews. We observed and interviewed students working on seven different projects. In some projects we tried to observe aspects of the whole life cycle. For other projects we constructed snapshots of the current work. Interesting episodes were recorded with a digital video camera or a digital still camera. The second round of fieldwork took place from November 2002 to January 2003 when we introduced our first prototypes of space and technologies into students' work.

The diversity of design representations

Students' project work proceeds through developing a large number of design representations. These are characterized by the expressive use of a diversity of materials and are sometimes animated and presented dynamically.

Figure 1: A diversity of design representations

As an example two students worked on a façade for ‚Möbel L' (a furniture house who sponsored a student project for their main inner city building). The students envisioned the façade of the building as a threshold between inside and outside. On their table are sketches of the form of the façade, detailed plans, drawings visualizing atmospheres and situations of use, 3D models, diagrams - a collage of visual and tactile material (Figure 1). One reason for this diversity of representations is that changing media and scale adds to the quality of the design process, with different techniques allowing to explore different aspects of the design idea. These heterogeneous representations are often manipulated simultaneously and they evolve in different versions. While working the students continuously switch between representations, as for example in Figure 2 where they work on a 3D model of the concept (left), on drawing and sketches (middle) or with the 3D model and diagrams in parallel (right).

Figure 2: Switching between design representations

The students' common field of work is constituted through this diversity of design artefacts and their relationships. These relationships are not fixed, they evolve over time, such as for example the notion of a façade 'to lean and sit on' (Figure 1d), which became stable – incorporated into their final drawings - only towards the end of the project. A crucial aspect of the design process is to maintain evidence of all the material that has been produced. It is essential to be able to read and re-read the material from different points of view and to be able to go back to a moment when a particular issue emerged.

Figure 3: Layers grouped together support different perceptions of a complex design problem

Architectural students' field of work is highly complex and they constantly invent and probe techniques for representing this complexity. One example is this representation of an urban planning project with layers for each type of elements (roads, rivers and lakes, railroads, settlements, industrial buildings, etc.) (Figure

3). The layers are made of transparent slides and collages of materials. There are two stacks of layers, one corresponds to the current situation, the second one visualizes the proposed interventions, e.g. populate an area, or extend roads. The model is animated and presented dynamically allowing to explore the relationships between elements as well as between current and future states through grouping and ordering the layers.

The distributed character of learning

As Lave and Wenger (1999) phrased it, learning takes place in a participation framework. It is a process by which newcomers become part of a profession. A good learning curriculum consists of situated opportunities for the improvisational development of new practice in a diversity of role configurations.

Students' learning happens in different places and in different cooperative arrangements. It is typically distributed in space and time. Activities take place in an environment, which is rich of interactions between students and with the teaching staff and external professionals. Students work individually or in small teams. Sharing a room with other project teams facilitates a 'ping-pong' of ideas, the exchange of knowledge and experiences across teams. They work at different times of the day, sometimes staying over night.

Figure 4: a) Digital pictures and recorded audio around a diagram, b&c) Multiple traveling - the picture of an event and its re-viewing in the context of a presentation

An interesting aspect of this distributedness is students' need to feel connected with the outside space of city, project site or people. Built into their work are excursions to the outside world, e.g. the site of a project, where they collect video and audio material, pictures, sketches, and objects, such as in the case of this project, which deals with redesigning an inner courtyard. In the first phase of the project the student interviewed people living in the area. She represented each person with a list of keywords and symbols around a map. Each list had a pin and a thread connected to another pin in the map showing where the person lives. When presenting the model she used electronic devices to augment her diagram, a digital camera and an audio recorder (Figure 4 a). Her diagrammatic representation of the project was connected to a whole range of material collected at the site.

Students and their teachers use the notion of 'multiple travelling' to capture this distributedness. The first journey when a project starts is to the place of an intervention itself with the aim to experience the authenticity of the place. A student who has travelled to Ghana as part of her project mentioned that, although she took pictures, made notes, carried out interviews, and produced videos, it was hard to capture the richness of the experience while being there: "It is your body that subconsciously absorbs the place. Back home you perform your second journey through the collected material, remembering with your body even subtle things like the smell of a place". This journey through the material has to be repeated again and again, with different layers and aspects coming to the surface (Figure 4 b,c).

Apart from this distribution in time and space, learning is distributed conceptually as well as in terms of control. Although supportive of students' ideas, teachers at the Academy constantly challenge their concepts. Creative work, they argue, requires to transform and re-program - to explore solutions and contexts, to shift perspectives, to carry out experiments, to present and perform, to have time and space for free play and day-dreaming, and to generate a 'different view'.

Figure 5: Examples of how students learn to see a place in a different way

An example is a feedback session with a student who proposed an underground parking space in her project of re-vitalizing an area with immigrant workers. Her teachers challenged her approach, asking her to transcend the traditional categories trying to combine them in new ways. To, for example, work with contradictions – 'the mosque, outside lively, inside an oasis of tranquillity'; to let market and street reach into the park; to use empty shops for parking; to connect living with the car, its sound machine being used in the living space. Other examples can be seen in Figure 5 where an ugly industrial skyline has been photomontaged into a ship and a table in a deserted courtyard turned into an elegant dinner arrangement. It also shows representations of a student idea for a temporary installation in a courtyard, which sets traces for future possible projects. Their project is an intervention rather than a finished plan for something to be built, challenging the notion of the 'completeness' of architectural solutions.

This juxtaposition of perspectives and questioning of concepts is supported in different ways. Students use their multiple travelling experiences, they are encouraged to collect and mobilize inspirational objects, to experiment with atmosphere and context. For example, one student, while working on a project about the beach, "started seeing beaches everywhere, also where the sunlight was reflected on the road. These constant changes of context helped her think differently about beaches".

Uses of space as a resource

Students working on a specific semester program are co-located in one of the Academy's large, high-ceiling spaces. Students' workspaces are spread through the room, with project-related material filling the tables, the moveable boards and the walls. Even in the absence of students there are physical traces of their work to be read in an open exhibition.

Artefacts such as large scale models are sometimes shared. They offer a platform for group discussions. This was the case in the project 'Learning from Tibet' where a series of interventions into an alpine environment was held together by a large plaster model which served as a point of reference for discussions, with students placing material such as threads or tape to mark forms of paths, and rivers on it. Each time we visited the project space we found new traces of students' discussions (Figure 6 a).

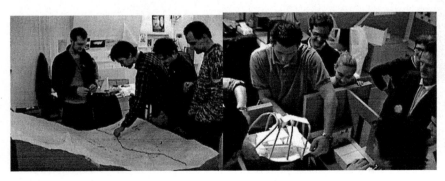

Figure 6: a shared model b) Placing elements in the shared model to demonstrate their relationship to the environment.

Students' work environment is in constant reconfiguration. Activities range from working alone or in groups, with different representations and materials, to having coffee, listening to music, partying and occasionally sleeping over night. One occasion for rearranging the space are project presentations or feedback sessions, which are often held in students' workspace. We observed a presentation of the work of first semester students whose project was to re-design their own working environment (Figure 6 b). A large shared model of the project space had been placed in the middle of the room. During the presentation students positioned their own models inside this space, demonstrating and arguing the relationship of their designs to the shared workspace. Some students used mobile furniture for their models, e.g. moving the model from a position where it was visible to the audience and could be pointed at to a position where it could be directly touched and modified (models are often composed by movable parts).

Student's flexibly adjust their workspace to the changing needs involved in developing a project, producing and exhibiting design presentations. Introducing a PC into the workspace reduces this flexibility, as the PC takes up much space and attention and is difficult to move with all its cables. This is one of the reasons why individual workspaces are not equipped with computers except when students bring their own laptop.

The PC also diminishes the presence of important aspects of work, hiding the work of some students to others. Figure 7a shows two students browsing pictures of a trip on a PC. Due to the particular position of the PC and the fact that the object of work (the pictures) is only accessible on the computer screen, this activity remains separated from what others in the room are doing. Moreover, when the computer is switched off, no traces of students' work are left. In contrast, browsing through printed photographs or slides on the table (Figure 7b and c) creates the kind of visibility that allows others to participate, directly or by being peripherally aware.

Figure 7: a) Browsing pictures on a PC, b) browsing printed photographs, c) browsing slides

One student group spread their pictures from the trip on the table, sorting them in rows. Other students came by, asking questions and together they started remembering, evoking encounters, telling each other stories (Figure 8a). All of a sudden, what had been constrained to the desktop, was available to all. He then played sound from a football stadium in Mexico. These interventions completely

148

changed the atmosphere in the project space, evoking some of the common aspects of students' work.

Figure 8: Making work visible a) on the table, b) and c) by projecting work on the PC onto the walls

Towards a ubiquitous computing environment: qualities and supporting technologies

Our aim is to develop an environment that reaches beyond the desktop computer, integrating the physical environment of space and objects. It is obvious that there is no single technical solution for complex learning processes such as the ones we briefly described. It even does not make sense to think primarily in terms of technical solutions but to look at the learning environment as a whole – the changing places and their characteristics, the multiple cooperative arrangements, the diversity and materiality of design representations, the need for experimentation and for seeing things differently.

Based on the analysis of the observations and of interviews with a small number of practicing architects we specified a set of qualities of the environment:

- creative density - the multi-mediality and diversity of design representations and their sharing
- the connecting of design-relevant materials – chronologically, conceptually, narratively, randomly, etc. – multiple travels that help create and explore different perspectives
- re-programming – to play with context, atmosphere, dimension
- configuring – the adaptability of a space to a diversity of uses and identities.

These qualities capture the crucial aspects of students' learning environment. They specify the ways, in which students explore, develop, share, criticise, and concretise their ideas. For the project team of designers, ethnographers, and architects the description of these qualities – through metaphors, text, images, video clips – served as key design representations, inspiring the design of the prototypes of space and technologies as well as helping to define and evaluate them.

Qualities

Multi-mediality and creative density: The multi-mediality of design representations plays a crucial role in envisioning particular aspects of a design. A conceptual model in its abstractness and lightness asks the architect a different question than a plan, a diagram or a model in a different scale. In many cases the nature of the materials chosen for a model play an important role, with their physical features carrying meaning and enabling students to represent more abstract kinds of information, such as fragility, denseness, atmosphere (Ormerod/Ivanic 2002). Fieldwork observations showed how engaging in an immersive mass of material – design representations in different media, inspirational objects, etc. - supports intensity in design situations. One aspect of this creative density is the chance to encounter surprising or interesting combinations of objects. Another aspect of creative density are spatial limitations or constraints that may provide stimulating perspectives, with things and spaces overlayering each other.

Connecting – multiple travels: Work at the Academy is distributed in time (covering several weeks or months), place (students move within and between the Academy and places outside), and conceptually (their concepts develop, teachers bring in their views). Students go back and forth between media and representations, 'circulating references' (Latour 1999) throughout the design process. One important aspect of connecting is the necessity to maintain the design material physically present so that it can merge with the ongoing design work, visible also to passers-by who are invited to comment. Often the sheer amount of material makes this impracticable. Here the notion of multiple travels is helpful as the possibility to create different perspectives and views of design-relevant materials. Drawing maps of one's own work is a way of connecting. Putting it on top of someone else's map, may help perceive one's own patterns differently. The connections the traveller forges may be of varying nature and quality: chronological, narrative, based on some random selection, driven by the desire to contrast and confront.

Re-programming: Part of the architectural students' training consists in learning to see things differently. This implies changing familiar images - mutating the city, the landscape, and objects of everyday life. An example is the students' projects for a Fitness Centre in a high rising building – e.g. inviting mountain bikers in, varying the temperature in the building so that different training conditions are provided. Students may vary the context of an object through simple projections, e.g. place a railway station in the midst of a jungle or igloos in the desert (without having to do complex renderings). They may play with dimensionality, scaling up and scaling down, changing familiar objects and thereby arriving at unexpected uses.

Configurability - adaptability to a diversity of uses and identities: Setting up one's own project space becomes one of the first opportunities for reflection.

Being able to configure and personalize it is part of opening up the design space. This includes playing with different contexts and media. The variety of cooperative arrangements together with the intensity of work make it desirable to be able to use the space for multiple purposes, solitary work as well as group discussions and presentation. An important experience is that a perfectly furnished space is often not the best solution to creative work. The students need to appropriate the space, struggle with its constraints, finding their own interpretation and set-up. Adaptability of a space means the possibility to reconfigure a space so that you can personalize, exhibit, build models, collect, have a nap, make coffee, interact with material and odd objects, etc.

Experimenting with space and technologies

We are currently pursuing a variety of technical and spatial solutions with the idea that these should be considered 'components' of a future ubiquitous computing environment that the students should be able to combine and tailor. First opportunities to introduce these components to students and teachers presented themselves from November 2002 to January 2003 in the context of a workshop and a series of individual projects.

The configurable space: An architectural space is not static, it constantly changes with people's activities. This is why the architects focused on the spaces at hand in the Academy, their re-programming for changing activities and needs (rather than creating new typologies). The space that was selected for the project within the Academy offers some possibilities for creating these conditions. It is located in one of the four towers of the Academy building that was constructed by Theophil Hansen. It is "far from perfect and cannot do everything". For example, it has no windows, with the light coming in from openings in the roof, and it has no natural ventilation. However, the lack of perfection, the spatial constraints are important, since they stimulate the creative appropriation of the space for different activities.

Four types of interventions in the space have been designed: a ,*grid*', an ,*interactive wall*' for storing models, materials, (technological) components, typological furniture, etc. (currently available as a mock-up), and, for the future, adjustable platforms (allowing to position objects at different heights or people to assume positions from unusual perspectives), as well as an elaborate lighting system. Multiple projections play a large role in the architects' vision of configurability. Here, for example, one of the teachers enjoys the atmosphere of the garden into which he will design a building (Figure 9a). The grid supports the visualizing, scaling, colouring, etc. of spaces, objects, and people. It is a simple infrastructure, which has been mounted on the ceiling. A sliding-door system provides the space with frames for multiple projections and for layering walls. The frames serve for hanging textiles and other materials, objects, plants, etc.

Figure 9: a) life size projections b) multiple traveling

We observed how a student group configured the workspace for a multi-media presentation, fixing a data projector for floor projections high up on the ceiling and hanging up double layers of translucent cloth. In their presentation the students created a very effective immersive environment, which worked really well with contrasting images of different qualities – sharp and blurred, narrative and symbolic (Figure 10a and b).

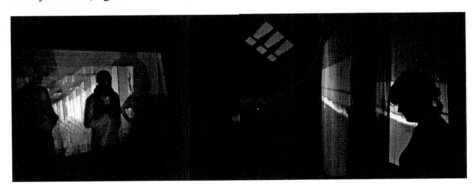

Figure 10: a) and b) Creating an immersive environment with multiple projections,

Another student group presented a movie of their trip, integrating the space into their performance. Seats were arranged like in the underground and passengers that had to stand were provided with a handle made from orange plastic. In this configuration they watched the movie which alternated sequences of traveling the underground (which accelerated, growing noisier and more hectic) with the presentation of stills at a calm and slow pace (Figure 10)[3].

Texture painter: Using a brush, which is tracked with a video camera, this is a tool for 'painting' objects such as models or parts of the physical space, applying

---

[3]: Another component, the *atmosphere configuring tool* enables students to configure the physical space - lighting and sound system, air conditioner, fans, projectors, etc. – helping them create and reproduce different atmospheres.

textures, images or video, scaling and rotating them. Students started animating their models with the help of the *texture painter*. One student studied soccer games to identify the most exciting camera views and to understand which kind of atmosphere the players need. He used the camera views to find out where to place few spectators so that the stadium looks jammed. He built a simple model of a stadium and used model and images together with the *texture painter* for projecting different atmospheres into this 'fragmented stadium' (Figure 11a and b). Another student painted images of his interventions onto projected images of two residential buildings, projecting detailed plans onto the space between them.

Figure 11: Painting a) spectators , b) a background onto models of a stadium, c) interventions into a space between two buildings.

The tool allows creating a kind of intermediary space between the physical and the digital, to connect the physical object (a model) with a digital representation (e.g. the rendered model, a video, an image). This gives the rendering a haptic, sensual quality.

Animating barcode: Reminiscent of Webstickers (Ljungstrand et al. 2000) the *animating bAR code* has a barcode reader attached to a PC on which a Java program is running that associates pictures, sounds and video clips to barcodes. The pictures are displayed with a projector so that users do not have to be near the PC screen. Students use the *animating barcode* as a tool for connecting and story-telling. For instance, one student in preparation of a feedback session attached barcodes to parts of his model, with the idea to make his model self explanatory, inviting the audience to discover the model. Another student used barcodes as a tool for turning her diary, which she had filled with notes, sketches, small images and objects collected during a trip, into "a book that speaks". Touching a sensor at the back of the book initiated the reader's journey with the possibility to turn the pages, activate the barcodes and triggered a series of projected images (Figure 12a).

Also two of the teachers used the barcodes for creating associations between pictures and a model of a building which they are planning, the site being a large garden with fruit trees and an old house. With the barcode reader they animated the model with sound and with projections of images of interiors of the old house, and of different perspectives onto the surrounding garden (Figure 12b).

Figure 12: a) Barcodes on the pages of a diary of a visit; b) on parts of a model

Touch sensors and sensitive samples: We are experimenting with various types of sensors to augment physical objects. For example, sensors have been installed inside a wooden box that recognize actions such as shaking, knocking, and stroking, with different actions activating different types of material – sound, images, video, and wind (Figure 13a). The "book that speaks" is equipped with a sensor that, when the book is picked up, activates instructions how to read the diary using the barcode scanner (Figure 13b).

Figure 13: a) Box with sensors inside, b) sensors on a diary c) Sensors connect a moving object (ball) with images and sound

One of the students prepared an elaborate presentation of her design ideas for an 'extreme stadium' in the area between Vienna's two large museums. She had prepared a soccer field and two slide shows, with one screen displaying cultural aspects of soccer (images, sound, video) and the second screen displaying her design ideas 'in the making'. The slide show was operated through a sensor that had been fixed underneath the soccer field. The presentation itself was designed as a soccer-game, with the building sites being the teams - stadium versus museums, explaining the design ideas being the team-tactics, and herself as the referee, with a yellow card and a whistle signaling a 'bad idea' and shooting a goal a 'good idea'. When the ball touched the goal a sensor triggered off a reporter's voice shouting 'goal, goal' and the cheering of the visitors (Figure 13c).

The Jacket: The *Jacket* is a machine that supports people during visits to create a personal perspective of places of interest. The *Jacket* helps collecting video, audio and information from sensors like the location, the direction from an electronic compass. This data is combined with information of time and visitor's actions. Particular actions of the visitor are also recorded like taking a picture or recording a sound. The multimedia path, which is created during the visit, can be then visualized and edited in the Atelier environment. The *Jacket* consists of two main components: the *Jacket* as a recorder that is worn to visit a place (iPaq, GPS receiver, digital camera, and sound recorder), and a 3D visualization tool for navigating, manipulating, and editing the collected information back in the studio (Figure 14 a and b).

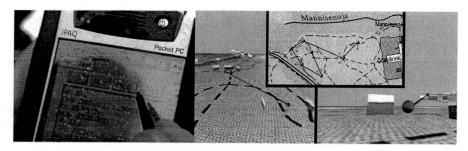

Figure 14: The prototype of the *Jacket* a) pocket PC with GPS to record a path, b) a 3D visualization application to navigate and manipulate the path on maps or plans.

Discussion

We explored two aspects of ubiquitous computing – (i) mixing physical objects and digital media and (ii) widening the possibilities of using space as a resource. Our interventions helped amplify aspects of architects' practices in several ways: Spatial design and technologies supported students' re-arranging and re-configuring of their workspace for different purposes; they helped preserve and enrich the landscape of design representations and enlarged the spectrum of media, integrating sound, video and digital pictures into students' predominantly physical work environment; finally, the possibilities of connecting and multiple traveling strengthened and enriched students' collaboration with each others and with their teachers.

Previous observations of practices and their settings within CSCW were used mostly, with some exceptions, to design features of desktop applications. Ubiquitous computing gives the opportunity to include the physical environment in the design thinking. This probably means that we will continue to observe practices in the same way but we will draw different design implications because we expect technology to support collaboration in a different way. Why and how can ubiquitous computing better support collaborative work? This question is new for CSCW research and will be debated in the next years as ubiquitous computing and its use will become observable.

Intermediary spaces

The *Animating bARcode* and the *texture painter* are examples of technologies where the physical object is part of the interface when interacting with digital media. For example, the *animating bARcode* makes it possible to access project files while maintaining the physical model present. The *texture painter* allows to animate the physical object itself. People's interactions with physical objects (and the associated) material are related to the physical space and available to others. These integrations of physical elements of the work environment with digital presentations preserves the reversibility of perception, a term Merleau-Ponty introduced for describing "the complex intertwining between the perceiver, the perceived and the physical environment that is the essential condition for our interaction with the world and with others" (Robertson 2002). These forms of embodied interactions support understandings of technological artifacts and social actions emerging in concert with other people (a phenomenon referred to as intersubjectivity; Dourish 2001). According to Dourish embodiment "offers opportunities for a much more direct apprehension of the modulating, mediating effect that computation plays in interaction", with the active nature of computers being important not as independent agents but "as augmentations and amplifications of our own activities."(p. 166)

Here the role of life size projections, intensified by multiple screens and data projectors (the 'grid') needs to be emphasized. Students re-experience their ride with the metro while watching the video of their trip and their teacher *is* sitting in the garden while looking at the model of his design and thinking about it.

Another interesting aspect of these intermediary spaces, that the mixing of physical and digital creates, is the transient and ephemeral way in which artifacts, people, and ambiences are encountered. This resonates with what architects see as an important aspect of their work – the peripheral presence of events or objects, with short-time events, fast, assembled, ad-hoc, such as film, video and fashion photography being important inspirational resources. (Wagner 2002).

Dynamic Objectifications

Students produce objectifications of their design ideas. These objectifications constitute the common field of work and they are the stuff that mediates their interactions with other students and teachers. The prototypes we presented support the objectification and concretising of the design in dynamic and interactive ways. The *texture painter* provides a fast and highly interactive way of experimenting with scale, colour, background, and social use of physical objects (introducing animated scenes of e.g. spectators into a stadium) – in the language of the architects their *re-programming*. The *animating bAR code* and touch sensors/sensitive samples allow connecting physical artifacts, such as a model or sample of material, with a diversity of multi-media objects. Moreover the *Jacket*, in combination with the 3D visualization tool, helps students to connect the studio with places, people, and artifacts outside. More importantly it supports them in creating digital representations through a performance in the physical environment. These connections can be configured and evoked in multiple ways, creating different stories or walking paths.

Conclusions

What did tangible computing support?

Interaction between students and with the staff, hence collaboration in learning, was observed in presentations and review meetings but also as an intricate part of students' everyday work. While in the context of our first experiments the prototypes were mainly used for presenting material in an interactive way, we can see more complex modes of support for collaboration.

Firstly, the prototypes (*animating bARcode, sensitive samples, texture painter*) help preserve and even extend the *multi-mediality* and *diversity of materials* and representations. More importantly, they help create and share different views onto the common field of work. We described as an important quality *creative density* - having the 'sea of design material' physically present so that it can merge with the ongoing design work, and be made available to others (students, teachers). This is an important aspect of learning at the Academy, as is making the trajectory of students' projects visible in the project space so that everyone gets a quick overview.

Secondly, the prototypes - not only sensors, barcodes, and projections but also the *Jacket* as a tool for sharing and *re-experiencing* visits – increase the possibilities of *connecting* work that is distributed in time and space, but also conceptually. From current observations we can already discern more experimental and also interactive ways of '*re-programming*' a design, material or place, playing with context, atmosphere and dimension. This is partly to do with the hands-on way, in which all kinds of material can be integrated into the flow of work and connected, partly it is to do with the embodied and 'performative' nature of how physical artefacts and digital objects are made to play together, integrating the physical space. This creates a high level of intensity and involvement.

Reviewing our method

To design and integrate computation in a physical environment we have carried out observations of current work, inferred current and desirable qualities of an environment in support of learning and collaboration, implemented a variety of simple prototypes, and experimented with them. Our analysis of students' first experiments with the prototypes maintains a view on the learning environment as a whole. This means that rather than focusing on a particular requirement and (prototypal) technology, we took account of the multiple facets of students' learning, trying to understand how and what the prototypes add to them. This experimental and explorative approach to enriching a learning environment with a variety of technologies provides us with some grounding for discussing useful features of tangible computing. The 'qualities' we defined and sought to amplify, although specific to our case (and to design work[4]), contribute to explaining the diverse roles artefacts, materials, and spatial arrangements may play in collaborative environments. We are aware that we have still a long way to go in order to create a ubiquitous/tangible computing environment in support of learning, which is sufficiently complex to add dimensionality to students' work and easy to use.

Acknowledgements

We are grateful to our co-researchers at the Creative Environments, Arts & Communication, Malmö University; the Space & Virtuality Studio, Interactive Institute; the Consorzio Milano Ricerche, DISCo University of Milano-Biccocca; the University of Oulu. We wish to acknowledge in particular the contributions of the Vienna Group – Michael Gervautz, Heimo Kramer (Imagination Computer Services), Rüdiger Lainer, Kresimir Matcovic, Thomas Psik, Andreas Rumpfhuber, and Dieter Spath, not to forget the students at the Academy. Finally we would like to acknowledge Infotech Oulu for supporting this research at the University of Oulu.

References

Bellotti, V., Bly, S. (1996): 'Walking Away from the Desktop Computer: Distributed Collaboration and Mobility in a Product Design Team', in: *Proceeding of the Sixth Conference on Computer Supported Cooperative Work*, ACM Press, MA Cambridge, 1996, pp. 209-218.

Bergquist, J., Dahlberg, P., Ljungberg, F., Kristoffersen S. (1999): 'Moving out of the Meeting Room: Exploring Support for Mobile Meetings', in S. Bodker, M. Kyng, K. Schmidt, K. (eds): *Proceedings of the Sixth European Conference on Computer Supported Cooperative Work ECSCW'99*, Kluwer, Dordrecht etc., 1999, pp. 81-98.

Brave, S., Ishii, H. and Dahley, A. (1998): 'Tangible Interfaces for Remote Collaboration and Communication', in: *Proceeding of the Eighth Conference on Computer Supported Cooperative Work*, ACM Press, MA Cambridge, 1998, ACM Press, pp. 169-178.

---

[4] Our project partners in Malmö are using the 'qualities' for conducting and evaluating similar experiments within students of interaction design.

Büscher, M., P. Mogensen, et al. (1999): 'The Manufaktur. Supporting Work Practice in (Landscape) Architecture', in S. Bodker, M. Kyng, K. Schmidt, K. (eds): *Proceedings of the Sixth European Conference on Computer Supported Cooperative Work ECSCW'99*, Kluwer, Dordrecht etc., 1999, pp. 21-40.

Dourish, P. (2001): *Where the Action Is: the Foundations of Embodied Interaction*, MIT Press, Cambridge MA.

Heath, C., Luff, P. Kuzuoka, H., Yamazaki K., Oyama, S., (2001): 'Creating Coherent Environments for Collaboration, in Prinz, W., Jarke, M., Rogers, Y., Schmidt, K., Wulf, V., (eds): *Proceedings of the Seventh European Conference on Computer Supported Cooperative Work ECSCW'01*, Kluwer, Dordrecht etc., 2001, pp. 119-138.

Heath, C., P. Luff, et al. (2002). 'Crafting Participation: Designing Ecologies, Configuring Experience', *Visual Communication*, vol. 1, no. 1, 2002, pp. 9-33.

Koleva, B. Benford, S. Greenhalgh, C. (1999): 'The Properties of Mixed Reality Boundaries', in S. Bodker, M. Kyng, K. Schmidt, K. (eds.): *Proc. of the Sixth European Conf. on Computer-Supported Cooperative Work ECSCW'99*, Kluwer, Dordrecht etc., 1999, pp. 119- 137.

Lainer, R. and Wagner I. (1998): ‚Offenes Planen. Erweiterung der Lösungsräume für architektonisches Entwerfen', *Architektur & BauForum*, vol. 196, September/October 1998, pp. 327-336.

Latour, Bruno (1999): *Pandora's Hope — Essays on the Reality of Science Studies*. Harvard University Press. Cambridge MA.

Lave, J. and E. Wenger (1991): *Situated Learning. Legitimate Peripheral Participation*. Cambridge University Press, Cambridge MA.

Ljungstrand, P., Redström J., and Holmquist, L. E. , Webstickers (2000): 'Using Physical Tokens to Access, Manage and Share Bookmarks to the Web', in: *Proceedings of DARE 2000 (Designing Augmented Reality Environments)*, April 12-14, Elsinore, Denmark. ACM Press.

Luff, P. and Heath, C. (1998): 'Mobility in Collaboration', *Proceeding of the Seventh Conference on Computer Supported Cooperative Work*, ACM Press, MA Cambridge, 1998, pp. 305-314.

Ormerod, F. and Ivanič, R. (2002): 'Materiality in Children's Meaning-Making Practices', *Visual Communication*, vol. 1, no. 1, 2002, pp. 65-91.

Orr, J. E. (1996): *Talking about Machines: An ethnography of a modern job*. Ithaca, New York: Cornell University Press.

Robertson, T. (2002): 'The Public Availability of Actions and Artefacts', *Computer-Supported Cooperative Work*, vol. 11, 2002, pp. 299-316.

Schmidt K. and Wagner I. (2002): 'Coordinative Artifacts in Architectural Practice', in M. Blay-Fornarino, A.M. Pinna-Dery, K. Schmidt, P. Zaraté (eds) : *Cooperative Systems Design. A Challenge of the Mobility Age*, IOS Press, Amsterdam, 2002, pp. 257-274.

Schmidt, K. (2002): 'Remarks on the Complexity of Cooperative Work', in H. Benchekroun and P. Salembier (eds): *Coooperation and Complexity*, RSTIA, Paris 2002 (forthcoming).

Wagner I. (2002): 'Open planning: objets persuasifs et fluidité des pratiques', in : *Proceedings Colloque Architecture des systèmes urbains*, Université de Technologie de Compiègne, July 5, 2001 (forthcoming).

Weiser, M., Gold, R., Brown, J. S. (1999): 'The Origins of Ubiquitous Computing Research at PARC in the late 1980s', *IBM Systems Journal*, vol. 38, no. 4, 1999, pp. 693-696.

K. Kuutti, E.H. Karsten, G. Fitzpatrick, P. Dourish and K. Schmidt (eds.), *ECSCW 2003: Proceedings of the Eighth European Conference on Computer Supported Cooperative Work, 14-18 September 2003, Helsinki, Finland*, pp. 159-178.

System Guidelines for Co-located, Collaborative Work on a Tabletop Display

Stacey D. Scott
Department of Computer Science, University of Calgary, Calgary, Canada
sdscott@cpsc.ucalgary.ca

Karen D. Grant
Department of Computer Science, Stanford University, Stanford, CA, USA
kgrant@cs.stanford.edu

Regan L. Mandryk
School of Computing Science, Simon Fraser University, Burnaby, Canada
rlmandry@cs.sfu.ca

Abstract. Collaborative interactions with many existing digital tabletop systems lack the fluidity of collaborating around a table using traditional media. This paper presents a critical analysis of the current state-of-the-art in digital tabletop systems research, targeted at discovering how user requirements for collaboration are currently being met and uncovering areas requiring further development. By considering research on tabletop displays, collaboration, and communication, several design guidelines for effective co-located collaboration around a tabletop display emerged. These guidelines suggest that technology must support: (1) natural interpersonal interaction, (2) transitions between activities, (3) transitions between personal and group work, (4) transitions between tabletop collaboration and external work, (5) the use of physical objects, (6) accessing shared physical and digital objects, (7) flexible user arrangements, and (8) simultaneous user interactions. The critical analysis also revealed several important directions for future research, including: standardization of methods to evaluate co-located collaboration; comparative studies to determine the impact of existing system configurations on collaboration; and creation of a taxonomy of collaborative tasks to help determine which tasks and activities are suitable for tabletop collaboration.

Introduction

Few existing technologies provide the rich, fluid interactions that exist during collaboration involving paper-based media. Typical desktop computers do not effectively support co-located, multi-user interaction because of their underlying one-user/one-computer design paradigm (Stewart et al., 1999). As computers become pervasive in society, digital information is more often required during collaboration. However, people often convert this information to paper-based media, make modifications, and then re-convert it back into digital form. Luff et al. (1992) observed an abundant use of paper in computerized workplaces, with considerable redundancy between the informational contents of the paper and computers used in these environments. Translating information from one medium to the other places overhead costs during co-located collaboration, such as the time and effort required to type in annotations made on paper documents, and the financial and environmental expense of printing and re-printing documents. In order to minimize these costs, improved technology is needed to support interaction with digital media during collaboration.

Advances in display and input technologies have led to a wide assortment of novel systems to support co-located collaboration. These systems range from extensions of the standard desktop computer (e.g., Bier & Freeman, 1991; Stewart et al., 1999), to electronic whiteboards (e.g., Fox et al., 2000; Streitz et al., 1999) and digital tabletop systems (e.g., Wellner, 1993; Deitz & Leigh, 2001). Technology that provides access to digital media on a tabletop can take advantage of the considerable experience people have with traditional tabletop collaboration.

Observations of traditional tabletop collaboration have shown that people's interactions are fluid and dynamic on a tabletop (Bly, 1988; Tang, 1991), and that collaborators are physically animated during these interactions (Scott et al., 2003). In order to effectively design a digital table, we need a clear understanding of these interactions, and of the ability of current technology to support them.

Design of digital tabletop systems is currently at a crossroads; technology is maturing, but it is not clear which tabletop system configuration is suitable for each collaborative environment or activity. At a recent international workshop organized by the authors of this paper (Scott et al., 2002), tabletop researchers were still debating the question: *what is the most appropriate type of tabletop system to build?* Answering this fundamental question could benefit the larger Computer-Supported Cooperative Work (CSCW) community as more researchers begin exploring co-located collaboration.

As of yet, there is no standard configuration for tabletop systems. Researchers investigating software interface issues for tables are often required to design and build their own system. Many researchers have used simple prototypes involving top-projecting a computer display onto a traditional table (e.g., Patten et al., 2001; Scott, et al., 2002; Shen et al., 2002). More elaborate systems have been built involving rear-projected tabletop displays (e.g., Cutler et al., 1997; Ullmer & Ishii, 1997) and self-illuminating displays (e.g., Streitz et al., 2002; Ståhl et al., 2002; Kruger & Carpendale, 2002). These systems also use a wide variety of input devices, such as mice (Scott et al., 2002; Kruger & Carpendale, 2002), pens (Grant et al., 2003), styli and/or direct touch (Shen et al., 2002; Streitz et al., 2002; Ståhl et al., 2002) and tracked physical input devices (Ullmer & Ishii, 1997; Underkoffler & Ishii, 1999; Patten et al., 2001).

Many digital tabletop systems have also been developed for a variety of specific purposes (e.g. Underkoffler & Ishii, 1999, Buxton et al., 2000). However, comparative studies have not been performed to determine the suitability of these existing systems for generalized use. In order to help researchers and practitioners make informed design decisions related to both system configuration and functionality, we performed a critical analysis of the current state-of-the-art in digital tabletop systems.

This paper first presents the investigation of past and present digital tabletop systems. Then, a set of design guidelines for collaborative tabletop systems that emerged from this investigation is presented. Examples are given of how these guidelines manifest in current system design. Directions for future collaborative tabletop research are then discussed, followed by our conclusions.

Investigating Existing Digital Tabletop Systems

In order to inform the design of future tabletop systems, we investigated the state-of-the-art in digital tabletop systems, gaining a deeper understanding of how their properties impact co-located collaboration. We gathered data covering user and task requirements. These data sources included:

- Literature on existing digital tabletop systems. A database was developed to classify pertinent details of each system, including details on input (e.g., was concurrency supported, what technology was used), on display (e.g., illumination type, size, height), on end users (e.g., was it collaborative, what was the user domain), and other critical characteristics;
- Human-Computer Interaction (HCI) and CSCW literature on design requirements, implications, and guidelines for co-located CSCW systems;
- CSCW literature involving observational studies of co-located collaboration involving traditional media originally performed for the purposes of informing distributed groupware;
- Relevant literature from the social sciences discussing interpersonal communication and tabletop collaboration;
- Our research experience with tabletop collaboration and digital tabletop systems, which includes building systems, observing how people use a variety of digital tabletop environments, and performing observational studies of collaboration on traditional tabletops in both casual and formal

settings; and
- Outcomes of an international workshop on collaborative tabletop systems.

The results of this analysis revealed four general classes of digital tabletop systems in the literature: digital desks, workbenches, drafting tables, and collaboration tables (see Figure 1 for examples). Digital desks are designed to replace an individual's traditional desk by integrating activities involving paper-based and digital media. Workbenches allow users to interact with digital media in a semi-immersive, virtual reality environment projected above a table surface. Drafting tables are designed to replace a typical drafter's or artist's table. They have an angled surface and are generally used individually. Collaboration tables are digital tabletops that support small-group collaborative activities, such as group design, story sharing, and planning.

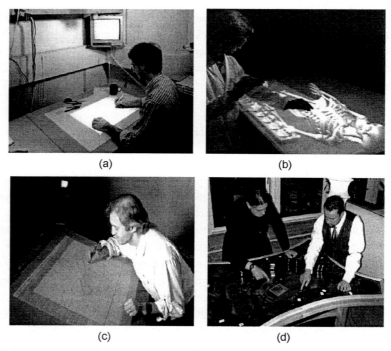

(a)   (b)

(c)   (d)

Figure 1. Examples of the four table types: (a) digital desk (from Wellner, 1993); (b) workbench (from Culter et al., 1997); (c) drafting table (from Buxton et al., 2000); (d) collaboration table (from Ståhl et al., 2002).

This paper focuses on the design of collaboration tables. However, the other three types of tabletop systems include useful features that can be leveraged to improve collaboration table design. Wherever appropriate in the following design discussions we describe some of these useful technologies and functionalities.

Our critical analysis revealed several implications for the design of collaborative digital tabletop systems, which have been synthesized into the set of design guidelines presented below. Although these guidelines focus on table systems for collaborative work, we draw on research from the entertainment (Mandryk et al., 2002; Ishii et al., 1999), social (Shen et al., 2002; Grant et al., 2003), and educational (Stewart et al., 1991; Bricker et al., 1999; Scott et al., 2003) domains.

Design Guidelines for Co-located Tabletop Collaboration

Through years of experience collaborating around tables, people have developed skills for interacting with each other as well as with objects on a table. When integrating computer technology into a table, designers must support these skills. Our guidelines are grounded in supporting users' previous experiences with traditional media on a table, while still recognizing that the addition of digital capabilities offers new possibilities and affordances.

We present eight collaborative design guidelines based on our critical analysis. Additionally, we discuss how current tabletop systems conform to the guidelines. These guidelines assert that technology must: (1) support interpersonal interaction, (2) support fluid transitions between activities, (3) support transitions between personal and group work, (4) support transitions between tabletop collaboration and external work, (5) support the use of physical objects, (6) provide shared access to physical and digital objects, (7) consider the appropriate arrangements of users, and (8) support simultaneous user actions.

Support Interpersonal Interaction

Technology designed to support group activities needs to support the interpersonal interaction at the heart of collaboration. Supporting the fundamental mechanisms that people use to mediate collaborative interactions is a minimal and necessary technological requirement. Interfering with these interactions can cause breakdowns in collaboration, especially when the technology hinders the conversation (Elwart-Keys et al., 1990). For example, when using the idea generation and organization tool COGNOTOR, groups often suffered from communication breakdowns because the system design imposed a communication process that did not support normal co-located conversation (Tatar et al., 1991).

Gutwin and Greenberg (2000) identified several low-level mechanisms, called the *mechanics of collaboration*, which people use to organize their collaborative activities and interactions. These mechanics increase workspace awareness (Gutwin et al., 1996) by conveying and gathering information about which actions are performed, when they are performed, and who is performing them[1]. It may not be necessary for co-located groupware to explicitly provide software support, such as awareness widgets (Gutwin et al., 1996), for each mechanic, but technology must not interfere. Furthermore, research demonstrating the collaborative importance of gesturing (Bekker et al., 1995; Bly, 1988; Tang, 1991), deictic referencing (Gutwin et al., 1996), and meeting coordination activities (Olson et al., 1992) reinforces the need for co-located tabletop technology to support the mechanics of collaboration.

Tabletop environments which accommodate separate, personal displays on the tabletop, such as AUGMENTED SURFACES (Rekimoto & Saitoh, 1999), INTERACTIVE WORKSPACES (Fox et al., 2000), and CONNECTABLES (Tandler et al., 2001) can hamper the use of certain communicative gestures, such as pointing to objects, because other group members may not understand what is being referenced or may not notice the gestures (Bekker et al., 1995).

The tabletop system needs to have an ergonomic form factor suitable for the collaborative activity being performed. For example, the story-sharing PERSONAL DIGITAL HISTORIAN (PDH) tabletop system is modeled after a household coffee table, which provides users with an appropriately informal environment where users can sit on comfortable sofas or lounge chairs while interacting with the table (Shen et al., 2002). In contrast, tabletop systems that have bulky components under the table, such as projectors and mirrors for bottom-projected displays (Ullmer & Ishii, 1997; Agrawala, 1997; Leibe et al., 2000), often require users to stand or sit awkwardly for extended periods of time, potentially impacting the comfort level of users and the naturalness of the interactions between users. The precise impact of the form factor of these systems on interpersonal interaction requires further investigation.

Support Fluid Transitions between Activities

Technology should not impose excessive overhead on switching between activities performed on a table, such as writing, drawing, and manipulating artifacts (Bly, 1988; Tang, 1991). For example, paint programs often distinguish between textual and graphical marks, forcing users to explicitly indicate their intention to write or draw. Studies of traditional tabletop design sessions revealed that people do not make this distinction and that they rapidly transition back and forth between writing and drawing (Bly, 1988; Tang, 1991). Technology that provides little or no overhead to performing or switching between activities

---

[1] The *mechanics of collaboration* include explicit and consequential communication, coordination of action, planning, monitoring, assistance, and protection. Full explanation of these mechanics is beyond the scope of this paper; the reader is referred to (Gutwin & Greenberg, 2000) for more details. However, it is important to mention that, while the mechanics of collaboration are based on studies of co-located and distributed collaboration, they were developed for improving distributed groupware system design. Thus, each mechanic may not have the same relevance for the design of co-located groupware since the communication environment is richer than in a distributed collaboration setting.

would allow users to transition easily between activities, focusing instead on communication.

A universal input device for all tabletop activities would make transitioning between activities smoother. Most current systems associate different input devices with different activities, such as a wireless keyboard for typing and a pointing device for selecting and manipulating virtual objects (Fox et al., 2000; Shen et al., 2002; Scott et al., 2002). Providing only one input mode and device, such as a stylus, ensures that there is no overhead from changing physical devices with shifts in activities. However, having a specialized input device for a particular task can optimize the completion of that task. Thus, the benefits of each approach should be considered carefully, especially with regard to how often transitions between activities that require separate specialized devices will be necessary during the collaborative tasks.

Most current tabletop research systems avoid this issue by focusing on a single type of activity such a sketching or moving objects around the table without providing any capabilities for modifying these objects (Kruger & Carpendale et al., 2002; Shen et al., 2002; Ståhl et al., 2002). One step towards providing seamless transitions between tabletop activities is the development of the BEACH architecture which underlies the INTERACTABLE tabletop system, along with other systems in the INTERACTIVELANDSCAPE (I-LAND) environment (Streitz et al., 1999). BEACH allows users to use pen gestures on the tabletop interface to perform certain frequent actions, such as rotating objects or making informal annotations on the table. While a wireless keyboard is still provided for more extensive text input, these pen gestures help users continue making interactions directly on the table for several different activities, thus, effectively supporting the users' transitions between activities.

Support Transitions between Personal and Group Work

Previous research has shown that people are adept at rapidly and fluidly transitioning between individual and group work when collaborating (Elwart-Keys et al., 1990; Mandviwalla & Offman, 1994). During a study of tabletop collaboration involving traditional media, Tang (1991) observed that users often maintain distinct areas on a tabletop workspace in order to mediate their interactions with the task objects and with each other. Allowing users to maintain these distinct areas may facilitate the transitions between individual and group work. However, the shape of a tabletop system may influence its ability to provide distinct workspaces. A study on seating preferences in a school library showed that students tended to avoid round tables because it was more difficult to partition them into individual workspaces as compared to square or rectangular tables (Thompson, 1973).

One method used to make these transitions fluid is to provide a separate personal display adjacent to the main tabletop computer display. The user can then easily shift her attention from the personal display to the group display with minimal effort. Separate displays also create obvious boundaries between the personal and shared workspaces, although as noted earlier, the separate displays may hamper interpersonal interaction. Collaborative environments such as INTERACTIVE WORKSPACES (Fox et al., 2000), AUGMENTED SURFACES (Rekimoto & Saitoh, 1999), and I-LAND (Streitz et al., 1999), provide mechanisms for secondary devices to be placed on or adjacent to the tabletop display. In the INTERACTIVE WORKSPACES and AUGMENTED SURFACES environments, participants are encouraged to use personal laptops that are linked to the tabletop display by underlying software architectures. In the I-LAND environment, participants can each use a personal CONNECTABLE (Tandler et al., 2001), which can combine with others to form a larger group workspace, allowing users to transition easily from individual to group work.

In contrast to this hardware approach, partitioning the software tabletop display space is another way designers have provided distinct workspaces. The PDH system provides a unique method of providing users with distinct work areas. Each corner of the tabletop display is designated as storage space for personal bookmarks while keeping the circular central area as a group space (Shen et al., 2002). PDH also provides each user with a system menu at the table edge, allowing them to access the system functionality without disrupting other users. These features allow users to attend to their own activities or the group activities without changing the entire display for each type of activity.

Partitioning the input space, or providing the ability to integrate personal computing devices is essential for supporting both personal and group spaces on the table. How to best support the transition between these two spaces still needs to be determined.

Support Transitions between Tabletop Collaboration and External Work

Most collaborative tabletop activities are part of a larger group effort that exists beyond the tabletop environment. Co-located group interaction is only one part of daily collaborative activity (Luff et al., 1992), thus group members must be able to incorporate work generated externally to the tabletop system into the current tabletop activity. It is important for collaborative tabletop systems to allow users to easily transition between mutually focused work and independent work done beyond the tabletop environment (Elwart-Keys et al., 1990; Mandviwalla & Olfman, 1994).

To ensure an easy transition between external work and tabletop collaboration, several systems support the use of off-the-shelf software (Fox et al., 2000). These systems allow participants to use previously generated files in the group setting. Transferring files either across a network or using storage devices is often more complicated and cumbersome than necessary. Transferring data from one display to another should be as simple as saying "I want this information displayed there" while gesturing to the appropriate data and display.

Several mechanisms exist to help facilitate importing and exporting of external work. Within the I-LAND environment, the PASSAGE mechanism allows users to easily move digital information from one computer to another (Streitz et al., 2002). Users associate digital information with any small object (e.g., a pen or key chain) by placing it on a 'bridge' associated uniquely with each computer in the environment. Moving the object to the INTERACTABLE bridge causes the digital information to appear on the tabletop. The hyperdragging technique developed for the INFOTABLE (Rekimoto & Saitoh., 1999) supports a seamless transfer of digital information between a table, wall display, and laptop computers. Hyperdragging uses normal mouse operations in combination with the physical relationship among the computers. The POINTRIGHT system (Johanson et al., 2002) in the Stanford IROOM (Fox et al., 2000) integrates displays on the table, wall and portable computers with a single set of mouse and keyboard controls. The CAFÉ TABLE (Kyffin, 2000), utilizes tagged objects, called tokens, which can be recognized by other computer systems in the users' environment, allowing for ease of data transfer.

Support the Use of Physical Objects

Tables are versatile work environments with a unique characteristic of providing a surface for people to place items during collaboration. These items often include both task-related objects (e.g., notebooks, design plans) and non-task-related objects (e.g., beverages, day-timers). Tabletop systems must support these familiar practices, as well as providing additional digital features. Research has shown that the versatility of paper contributes to its persistent use in many work environments, even along-side computers meant to replace it (Luff et al., 1992). Technology that allows the seamless integration of digital and physical objects at the table will support the practices mentioned above, allowing users to apply the years of experience they have accumulated collaborating around tables.

To support the practice of using physical objects on a table, researchers have begun offering tangible user interfaces (TUIs) as an alternative to standard computer input devices. Some systems use generic items, such as bricks, for generalized tangible input (Rauterberg et al., 1997; Fitzmaurice et al., 1999; Patten et al., 2000). Other tabletop systems provide specialized artifacts related to the application task. For example, the URP system uses pre-existing building models as input to an urban planning system (Underkoffler & Ishii, 1999), while the ENVISIONMENT AND DISCOVERY COLLABORATORY (EDC) (Arias et al., 1999) has tracked objects representing components of a neighbourhood (e.g., trees and buildings) for simulation and design tasks. The METADESK system handles physical objects by providing specialized tools for generic tasks (Ullmer & Ishii, 1997).

Instead of tagging objects, some current systems use computer vision technology to allow objects to retain their physical form and be used as intended, as well as be recognized by the system. Matrix codes have been placed on objects, such as textbooks (Koike et al., 2000) and videotapes (Rekimoto & Saitoh, 1999), to be captured and interpreted by overhead cameras. Radio frequency identification (RFID) tags have been embedded in clear acrylic tiles by Rekimoto et al. (2001) to create modular graphical and physical interaction devices. The disadvantage of using tagging technology is that objects must be pre-tagged to be interpreted, limiting the possible system input. Alternatively, Wellner's DIGITALDESK (1993) reads and interprets information created with a standard marker on paper (see Figure 1). The DESIGNER'S OUTPOST (Klemmer et al., 2000) captures and interprets regular Post-it Notes™, while PINGPONGPLUS (Ishii et al., 1999) augments the interaction between an unenhanced ping-pong ball and a ping-pong table. These three systems bring in physical artifacts, not previously enhanced by technology.

There are many digital or physical objects that users may want the system to recognize (e.g., laptop computer, daytimer, ping pong ball), but tabletop systems must also allow users to interact with objects that are not interpreted by the system (e.g., coffee cups, notebooks). Using a robust surface such as the DIAMONDTOUCH display (Deitz & Leigh, 2001) encourages users to treat the system surface as a table, not as a delicate display. Systems using self-illuminating displays can be enhanced by providing a boundary around the display on which to place objects (Streitz et al., 1999; Fox et al., 2000). Finally, although a system may ignore a coffee cup placed on the table as input, there needs to be a mechanism that recognizes the placement of an object and does not display relevant information in the physical space occupied by the item.

Provide Shared Access to Physical and Digital Objects

Tables are an ideal environment for sharing information and objects with others. It is common to see work colleagues, schoolmates, and family members gathered around a table discussing some object. For collaborative designers, sharing a work surface can enhance the design process (Bly, 1988). Furthermore, pointing or motioning to a shared object during a discussion provides a clear spatial relationship to the object for both the gesturer and the other group members, facilitating the group communication (Bekker et al., 1995; Tang, 1991). In contrast, situations in which everyone has a copy of a digital object, a gesture made to one copy of the object forces the other group members to perform a spatial translation to determine the specified location on their own copies. This creates cognitive overhead to using important communicative tools such as gestures and deictic references (Bekker et al., 1995; Bly, 1988; Tang, 1991;

Gutwin et al., 1996). Interacting with shared artifacts can also help maintain the group focus and facilitate awareness within the group because body positioning and eye gaze of group members attending to the same object can be easily interpreted by other group members (Suzuki & Kato, 1995).

Depending on the nature of the collaborative task, participants may be working primarily on a single object, such as one large design sketch, or they may be working on a series of related objects. Design tasks are a major application area where the sharing of common objects is essential. Arias et al. (1997, 1999), Underkoffler & Ishii (1999), Fjeld et al. (2000), and Eden et al. (2002) have built collaborative tabletop systems for urban planning. The collaborators typically gather around the design plan, and manipulate additional icons or physical pieces to add or delete design elements. Not only does a single representation of the design object ensure that each participant sees the same updated plan, but each participant can also see others place new elements as the actions happen. Furthermore, gestures can be easily interpreted during discussions. The shared object may be one large object such as a human skeleton (Cutler et al., 1997) or composed of several smaller pieces that comprise an organization scheme (Grant & Winograd, 2002).

When people are located at various positions around the table, the orientation of a shared object can become an issue. Orientation of an object can be both a problem and a potential resource for group interaction (Tang, 1991; Kruger & Carpendale, 2002). It may be difficult for one group member to read a document that is oriented toward the other side of the table, but collaborators often use temporary and partial rotation of objects for communicative purposes, such as directing the group's focus, sharing information, and assisting others (Kruger & Carpendale, 2002). Providing flexible, user-controlled orientation of shared objects on the table would facilitate this communicative function. Systems that support the maintenance of personal and group workspaces through appropriate orientation of objects towards the users around the table (e.g., Rekimoto & Saitoh, 1999; Tandler et al., 2001), partially provide this functionality. Various approaches to integrating orientation into a table interface are discussed in the next section.

Additionally, occlusion can be an obstacle to fluid interaction with a shared object. When using top-projected displays (e.g., Omojola et al., 2000, Patten et al., 2001; Rekimoto & Saitoh, 1999; Underkoffler & Ishii, 1999), one collaborator's hand can block the projection, obscuring the shared object for the other participants.

Consideration for the Appropriate Arrangements of Users

During tabletop collaboration, people sit or stand around a table at a variety of locations, both in relation to the table and in relation to other group members. Several factors can influence people's preferred locations, which in turn can influence the interpersonal interactions within the group (Sommer, 1969). Physical properties of the table, such as size or shape, can influence seating positions. People typically have various "distance zones" at which they interact comfortably with others (Hall, 1966).[2] Group members may temporarily be permitted to interact within a person's "intimate" space, but interaction at this distance for prolonged periods will often feel socially awkward. People generally feel comfortable working at "arm's length" since this preserves their personal space (Hall, 1966). Culture and age can also affect a person's preferred interaction distances (Hall, 1974). For example, young children tend to prefer closer interactions than adults (Aiello, 1987). Consequently, children tend to favour side-by-side or corner seating arrangements during tabletop activities compared to the face-to-face seating arrangement more commonly preferred by adults (Sommer, 1969).

The group task can also influence users' preferred locations at the table. Activities that require coordinated actions may best be supported by close user positions, because this positioning can enhance workspace awareness (Suzuki & Kato, 1995; Sommer, 1969). When the group activity is focused on conversation, adults generally prefer to sit in a face-to-face or corner seating arrangement (Sommer, 1969). In order to support these different kinds of tabletop activities, the technology must be flexible enough to allow users to interact from a variety of positions around the table.

Many current systems have cumbersome technology that renders one or more sides of the table unavailable to users (e.g., Wellner, 1993; MacKay, 1993; Culter et al., 1997). Other tables also incorporate a vertical display attached to one side of the table, which leaves only one side of the table with optimal viewing conditions (e.g., Rauterberg et al., 1997; Koike et al., 2000; Patten et al., 2001; Rekimoto, 2002). There are also table systems that provide vertical displays near the table without hindering the use of any sides the table (e.g., Arias et al., 1999; Fox et al., 2000).

When users are sitting at various locations around a table, the displayed information may not be oriented appropriately for all users. A non-oriented interface (e.g., Mandryk et al., 2002) would be appropriate for horizontal displays, but is unrealistic for work practices where rotation-sensitive components (Fitzmaurice et al., 1999) such as menus and text are present. As a result, providing support for orientation is a challenge and a salient issue for tabletop system research.

There are two main approaches to the orientation problem: having a system automatically present information in the "best" orientation and allowing users to manually rotate information themselves. The CONNECTABLES (Tandler et al., 2001) and INFOTABLE (Rekimoto & Saitoh, 1999) systems automatically orient

---

[2] Hall identified four distance zones: Intimate (touching – 18 inches), Personal (1.5 – 4 feet), Social (4 – 12 feet), and Public (+12 feet).

information towards a user while assuming that a user's position will be based on their static "personal" display space. This could potentially lead to inappropriately oriented objects if users move around the table. Hancock (2001) used a neural net to predict the location where users were seated based on input from a tracked stylus input device so that information was automatically projected toward each user, even if the users moved around the table. Automatically orienting information allows for ease of reading and interaction with oriented components such as menus, but it limits the use of orientation as a communicative function, as discussed in the previous section. A hybrid approach where rotation-sensitive components would be automatically oriented and users could also easily control orientation for communicative purposes might be more beneficial.

Support Simultaneous User Actions

When multiple people engage in tabletop activities, they often interact with artifacts on the table surface simultaneously (Tang, 1991; Scott et al., 2003). Traditional computer technology does not support multi-user, concurrent interaction. Instead, users are forced to share the available input device when working together at a single computer (Inkpen et al., 1995). This limitation still exists in large-screen displays used by many existing tabletop systems, sometimes interfering with users' actions during collaboration (Ståhl et al., 2002; Shen et al., 2002).

Teamwork is often comprised of a variety of collaboration styles, including working in parallel, working sequentially in tightly coupled activities, working independently,[3] and working under assumed roles, such as director and actor (Cockburn & Greenberg, 1995; Scott et al., 2003). On systems that don't provide support for concurrent interactions, users can adapt to technology limitations and learn to take turns (Shen et al., 2002). However users may have more difficulty working independently because they must monitor their collaborators to know when the system is available. Thus, providing concurrent interaction would free users to focus on the task at hand, allowing them to take advantage of these different interaction styles to suit the task requirements and the group dynamics (Mandviwalla & Offman, 1994; Scott et al., 2003). In collaborative systems where concurrency is not supported, users have requested the ability to interact simultaneously (Shen et al., 2002, Grant et al., 2003). In addition, users have appreciated the ability to interact simultaneously when this functionality has been provided (Hancock, 2001).

Providing concurrent, multi-user interaction is both a hardware and software consideration. The tabletop system must provide multi-user input capabilities,

---

[3] When independent interaction is coordinated it is sometimes referred to as the divide-and-conquer collaboration style (Gutwin et al., 1996).

several directions in order for our field to further support effective collaboration. These research directions include the standardization of methods to evaluate co-located collaboration, the implementation of more comparative studies to understand the impact of system configurations, and investigations to elucidate which tasks are most suitable for tabletop collaboration.

Our guidelines should be useful signposts for tabletop system and interface designers to use when considering important collaboration support issues. However, we also need further development of a robust evaluation methodology. Recently, attempts have been made to use conversational analysis as a measure of collaboration. Gale (1998) used the Conversation Games Analysis (Carletta et al., 1997) to determine the effectiveness of various collaborative settings for a remote repair task involving an expert and a trainee. The effectiveness of the COGNOTOR system to support co-located brainstorming was evaluated using research theories from Psycholinguistics, which helped reveal that the underlying conversational model that the system supported did not match the conversational model that people use when talking in a co-located situation (Tatar et al., 1991).

Evaluating collaboration on digital tabletop systems could benefit from comparisons to a control condition involving traditional media. Although there may be some limitations to this control setting as traditional media may afford different collaborative interactions and perhaps less functionality than digital media, studies based on traditional tabletop collaboration have provided applicable lessons for CSCW in the past (Bly, 1988; Tang, 1991; Grant et al., 2003). Time and time again people abandon technology to use traditional media in their co-located collaborations (Luff et al., 1992); thus, using traditional tabletop collaboration as somewhat of a benchmark for evaluating our system designs might help make our digital tabletop systems as preferable, if not more, as using paper-based media.

Additionally, further work is needed to understand the suitability of particular input and output configurations for tabletop systems before standard configurations are adopted. Each decision on system configuration affects the usability of a tabletop display system in a number of ways. For example, decisions about the size and resolution affect how many collaborators can gather around a table. Projection technology (e.g., top-projected, bottom-projected, self-illuminating) affects the viewing angle, brightness, and robustness of the system but also influences interaction. In addition to influencing individual interactions, decisions on input technologies and tracking technologies influence how well a system provides support for collaborative activities.

The fundamental issue of when and whether a computer tabletop is the best display configuration for a particular task and user group needs further research. For instance, collaboration involving several people discussing textual information intuitively does not seem appropriate for a tabletop environment because of possible orientation issues, but research has suggested that orientation such as multiple input devices or touch screens that detect simultaneous, multiple touches. The software must also support interacting with multiple software components at once. For example, single display groupware (Stewart et al., 1999) allows users to manipulate group widgets on a shared display and provides multiple, on-screen cursors. Tabletop systems that provide a tangible user interface must intelligently handle manipulation of multiple input objects at once.

Currently, only a few tabletop display systems support synchronous collaboration. The majority of current systems require turn-taking with only one input device and one active input channel (i.e. cursor) (e.g., Wellner, 1993; Fox et al., 2000; Scott et al., 2002). These systems may be collaborative in the sense that multiple people can gather around and discuss the digital information, but only one person can manipulate digital artifacts at any given time and control must be passed for a second user to interact. Providing each user with an input device, even though the system cannot interpret concurrent input, requires that users take turns but does not require the passing of control. This is the approach taken by the PDH system (Shen et al., 2002) and the ITABLE (Grant & Winograd, 2002) using ultrasonic pens, and is also inherent in any system that uses standard touch-sensitive screens (e.g., Streitz et al., 1999; Ståhl et al., 2002).

Recent efforts have been made to create technologies that allow for multiple, concurrent interactions. DIAMONDTOUCH (Deitz & Leigh, 2001) enables multiple concurrent users as well as multiple simultaneous touches from a single user. SMARTSKIN (Rekimoto, 2002) uses similar technology that allows for multiple concurrent interactions as well as supporting gestural input. Many systems that use tangible user interfaces (TUIs) for specialized input can simultaneously track multiple physical tokens (e.g., Fitzmaurice et al., 1995; Patten et al., 2002; Eden et al., 2000; Mandryk et al., 2002); however, the latency of a system may increase as more tokens are manipulated concurrently.

There are many methods of providing multiple, concurrent input to a tabletop display system. Research is required to determine which input mechanism (e.g., mice, gestures, touch, stylus, or TUI) is the most beneficial under different collaborative situations. The speed and accuracy of various input devices has been well documented, but their impact on collaborative issues such as communication and awareness of activities has not. For example, collaborators are more likely to see another collaborator access an icon when using a touch sensitive display since their whole arm is moving in space than when using a mouse when only a small cursor moves. This increased awareness may be worth a small decrease in speed of interaction in certain collaborative circumstances.

Directions for Future Research

To varying degrees, current tabletop systems satisfy the eight system guidelines presented. However, as a research community we need to make progress in of tabletop items plays a key communicative role (Kruger & Carpendale, 2002). Thus, further investigation into the tradeoffs of using various types of information on the table (e.g., orientation-dependent versus non-orientation-dependent) is needed. The creation of a taxonomy of collaborative tasks might help determine which activities and tasks are better suited to a tabletop environment and why.

Conclusions

Based on an investigation of the current state-of-the-art in digital tabletop displays and our experience building tabletop systems and applications, we have presented eight guidelines for designing collaborative tabletop display systems. These guidelines stress the importance of allowing tabletop collaborators to easily integrate the collaborative work they perform on the tabletop into the larger context of their working environment. Thus, work that users have performed individually or perhaps as part of other CSCW systems, such as distributed groupware systems, must be easily accessible from the tabletop workspace. Likewise, work performed on the tabletop system must be accessible from the users' other work environments.

The design guidelines also stress the importance of supporting users' familiar work practices at tables, such as using physical objects (e.g., paper, design models, drinks) and sitting at different positions around the table. Supporting these work practices provides the potential for a tabletop system to support a variety of tasks, just as traditional tables provide a flexible workspace for a multitude of activities, such as drawing, designing, debating, planning, and so on. Once these foundational systems become available, collaboration researchers can focus on designing applications to supporting such various types of tasks.

In some cases, small changes in system design can result in large changes in the ability of a system to support collaboration. In other instances, there are research questions that need to be investigated and obstacles to overcome. We have presented a number of these obstacles and research directions identified from own work, our critical analysis of current state of the digital tabletop research, and discussions with other designers at a recent international tabletop workshop. We anticipate that this field will continue to develop and impact not only our research community, but also provide insight into human-computer interaction as a whole.

Acknowledgements

This research has been partially funded by the Natural Science and Engineering Research Council of Canada (NSERC), National Science Foundation (NSF) Grant IRI-9817799, Mitsubishi Electric Research Laboratories (MERL), the New Media Innovation Centre (NewMIC), and the National

Science Foundation (NSF) Grant IRI-9817799. We gratefully acknowledge all of the participants of the Co-located Tabletop Collaboration: Technologies and Directions CSCW2002 workshop, whose insightful discussion contributed greatly to this research.

References

Aiello, J.R. (1987). Human Spatial Behavior. In D. Stokols & I. Altman (eds.): *Handbook of Environmental Psychology*, vol. 1, Toronto, ON: John Wiley & Sons, pp. 389-505.

Agrawala, M., Beers, A.C., Fröhlich, B., Hanrahan, P., MacDowall, I., and Bolas, M. (1997). The Two-User Responsive Workbench: Support for Collaboration through Individual Views of a Shared Space. In *Proceedings of the ACM Conference on Computer Graphics and Interactive Techniques (SIGGRAPH) '97*, pp. 327-332.

Arias, E.G., Eden, H., and Fischer, G. (1997). Enhancing Communication, Facilitating Shared Understanding, and Creating Better Artifacts by Integrating Physical and Computational Media for Design. In *Proceedings of the Symposium on Designing Interactive Systems (DIS) '97*, pp. 1-12.

Arias, E.G., Eden, H., Fischer, G., Gorman, A., and Scharff, E. (1999). Beyond Access: Informed Participation and Empowerment. In *Proceedings of the Conference on Computer-Supported Collaborative Learning (CSCL) '99*, pp. 20-32.

Bekker, M.M., Olson, J.S., and Olson, G.M. (1995). Analysis of gestures in face-to-face design teams provides guidance for how to use groupware in design. In *Proceedings of the Symposium on Designing Interactive Systems (DIS) '95*, pp. 157-166.

Bly, S.A. (1988). A Use of Drawing Surfaces in Different Collaborative Settings. In *Proceedings of the ACM Conference on Computer-Supported Cooperative Work (CSCW) '88*, pp. 250-256.

Bier, E.A., & Freeman, S. (1991). MMM: A User Interface Architecture for Shared Editors on a Single Screen. In *Proceedings of ACM Symposium on User Interface Software Technology (UIST) '91*, pp. 79-86.

Bricker, L.J., Bennett, M.J., Fujioke, E., & Tanimoto, S.L. (1999). Colt: A System for Developing Software that Supports Synchronous Collaborative Activities. In *Proceedings of Educational Media (EdMedia) '99*, pp. 587-592.

Buxton, W., Fitzmaurice, G.W., Balakrishnan, R., and Kurtenbach, G. (2000). Large Displays in Automotive Design. In *IEEE Computer Graphics and Applications*, 20(4), pp. 68-75.

Carletta, J., Isard, A., Isard, S., Kowtko, J.C., Doherty-Sneddon, G., & Anderson, A.H. (1997). The reliability of a dialogue structure coding scheme. In *Computational Linguistics*, 23, pp. 13-31.

Cockburn, A. & Greenberg, S. (1996). Children's Collaboration Styles in a Newtonian Microworld. In *Conference Companion of ACM Conference on Human Factors in Computing Systems (CHI) '96*, pp. 181-182.

Cutler, L.D., Fröhlich, B., and Hanrahan, P. (1997). Two-Handed Direct Manipulation on the Responsive Workbench. In *Proceedings 1997 Symposium on Interactive 3D Graphics*. pp. 107-114.

Deitz, P. and Leigh, D. (2001). DiamondTouch: A Multi-User Touch Technology. In *Proceedings of the ACM Symposium on User Interface Software and Technology (UIST) 2000*, pp. 219-226.

Eden, H., Hornecker, E., and Scharff, E. (2002). Multilevel Design and Role Play: Experiences in Assessing Support for Neighborhood Participation in Design. In *Proceedings of the Symposium on Designing Interactive Systems (DIS) 2002*, pp. 387-392.

Elwart-Keys, M., Halonen, D., Horton, M., Kass, R., and Scott, P. (1990). User Interface Requirements for Face to Face Groupware. In *Proceedings of the ACM Conference on Human Factors in Computing Systems (CHI) '90*, pp. 295-301.

Fitzmaurice, G.W., Ishii, H., and Buxton, W. (1995). Bricks: Laying the Foundations for Graspable User Interfaces. In *Proceedings of the ACM Conference on Human Factors in Computing Systems (CHI) '95*. pp. 442-449.

Fitzmaurice, G.W., Balakrishan, R., Kurtenbach , G., and Buxton , B. (1999). An Exploration into Supporting Artwork Orientation in the User Interface. In *Proceedings of the ACM Conference on Human Factors in Computing Systems (CHI) '99*, pp. 167-174.

Fjeld, M., Voorhorst, F., Bichsel, M., Krueger, H., and Rauterberg, M. (2000). Navigation Methods for an Augmented Reality System. In *Extended Abstracts of ACM Conference on Human Factors in Computing Systems (CHI) '00*, pp. 8-9.

Fox, A., Johanson, B., Hanrahan, P., and Winograd, T. (2000). Integrating Information Appliances into an Interactive Workspace. *IEEE Computer Graphics and Applications*, 20(4), pp. 54-65.

Gale, C. (1998). 'The Effects of Gaze Awareness on Dialogue in a Video-Based Collaborative Manipulative Task,' in *Conference Summary of the ACM Conference on Human Factors in Computing Systems (CHI) '98*, pp.345-346.

Grant, K.D., Graham, A., Nguyen, T., Paepcke, A. and Winograd, T. (2003). Beyond the Shoe Box: Foundations for Flexibly Organizing Photographs on a Computer. *Submitted for Publication*. http://dbpubs.stanford.edu:8090/pub/2003-3.

Grant, K.D. and Winograd, T. (2002). Flexible, Collaborative Organization on a Tabletop. In *CSCW2002 Workshop on Co-located Tabletop Collaboration: Technologies and Directions.*

Gutwin, C., & Greenberg, S. (2000). The Mechanics of Collaboration: Developing Low Cost Usability Evaluation Methods for Shared Workspaces. In *IEEE 9th International Workshop on Enabling Technologies: Infrastructure for Collaborative Enterprises (WETICE'00).*

Gutwin, C., Greenberg, S., and Roseman, M. (1996). Workspace Awareness in Real-time Distributed Groupware: Framework, Widgets, & Evaluation. In *Proceedings of the HCI '96*, pp. 281-298.

Hall, E.T. (1966). *Distances in Man: The Hidden Dimension*. Double Day, Garden City, NY.

Hall, E.T. (1974). Proxemics. In S. Weitz (ed.), *Nonverbal Communication: Readings with Commentary*, Oxford University Press, Toronto, ON.

Hancock, M.S. (2001). A Feed Forward Neural Network for Determining a User's Location. Simon Fraser University Technical Report TR 2001-2. December, 2001.

Inkpen, K., Booth, K.S., Klawe, M., Upitis, R. (1995). Playing together beats playing apart, especially for girls. In *Proceedings of the Conference on Computer-Supported Collaborative Learning (CSCL) '95*, pp. 177-181.

Ishii, H. Wisneski, C., Orbanes, J., Chun, B., and Paradiso., J. (1999). PingPongPlus: Design of an Athletic-Tangible Interface for Computer-Supported Cooperative Play. In *Proceedings of the ACM Conference on Human Factors in Computing Systems (CHI) '99*, pp. 394-401.

Johanson, B., Hutchins, G., Winograd, T., Stone, M. (2002). PointRight: Experience with Flexible Input Redirection in Interactive Workspaces. In *Proceedings of the ACM Symposium on User Interface Software and Technology (UIST) 2002*, pp. 227-234.

Klemmer, S.R., Newman, M., Farrell, F., Meza, R., and Landay, J.A. (2000). A Tangible Difference: Participatory Design Studies Informing a Designers' Outpost. In *CSCW2000 Workshop on Shared Environments to Support Face-to-Face Collaboration.*

Koike, H., Sato, Y., Kobayashi, Y., Tobita, H., and Kobayashi , M. (2000). Interactive Textbook and Interactive Venn Diagram: Natural and Intuitive Interfaces on Augmented Desk System. In *Proceedings of the ACM Conference on Human Factors in Computing Systems (CHI) 2000,* pp. 121-128.

Kruger, R., & Carpendale, M.S.T. (2002). Orientation and Gesture on Horizontal Displays. *UbiCOMP 2002 Workshop on Collaboration with Interactive Walls and Tables.*

Kyffin, S., Living Memory Project Brochure, Philips Design. (2000). http://www.design.philips.com/lime/download/brochure.pdf

Leibe, B., Starner, T., Ribarsky, W., Wartell, T, Krum, D., Singletary, B., and Hodges L. (2000). The Perceptive Workbench: Towards Spontaneous and Natural Interaction in Semi-Immersive Virtual Environments. In *Proceedings of the IEEE Conference on Virtual Reality 2000.* pp. 13-20.

Luff, P., Heath, C., and Greatbatch, D. (1992). Tasks-in-Interaction: Paper and Screen Based Documentation in Collaborative Activity. In *Proceedings of the ACM Conference on Computer-Supported Cooperative Work (CSCW) '92,* pp. 163-170.

Mackay, W., Velay, G., Carter, K., Ma, C., and Pagani, D. (1993). Augmenting Reality: Adding Computational Dimensions to Paper, In *Communications of the ACM* 36(7), pp. 96-97.

Mandryk, R.L., Maranan, D.S., and Inkpen, K.M. (2002). False Prophets: Exploring Hybrid Board/Video Games. In *Extended Abstracts of ACM Conference on Human Factors in Computing Systems (CHI) 2002.* pp. 640-641.

Mandviwalla, M. and Olfman, L. (1994). What Do Groups Need? A Proposed Set of Generic Groupware Requirements. In *ACM Transactions on Computer-Human Interaction,* 1(3), pp. 245-268.

Olson, G.M., Olson, J.S., Carter, M., & Storrøsten, M. (1992). Small group design meetings: An analysis of collaboration. In *Human-Computer Interaction,* 7, pp. 347-374.

Omojola, O., Post, E.R., Hancher, M.D., Maguire, Y., Pappu, R., Schoner, B., Russo, P.R., Gershenfeld, N., and Fletcher, R. (2000). An Installation of Interactive Furniture. In *IBM Systems Journal,* 39(3/4) pp. 861-879.

Patten, J., Ishii, H., Hines, J., and Pangaro, G. (2001). A wireless object tracking platform for tangible user interfaces. In *Proceedings of the ACM Conference on Human Factors in Computing Systems (CHI) 2001.* pp. 253-260.

Rauterberg, M., Bichsel, M., Leonhardt, U., and Meier, M. (1997). BUILD-IT: a computer vision-based interaction technique of a planning tool for construction and design. In *Proceedings of the IFIP International Conference on Human-Computer Interaction (INTERACT) '97.* pp. 587-588.

Rekimoto, J. and Saitoh, M. (1999). Augmented Surfaces: A Spatially Continuous Work Space for Hybrid Computing Environments. In *Proceedings of the ACM Conference on Human Factors in Computing Systems (CHI) '99,* pp. 378-385.

Rekimoto, J., Ullmer, B., and Oba, H. (2001). DataTiles: a modular platform for mixed physical and graphical interactions. In *Proceedings of the ACM Conference on Human Factors in Computing Systems (CHI) 2001,* pp. 269-276.

Rekimoto, J. (2002). SmartSkin: An infrastructure for freehand manipulation on interactive surfaces. In *Proceedings of the ACM Conference on Human Factors in Computing Systems (CHI) 2002,* pp. 113-120.

Scott, S.D., Lesh, N., and Klau, G.W. (2002). Investigating human-computer optimization. *Proceedings of the ACM Conference on Human Factors in Computing Systems (CHI) 2002*, pp. 155-162.

Scott, S., Grant, K., Carpendale, S., Inkpen, K., Mandryk, R., & Winograd, T. (2002). Co-located Tabletop Collaboration: Technologies and Directions. Workshop at CSCW2002 (In *Extended Abstracts of the ACM Conference on Computer-Supported Cooperative Work (CSCW) '02*, p. 21.).

Scott, S.D., Mandryk, R.L., & Inkpen, K.M. (2003). Understanding Children's Collaborative Interactions in Shared Environments. In *Journal of Computer-Aided Learning*. (in press).

Shen, C., Lesh, N., Vernier, F., Forlines, C., & Frost, J. (2002), Sharing and Building Digital Group Histories. In *Proceedings of the ACM Conference on Computer-Supported Cooperative Work (CSCW) 2002*, pp. 324-333.

Sommer, R. (1969). *Personal space: The behaviour basis of design*. Prentice-Hall, Englewood Cliffs, N.J.

Ståhl, O., Wallberg, A., Sderberg, J., Humble, J., Fahln, L.E., Lundberg, J., Bullock, A. (2002). Information Exploration Using the Pond. In *Proceedings of the Conference on Collaborative Virtual Environments (CVE) 2002*, pp. 72-79.

Stewart, J., Bederson, B.B, and Druin, A. (1999). Single Display Groupware: A Model for Co-present Collaboration. In *Proceedings of the ACM Conference on Human Factors in Computing Systems (CHI) '99*, pp. 286-293.

Streitz, N., Prante, T., Mueller-Tomfelde, C., Tandler, P., and Magerkurth, C. (2002). Roomware - The Second Generation. In *Extended Abstracts of ACM Conference on Human Factors in Computing Systems (CHI) 2002*, pp. 506-507.

Streitz, N.A., Geißler, J., Holmer, T., Konomi, S., Müller-Tomfelde, C., Reischl, W., Rexroth, P., Seitz, P., Steinmetz, R., Steinmetz, R., and Steinmetz, R. (1999). i-LAND: An interactive Landscape for Creativitiy and Innovation. In *Proceedings of the the ACM Conference on Human Factors in Computing Systems (CHI) '99*, pp. 120-127.

Suzuki, H. and Kato, H. (1995). Interaction-Level Support for Collaborative Learning: AlgoBlock - Open Programming Language. In *Proceedings of the Conference on Computer-Supported Collaborative Learning (CSCL) '95*, pp. 349-355.

Tandler, P., Prante, T., Müller-Tomfelde, C., Streitz, N., and Steinmetz, R. (2001). ConnecTables: Dynamic Coupling of Displays for the Flexible Creation of Shared Workspaces. In *Proceedings of the ACM Symposium on User Interface Software and Technology (UIST) 2001*, pp. 11-19.

Tang, J.C. (1991). Findings from observational studies of collaborative work. In *International Journal of Man-Machine Studies*, 34, pp. 143-160.

Tatar, D.G., Foster, G., and Bobrow, D.G. (1991). Design for Conversation: Lessons from Cognoter. In *International Journal of Man-Machine Studies*, 34, pp. 185-209.

Thompson, J.J. (1973). *Beyond Words: nonverbal communication in the classroom*. New York: Citation Press.

Ullmer, B. and Ishii, H. (1997). The metaDESK: Models and prototypes for tangible user interfaces. In *Proceedings of the ACM Symposium on User Interface Software and Technology (UIST) 1997*, pp. 223-232.

Underkoffler, J. and Ishii, H. (1999). Urp: A luminous-tangible workbench for urban planning and design. In *Proceedings of the ACM Conference on Human Factors in Computing Systems (CHI) 99*, pp. 386-393.

Wellner, P. (1993). Interacting with Paper on the DigitalDesk. *Communications of the ACM*, 36(7), pp. 86-96.

K. Kuutti, E.H. Karsten, G. Fitzpatrick, P. Dourish and K. Schmidt (eds.), *ECSCW 2003: Proceedings of the Eighth European Conference on Computer Supported Cooperative Work, 14-18 September 2003, Helsinki, Finland*, pp. 179-198.

Assembling History:
Achieving Coherent Experiences with Diverse Technologies

Mike Fraser[1], Danaë Stanton[1], Kher Hui Ng[1], Steve Benford[1], Claire O'Malley[1], John Bowers[2], Gustav Taxén[2], Kieran Ferris[3], Jon Hindmarsh[4]

[1]Mixed Reality Laboratory, University of Nottingham, UK.

[2]Royal Institute of Technology (KTH), Stockholm, Sweden.

[3]University of Limerick, Ireland.

[4]King's College London, UK.

{mcf, des, khn, sdb, com}@cs.nott.ac.uk, {bowers, gustavt}@nada.kth.se, Kieran.Ferris@ul.ie, Jon.Hindmarsh@kcl.ac.uk

Abstract. This paper describes an activity designed for a site of special interest in which clues to its history are gathered as visitors explore the site before interacting with two displays which reveal details of key past events. We investigate a design approach in which electronically tagged paper is used both to weave the visit together and configure the interactive displays so as to provide variable access to a common information space. An analysis of visitors' interactions throughout a week's public exhibition shows how features of our approach can support people in making connections between displays, locations, and historical events. In addition to situating our work in relationship with CSCW's emerging concern for technologies and collaboration in museums and allied public settings, we examine general questions of how to design activities to establish coherence of experience across diverse interfaces. This is a timely issue as interactive technologies proliferate and take on ever more variable physical forms.

Introduction

Many researchers, following Weiser (1993), suggest that computers are more and more mass-market products with the potential of becoming part of the fabric of everyday life, rather than tools requiring expert skill and encountered in laboratories or high-tech offices. Our encounters with information technology are less exceptional, more everyday, and increasingly domestic, leisure-related and in public places. This proliferation of interaction devices and information displays raises new problems. In particular, how are these technologies to be coherently interrelated in ways which make sense to, rather than overwhelm, their users? Accordingly, CSCW and HCI research is beginning to complement its interest in the design of individual devices and displays with a concern for how they might be *coherently assembled*. It is this problem of the practical assembly of artefacts to support coherent experience that we focus on.

Assembling Visiting Experiences in Museums

Museums, exploratoria and galleries are relevant areas to study how information can be assembled, as well as promising domains for evaluating designed solutions. Indeed, several researchers, have begun to examine people's encounters with technologies in such public places. Büscher et al. (1999) describe a media art exhibition space and characterise the ways in which people move between artefacts, learn about them and cooperate with each other in making sense of them. On the basis of these observations, the authors make proposals for the design of technical infrastructures which intelligibly interconnect large scale, multi-user virtual environments. While Büscher et al. are concerned to inform requirements for general purpose platforms on the basis of studying public places, we are interested in effectively deploying technologies within those places themselves. We share the insight though that exhibition spaces are sites where multiple interactive artefacts may be found, whose interrelations are not always coherently designed.

Traditional museums have commonly utilised multiple displays (cabinets, vitrines etc.) for showing items from their collections. Presenting items in separate displays enables taxonomies of items to be made visible, or comparisons between items to be made with respect to particular highlighted features. As collections grow, many museums experience a problem of selecting what to display and what to keep in storage. New displays are introduced to accommodate new acquisitions and to house visiting exhibitions. These must coexist with a legacy of older displays, embodying older taxonomies or design aesthetics.

For many museums, interactive exhibits offer an alternative to traditional ideas of museum pedagogy and principles of exhibition (Benelli et al. 1999, Caulton 1998, Bitgood 1991). For example, an 'interactive' may enable a richer impression to be given to visitors of the history or use-context of an artefact which the mere display of the artefact alone might not make so clear. Multimedia applications can also bring items (virtually) 'out of storage' (Ciolfi et al. 2001). Consequently, museums have often been at the forefront of deploying new interface technologies, ranging from immersive displays to extend the imaginative presentation of artefacts, to mobile devices that present information in context and in a personalised or intimate way as part of a museum tour (Aoki and Woodruff 2000, Benelli et al. 1999, Grinter et al. 2002, Schnädelbach et al. 2002). However, such innovations introduce further displays into the museum environment that might uneasily coexist with traditional display techniques.

Whatever the value of these introductions of information technology, the practical condition many museums find themselves in is one of multiple coexisting displays and devices of varying age, rationale, design aesthetic and material manifestation. Displays differ in terms of the kinds of activity they support, personalisation, physical scale, cost, portability, commodity or bespoke, and many other factors. And yet, they also need to be embedded within an overall visiting experience which can be collaboratively made sense of by groups of co-visitors. We aim to provide *assemblies* of artefacts to support a coherent experience for visitors. How can visitors make connections between their experiences at different displays in order to gain new insights or make sense of complex information? As we will shortly describe, we designed a site-specific experience involving an assembly of technologies to investigate these issues.

Designing Public Experiences

In addition to the goal of assembling displays and interaction devices into a coherent experience, our work is also informed by several key issues in the design of public visiting experiences which emerge from social scientific studies of museums and related settings.

vom Lehn et al. (2001, see also Heath et al. 2002, Hindmarsh et al. 2002) describe how people engage with a variety of interactive exhibits. They reveal how companions shape each others' experience and how passers-by often draw on the activities of others to learn how to use and appreciate interactive exhibits. Interaction, then, should not refer to just the interaction of a single 'user' with an exhibit but should address the multiple ways in which people engage with each other in, around and through the display. Our work builds on this and other sources (e.g. Caulton 1988) on visitor conduct and exhibit design. In particular, we were concerned to:

- support a range of ways in which our assembly of artefacts could be oriented towards (casually, as fun, or for serious visitors and organised school trips)
- encourage collaboration within small groups, often composed of children and adults
- recognise that the overall experience must be managed (coping with bottlenecks, failures, special needs)
- be sensitive to questions of costs and scalability
- recognise the need to provide 'take home' materials (for use in schools or as souvenirs)
- allow flexibility in how the overall experience could be acted out (i.e. avoiding a fixed order of activities)
- explicitly provide for different means for engaging with our artefacts (hands on, overseeing, passing by etc.).

A Set of Principles for Assembling Artefacts

Let us introduce our approach for addressing these requirements. First, coherence is given to the experience by defining a *unifying overall activity* in which the visitors are to be engaged. In our case, we indicated to visitors that they would be doing a 'history hunt' in which they would collect 'clues' around the site. Secondly, an underlying *common information space* (cf. Bannon and Bødker 1997) is designed which contains a variety of interrelated items that can be revealed as the activity progresses. In our case, this concerned two different historical events which implicated different parts of the site. Thirdly, *an assembly of interactive displays* is used with each display supporting a particular part of the overall activity and revealing a sub-set of the common information space. We describe these shortly. Our aim was that the progressive unfolding of events using different displays would give an intrinsic 'structure of motivation' (see Bowers 2001) for engaging with the overall activity and discovering a variety of details about the site. Fourthly, to promote the coherence of the experience, *common interaction techniques* are provided across different displays. In our case, we rejected standard desktop multimedia interaction techniques and devices throughout in favour of designing a set of overlapping techniques which were idiomatic for the site and the clue-seeking activity. Finally, to further enhance the integration of the visit, a *portable artefact* is provided to enable visitors to accumulate a record of their visit and support their identification as they move around the site.

Paper as 'Glue'

Our approach to assembling multiple displays is to use paper as the glue that holds an experience together. Museum visitors are provided with sheets of paper on which they make a visual record of the locations and displays they have visited. These sheets are pre-printed with information to guide and structure the visit, for example clues, maps and suggested activities. Each sheet is also electronically tagged using RFID technology so that it can be used as input to various interactive displays (Want et al. 1999), and can hold a computer-readable history of the visiting experience. Visitors engage in a series of different activities throughout a visit, some of which involve following suggestions from the paper, others annotating the paper with information that they have found, and yet others using the same paper to obtain further information from interactive displays.

The key idea is that the combination of a visual record and an electronic record on a single artefact – a piece of paper – can provide both visitors and displays with the information required to assemble a coherent experience. For the visitor the instructions on each piece paper can be part of a unifying overall activity (e.g., a treasure hunt, mystery or scientific field trip). For the display, the tag on each piece of paper can index into a common information space, and can also provide valuable context information in terms of previous displays visited (and activities at these) that can be used to shape and personalise their experience.

There are many possible approaches to interaction across different displays, for example, directly picking and dropping digital information (Rekimoto 1998). Our approach builds upon previous research in which paper has acted as the interface between the physical world and digital content. The Campiello project explored how different kinds of paper (tourist guides, maps, flyers and newspapers) could be associated with digital content (through computer-readable check boxes, stickers and DataGlyphs) and used to support community activities within a city (Grasso et al. 2000). In PaperLink, a highlighter augmented with a camera allowed people to manipulate digital information on physical paper (Arai et al. 1997). Others have focused on augmented desks (Wellner 1993) and books (Back et al. 2001) that mix paper with digital content.

These projects have been motivated in large part by some of the important features of paper: it is inexpensive, adaptable, foldable, annotatable, familiar, scaleable, durable, failsafe, shareable, legible, and portable. In our particular application, paper allowed the right kind of flexibility in the ordering of component activities (sheets could be shuffled); was easily shareable amongst a small group; was familiar to adults and children alike; was inexpensive and flexible as a medium for both writing and drawing; and could be taken away afterwards. In short, we felt that the use of paper as a portable artefact would address the exhibition specific requirements bulleted above while – with tagging technology – support the technical integration of an assembly of artefacts.

The History Hunt

We have tested our approach by creating a public exhibition in collaboration with Nottingham Castle Museum, a heritage site at which many significant historical incidents have occurred over several centuries. Our goal was to enable exploration of the complex 'layered histories' of this site, comparing key events across time and space. Our experience has taken the form of a 'history hunt', in which visitors explored the castle grounds, gathering clues and interacting with a number of displays, in an integrated, yet flexibly structured, activity that revealed historical events.

We designed and staged our public experience over the course of four months. The research process included consulting museum personnel over exhibit content and requirements. As many visitors are families or groups with children, we also staged a number of preliminary trials involving a head teacher and a class of 10 year-old school children. The final exhibition was open to the general public during a week in the summer of 2002.

The Historical Background

The castle was first built in 1067. Over the past millennium, various significant historical events have taken place at different locations around its site. Following the end of the English Civil War, the year 1651 marked the destruction of the Castle. Around 20 years later, the Duke of Newcastle built a Renaissance-like 'Ducal Palace' on the site of the castle remains. Notably, what is left on the site bears little relation to the more complex medieval castle. In order to give visitors some sense of the castle, the museum (now primarily housed in the newer building) employs various mechanisms and technologies such as slideshows, medieval artifacts with associated text, interactive kiosks, signposts, guides, brochures and textbooks. Nonetheless, museum staff are constantly searching for further ways to help visitors to understand the castle as it used to be, and the part it played in key historical events. As part of this process, previous work has exhibited the castle's medieval form as a 3D reconstruction accessed through a mobile location-sensitive display (Schnädelbach et al., 2002).

A Tour through the Experience

The history hunt involves two different kinds of activity. The first is searching the castle grounds for information about a key historical figure and recording this on paper. The second is electronically tagging the paper and using it to reveal more information about this figure at two interactive displays, the Storytent and the Sandpit. A typical experience unfolds as follows.

Arrival: Visitors arrive at a gazebo located near the main entrance to the Castle. They are given a pack of paper clues and informed that they are on the trail of a historical character who featured in a particular period of the castle's history (either Richard I or Edward III). There are three or four clues in each pack, and it is made clear that visitors can complete as many as they like in any order that suits.

Searching the grounds: The clues guide them to locations that feature in the story of their character. These places today often only minimally resemble their appearance in history. For example, the Castle Green, now an open area of grass, was once the location for a large building called the Great Hall. The clues ask visitors to record some information, either by drawing a key feature (e.g., an image of a sword on a wall, a bridge, a heraldic lion) or making a rubbing (the Green in particular has several engravings set into the paths for just this purpose).

Tagging the clues: the visitors return to the gazebo where a member of the project team attaches an RFID tag to each completed clue. The identity of each tag has already been associated with the unique combination of character and location for this clue (e.g., Richard I at the Gatehouse). It would be possible to pre-tag the paper clues before the experience. However, we opted for a manual process in this first attempt in order to reduce the number of tags required. This also created an opportunity to capture information from the visitors about the number of clues answered and to manage the flow of visitors to the next stage.

At the Gatehouse: the visitors now make their way to a room in the gatehouse where they encounter two different interactive displays that tell them more. The Storytent (Green et al., 2002) reveals a single scene related to each clue (e.g., a scene showing Richard I laying siege to the Gatehouse). The Sandpit allows visitors to dig for other pictures that are more broadly related to either the character or location associated with each clue (e.g., other images associated with either Richard I or with the Gatehouse).

Depart: visitors take their paper clues with them.

We now describe three essential elements of the experience in greater detail: the clues, the Storytent and the Sandpit.

Drawing on Paper Clues

Although all the clues in a pack could be assembled into a whole story, each clue was designed to be standalone so that visitors with little time did not need to complete all the clues to participate. The clues shared a common structure as shown in figure 1. The bottom section directed the visitor to a location around the castle, and instructed them to draw or rub an image of a prominent feature. The middle section provided space for this drawing or rubbing. The top section contained some further information written in ultraviolet ink so that it was not normally visible, but could be revealed under an ultraviolet light in the Storytent later on. A map of the castle grounds was copied on the reverse to help visitors navigate around the site. The RFID tag was attached to the reverse of the paper using a small Velcro tab to allow re-use.

On occasion, clues were scanned and reused as part of the content of the Sandpit so that visitors might encounter previous visitors' drawings.

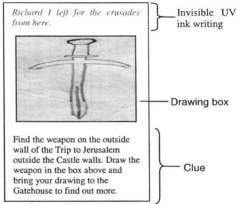

Figure 1: Paper layout design for clue

Revealing Scenes in the Storytent

The Storytent is a projection screen in the form of an A-frame tent (see figure 2). Two projectors throw different, but synchronized, images onto its surfaces while surrounding speakers play out sounds. Visitors can either sit inside the tent or stand outside in order to view its images. The overall effect is to establish a more personal and intimate space inside the tent, set within a larger, more public space outside, but with access to its information available from both.

Visitors entered the Storytent and placed their clues one at a time on a turntable device, a rotating platform that uses a potentiometer to sense its movement, contains an embedded RFID tag reader, and has an ultravoilet lamp pointing onto its surface (see figure 2 inset). The tag reader would then identify the clue and

186

load the corresponding images and sounds associated with its combination of character and location. One side of the tent would now display a 3D reconstruction of the Castle as it would have appeared at the time of this character, viewed from this particular location. Visitors could rotate the turntable in order to rotate their viewpoint within the model and so explore it in some more detail. The other side of the Storytent would display an image depicting a key event from history involving this character and this location. These images were usually taken from the museum's collection of paintings and tapestries. Ambient sounds relevant to the event would also be played.

Finally, the ultraviolet lamp just above the turntable would reveal the secret writing that tied the clue, the drawing made by visitors, the different images and sounds together. For example, on placing the clue for 'Richard I at the Gatehouse' on the turntable, the tent would display a 3D image of the Gatehouse as it would have appeared in his time, a 2D painting of him laying siege to the castle and play a battle sound. The secret writing would then explain how Richard fought a battle at this location to capture the castle back from his brother John.

Overall, there were seven different clues (four for the time of Richard I and three for the time of Edward III) that would trigger seven different scenes. The scenes could be viewed individually as stand-alone fragments, although the combination of scenes for each character would tell a complete story.

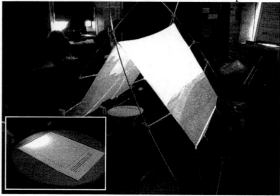

Figure 2: The Storytent, with close-up of the turntable interaction device with a clue placed on top

Sifting for Images in the Sandpit

Our second display, the Sandpit, is an interactive floor projection. Visitors stir up sand in order to sift for buried images. In this case, the sand is a graphical simulation and sifting is achieved by pointing the beams of flashlights at the image on the floor. The flashlight beams are video tracked in the manner of Green et al. (2002), so that each controls a cursor (a sparkling light) that appears to dig into the sand. After digging for while, visitors begin to uncover digital images that then move up to the surface before fragmenting, spinning around and disappearing (figure 3). Two flashlights can be used simultaneously, in which case visitors can more effectively dig together.

Next to the Sandpit is a small raised sandbox covering an RFID tag reader (figure 3 inset) Placing a tagged clue into the sandbox selects a set of images to be buried in the sand. These images are related either to the character or the location associated with the clue. The Sandpit generates sound for ambience and also feedback to indicate when a tagged clue has been recognised.

Figure 3: The Sandpit, with close-up of the sandbox device and a clue placed on top

The Sandpit was positioned in the gatehouse, opposite the tent, and separated from it by a distance of approximately two meters. The Storytent was configured so that the side showing the 2D images became the 'public facing' side, directly facing the sandpit (that displayed some of the same images). The side showing the 3D model was the more private side that was hidden away from the Sandpit.

These two displays have been designed to play complementary roles within the overall assembly that is the history hunt. In particular, they support different ways of accessing a common database of historical information. This database is organised as a time-space matrix, currently defined by two times (the times of Richard I and Edward III) and five locations (the Green, the Drawbridge, the Gatehouse, the Trip to Jerusalem Inn and a secret passage called Mortimor's Hole). Each clue indexes into one cell of this matrix (i.e., a specific combination of character and location). The Storytent focuses down on a particular event by retrieving and displaying information from this cell. The Sandpit on the other hand, suggests connections to other events by retrieving information from neighboring cells (same time or same location).

We now turn to an evaluation of the history hunt, focusing on how visitors were able to make connections between the different activities and displays.

Making Connections

Our exhibition was open to the public for three and a half days between 10am and 4pm. In that time, more than 200 visitors tried out the experience. Visitors ranged from individuals to groups of seven or eight; and from very young children to elderly citizens. Some participants completed all the clues, some completed only one or two.

We have conducted a qualitative analysis of the role of our paper clues in binding visitors' activities into a coherent experience. We have focused our analysis on audio-video recordings of the displays in the Gatehouse. Where possible, we have supplemented these with observation and further video recording of visitors exploring the grounds. We also asked some visitors (primarily children) to recount the stories that they had discovered after the experience.

Our primary analytic concern has been to look for evidence of whether visitors can understand and assemble a coherent experience through their use of the paper clues. We have focused in particular on the role of the clues in visitors making connection between their activities, the displays and the history of the museum. Our observations reveal three broad kinds of connections:

- **Activity connections:** associations made between the displays and visitors' activities from the exploration phase.
- **Event connections:** associations made between displays and historical events related to those activities.
- **Display connections:** associations made between displays.

These connection types are not mutually exclusive, nor are they entirely exhaustive. However, they do provide a useful vehicle to study how visitors assemble a coherent experience. In the following sections, we describe how such connections occur, illustrating this with examples from the Storytent and the Sandpit. Our illustrative examples primarily come from a single group: 'J' and 'L' are two 10-year old girls and their mother is 'C'. This group's interactions included many of the key connections we have repeatedly observed throughout the data.

Activity Connections

Activity connections are those made between the information revealed at the display, and the paper-based activities undertaken during the exploration phase. Our interest in activity connections lies primarily in finding out how important drawing and exploring were to the overall experience.

Activity connections were made frequently by almost all visitors. In the Storytent, such connections were made with both the 2D images projected on one side of the tent and the 3D views projected on its other side. For example, J and L are sitting in the tent watching the 3D view, and placing their clues onto the turntable (figure 4).

J: puts down clue with drawing of sword on Turntable

J: "Look there it is", as she points at the 3D Trip to Jerusalem on the side of the tent.

L: looks where J is pointing.

Figure 4: J (closest to camera) points out the connection between the 3D model and their drawing

As with the real inn, the 3D model of the Trip to Jerusalem has a sword hanging on the wall. It is unclear from the video whether J is pointing at the virtual sword itself (although this seems likely), or the inn as a whole. Nonetheless, J can animate the 3D graphic for L, at the same time showing that the 3D model bears a direct relationship to their earlier drawing activity. J is able to indicate a relationship between current and past activities to set the scene for L. We have also seen examples of visitors relating the 2D images presented on the tent to their activities during exploration.

Examples of activity connections also occurred frequently at the sandpit. In this case, J (on the right in figure 5) and L (on the left) are both using torches to uncover images in the sand. L's digging has uncovered the image of another child's drawing of a lion.

L: "There's the lion"

J: (inaudible)

C: "It's not as good as yours"

Figure 5: C points at the picture of a lion, saying to J "its not as good as yours"

C situates the appearance of the lion picture within the context of the group's own drawing activities. The comparison by C can also be heard as confirmation to the girls that this is not just any lion, it is indeed *the* lion, the lion of their drawing experiences. This last comment also reveals the value of the drawing. It is personalized, owned and worthy of comparison with others.

What is key to these examples is how important the activity of drawing on the clue is to making subsequent connections. The paper acts as both a record of activity and a reminder of the location of events depicted in using the displays.

Also, the act of drawing on the paper represents a significant investment in time and effort by visitors and they are rightly interested in obtaining a suitable reward for this. Our data repeatedly show that visitors entering the Gatehouse were keen to interact with technology so as to understand more about their clues (the first example in the Storytent above occurs immediately after the group has arrived at the gatehouse and entered the tent). There is a sense in which, by investing in their drawings, visitors buy into the experience at the outset. Rather than approaching the interactive displays cold, they are already 'playing the game' when they arrive at the Gatehouse and so may be better prepared to use the technology to make connections between different parts of the experience.

Event Connections

While activity connections are useful ways for visitors to make the experience more coherent, we were interested in whether and how visitors could make sense of the underlying historical events. Event connections go further than activity connections in the sense that they relate the paper clue and the information revealed at the display to the historical events being hunted.

Event connections occurred relatively often during the use of the displays, although generally they were not as common as activity connections. We found many examples of visitors making event connections for one another. In one example, three teenage children have just entered the tent. They begin by placing a clue on the Turntable and rotating the 3D view.

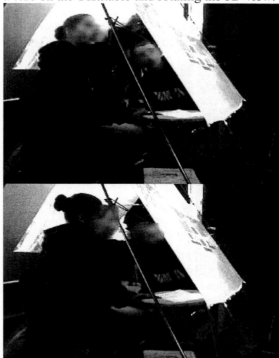

G: *"You can see it all - oh right so there's the castle, look - and so this'll be"*

B: *"Oh that's that pub"*

G: *"Yeh, that's the pub - so that's why ... Richard I set off from his crusades from here"*

Figure 6: a) G (closest) points at the virtual castle, saying "so there's the castle"
b) G points at the pub model, saying "yeah that's the pub"

As G rotates the view, the model of the castle comes into view and she points it out (figure 6a). As the group 'get their bearings', B points out that "that's that pub". G agrees (figure 6b) and now moves her gaze down to the Turntable to read the UV writing, "Richard I set off from his crusades from here".

Here we see a number of features of the Storytent being used to make event connections. The ability to rotate the 3D viewpoint provided by the turntable, combined with the recognizable features seen in the model, as well as the associated sound events, allow the participants to connect their activities to the history being depicted. The UV writing which is now revealed on the clue (the artefact that triggered this 3D information) then provides the critical link to the historical event.

The sandpit can also be used to make event connections via the relationships between the images buried in the sand. Although it provides a less direct relationship between the use of the paper clue and the events in question, visitors do discuss some images as they might relate to hunted historical events.

Let us return to the example of L, J and C at the sandpit: L and J are still digging in the sand. L uncovers a picture of King John I (Richard I's brother and rival) etched into a paving stone in the castle grounds. During their exploration, the girls have used a crayon to rub this image. The clue relates to the location of the Great Hall, where John was banished to France by Richard.

C: *"That's a rubbing isn't it. Down on the pavement wasn't it? On the Castle Green where the Great Hall was."*

Figure 7: Above left: making a rubbing of John. Below: C points with a clue, "that's a rubbing" as L uncovers the original engraving (top right) with her torch

Here C points to the emerging image of John (figure 7). Her comments to the girls describe a range of hints to the historical event. Firstly, she provides an activity connection, "that's a rubbing" to remind the girls of their initial use of the relevant paper clue. Secondly, she notes the location of the activity, "down on the pavement ... on the Castle Green". Finally, she describes what used to be located there in the time of Richard I: "where the Great Hall was".

Although the Sandpit and Storytent differ significantly in how they provide information, we see related activities in making event connections. The sandpit may also allow visitors to 'get their bearings'. In this example, C provides enough information for L and J to understand the elements of the historical circumstances.

Parents occasionally climb into the Storytent when in small family groups. However, some favor staying outside to allow their children to experience the display. This option may prevent parents from getting very involved and animating the historical event, often leaving the children to discover connections for themselves, supported by the UV writing (see Stanton et al. 2003). This example shows that, in contrast, the sandpit can be more open (in terms of both space for visitors, and the images shown), and therefore can provide parents such as C the opportunity to describe, reiterate and animate history through event connections.

However, there is less visible evidence that visitors were able to put together the 'bigger picture', i.e., to construct an overall narrative connecting events, locations and times of historical significance at the Castle. It was difficult to elicit this from casual visitors during the exhibition, for various reasons (e.g., them only completing one or two clues due to pressure of time, and dropping in and out at various points). It may be that by deliberately designing the clues to be 'standalone' so as to support a variety of visiting experiences, we ended up downplaying the relationships *between* events associated with different paper clues.

There were however, two opportunities to focus on this issue in more detail. One came from two formative evaluation sessions in which groups of children from a nearby school (not local and therefore unfamiliar with the Castle) participated in a school field trip prior to the pubic opening. These children (about 10 in each session) were given the clues in pairs, in random order. Once they returned to the gatehouse, they were asked to sequence the clues. They all achieved this successfully. They were then prompted, during their interaction with the Storytent, to explain what was going on in relation to the scenes they witnessed there. Given scaffolding from one of the project team, nearly all of the children managed to identify the 3D scenes with the actual locations visited, as well as their historical significance.

A second opportunity to evaluate this aspect of the exhibition came from monitoring 11 children who took part in the public experience (3 pairs and 2 groups of three, aged between 4 and 14 years). These children completed all of the clues. All bar one of the pairs (who were the youngest children) were able, with very little prompting, to construct accurate narratives linking the paper clues with the scenes they encountered using the Storytent. It seems that with some additional scaffolding, visitors are able to assemble an overall experience spanning multiple activities, clues and displays. We return to this issue below.

Display Connections

Display connections are those directly made between different displays in the exhibit. As noted above, we had aligned the Storytent so that the side showing the 2D images faced the Sandpit (that displayed some of the same images drawn from the shared database). We observed a few examples of visitors spotting connections between the images on the two displays. For example, when J first starts to use the Sandpit, she uncovers an image that had appeared on the 'public' side of the Storytent earlier while the group was waiting its turn. She states to L "that one's on there", making an (asynchronous) connection between the displays.

For the same image to appear on the Storytent and the Sandpit *at the same time* requires what seems like a fairly unlikely set of conditions to occur (the clue on the sandbox relates to the clue on the turntable; and the correct image is then uncovered at the Sandpit). Nonetheless, we have seen examples of visitors making immediate connections between the two displays. For example, J uncovers an image of Edward III's coat-of-arms at the same time as it is showing on the side of the tent. C (figure 8, rightmost in circle) turns to the tent, notices the coat-of-arms on display, and points to show J (figure 8, leftmost in circle).

C: "That's the same as on there look"

Figure 8: C points "that's the same as on there look"

In the example above, the visual association indicates that the group using the Storytent and the group using the Sandpit are both using clues for, and finding out about, Edward III. The connection made by C therefore presents at least the possibility to the girls that there is a deeper connection discoverable between the displays and possibly even between the groups of visitors. As a further note, display connections are almost always made while at the Sandpit as the tent is a more intimate and immersive environment that usually shields visitors aurally and visually from the majority of occurrences 'outside'.

Summary: Assembling the Bigger Picture

In summary, our analysis suggests that some features of the history hunt do support visitors in making connections between activities, displays, and historical events:

- the initial activity of making drawings and rubbings seems highly significant. Not only might it aid recall, but it enables visitors to invest in the experience before they reach the interactive displays.
- the use of the paper clues to directly trigger information on the displays may serve to emphasise connections. The displays further reinforce these by revealing more information on the paper clues (the Storytent) or showing other visitors' clues (the Sandpit).
- physical proximity combined with content drawn from a common database may help establish a sense that individual displays are part of a larger whole.

However, while making such connections may well be part of the overall work of assembling a coherent experience, our analysis suggests that more work needs to be done before visitors (certainly casual ones) are easily able to assemble the 'big picture', a sense of the clues connecting to an instructive episode of past history.

Discussion

In this paper we have described the assembly of technologies which we designed for an interactive exhibition at Nottingham Castle. In particular, we have highlighted how multiple displays and devices can be integrated into a coherent experience by the use of a simple familiar portable artefact – paper. This artefact not only enables related information to be retrieved and viewed in contrasting ways on different devices, it also allows that information to be related to the exploration of the site visitors had previously engaged with. In this sense, paper 'glues' together the technically mediated and 'on foot' parts of the visitors' experience as a series of historical events are revealed. Let us bring out explicitly a number of features of our analysis which may have further implications for the design of visitor experiences and more generally for the coherent integration of multiple public displays in cooperative settings.

Flexibility of Activity Organisation

Informed by relevant social scientific studies of visitors to interactive exhibits (e.g. vom Lehn et al. 2001, Heath et al. 2002, Hindmarsh et al. 2002), we set out to design an experience which could be engaged with in a variety of ways. We wished to support both single visitors and groups of varying sizes. We wished to accommodate visitors with varying amounts of time at their disposal. Also, we wished to provide something that would be engaging for inter-generational groups and which also might stimulate serious scholarly visitors. To accomplish this, we decided to organise the overall activity in an 'atomic' fashion. That is, one searched for clues which could vary in number depending upon one's available time or patience. A pack of clues could be dealt with more or less completely and in any order. It was not essential for one clue to be understood in sequence with any other. However, if multiple clues were investigated, a combined picture of historical events might (in principle) emerge in the understanding of the visitors. That is, the item-by-item, atomic nature of clues did not rule out people, in their understandings, combining the clues into some overall sense of the historical period. Indeed, we hoped the possibility that an understanding might emerge from particulars was further reinforced by the clue metaphor.

This approach could be contrasted with one where a narrative or some similar overall organisation is given to the experience such that one element needs to be encountered for subsequent ones to make sense. Although so-called 'non-linear' highly branching narratives can be devised which are flexible in their order of composition, we opted for the even more loosely structured approach of 'clues' to maximise flexibility in the face of the practical exigencies of working on-site under unpredictable conditions. Our experience of participatory events suggests that an approach with flexible technical structuring while allowing latitude for participants to themselves make, suggest or guess at connections has a lot to commend it.

However, it must be admitted, as discussed above, we did not note people spontaneously connecting together the clues to construct a historical narrative for themselves particularly frequently. This does not mean that we are forced to give up our flexible approach in favour of a more fixed narrative structure for activities. A possibility to examine in future work might be, for example, to identify a role for a human helper in engendering a historical narrative sense from given fragments (compare with the role that actors and invisible 'stage hands' had in the on-line participatory narrative described by Drozd et al. 2001). Alternatively, the clues or displays themselves might provide greater scaffolding by, for example, directly suggesting relationships to other clues or encouraging visitors to return outside to explore the site some more. However, this has to be balanced against meeting the needs of the short-term visitor.

Assembly as a Social Accomplishment, Technically Provided For

Our analyses of people interacting with the displays in the Castle Gatehouse have focussed on how people make various connections in their talk and gesture as they engage with the displays and devices we have set before them. Visitors make connections between the activities they have been engaged in while exploring the site, the historical events that occurred at those various locations, and invisible writing, images, sounds and 3D models which are presented at the Gatehouse. Through making these connections, participants assemble some sense of the history of the site and how they have hunted it down during their visit. Naturally, the depth and sophistication of this sense varies between visitors, in relation to their interests and whatever they have actually done during their visit. The point here is that in assembling such understandings participants are assembling relations between different displays, devices and the site itself. In this sense, 'assembling' is a practical social interactional accomplishment which is technologically provided for (cf. Hindmarsh et al. 2002).

Such sense-assembling *activities* are supported by an organised collection of technologies – an assembly in the *technical* meaning. We wished to combine displays and devices in a systematic fashion to enable visitors to create a coherent visiting experience for themselves. The manner in which we did this is, we believe, instructive and worthy of investigation in other contexts. We provided a sense of a *unifying overall activity* with an underlying *common information space* explored using an *assembly of interactive displays* which manifest *common interaction techniques* and are integrated by means of a simple *portable artefact*. We do not wish this to be thought of as a universal recipe for getting technologies to interwork coherently in public settings regardless of the details of the application domain. Rather, it highlights five areas of design concern which would need to be addressed in realising a particular strategy for experience design – one where activities are flexibly structured and latitude is recognised for participants to develop their own sense of what is going on.

Paper

Our 'portable artefact' is none other than paper. We have exploited a number of features of paper in our work: its portability, shareability, familiarity, its ability to be a medium for drawing and so on. These features have been written about in the CSCW, HCI and allied literatures before. What is more novel with our approach is how we use paper artefacts to integrate a variety of devices and displays in a flexible fashion. By attaching tags, pieces of paper can be used to configure devices and retrieve information and, because a common information space has been used, this enables subtle relations between displays to be noticed and explored, at least in principle.

In a sense, we are rediscovering a well-known feature of paper but are drawing less common design conclusions from it. It is often noted that people make use of paper for swift and convenient note-taking while working with information displays (cf. Luff et al. 1992). Such written paper notes can then be consulted when a fresh screen-full of information appears rather than rely on memory, or be carried to other, physically distant displays to enable their contents to be compared. This enduring use of paper to support the juxtaposition of display contents is often taken as an indication of the requirements portable digital artefacts (PDAs, digital paper and such like) have to meet or the applications which are worth developing for them. Our current work has a different orientation (see also Mackay 2000). Rather than design advanced portable artefacts on the basis of what we know about how paper is used, we have used paper itself to support the coherent integration of assemblies of advanced technologies (cf. Grasso et al. 2000).

The portability of paper could be further exploited in encouraging reflection and assembly of a sense of the history of the Castle off-site after the visit. For example, a class back in school could use the clues to assemble the bigger historical picture as an interactive wall display for the classroom. Children back at home could create an interactive storybook so that they could recount their visit to family and friends. Such further assembly would require developing new interactive displays: walls and desks for the classrooms and interactive books and souvenirs for the home. Eventually these might also exploit the electronic tagging of the clues, although in the short term it would be easier and more cost effective for the clues to also contain manual links to the digital content (for example, URLs for accessing the 2D and 3D images from the museums website). In these and other ways, we can think of deepening our exploitation of interactionally relevant features of paper in simultaneously supporting the interworking of technology and human sense-making activities.

CSCW and Designing for Museum Settings

Increasingly CSCW research is broadening its purview beyond work settings narrowly conceived to study cooperative activity in leisure, domestic and entertainment settings. Our work is consistent with this trajectory in its concern for a public setting where leisure-related and educational activities take place. However, we believe that investigation of such settings brings issues of general importance to CSCW into focus. How to combine a variety of information displays and interaction devices in an integrated fashion is a matter of general concern and not confined to museum settings. How to technically support activities coherently while flexibly allowing participants to manage local contingency has been a core CSCW issue at least since the early days of groupware and structured computer-mediated communication systems (cf. Bowers and Churcher 1988). Here, we are attempting to strike a balance between technical provision and giving participants resources with which they can assemble their own sense-making activities – a notion of what 'computer support' might mean in CSCW of more general applicability. We have worked with rich digital materials and physical interaction techniques in relation to a real historical site. As such our work furthers the concern in CSCW for 'mixed reality' research. However, we have been most conscious of the practical exigencies of bringing such technologies into the wild and, accordingly, developed a use of paper as a means for bridging mixed reality design with intelligible public experience. In all these respects, museums are far from being institutions frozen in the past but offer CSCW timely research opportunities of genuine technical, conceptual and practical value.

Acknowledgments

The work reported in this paper comprised the first 'Living Exhibition' of the SHAPE project funded by the Disappearing Computer initiative of the European Community's FET IST programme. We would like to thank all of our SHAPE colleagues for their invaluable contributions. We would also like to thank Denny Plowman and all Nottingham Castle Museum staff for their help and support for our work. We are also very grateful to Ella Roberts and the staff and children of Outwards Edge Primary School for participating in the design workshops and helping to create the history hunt.

References

Aoki, P. & Woodruff, A. (2000). Improving Electronic Guidebook Interfaces Using a Task-Oriented Design Approach, Proc. DIS 2000, 319-325, ACM Press.

Arai, T., Aust, D and Hudson, S. (1997). PaperLink: A technique for hyperlinking from real paper to electronic content, Proc. CHI 97, Atlanta, GA, ACM Press.

Back, M., Cohen, J., Gold, R., Harrison, S., Minneman, S. (2001). Listen reader: an electronically augmented paper-based book, Proc. CHI 01, 23-30, Seattle, WA, ACM Press.

198

Benelli, G., Bianchi, P, Marti, E., Not, E. & Sennati, D. (1999). HIPS: Hyper-interaction within physical space, Proc. International Conference on Multimedia Computing and Systems, 1075-1078, Florence, Italy, IEEE.

Bitgood, S. (1991). Hands-on, participatory and interactive exhibits, Visitor Behavior, 6, 4, 14-17.

Bowers, J. and Churcher, J. (1988). Local and Global Structuring of Computer Mediated Communication. Proc. CSCW 1988, Portland, OR , ACM Press.

Bowers, J. & The SHAPE Consortium (2001). TONETABLE: A Multi-User, Mixed-Media, Interactive Installation, Proc. Digital Audio Effects (DAFX-01), Limerick, Ireland.

Büscher, M., Hughes, J., Trevor, J., Rodden, R., O'Brien, J. (1999). Supporting cooperation across shared virtual environments, Proc. GROUP'99, November 1999, ACM Press.

Caulton, T. (1998). Hands-on exhibitions, London: Routledge, 1998.

Ciolfi, L., Bannon, L. and Fernström, M., Envisioning & Evaluating "Out-of-Storage" Solutions, in ICHIM (1), 595-607, 2001.

Grasso, A, Karsenty, Susani, M. (2000). Augmenting paper to enhance community information sharing, in Proc. DARE 2000, 51-62, Elsinore, Denmark, ACM Press.

Green, J., Schnädelbach, H., Koleva, B., Benford, S., Pridmore, T. and Medina, K. (2002). Camping in the Digital wilderness: tents and flashlights as interfaces to virtual worlds, in Proc. ACM CHI 2002 Conference Abstracts, 780-781, ACM Press.

Grinter, R., Aoki, P., Hurst, A., Szymanski, M., Thornton, J., and Woodruff, A. (2002). Revisiting the Visit: Understanding How Technology Can Shape the Museum Visit. In Proc. CSCW 2002, New Orleans, USA, ACM Press.

Heath, C., Luff, P., vom Lehn, D., Hindmarsh, J. and J. Cleverly (2002). Crafting Participation: Designing ecologies, configuring experience. Visual Communication, 1, 1, 9-34.

Hindmarsh, J., Heath, C., vom Lehn, D., Hindmarsh, J. and J. Cleverly (2002). Creating Assemblies: Aboard the Ghost Ship. In Proc. CSCW 2002, New Orleans, USA, ACM.

Hood, M. (1983). Staying Away: Why people choose not to visit museums, Museum News, 61, 4, 50-57.

Luff, P., Heath, C. and Greatbatch, D. (1992). Tasks-in-interaction: paper and screen based documentation in collaborative activity, Proc. CSCW 1992, Toronto, Ontario, Canada.

Mackay, W.E. (2000). Is Paper Safer? The Role of Paper Flight Strips in Air Traffic Control. ACM Transactions on Computer-Human Interaction, 6, 4, 311-340, ACM Press.

Schnädelbach, H., Koleva, B., Flintham, M., Fraser, M., Chandler, P., Foster, M., Benford, S., Greenhalgh, C., Izadi, S. and Rodden, T. (2002. The Augurscope: A Mixed Reality Interface for Outdoors, in Proc. ACM CHI 2002, 9-16, ACM Press.

Rekimoto, J. (1998). Multiple-Computer User Interfaces: a Cooperative Environment Consisting of Multiple Digital Devices, Proc. CoBuild98, 33-40, Heidelberg: Springer.

Stanton, D., O'Malley, C., Fraser, M., Ng, K-H. and Benford, S., Situating Historical Events through Mixed Reality: Adult-Child Interactions in the Storytent, to appear in *Proc. CSCL 2003*, Bergen, Norway.

vom Lehn, D., Heath, C. and J. Hindmarsh (2001). Exhibiting Interaction: Conduct and Collaboration in Museums and Galleries, Symbolic Interaction, 24, 2, 189-216.

Want, R., Fishkin, K., Gujar, A., Harrison, B. (1999). Bridging Physical and Virtual Worlds with Electronic Tags, Proc. CHI 99, Pittsburgh, ACM Press.

Weiser, M. (1993). Some Computer Science Issues in Ubiquitous Computing, Communications of the ACM, 36, 7, 75-84, ACM Press.

Wellner, P. (1993). Interacting with paper on the Digital Desk, Communications of the ACM, 36, 7, 87-96, 1993, ACM Press.

K. Kuutti, E.H. Karsten, G. Fitzpatrick, P. Dourish and K. Schmidt (eds.), *ECSCW 2003: Proceedings of the Eighth European Conference on Computer Supported Cooperative Work, 14-18 September 2003, Helsinki, Finland*, pp. 199-218.

Learning and living in the 'New office'

Eva Bjerrum & Susanne Bødker

Centre for New Ways of Working, University of Aarhus, Denmark

(ebjerrum, bodker)@daimi.au.dk

Abstract. 'Knowledge sharing' and 'learning' are terms often connected with the 'New office', the "modern" open office space. Work in these settings becomes more and more distributed, mobile and characterised by temporary constellations of collaborators. The workers are mobile and work wherever they are. Based on nine case studies, this paper describes how the 'New office,' intended to support learning and peripheral participation often gets directly counterproductive to this purpose. It lacks places to dwell and return to, places to meet coincidentally, shared artefacts and possibilities of leaving traces of current and past activities. These problems are due to a combination of problematic architecture and insufficient technology, and not least to insufficient design processes, where the actual needs of the people in the organisation are rarely considered, and where people are rarely involved in the design and introduction processes. Through exploratory design we have pursued ways of improving legitimate peripheral participation, through architecture, physical artefacts and materials in the rooms as well as through virtual extensions of these artefacts, in order to explore alternatives and raise further research questions regarding 'the new office'.

Introduction

Our starting point in this paper is that CSCW has analysed and conceptualised many cooperative artefacts, though never the "modern" open office space, that are dominating discussions of new ways of working, flexible offices and the learning organization. It is our basic suspicion that many organizations introduce open, flexible office solutions to support learning, yet it seems that they are often running the risk of throwing the baby out with the bath water - of neglecting some of the mechanisms that make learning and peripheral participation happen. They implement office design in a way that is contradicting to how CSCW views cooperation as basis for learning and knowledge sharing, and hence the actual office design becomes counterproductive to the ideas as such.

'Knowledge sharing' and 'learning' are terms often connected with the 'New office', the "modern" open office space. At the same time as offices move from hallways to open spaces, work in these settings becomes more and more distributed and mobile. The workers are "always on" and able/demanded to work wherever they are. Work is increasingly characterised by temporary constellations of collaborators because people work in projects, and because people move about between employments much more than previously (Sennett 1998, Nardi et al. 2000). Traditionally, office workspace has been designed to fit with the organizational hierarchy, regarding location, size as well as furniture. Office design was mostly seen as a cost, a way to support quiet work and show people's status. This way of thinking lives on, and is in many ways conflicting with the demands from more recent ways of organizing work. Hence, there are many good reasons for rethinking the workplace design to support work as it actually takes place in the office.

The ideas and theories behind the *'New office'* are as follows: (Raymond & Cunliffe, 1997) describe the purposes of the new office as to attract and retain staff and to revolutionize corporate culture. Administrative work must take place in different work settings emphasizing learning and overhearing of the activities of others. Flexibility is essential for learning, and *"flexible working needs flexible settings, places that can change to accommodate whatever is happening now or tomorrow"* (p.2).

Worthington et al. (1998) focus on different activities and functions and divide the workplace into different types of rooms. Their typological model, called "The responsible workplace model", distinguishes four basic types of offices - hives, dens, cells and clubs - based on different levels of interaction and autonomy. The dens for group processes, the hives for individual process work, the club for transactional knowledge work and the cell for concentrated study. In their definition, the new workplace consists of shared open spaces for interaction and communication, shared offices for confidentiality and concentration, project rooms for teamwork, café areas for informal meetings, external and internal meeting rooms, mobile and modular furniture, as well as wireless LANs and a variety of mobile technologies. Myerson & Ross (1999) use four key themes to describe the new office: Team, Exchange, Community and Mobility; team offices which encourages team-building and group working; exchange offices which promote sharing and presentation of knowledge; community offices designed for greater social cohesion and mobility offices, designed for work everywhere. Many of the theories behind the new office are focussing on designing space and rooms to support particular activities and work processes.

We welcome these new initiatives: The idea that you can choose a setting depending on the task you're working on; the idea that a workplace is an important meeting place for flexible workers; and the idea that you can easily get in touch with your co-workers, cooperate and share knowledge.

Whereas, however, ideas and theories behind the 'New office' are challenging and exciting, everyday living and learning in the 'New office' is often much more problematic as we shall see in the following. And the appropriate technology is indeed lacking behind.

Empirical background

Centre for New Ways of Working does research on office workspace and technology from a perspective that emphasises the intertwined nature of organisation, physical space and technology. The research is action-oriented, interdisciplinary, and analytical as well as design-oriented.

Title	Resources/duration	Purpose	Methods
C1.Engineering company	3 months	Exploratory design of CSCW	Observations, interviews, workshops, video proto-types
C2. Design firm	3 months	Exploratory design of AR technology	Observations, interviews, workshops, video proto-types
C3. Telecom industry	1 year, 55 subjects	Analysis of work patterns	Registration of work patterns Interviews
C4. County office	6 months 26 subjects	Analysis of work patterns Mobile work and technology	Observations, Registration of work patterns Interviews Workshops
C5. The State Agency	Several visits	Example material for book	Interviews
C6. Research organization	Long-term study	Analysis of work patterns Design of new building	Registration of work patterns Interviews Workshops
C7. Dot.com	Long term study 1 month per year	Knowledge management	Observation interviews workshops
C8. Advertise-ment bureau	Visit	Example material for book	Interviews
C9. Professional organization	Several visits	Example material for book	Interviews

Figure 1. Case studies – work setting of each case described in figure 2

The paper is based on several empirical studies of modern office space and office buildings, in particular such that are claimed to be "new" or even "innovative", and it will draw on examples from these studies when necessary. These studies are of a varying nature – from yearlong empirical investigations combined with participatory redesign of technologies and spaces, to one-day site visits and accompanying interviews with key persons (see figure 1 for overview of cases). Common to the studies, however, is the overlaps in methods that make it possible for us to compare across studies, qualitatively and to some extent quantitatively. It is these comparisons that form the basis for the examples used in the paper. Hence our references to the cases must be seen as examples of more general findings, rather than as solitary empirical findings.

Furthermore, the paper will draw on our past studies of more traditional office settings (see e.g. Trigg & Bødker 1994) and our own exploration of ways of working and IT-support in an open flexible office, that was set up for exploration in our own physical and organisational environment. This open, flexible office constitutes a microcosm (Engeström 1987) in which we

- gain our own experiences with working in a flexible environment,
- draw on experiences from the case studies to explore the relevance of the experiences gained in the flexible office,
- in particular we explore various CSCW technologies to understand the possibilities of supporting awareness and cooperation in the office,
- and we use those experiences to raise further questions to the case studies (bringing experiences from the microcosm to more general real-world settings).

The use of the flexible office is developed through a participatory process including regular office meetings where problems are dealt with and discussed and prototyping experiments to explore cooperation possibilities in the office.

CSCW and the office

In a certain way, the interest in offices among CSCW researchers started before CSCW, not least with the studies of Suchman & Wynn (1984) of procedures and problems in the office. In these studies, they pointed out how much work in, what at first glance seemed to be highly routinised office settings, is based on joint problem solving, based on the peripheral overseeing and overhearing of the work of co-workers in the office. Since then, surreptitious monitoring has been found in many settings to be the basis for learning and knowledge sharing. In these processes it is equally well demonstrated that it is through the joint access to materials and artefacts that these processes take place as much as it is through conversation (Wagner et al. 1999, Robinson 1993). Teasley et al. (2000) in particular point out how 'at a glance' visibility of a permanent record of group activity and decisions is essential for teams working in shared large workspace.

In her book about the development of office technology, Yates (1989) points out how such technologies, by structuring and enabling communication have made distributed organisations possible.

In some ways, the "new" office technologies are a continuation of these developments. Shared electronic document repositories are a continuation of the advanced, yet individual and paper-based, desks that Yates describes, and wireless laptops and mobile telephones an extension of the communication technologies that made distributed organisations possible.

Title	
C1.Engineering company	The Engineering Company is located in a new building with a perfect view from most windows. The public areas of the building consist of a reception, stairways, café areas, and cafeteria area with meeting rooms. The office space consists of two floors of open-space office with flexible quiet/meeting rooms to one side. For the majority of people they have their own desk somewhere in the open space, together with other people from their group or project. Desks are moved when necessary. Managers have desks in the open space as well. People have regular PCs. Some people use CAD stations with larger computer screens and a small number of laptops are available. The network and the telephones are stationary. Materials are kept on shelves. There are hardly any pin boards anywhere, and there are whiteboards only in the meeting rooms. The company is continuously experimenting with the use of their office space, hence they experimented with open offices before they moved into this building, and they are continuing to experiment.
C2. Design firm	The office is the home of three independent industrial designers and a similar number of hired staff. The office space is open, and filled with models, mock-ups and materials. People move about, and change the location of their work, partly as a result of the task they are doing and the tools they need, and partly when they change between the projects that they are working on. The CAD workstations used are not movable, and hence are in some ways determining where certain tasks take place. People cooperate around projects, and move between places as they move in and out of discussions or situations of practical cooperation. The designers use the stuff left in the office space to seek inspiration from past projects, and visitors are left in no doubt what the firm is doing and which projects they are proud of.
C3. Telecom industry	A department with 55 people is placed in 6 different locations. The company wanted to make a new office design to obtain increased knowledge sharing and cooperation and they wanted to implement a strategy for flexible working arrangements. In all 6 places the employees were placed in a traditional office environment with hallways and offices. Most of the technical solutions were stationary although most of the employees were flexible workers.
C4. County office	The Office is currently located in two different locations, each with traditional hallways and individual offices. People work on a variety of matters regarding the relationship between the county and local business: tourism and EU lobbyism are two such instances. The County office has flexible working hours and some people travel extensively and work from a distance (Figure 6). At the same time all employees use the same PC platform. This causes problem to e.g. the EU lobbyists who need to exchange electronic documents with numerous agencies, which typically use Microsoft products. It is typical to the Office, that while each employee cooperates with many people outside the office, there is little cooperation between employees in the office (Bjerrum & Brinckman, 2001).
C5. The State Agency	In the State Agency's new building there are 450 employees The Agency moved into a new building a year ahead of our studies. This building was planned with new office design. The main idea was to gain increased knowledge sharing, increased efficiency and more flexibility. The office is dominated by big open spaces. Most of the employees own their desks, 30 work at different places in a hotelling concept. In the building there are 36 meeting and project rooms. Some people use laptops and some stationary PCs. There are project rooms, hives or offices and café areas spread all over the building. There are no colours (except for the clothes the employees are wearing) and there is nothing on the walls – no paintings or whiteboards - because the house rules prevent that.
C6. Research organization	The research organization is now placed in a traditional office environment with hallways and offices. The organization manages research cooperation between universities and industry. The plans for the new building are to make a range of different solutions for different people and work processes. There will be room for group work, individual work, formal and informal meetings. Everybody will have his or her own desks. There will be no rules except that people can fill the walls and desks with projects and paintings - both professional and personal stuff. Rooms will be equipped with whiteboards and pin boards. Wireless networks will be in place, and telephone arrangements are currently investigated.

C7. Dot.com	The Company is an internet start-up that has emerged out of a more traditional IT-firm. It is placed in an old building with a large staircase in the middle. There are 25 employees placed in open spaces all the way through. They all have their own desk and most have laptops and cellular phones. There are no white boards or pin boards except in the meeting room. The company builds knowledge management software and is concerned with the knowledge sharing in the company itself.
C8. Advertisement bureau	This bureau has created a workplace like a home from the seventies in an apartment with children's room, kitchen, and living room – even a cocktail cabinet. All the employees have laptops and cellular phones. The price for a worked through concept is a lack of white board and pin boards and personal stuff.
C9. Professional organization	The professional organization with 100 employees moved into a new building in 1999. The employees are all placed in open spaces all the way through - except for the management who launched the idea. The idea was to mix different cultures and increase knowledge sharing but also with a focus on interior design. There was an enormous resistance towards the ideas in the new building especially from the development department. The Development Departments answer to the New Office was to create "offices" with a lot of walls in the open space. The professional organisation is now in the middle of a reorganization of the workplace. They are prepared to start all over again and this time they involve all the employees in the process.

Figure 2. Case work settings. Most cases are documented further in Bjerrum & Nielsen (in press)

When it comes to learning in this perspective we find Lave & Wenger's (1991) definition of learning as legitimate peripheral participation useful, because it emphasizes what the main argument for the 'new office' is about: learning and peripheral participation in activities of other people in the room. The concept of legitimate peripheral participation emphasizes the social nature of learning, and the potentiality as well as actuality of being located in a physical and organizational space. In continuation of the same line of thought we see knowledge not as a commodity, or object that can be placed in the common space to be shared, but as deeply process-oriented and interpersonal (Nonaka & Takeuchi, 1995). Activity theory and distributed cognition are other relevant theories that we find of greater importance if we move on to an analysis of shared artefacts and representations in the office (see e.g. Bertelsen & Bødker, 2001, Bødker et al. 2001 or Olson et al. 1998).

Nardi et al. (2000) point out that knowledge workers are becoming increasingly dependent on personal knowledge networks across organisational boundaries and physical locations. In the current societal condition workers are furthermore expected to move between places and locations of work, rather that to spend their lives as a "company man" (or woman) (Sennett, 1998). Because of the ongoing moving about, the responsibility of learning is increasingly put in the hands of individual participants (Nardi et al. 2000) and their personal networks whereas the role and mechanisms of the organization of supporting collective learning, to knowledge maintenance and innovation are loosing out.

Bødker & Christiansen (2002) develop the connection between place, identity, materials and learning, what they call dwelling, by pointing out that it is important to dwell in order to develop routines and to learn. Dwelling means that one is able to move and come back, to repeat what one is doing. Such dwelling is the starting point of imagining something different. In other words to have an environment that is recognizable is an element of developing routines, and routines, even in the flexible work setting is a precondition for legitimate participation. Routines are preconditions for innovation, for creating something new (Engeström 1987).

Harrison & Dourish (1996) talk about the importance of place as well as space. Suchman (1993, 1996) describes how airport workers create such places, as centres of coordination to orient in a large, unstructured physical space. Bertelsen & Bødker (2001) discuss a case where learning and knowledge sharing is connected to movement in a large but well-defined physical space (a waste water plant).

These perspectives will be applied in the following to analyse findings from our studies of the 'New office' design.

Findings from the field

Our studies of office space and interviews with decision makers show that the *main reason* for implementing new office design is the wish for increased learning and collaboration among managers and employees. As we shall see from the following, we find in our cases different solutions, which do not support:

- Rendering work and activities visible.
- Learning through other means that hearing.
- Participation while away.
- Mobility.
- Transition between locations and cooperative situations.

In the following we will describe these finding through different examples from our different cases (Figure 1) and a more detailed presentation in Figure 2. For pedagogical reasons and to allow us to go into some level of detail, we shall use some of the cases as more dominating examples than others. This is not because they are particularly better or worse than others.

Rendering work and activities visible

New office buildings, such as the State Agency (C5) or the Engineering Company (C1), are often very anonymous. They all look the same and they all look very nice. The office building and the office design rarely show the company story, they do not show to customers whether they have entered an auditing firm or an engineering company.

There are exceptions to this, e.g. the Advertisement Bureau (C8). It is awful but has been useful in many ways because it shows identity and a certain style for customers and employees to identify with. However, this is primarily a matter of branding and not of asking whether employees feel comfortable working in the kitchen or the children's room (Figure 3).

One matter, however, is a building not showing the history or company vision or product to outsiders, another is people in the building and their professional and personal identity.

Figure 3. Showing corporate identity

The new office buildings are often characterized by very restrictive "exhibition" rules (E.g. C5). People are not allowed to show their sketches or pictures at the walls. The architects or the management are afraid that people will put up stuff that will remove a nice general impression. That it will be pure disorder and anarchy, as one manager said (C1, similar statements from C7).

We recently visited a company where they had the following rules for *good* conduct in an open space (figure 4).

A common rule is a "clean desk policy" that requires from workers, whether they have a permanent desk or not, to clean up their desk every day. Hence, they are prevented from leaving "stuff" around that reminds others or themselves of what they do, here and now, or over time. This type of clean desk policy is in harsh contrast to the piles of material found in creative offices of designers (Wagner 1999, and C2), but also to what we find by a simple at a glance inspection of a random office section in a university department or a research organization such as C6.

> - Abandoned cellular phones will be removed.
> - You'll have to clear your desk even if you come back the next day.
> - Common areas and quiet places must be cleared after use. Take care to make them presentable. Remove paper, binders and other unnecessary materials.
> - Don't place things on the top of the bookcases.

Figure 4. House rules - good conduct

Even if there is no strict clean desk policy, the open space impression is very important and our cases show that whiteboards and pin boards are rare (see e.g. the Engineering Company, C1). And the house rules further reinforce our impression that the buildings look the same. The office design looks the same. The furniture looks the same. The empty walls look the same. There are very few, stable "landmarks" in the office landscape. It is difficult to know where one has to locate oneself to casually meet somebody, and even more importantly, creating what Suchman (1993, 1996) calls "centres of coordination" – places to coordinate with other people, e.g. in a open landscape such as, in the case of Suchman (1993, 1996) an airport tarmac.

The empty desks and walls make it virtually impossible to share "stuff" while working in the office. The moving about, the clean desks and lack of information on the walls are counterproductive to sheer coordination: When walking through the office landscape it is difficult to sample impressions of who is doing what, and hence be a legitimate peripheral participants in projects and topic areas other than your own. This means that unless a person happens to be located in hearing distance, it is necessary to turn to the company intranet to identify a person working on a particular topic. We conclude that there is a tendency that new office designs are driven by architects' focus on a particular kind of anonymous aesthetics more than by people's need for dwelling, i.e. occupying a space, individually or together, and for showing their work and personality.

Learning through other means than hearing

As described above, the open office is one where whiteboards and pin boards are rare, and where there are few other places for projects or teams to post material for mutual monitoring of a process or for mutual creation of a product. In our perspective on learning, the open office has on the one hand a lot of potential for being the centre of a lot of legitimate peripheral participation. This is by virtue of being open and flexible so as to allow for moving nearer to where things happen and to allow for overhearing and over-seeing. Yet, conversation requires co-locatedness in time. In particular, the lack of shared artefacts, such as sketches and drawings makes legitimate peripheral participation difficult. Accordingly it appears to be an assumption behind the new office design that learning is entirely an effect of talking and listening, which we propose that it is not (see Bødker & Graves Petersen 2000).

Furthermore, the functional spaces are equally separated by house rules - you may start a conversation in the common quiet area, but in order to continue, the co-operation needs to move elsewhere. A discussion may start in the café area, but due to the lack of shared artefacts there (whiteboards or computers) a focussed discussion need to move to a meeting room. Teasley et al. (2000) mention nine kinds of work taking place in a software design team and focus, similar to us, on the transitions that happen between those.

Trailing after the open office design, the newest trend is the establishment of a new type of rooms, called "innovation rooms" or "experimental rooms". In such rooms, you get all the gadgets and offbeat objects that lack in the rest of the anonymous offices (Figures 5 and 6). You can walk into a specific room to be creative, to brainstorm, to play or to write on the ceiling.

Figure 5. Brainstorm room   Figure 6. Working/meeting

We suspect that the need for such add-ons is symptoms of the lack of learning, creativity and knowledge sharing in the open office. And we worry that these rooms are exaggerations that add yet another place with artificial rules where one needs to behave in certain ways - creative ideas don't always show up because you make an untraditional design of a room. Rather, in our cases we find that people use posters and materials from past projects, etc. (e.g. the Design Firm, C2). These innovation rooms are different from the "war rooms" described by Teasley et al. (2000), because the war rooms are not 'add-ons' but part of an integrated strategy where people are continuously located in the room, with a documented effect on productivity, learning and cooperation.

Participation while away

In three case studies (the Telecom Industry, C3 the Research Organisation, C6 and the County Office, C4) we have looked at workplace and location of activities. The participants registered their working patterns and locations for a period of 7 weeks; the study involved 55, 24 and 17 participants respectively. In all cases there was a span of working patterns, from very few people spending all their working hours at the workplace (typical secretaries) to mobile people spending most of their time outside the workplace working through a combination of mobile work, external meetings and working from home (Example working patterns in figures 7 and 8). Our studies show that people in general only are in their office half their working time. In different national institutions the utilization of a workplace was measured four times a day (within normal working hours). The conclusion of the Building Management of the Danish State was that the workplace in general is used less than 50% of the time (Mosbech, 2001). Observations of hundreds of cases show that office workplaces are rarely occupied for more than one third of the time that they are available even during the core eight-hour working day (Duffy 2000).

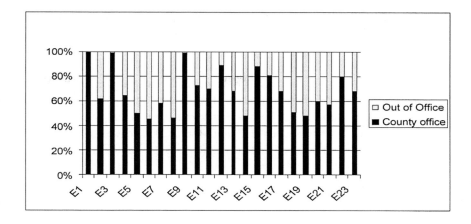

Figure 7. Working patterns – C4. The X-axis represents 23 employees. The Y-axis represents 100 pct. working time accumulated over 8 weeks

The differences in working patterns show the need for rethinking the workplace. It is obvious that mobile and non-mobile workers don't need the same office solutions, roomwise, or with respect to furniture and technology. They need different choices, e.g. with respect to "owning a desk", with respect to mobile, wireless or traditional telephones, and with respect to computers. In C4, where the highly mobile EU lobbyist may desire an advanced mobile telephone and a laptop with wire-

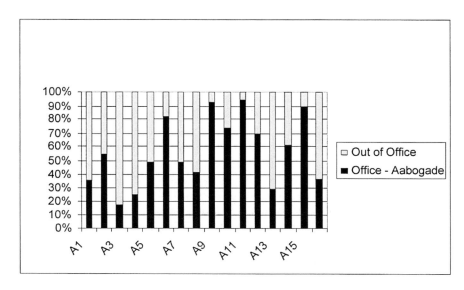

Figure 8. Working patterns - C6. The X-axis represents 23 employees. The Y-axis represents 100 pct. working time accumulated over 5 weeks

less Internet connection, the secretary may have greater need for a desk with a stationary PC and a large computer screen. And while the secretary may be content with sharing document formats inside the walls of the County, this is highly insufficient for the EU lobbyist.

Our studies further show that the more people are away, the more important their workplace is. They enjoy the qualities of place when they are there, and they need a workplace where it is possible to get both a professional and social contact to colleagues. This is in essence what Bødker & Christiansen (2002) call dwelling. They point out how too much movement and too much change in the surroundings prevent routines in developing, be they routines by which work can be left for later, similar matters dealt with at a later instance, or conversations to be left for later. In many ways, the familiarity of the surroundings is a precondition of learning.

Transition between locations and situations

Through the emphasis on functional space (e.g. dens, hives, club, cell) (Wortington et al. 1998) the new offices at a first glance seem to support casual encounters as well as focused ones. However, if we look at the Engineering Company (C1), the café, intended for casual encounters, has neither whiteboards nor tabletop space. Accordingly, people may start a casual conversation in the café, but there are no means there for changing this into more focused work. Hence, people need to move to a meeting room to continue such focused affairs. This is indeed a transition in type of work (Teasley et al. 2002) or mode of cooperation (Simone & Schmidt, 1996) that leads to a transition in location. Similarly, in the open office, people may pass by somebody's desk and ask a question, e.g. regarding a CAD drawing on the person's screen. However, a more detailed conversation cannot continue there without disturbing the rest of the office. And materials are not easily moved away from the CAD screen and into the meeting room. The only thing that can be moved is the entire desk with its telephone, PC and everything else.

While the different modes of cooperation may be supported in various physical locations, the transitions between casual and focussed suffer from the physical separation of places, and the artefacts available for cooperation in those places. We are not arguing that e.g. cafés should be jammed with boards and computers. We are considering how transitions can be supported, and e.g. how electronic documents may be carried from one location to another, and from one type of computer screen to another (e.g. PC and wall-mounted screen), through lightweight technologies. There are many proposals for such technologies in the CSCW literature, and we are continuously exploring the usability of such proposals in our actual settings (Bødker et al 2000, in preparation, Bødker & Christiansen, in preparation).

Processes, processes and processes

Our case studies point out that the processes of designing and introducing new office design are highly important for the success of the project. As is fairly well known from computer technology there is a harsh difference between designing for idealized work processes and for how work actually takes place (Suchman 1987). And, as is equally well documented, the processes through which people get to experience their future technologies; work processes etc. are very essential (see e.g. Ehn 1988, Bødker 1999). The lack of process is typical in many 'New office' implementations. And we often meet the following problems:

Not to investigate. There are many examples where companies implement new office design as a "general solution" without investigating the work processes, the tasks, meetings, etc. in the workplace. Our Dot.com (C7) is a modest example of this, primarily driven out of sheer lack of appropriate space. The Professional Organization (C9) shows many of the problems that occur when people are forced to work in open spaces: complaints about noise, building fences and walls of book shelves, or working from home to get things done.

Not to participate. The management initiates and sells the idea of efficient learning and cooperation in open spaces. But the managers stay in their own big private offices. In a Danish County they made the following principles for what they called "The New Office". Top and middle management were to have individual offices - 4 modules for top management and 3 for middle management. Ordinary employees, on the other hand, were to have group offices with varied space. This particular top management claimed that the new group office space would support knowledge sharing, cooperation, openness and flexibility. However, the principles for assigning spaces still show a deep connection between status and office size.

Not to continue. The process stops when people have moved in, before the actual experiences begin. A typical mistake is to close down all the groups, meetings and activities related to new office design once people have moved into the new building. Experiences from our own experimental office show, however, that improvements can be made, and are necessary based on the actual experiences. It is an ongoing process where work, its technologies and surroundings are under continuous development.

Preventing or supporting learning in the 'New office'?

There should be no doubt that we see many of the new office design as refreshing alternatives to classical office hallways or cubicles. However, it is necessary to understand the workplace both in terms of actual and desirable contact between people and new rooms and facilities, in order to support cooperation and learning. We see a number of ways where the new office design seems to go too far, risking of preventing rather than supporting learning:

- The focus on anonymous aesthetics
- The lacks of corporate and personal identity in the new office buildings
- Open spaces all the way through
- The house rules
- Lack of concern for actual work and different needs
- Lack of mobile (or movable) technology
- Lack of concern for processes of design and implementation

There is a tendency that new office designs are driven by architects' more than by people's need for dwelling and for showing their work and personality.

Functional separation means difficult transitions between locations and between modes of cooperation. This is partly because cooperation is seen as carried out entirely by conversation and not through shared artefacts as well. Our own flexible office has been set up partly to explore for ourselves some of the potentials and problems of the open, flexible office, and partly because we want to do action-oriented research, exploring physical space, furniture, technologies etc. In our own office, we can work with design alternatives before or alongside our cooperation with larger empirical settings (e.g. County Office, C4). Obviously, we do this type of research because we are interested in CSCW technologies at large, and not because we believe that there are any "quick technological fixes" to the problems described above. Accordingly, we turn to our own flexible office, in order to explore the questions raised in this microcosm and to discuss the possibilities of using CSCW technologies to augment new offices and hence re-enforce possibilities and counteract some of the here-mentioned problems.

Our microcosm

Our experimental office is the setting for our design ideas. In this office, four-six researchers are working in an open space with four desks. They have an additional informal meeting room (with a couch) for small meetings, extensive telephone calls, and quiet reading. From the beginning they decided not to own their desk, but make use of whatever desk was available. They have laptops with wireless network connections working in the entire building. The researchers all do field work where they are away from the office for shorter or longer periods, and several of them live at a distance and work at home some days. As a main rule the researchers do not work on the same project. They have been cooperating on many smaller assignments across and between various constellations of people and they have all participated in the development of the experimental office itself.

Overall, this flexible office experiment is meant to raise and explore further research questions as well as to inform the building of our own new office building. The use of the flexible office setting has been monitored through participant observation and regular office meetings where problems are dealt with and discussed. Furthermore, we are doing prototyping experiments to explore cooperation possibilities in the office. In particular we have experimented with shared itineraries and awareness support, as well as with physical and virtual means of creating "a place of your own" and of various projects in the room (see further in Bødker & Christiansen, 2002).

Our experiment has been one where we have provided means that looked very much like what we see in many open office spaces: activity-based spaces (meeting room vs. office), movable furniture and laptop computers, and some amount of change in whom and how many use the office. Indeed the office is much smaller than what we find many places, and as such not all aspects are comparable to a large flexible office space.

In the beginning the office was dedicated to six (mobile) researchers sharing four desks so it did make sense not to "own" a specific desk. After a while, there were only four researchers left and it began to feel awkward to change table all the time and to clear the desk when they knew that there were plenty of room for the four of them. So the researchers agreed to change the concept and got a desk for each person. And indeed this decision changed how people used their desks, and how people, who came to see them, oriented themselves in the office - aspects that we shall return to.

By drawing on the findings from our case studies we initiated the exploration of the flexible office at a different technological state than many other organisations:

- Wireless LANs, laptops and mobile phones were deployed to support easy transition between different rooms at the workplace while travelling and while at home.
- The office had ample supply of whiteboards and pin boards and there were no rules for what could be posted or left in the room.
- We have been working in close cooperation with projects where electronic whiteboards were already being explored. The workers in the flexible office have had access to the use of these throughout the project in one adjacent meeting room (Bücher et al. 2001, Bødker et al. 2001).

Starting from there, the following experiences of relevance here, were accumulated in our discussions:

We lack multi-level access to people's itineraries. One type of information is needed for people who come to seek somebody working in the office. Another type may be needed for the office community to answer urgent phone calls and to get a sense of who to expect on a given day. Surely it is even better if this information can be accessed remotely, so that an absent co-worker may contact a person who is actually in on a given day, and so that the information may be updated e.g. from home or from a train if plans are changed.

We lack personal space in the shared office. It was important for the researchers to make the office "their own", both as a group and as individuals. Though they all had a cart each for their "stuff" it was at times important to leave material out. To place sticky notes somewhere to remind oneself of the coming day, and even to put up pictures of children, etc.

We lack project space in the shared office. Similar to the private space, it is important for projects to have a place of their own, and to remind the project group itself as well as others of what the project is about and what it has achieved (similar to Teasley 2000).

We lack support for directly moving documents between electronic boards in various locations, and between PCs and electronic boards.

If we return to our studies of other organizations we see striking similarities in the two sets of experiences: the anonymity is a problem in this office at several levels: for visitors, among co-workers and for the individual researcher. The anonymity is a problem regarding coordination, knowledge sharing and dwelling.

The original decision - a new desk every day - was abandoned as soon as there were only four users of the office. And soon, artefacts and documents were left on the desk, personal space created, etc.

Exploration through mock-ups and prototyping

Our experiences in the flexible office formed the basis of several design explorations (Further in Bødker & Christiansen, in preparation). The purpose of these explorations is double: to create visions and challenges to be pursued in technological design (as opposed to designing technological gadgets with no anchoring in use) and to help the inhabitants of the office shape their requirements for a future office building.

In order to find out the kind of information about co-workers needed by other co-workers and by visitors to the flexible office, a two-level whiteboard with shared itineraries was set up: in the hallway the inhabitants posted one level of information for visitors, and visitors could place notes for the inhabitants. Inside the office, a more detailed calendar was set up to give an overview of where all inhabitants were for all days of the coming week/month. Experiments with information contents inside and outside the office were carried out for a month, and documented in daily pictures of the two boards. We further explored the physical placing of boards in the room (both inside the room and in hallway) in a workshop of all inhabitants and a couple of additional researchers.

The findings from this experiment are that it is important to be able to up-date shared itineraries information once, and that it is far from trivial to filter this information so that the right level of information reaches the people who pass by the door, and the right level reaches people in the office.

The second kind of exploration took place mainly in a workshop and aimed at exploring the possibilities of providing electronic panels with personal stuff – from post-it notes to pictures of one's family. The overall idea was to provide some kind of electronic panel at each desk where this personal stuff would pop up in a non-intrusive way, whenever somebody occupied the desk (e.g. placed the personal computer there). We explored with three different solutions: panel, desktop or wall that turned out to have different potentials and problems vis-à-vis personal and shared access. The wall turned out to be the more communal, but the least supportive of the attention of the individual user, e.g. the least suited for placing sticky notes. The wall worked well for shared project spaces as well as individual use. The screen embedded in the desktop was good for personal use, but more difficult as support for awareness by people passing by. The panel rising from the desktop had qualities somewhere between the two. However, such panels certainly do not replace piles and artefacts of the physical desktop.

The third kind of exploration was focussing on the right kind of display for the right job – electronic boards for meeting rooms, boards for shared information in offices, other representations on the PC or on small palm tops. Not least we have explored possibilities of smooth transitions, of using small devices to move documents from one location to another, instead of logging on and off servers to retrieve documents. The topic of collaborating on shared documents in front of large interactive boards and similar support for direct cooperation has been dealt with in our cooperation with the WorkSPACE project (Bücher et al. 2001). The work on easy ways of moving documents between display screens was started some years ago and discussed in (Bødker et al 2001). We have added a small experiment that made it possible to use a PDA to pick-and-drop (Rekimoto 1997) documents from a board or PC onto the PDA and vice versa.

From microcosm back to the real world

This section connects our experiences and technological explorations from the flexible office back to the real world cases that we started out with. We formulate questions or challenges rather than answers.

CSCW technology

We have found that in most organizations there is a large diversity in how much time people spend at their desk, at home, and in various other locations. In a case such as the County Office (C6) these other locations include for some people mainly other parts of a large administration building, for others locations within the boundaries of the county and for still others, a hotel room in Brussels. This means that while there is a need in the organization to support transition between different rooms at the workplace while travelling and while at home, the challenge is to provide a variety of solutions, and a flexible infrastructure to support this.

We have explored the possibility of substituting whiteboards and pin boards with lightweight electronic solutions. In the Engineering Company, C1 we explored mock-up information kiosks to be placed in the open café areas, hallways and other "in-between" places. The question is how far such solutions may help people learn about each other and about projects? To what extend will they help provide project space in the shared physical and virtual space? And to what extent may these same types of solutions help people create personal space?

We have seen no uses of electronic whiteboards in any of our case studies. We have discussed the use of such in several cases, e.g. Engineering Company, C1. Provided that meetings are about electronic materials such as e.g. CAD drawings, or that electronic materials can be made useful for people when returning to their own offices, the question is how far we can go in employing electronic boards or electronic pens on regular whiteboards in organisations such as our cases? And how may transitions be supported?

Multi-level itineraries we see as a supplement to shared electronic calendars. Electronic calendars are useful for planning joint meetings or for finding very specific details about a particular person. In larger organisations, however, we hear many complaints that it is difficult to locate each other. The question is how useful electronic calendars are for this purpose? If an organisation chooses another form of shared itineraries, what form should they take, and how do they get updated together with the calendars?

Process experiences

Through the process we have gained experiences with participatory activities to involve office inhabitants in design and tailoring of their own office environment and technology. In accordance with the findings, it is important to continue participatory activities when people have moved into new buildings, and not just during the design process. We continue to do real life projects in which the next step is to develop a toolbox of methods helping these design and monitoring processes, emphasizing *design in use*.

Our studies have pointed to a need to extend participatory design concerns in the direction of the combined office design and technology. One aspect is to work with the actual users and their actual needs, the other to expand on ways of doing cooperative tailoring (Trigg & Bødker 1994) and cooperative reflection based on experiences with actual use. These elements we will continue to develop.

Conclusion

In the current situation, an optimal design of the 'New office' must include design of information technology. The large open-plan offices in many organisations are the architects' version of "anything, anywhere." And, as discussed e.g. by Bertelsen & Bødker (2001) information technological "anything anywhere" often becomes "nothing, nowhere." We have demonstrated that the architectural version is nowhere different. New computer artefacts, and new buildings do not as such make knowledge sharing and learning happen. We see a danger in the recent development that learning and communication is prevented, and that the 'New office' leads to conformity and anonymity rather than cooperation and creativity.

Through our exploratory prototypes we have pursued ways of improving legitimate peripheral participation, through architecture, physical artefacts and materials in the rooms as well as through virtual extensions of these artefacts.

Acknowledgments

Many people have been involved in the studies and experiments behind this paper. We thank Ole Nielsen for his involvement with several site visits and for providing the basis for a students' project, Wendy Mackay, John B Simonsen, the students in the "augmenting artefacts for design" and "designing interactive systems" courses, Claus Bossen, Ellen Christiansen, Ole Iversen and Werner Sperschneider for their involvement in the flexible office and case studies, Kaj Grønbæk, Peter Krogh, Jannie Friis Kristensen, Preben Mogensen, Christina Nielsen and the entire I-Room crowd for their participation in the design experiments. Funding was provided by CIT and the Alexandra Institute through Centre for New Ways of Working.

References

Baldry, C., Bain, P. & Taylor, P. (1998). 'Bright satanic offices': intensification, control and team taylorism. In Thompson, P. & Warhurst, C. *Workplaces of the future*, Macmillan, pp.163-183.

Bertelsen, O.W. and Bødker, S. (2001). Cooperation in massively distributed information spaces. In *ECSCW 2001: Proceedings of the Seventh European Conference on Computer Supported Cooperative Work*, Kluwer Academic Publishers, pp. 1-18.

Bjerrum, E. & Brinkman, S. (2001). *New Ways of working i Århus Amt*. Alexandra Instituttet.

Bjerrum, E & Nielsen, O. (in press). *Bliver man lidt småsær af at have eget kontor?* Jyllands Postens Forlag.

Bødker, S. & Christiansen, E. (2002). Lost and Found in Flexibility, *IRIS 2002*, CD-ROM

Bødker, S. & Christiansen, E. (in preparation). IT-support for social awareness: Why, how and where?, in preparation for journal publication.

Bødker, S. & Petersen, M.G. (2000). *Design for learning in use*, Scandinavian Journal of Information Systems, vol. 12, pp. 61-80.

Bødker, S., Krogh, P & Petersen, M.G. (2001). The interactive design collaboratorium. In Hirose, M. (ed.) *Human Computer Interaction. Interact '01*, IOS Press, pp 51-58.

Bødker , S., Kristensen, J.F., Nielsen, C. & Sperschneider, W. (in preparation). Technology and design work on the boundaries.

Büscher, M., Mogensen, P. & Shapiro, D. (2001). Spaces of Practice. In W. Prinz et al. (Ed.), Proceedings of the *Seventh European Conference on Computer Supported Cooperative Work*. 139-158. Kluwer Academic Publishers.

Duffy, F. (2000). *New Ways of Working-Know Thyself*. COWI Aarhus 2/11, unpublished lecture.

Ehn, P. (1988). *Work-oriented design of computer artifacts*. Falköping: Arbetslivscentrum/Almqvist & Wiksell International, Lawrence Erlbaum.

Engeström, Y. (1987). *Learning by expanding*. Orienta-Konsultit.

Harrison, S. & Dourish, P. (1996). Re-Place-ing Space: The role of place and space in collaborative systems, *Proceedings of ACM CSCW'96 Conference on Computer-Supported Cooperative Work*, pp. 67-76.

Lave, J., & Wenger, E. (1991). *Situated learning: Legitimate peripheral participation*, Cambridge University Press.

Mosbech K. (2001). Oral presentation at "Banestyrelsen" Copenhagen. December 2001.

Myerson, J. & Ross, P. (1999). *The creative office*, Laurence King Publishing.

Nardi, B, Whittaker, S. & Schwarz, H. (2000). It's Not What You Know, It's Who You Know: Work in the Information Age, *First Monday Volume 5, Number 5 - http://firstmonday.org/issues/issue5_5/*

Nonaka, I. & Takeuchi, H., (1995). *The knowledge-Creating Company*, Oxford University Press.

Olson , J. Covi, L., Rocco, E., Miller, W. & Allie P. (1998). A room of your own: what would it take to help remote groups work as well as collocated groups? *Conference on Human Factors and Computing Systems*, ACM Press New York, NY, pp. 279 – 280.

Raymond, S. & Cunliffe, R. (1997). *Tomorrow's Office*, E&FN Spon.

Rekimoto, J. (1997). Pick-and-Drop: A Direct Manipulation Technique for Multiple Computer Environments. *Proceedings of the ACM Symposium on User Interface Software and Technology*, p.31-39

Robinson, M. (1993). Design for Unanticipated Use. In G. deMichaelis & C. Simone (eds.), *Proceedings of the Third European Conference on Computer-Supported Cooperative Work*. Kluwer, pp. 187-202.

Schmidt, K. & Simone, C. (1996). Coordination Mechanisms: Towards a Conceptual Foundation of CSCW Systems Design. *Computer Supported Cooperative Work* 1996 v.5 n.2/3 p.155-200.

Sennett, R. (1998). *The Corrosion of Character. The Personal Consequences of Work in the New Capitalism.* W.W.Norton and Co.

Suchman, L. & Wynn, E. H. (1984). Procedures and Problems in the Office. *Office: Technology and People 2*, 2 (Jan 1984), 133–154.

Suchman, L. (1987). *Plans and Situated Actions*, Cambridge University Press.

Suchman, L. A. (1993). Centers of Coordination: A Case and Some Themes. Presented at the NATO *Advanced Research Workshop on Discourse, Tools and Reasoning*, Lucca, Italy, November 2-7.

Suchman, L. A. (1996). Constituting shared workspaces. In Engeström, Y. & Middleton, D. (eds.). Cognition and Communication at Work. Cambridge University Press, pp. 35-60.

Teasley , S. Covi, L., Krishnan, M.S. & Olson, J (2000). How does radical collocation help a team succeed? *Proceedings of the 2000 ACM conference on Computer supported cooperative work*. ACM Press New York, NY, pp. 339 – 346.

Trigg, R, & Bødker, S (1994). From Imlementation to design: Tailoring and the emergence of systematization in CSCW, in Futura, R. & Neuwirth, C: *Proceedings og CSCW 94*, ACM press, pp. 45-54.

Wagner, I., Buscher, M., Mogensen, P. Shapiro, D. (1999) Spaces for creating context & awareness - designing a collaborative virtual work space for (landscape) architects. *Proceedings of the Eighth International Conference on Human-Computer Interaction v.2* p. 283-287.

Worthington J., Duffy F., Greenberg S., Myerson J., Powell K. & Thompson T. (1998).*The architecture of DEGW*, Birkhaüser Verlag

Yates, J. (1989). *Control through Communication*, John Hopkins Press.

K. Kuutti, E.H. Karsten, G. Fitzpatrick, P. Dourish and K. Schmidt (eds.), *ECSCW 2003: Proceedings of the Eighth European Conference on Computer Supported Cooperative Work, 14-18 September 2003, Helsinki, Finland*, pp. 219-238.

Seeing What You Are Hearing: Co-ordinating Responses to Trouble Reports in Network Troubleshooting

Steve Whittaker[1] and Brian Amento[2]

Sheffield University, UK[1], AT&T Labs-Research, USA[2]

s.whittaker@shef.ac.uk, brian@research.att.com

Abstract. Real time team co-ordination is a central problem for CSCW, but previous attempts to build novel systems to support it have not been greatly successful. One reason for this is that teams have often evolved highly effective work practices involving paper. In contrast to these prior negative findings, we present an instance of a successful digital system to support real-time co-ordination. Our system is designed to co-ordinate rapid responses to serious network failures in a telecommunications company. A critical reason for our system's success is that (in contrast to many prior studies) the primary data in our setting is *speech*. The support team must co-ordinate responses to trouble reports sent in voicemail messages. Our fieldwork suggests that because speech is ephemeral and not inherently visual, existing paper practices make it hard to extract information from those messages in order to construct shared visual representations of the major elements of the work. This in turn makes it difficult to co-ordinate work. Our novel system makes visible the content of these messages along with the actions that team members are taking to deal with them. An 8-month system field trial showed that making important aspects of individual work visible enhanced awareness and team co-ordination.

Introduction

Real-time team co-ordination is a central problem for CSCW (Hutchins, 1995, Malone and Crowston, 1992). This problem is made even more demanding when there are requirements for teams to respond to rapidly changing situations. Empirical studies of air traffic control (Hughes et al., 1992), team navigation (Hutchins, 1995) transport co-ordination (Heath and Luff, 1992), managing the space shuttle flight (Patterson et al., 1999) and neurosurgery (Nardi et al., 1993) have documented the major challenges of such real time co-ordination. The complex cognitive demands of such situations mean that work is necessarily distributed among different team members often with different areas of expertise. This in turn requires that teams co-ordinate their individual work, sharing the results of their individual activities and redistributing individual work-loads when necessary.

Two important methods for achieving real-time team co-ordination are awareness of the actions of others, and access to shared visual representations. Heath and Luff (1992) document the importance of a shared physical space in affording lightweight access to, and awareness of, the work of others. Hughes et al., (1992) describe how paper flight strips serve as a shared visual representation that promotes co-ordination between air traffic controllers. The shared visual representation makes important parts of individual work visible to others -- facilitating awareness and co-ordination. Shared visual representations support critical cognitive and social functions: they both serve as an attentional focus, as well as a record of progress through the task, allowing team members to co-ordinate their individual contributions to the collective task.

But prior CSCW systems to support real-time co-ordination that have been based on these insights have not been greatly successful. One reason for these failures is the nature of pre-existing work practices. Teams have often evolved highly effective work practices that are associated with paper. These paper-based processes allow workers to exploit shared representations, making work visible and shareable in ways that are hard to duplicate using digital media (Hughes et al., 1992, Sellen and Harper, 2002, Whittaker and Schwarz, 1999).

Figure 1 – The Network Operations Centre

In contrast to these prior negative findings, we present an instance of a successful digital system to support real-time co-ordination. Our system is designed to co-ordinate responses to serious network failures in the Network Operations Centre (NOC) of a telecommunications company, where complex problems must be diagnosed and responses co-ordinated within minutes. We will argue that a critical reason for our system's success is that (in contrast to prior studies) the primary data in our setting is *speech*. The support team must respond to trouble reports that are sent in as voicemail messages. Our fieldwork suggests that because speech is ephemeral and not inherently visual, it is hard to construct shared visual representations of the major elements of the work using paper-based processes. This in turn makes it difficult for the support team to co-ordinate work. This emphasis on co-ordinating *spoken* as opposed to textual information is consistent with the focus of other recent successful CSCW systems (Hindus et al., 1996, Patterson et al., 1999).

The structure of the paper is as follows: we first describe the setting for our study, the Network Operations Centre, and the work that gets carried out there. In particular, we describe 3 months of fieldwork documenting the co-ordination problems resulting from the use of the existing voicemail system. We next describe and motivate our system that was designed to assist with processing and co-ordinating responses to incoming network trouble reports. We report the results of an 8-month field trial of the system in operation, documenting its successes and failures. We conclude with a discussion of the theoretical and practical implications of our study.

The Network Operations Centre: Setting and Fieldwork

The Network Operations Centre

The setting for our work was the Networks Operations Centre (NOC) of a large telecommunications company (BigTel). We made multiple visits to the NOC over a three-month period, interviewing various personnel and observing NOC operations in order to understand the operation and demands of network trouble-shooting. We interviewed 15 support and technical engineers as well as their managers, and carried out 8 days of observations of NOC activities. All interviews were conducted during low tempo work periods. The fieldwork constituted about 100 hours of interviews and observations, and this provides the basis for the new system we implemented and evaluated in the NOC.

The goal of the NOC is to control the running of large numbers of national and international data networks, in particular to diagnose and repair network failures. Network failure is particularly costly to BigTel, because the company negotiates contracts with large companies that guarantee very high levels of trouble-free operation. These contracts contain penalty clauses, in which BigTel has to compensate these customers for even short periods of network malfunction. And a single malfunction may affect several large customers. This means that network failures need to be addressed within minutes of their detection.

The NOC is a complex open-plan working environment resembling a "warroom" (see Fig. 1). It contains about 40 office cubicles each containing multiple computers and telephones. At any one time, about 20 of these offices are staffed by managers, technical and customer-support engineers. As Fig. 1 shows, the room is about 15 metres high, and one wall is entirely taken up with large screens displaying various types of data that are relevant to predicting and diagnosing networking problems. Some of these screens contain detailed information to help engineers address emerging networking problems, e.g. networking node diagrams showing routing information and network load in the BigTel network. Others contain information about incoming customer reports concerning recently detected faults in the network, or roster information about which engineers are manning the current shift. Yet other screens provide information about news and weather. These are important because cataclysmic news events, such as earthquakes or terrorist strikes can have large effects on network traffic loads, vastly increasing the likelihood of failure.

There are three types of personnel in the NOC, technical engineers, support engineers and managers. The role of the technical engineers is to anticipate, diagnose and repair networking problems. The role of the support engineers is to interact with customers, both to interpret and evaluate incoming customer reports of networking problems, to determine their severity and importance. If customers report severe problems, support engineers may escalate these, so that they are dealt with immediately by a critical response team. Customer support engineers also interact with customers about the current progress of the technical engineers' repair efforts and their likely outcome. Engineers work 8-hour shifts and on any shift there are about 10 technical engineers and between 2 and 5 customer support engineers.

In what follows our main focus is on support engineers and their work processes. Over previous months they had experienced some problems in executing their work. Our remit was to identify possible reasons for their problems and to devise software that might address these.

Customer Support in the NOC

BigTel receives many reports of network failure through a web-based system, allowing customers or account representatives to enter a description of their networking problem. These failure reports are known as BMP (Business Management Process) reports. Most problems are taken care of using this system. A technical engineer will pick up a BMP report, fix the problem and then close the BMP ticket.

However a second, more important, set of failure reports are received in voicemail. These are the sole responsibility of the support engineers and are known as "trouble reports". Important customers and account representatives are given a direct support hotline that they can use to escalate problems that they feel are not being dealt with quickly enough using the online BMP system. Customers may also leave voicemail when networking failures mean that they cannot access the web to register their problem - making the phone their only possible communication mode. If the customer problem is indeed serious, or if multiple customers are reporting similar problems suggesting a large-scale network failure, the support engineer may then decide formally escalate the problem. Escalation leads to the immediate creation of a critical response team of 3-10 technical and support engineers who are standing by for such a situation. The team's goal is to diagnose and repair the escalated trouble immediately.

It should be noted at this point that escalations are unusual. Most trouble reports do not require escalation. There are highly effective automatic diagnostic processes in the network. This often means that by the time that the trouble is formally reported by the customer, the technical engineers have already fixed the problem, or are in the process of doing so. Nevertheless, the support engineer's role is important: (a) to escalate when necessary, (b) to identify those few cases that have not been reported elsewhere ensuring that appropriate remedial action is undertaken, and (c) for more usual cases to report back to the customer that their troubles are being dealt with.

The decision to escalate depends on a number of factors, including the seriousness of the problem, the number of customers reporting it, and the identity of the reporting customers. Often the decision to escalate depends on the number of incoming trouble reports. Networking failures seldom come in isolation, so that if the support engineer detects that multiple incoming trouble reports are related, this may be cause for escalation. For example, a major failure of the network can mean that multiple customers in one part of the country will suddenly all report concurrent problems. In order to detect such patterns, the customer engineers need to be aware of the details of the trouble reports that their colleagues are currently processing, along with other more general information provided by the wall screens shown in Fig. 1.

If the customer support engineer decides to escalate, this process involves setting up two different conference calls: one used by the escalation team to diagnose the technical repairs of the network and the second to interface to the customers. The technical discussions are often fraught and complex, and the aim is for the support engineer to serve as a conduit between customer and escalation team on these two separate calls, relaying relevant information between them.

The final job of the customer support engineer is accounting for their activities. At the end of their 8-hour shift, each support engineer generates an activity summary. The support engineer must state: which trouble reports they processed, when they processed them, the content of each report, and the action taken in response to the call. These activity summaries are important because they help BigTel to determine responsiveness to customer problems. Sometimes there are requirements to follow up on a previously dealt with call (*"What did we do about customer X's problem?"*), and these reports are the main source of information for such follow up activity. It is also important for the company to be able to determine the precise time a call was received, along with the exact details of the remedial action. This enables the company to determine whether legitimate problems were responded to as quickly as possible.

The critical duties of the support engineers are therefore to process incoming calls, to decide for each whether it warrants escalation, if necessary to co-ordinate that escalation with technical engineers and customers, and to summarise the results of their activities with respect to each trouble report.

Our interviews and observations revealed some important problems experienced by the support engineers. These stemmed from difficulties in: (a) processing incoming voicemail messages to determine what action is required; (b) coordinating with others about how to address the trouble reports; (c) generating reports of their actions to support follow up and audit activity.

The Problems of Processing and Co-ordinating Reponses to Trouble Reports

Processing Messages

One major barrier to the effective processing of incoming trouble reports is that these are *spoken.* Often voicemail messages contain quite complex information such as caller name and callback number, account names, times and BMP ticket numbers. And the technical details of the trouble itself may involve technical terms and acronyms. In addition, the trouble report may be unclear because it was generated under the duress of system failures at the customer site.

Here is an example anonymised trouble report:

> "this is [** - identifying information removed] GNOC, we have 198 T3s down at 0914 EST, not counting each PVC. Frame Relay state that they have failed cons between [**] and [**]. As of 0935 EST, 25 T3s were restarted."[1]

The engineers were unanimous about how difficult these voicemail messages were to process. One support engineer noted how hard it was to determine what the message was about and what action needed to be taken. These problems were also exacerbated by the need to process messages rapidly:

> "we need to respond to those calls immediately because the network may be down but it can take several minutes to process one call because the information in there is so complicated"

Processing each message often involves replaying it several times with pen and paper at hand to take detailed notes of exactly what was said. Clearly, taking minutes to process a message is unacceptable, given the requirement that problems be addressed immediately.

Overall our informants were concerned about their ability to extract information from these messages, because of the general difficulty of extracting information from speech, the complexity of the messages, and the time pressure of needing to respond rapidly. These factors together meant that engineers were unconfident of the quality of the extracted information in their handwritten notes.

Co-ordinating with Others

In addition to these problems of extracting information from the voicemail trouble reports, a second set of concerns surrounded the co-ordination of work between support engineers.

---

[1] GNOC stands for global network operations centre, T3s are high bandwidth networks, EST is US eastern standard time, PVCs are permanent virtual circuits, Frame Relay is a type of network technology and cons. is an abbreviation for connections.

All incoming verbal trouble reports are delivered into a single shared voicemail box. All members of the customer support team have access to the mailbox, and they take turns to access the calls. Their workflow process is the following.

Given the need for immediate processing of voicemail trouble reports, it is imperative that one of the customer support engineers processes each trouble report the minute it arrives. All support engineers constantly monitor their voicemail. As soon as the 'message wai ting" light appears, anyone who is not directly engaged in processing other messages, or interacting with another customer picks up the new message. They then process the message, taking notes on paper as described above. They then delete the message. The reason for deleting the voicemail message is to prevent duplication of effort. Deletion stops a second engineer from inadvertently picking up the message and processing it.

The engineer responsible for the message then decides what action should be taken, i.e. whether the message warrants escalation, whether the fault is already being dealt with or whether to file a routine BMP ticket. Once this action has been carried out and the problem addressed, the engineer notes the results, and then proceeds to the next message.

Our observations suggested a number of co-ordination problems resulting from this process. The practice of deleting messages from the shared voicemail box and the inability to share private handwritten notes about messages means that each support engineers' work is largely inaccessible to others. In consequence engineers have little idea about what troubles their colleagues are dealing with. More specifically the following co-ordination difficulties arise:

(1) *Determining the number of outstanding trouble reports and who has responsibility for each.* The 'message waiting" light in the voicemail box indicates that there is at least one message to be processed but it does not indicate the exact number if there is more than one message. This makes it hard for the team of support engineers to determine their outstanding workload, as one cannot see at a glance how many unprocessed messages have arrived. It also makes it difficult for support engineers to allocate responsibility for incoming messages. We observed shouted conversations between engineers across cubicles to determine whether a colleague intended to take a new call: *"Are you taking that?"*. And when there were multiple unprocessed messages, one engineer shouted to another: *"There's more than one in there. Can you get the other?"*. Such shouted conversations are not ideal because the NOC can be a noisy environment, especially when there is an escalation taking place.

(2) *Determining relations between reports and who has responsibility for each.* Once an engineer has processed a message it is deleted from the system, and its details recorded on paper. But other engineers in the team cannot see these individual notes, so they have no idea about the details of the messages taken by others. This is problematic because the decision to

escalate may in part be determined by the fact that there are multiple related trouble reports, indicating a more serious network failure. The fact that engineers cannot currently 'share notes' means that they do not have access to others' reports, and so cannot make these connections. Not knowing who is responsible for each report can also mean that workloads may end up being distributed unequally, with team members being unaware that other team members are highly overloaded. We occasionally observed engineers seeking each other out to determine who had taken a particular prior call and what it was about (*'Did you take a call from X about Y?'*). Again however, the working environment was not conducive to such conversations.

(3) *Duplicate reports.* A related problem (also concerning detecting relations between messages) arises when there are multiple trouble reports from the same customer. The customer may call multiple times if their problem is changing rapidly, or they feel it is not being addressed quickly enough. These repeat calls should logically be dealt with by the same engineer, but private note-taking can mean that support engineers may be unaware of previous messages from the same caller if these were dealt with by someone else and if these prior calls are not explicitly referenced in the current trouble report call.

(4) *Handovers of outstanding trouble reports across shifts.* Sometimes a trouble report is still unresolved at the end of the shift, but engineers have no way to publicly record these outstanding calls for the next shift. It is therefore common practice for the shift supervisor to talk to every engineer at the end of the shift, to find out the status of their calls. S/he then informs the next shift supervisor about these unresolved calls, so they do not 'fall on the floor'.

To summarise, the voicemail system and the current practice of taking private notes about each message leads to a number of co-ordination problems. One major difficulty is that the combination of voicemail and private handwritten notes makes the engineers work *invisible* to others. Individual engineers have no clear idea about how many new unprocessed calls there are. They also don't know which calls have been processed by which people, what these were about, or whether they have already been dealt with. As we have seen, engineers sometimes resort to shouted conversations across cubicles about who is doing what, but these types of conversations are the exception rather than the rule.

Accounting for Activities and Following Up

The support engineer's final task is to record their activities in summary reports. Towards the end of every shift they generate a detailed report of each trouble report they have handled including: caller name and callback number, account names, times, BMP ticket numbers. They also note down the main reported problem and the action that they took (escalate, call back, etc.). These summary reports are based on their earlier handwritten notes, and written up in a word processing program.

These summary reports are then combined by the shift supervisor into various daily and monthly reports containing information about the total number of reports processed, the time to resolve each report, along with details of prevalent problems occurring during specific periods. These are used for quality assurance but also to determine the validity of customer follow up queries (*'why did it take 25 minutes to address network problem X on Dec.15th?'*).

According to our informants, one problem with these summary reports is that they are laborious to construct, and sometimes inaccurate. Engineers have to type up their notes about trouble reports that they have often processed several hours ago, based on their minimal notes taken under time pressure, with no access to the original voicemail message. All the engineers complained about these accounting practices and requested tools to help them better record the facts about their calls. Supervisors were also interested in better tools here, because they understood that there were often inaccuracies in summary reports. Another problem with the reports is that they are largely generated by individuals working independently. Engineers individually type up their notes, without consulting together on cases that overlap. Again, discovering and documenting these overlaps may be important for quality control or diagnostic reasons.

To summarise, engineers and their supervisors have to compile summary reports that are used for accounting and analysis. Both engineers and supervisors are concerned about the accuracy of the information in these reports, given that they are reconstructed from fairly sketchy notes, along with complaining about how laborious it is to construct these. Finally report generation is not co-ordinated between engineers, because of difficulties of sharing notes and information about relationships between calls.

Summary

In conclusion, support engineers experience 3 major problems stemming from the fact that they are processing complex speech data:

1) It is difficult to extract complex information from speech under time pressure. As a result, extracted information can sometimes be inaccurate;

2) The combination of voicemail and private note-taking means that engineers are unaware of the work of others, i.e. what calls others have taken and what these are about. This makes team co-ordination extremely difficult;

3) Post-hoc accounting reports are laborious to construct, are felt to be somewhat inaccurate, and fail to capture overlaps between related calls.

System

System Design Goals

The system we designed and evaluated was intended to support three main tasks that users had stated were problematic in their existing set-up. It was intended to assist with:

1) *Message Processing* – to improve the ease and accuracy of information extracted from speech under time pressure;

2) *Team co-ordination* – to provide a shared visual representation of the set of trouble reports to promote team co-ordination and awareness, showing:
   a. Outstanding unprocessed messages;
   b. Information about the content each message along with information about who has taken responsibility for it.

3) *Accounting and report generation* – to improve the ease with which engineers could generate detailed reports of their message processing activities, and help co-ordinate report writing.

System Design Rationale

The system is shown in Fig. 2 (with identifying information removed). Here we present the final design, but the actual system was developed over a period of several months, beginning with requirements derived from our initial fieldwork. We then iterated a series of designs with the engineers, using a variety of techniques including mockups. We worked with engineers and managers in soliciting feedback about these early designs.

The design of our system was influenced by work on both email interfaces and speech visualisation (Whittaker et al., 2002). Our fieldwork suggested that major problems with the existing voicemail system were that; (a) it made work invisible, making it hard for users to co-ordinate their activities; (b) it did not provide effective support for extracting complex information from spoken messages; (c) it offered little support for archive creation and management.

To make work visible, shareable and archivable, our system provides a visual interface to the shared voicemail box. It also allows users to take and share notes about individual messages. Our interface is similar to an email user interface in providing a header list showing important information about caller name, date, time and topic of incoming voicemail messages. More importantly it also supports access to the *content* of those voicemail messages using automatic speech transcription (ASR). Finally it provides tools for managing voicemail archives.

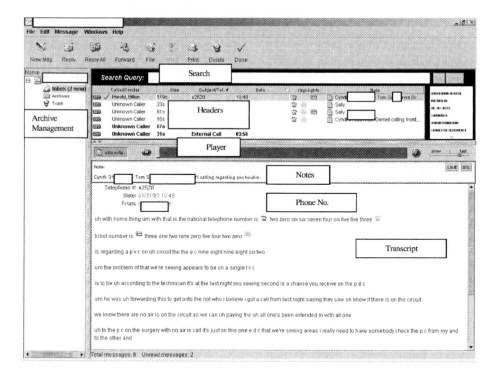

Figure 2 – User Interface

Before deciding on this design, we explicitly considered other types of system. It is possible that more traditional CSCW systems such as shared workspaces, workflow systems or shared databases such as Lotus Notes might potentially address some aspects of the support engineers' work in allowing them for example to share their notes on-line. However these technologies have the limitation that they are text-based. As a result, they do not provide direct access to the support engineer's primary work data, namely the speech messages, nor do they offer support for extracting information from these messages. They also do not address the problem that engineers' notes can be inaccurate. Access to voicemail message content seemed to be critical for team co-ordination, along with tools for managing speech archives.

The need for access to message content and archiving argues against two other potential designs. Voiceloops (Patterson et al., 1999) supports co-ordination for the space shuttle mission by broadcasting spoken communications on multiple audio channels, allowing distributed teams to communicate and listen in on relevant conversations. However Voiceloops does not provide a *record* of conversations, so it does not support extraction of complex information from speech (which may require multiple listenings). The absence of a conversational record also means Voiceloops also does not straightforwardly support archive creation and management. For related reasons, we rejected a different design where the system simply records message ID, caller phone number, time and ID of the person responsible for the call. Again such a system fails to allow users access to message content, i.e. to provide tools for extracting information from messages, or for creating effective archives. So, while both these potential designs offer some support for team co-ordination, neither helps engineers with the analysis and management of their primary work data -- which is *speech.*

System Features

The three main goals of the interface (shown in Fig. 2 with information anonymised) are therefore to provide the team with tools for extracting information from messages, for sharing the notes that engineers took about each message they had processed, as well as creating and managing archives. The interface to the system has five major elements: header information, message body (transcript), speech player controls, note-taking, and archival features (folders).

(1) *Header information* includes caller name (extracted where possible from telephone caller ID information using reverse lookup), message length, date/time, along with message highlights (explained below) and notes that have been taken about the message (again explained below).

(2) The *message body* (shown in the bottom third of the interface) is generated by applying ASR to the message. ASR is an imperfect technology and currently ASR generated transcripts contain about 20% errors. Despite these errors, transcripts can still expedite processing of voicemail messages in the following way: users read the transcript to determine the gist of the message, but in places where the transcript is unclear due to ASR errors, they access the original speech. They access the underlying speech by highlighting the unclear region of the transcript with their mouse and then hitting the play control in the player shown in the centre of the interface. For example, the initial part of the transcript '*uh with the home thing um"* is hard to understand, so the user might highlight this and play the underlying speech. In contrast, what follows is much clearer, where the caller provides a telephone number, ticket (BMP) number, and nature of the problem (a PVC with circuit number 989862).

It might appear to the sceptical reader that the ASR transcripts are almost unintelligible. However, other research has shown that this combination of reading transcripts and playing underlying speech is an effective way to process complex speech data (Whittaker et al., 2002). Another point to bear in mind is that the transcripts are being processed by domain experts, who are familiar with both the terminology and the class of reported problems.

The transcript also contains 'highlights" to help with message processing. Our interviews and analysis of the engineers' notes showed that there were certain critical pieces of information that engineers needed to extract from every message such as caller name, caller telephone number, and BMP number. We therefore used methods from AI to identify regions in the transcript where such information occurred. This is made possible because the target information has a predictable structure, e.g. a BMP number is composed of exactly nine digits. In the transcript in Fig. 2, the phone number is delineated in the transcript by the two small phone icons, and the BMP ticket number by two small 'BMP' logos. These icons allow the user to quickly scan the transcript to focus on this information, if, for example, they want to rapidly determine which problem is being reported in order to call back immediately. As with ASR, these AI techniques are not 100% accurate, but the philosophy is the same as with the overall transcripts. Users can quickly identify where in the message, the phone number, caller name and BMP ticket numbers occur. Then can then click on the relevant part of the message to play this information.

As Fig. 2 shows, we also present highlight information about caller name, caller phone number and BMP ticket number in the message header. By mousing over the relevant icon in the header, the user can quickly access this information without having to click on the message itself. We hoped that such header information would also help provide different members of the support team with important high-level awareness information about messages being processed by others.

(3) The system also supports *note-taking*. Our fieldwork had suggested that note-taking was essential to the processing of messages, and also potentially to team co-ordination. The interface allows users to type a short summary of the message in the notes field (shown in the centre of Fig 2). Notes usually include information about: the person taking the call, the caller name, phone number, BMP ticket number, nature of the problem and action taken. In Fig. 2 the notes indicate who has taken the call ('Cyndi'), the phone num ber, caller name ('Tom S.'), company and trouble description ('pvc trouble'). As with message highlights, these notes can be viewed in the message header pane, without needing to access the body of the message. One way of viewing these notes is that they provide a high level summary of message details. Our intention was that being able to see these header notes would promote awareness between engineers about who had taken which call, along with a brief summary of what the call was about.

(4) The *player controls* are standard, allowing users to select a region of the message and then to start, stop or pause playing. They also allow users to speed up playback.

(5) *Archives.* Finally, as with email, messages can be filed in the archives which operate like a standard email folder structure. And, of course the fact that we have a textual transcript for each message means that these archives (and the inbox) are searchable, allowing users to easily access specific information from the archive.

In conclusion, the system was intended to support the engineers' work processes in the following way:

1) Both the transcript and the highlight information we provide in the message headers should *expedite message processing*. While neither provides users with perfect information about the original message, they should nevertheless allow users to home in on the relevant parts of the message, playing the underlying speech where necessary.

2) The visual representation of the message inbox should make team work more visible promoting co-ordination and collaboration:

   a. The list of messages in the inbox should allow all team members to see the current workload of unprocessed messages

   b. Both the transcript, user notes and highlights should provide support engineers with access to, and awareness of, others' work

3) Transcripts, notes and the archive should assist users in generating reports, and in collaborating in the production of those reports.

Observations of the System in Use

After extensive design iterations involving the users, we installed the system and observed it being used over an 8-month period. Given the critical nature of the application, we designed our system so that it operated in parallel with the original voicemail system. This ensured that even if our system malfunctioned, the users would still be able to access trouble reports using their original system.

We collected various types of information in order to evaluate the system:

1) Observations of 11 support engineers and managers using the system.

2) Interviews and questionnaires, conducted before and after the system was installed. These addressed: how easy it was to extract information from incoming voicemail messages, whether the system was effective in supporting work, co-ordination with others, whether the system had changed the way that they worked, the main advantages and disadvantages of the system compared with the prior voicemail system, changes they wanted to make to the system.

Findings

Message Processing

It was clear from engineers' comments and questionnaire responses that once the transcript was available, the combination of reading the transcript and playing relevant regions helped them to process messages relatively effectively. Once we had ironed out initial problems, the engineers usually relied on our system for accessing messages. This happened despite the fact that their original voicemail system was still available, and they were familiar with using it for carrying out their work. Users quickly adjusted to a method of reading the transcript to get the gist of message and then playing important or unintelligible parts of the transcript. They were also very positive about the extracted phone numbers and BMP tickets. Despite this improved ability to process messages, the engineers were nevertheless dissatisfied with the quality of the ASR transcripts we generated. They pointed out various acronyms and technical vocabulary that were incorrectly transcribed. Although various system iterations improved this technical vocabulary (reducing overall recognition word error rate from 30% to 20%), the engineers still maintained that they wanted absolutely correct recognition. One issue we were careful to explore was whether inaccurate transcripts ever misled engineers about important aspects of a call. Our interviews and questionnaires indicated this was not the case: engineers did not rely exclusively on the ASR transcript for message processing. Instead, as we had intended, they used the transcript to direct their attention to critical parts of the call, which they made sure they listened to. They then recorded these important aspects of the call in the notes field. Another initial problem with the system was caused by ASR processing taking several minutes to complete, which forced the users to fall back to the original voicemail system because of the requirement for immediate responding. However once we modified the system to conduct multiple ASR passes (Whittaker et al., 2002) we were able to generate ASR transcriptions almost real-time, and this promoted greater usage.

Co-ordination and Collaboration

The system was highly successful in promoting team co-ordination. The engineers quickly abandoned taking handwritten notes on paper. Instead they used the system notes facility to enter information about: (a) who was responsible for the call; (b) caller name; (c) caller number; (d) customer name; (e) problem; (f) action taken. This notes information can be seen in Fig. 2.

The engineers were enthusiastic about their new ability to see the work of others. As one engineer commented:

'Now we can see who's dealing with what call and what they decided to do about it. That helps me with handling my calls"

This comment also reveals the importance of having access to the *content* of the calls that others are processing. Engineers confirmed that both others' notes and transcripts could be critical resources when attempting to co-ordinate. This validates our original design intuition that engineers needed to have visible access to message *content* rather than more abstract properties of the message.

The interface also allowed them to see at a glance whether there were new unprocessed messages, along with each team member's respective workload. For example, Fig. 2 shows two new unprocessed messages and four processed messages (two of the messages are being handled by Cyndi and two by Sally).

The system also promoted lightweight awareness of the actions of others. In the process of accessing a new message from the mailbox, users were able to see at a glance from header data, what their colleagues were currently working on.

The engineers were less positive about their ability to track precise message status. They pointed out that our initial system did not distinguish between messages that were currently being processed and those that were completely dealt with. At their request, we introduced message flags that could be used to signal status (e.g. the first message in Fig. 2 is 'done' as indicated by the tick mark (visible on the left hand side of the headers), the next three have been accessed but not yet discharged, as indicated by the fact that they are unbolded, and the final two are completely new unaccessed messages, as indicated by the fact that they are bold). This status flag was also useful for handovers between shifts. Supervisors no longer had to talk to all team members to compile a list of outstanding messages, in order to hand this over to the next shift supervisor. Instead this information was visible at a glance.

Although engineers reported benefits for the new system for co-ordinating with others, we also explored potential privacy concerns. Making people's work more visible helps promote co-ordination and awareness, but it also makes it more straightforward to monitor various individual's work. This seemed to be less of a problem than we had anticipated, for two reasons. First, users felt that the perceived advantages of greater visibility for co-ordination outweighed possible privacy concerns. In addition, several engineers pointed out that they already had to produce careful accounts of their activities at the end of the shift, in their summary reports, so greater accountability during shifts made little difference to them.

Archiving, Accounting and Follow-up

Finally, the engineers were extremely positive about the system's ability to support the generation of summary reports. Instead of relying exclusively on minimal handwritten notes to write up these reports, they could refer to the transcript or replay parts of the original message. In cases where two engineers had worked on different aspects of a problem, they could co-ordinate their write-up of the trouble. And in addition, for supervisors the system made it straightforward to carry out various audit tasks such as counting the number and times of various calls. Furthermore, if there were specific follow-up questions about how a particular call or set of calls had been dealt with, then it was extremely easy to use system search to access quite fine-grained details of these messages. For example archival system search could be used to answer the follow-up question: *'what action did we take about the persistent ** failure on Nov. 4th?"* The system allowed people to search for and access details about all prior messages, along with the engineer's notes associated with the message.

Previously they had to access large numbers of private notes and written reports to find this type of information.

Other NOC workers' reactions to the system

There were also strikingly positive reactions to the system from other people in the NOC who had observed it being used by the support engineers and their management. Overall we received extremely positive feedback about the system from both technical and managerial staff who were not part of the support team. Recall that the customer engineers work side-by-side with technical engineers, whose job is to anticipate and fix network problems. Four months after we had installed the system, the manager of the technical engineers contacted us, saying that his team had observed the support engineers using the system, and felt that it would be invaluable for their work too. He wanted us to install the system for the technical engineers. Furthermore, the NOC general manager also independently contacted us about displaying the system on one of the NOC walls. This he argued would increase the technical engineers' awareness of the workload and specific problems that the support engineers were currently dealing with. It could also inform them about potential problems that might end up being escalated to them. Together these observations provide additional evidence for the utility of our system.

Summary

Overall our system was successful in supporting both team co-ordination and archiving. The visible list of messages, along with notes and accessible transcripts made it possible for the support team to remain aware of each other's work in a way which was not possible with the voicemail system. In addition, the notes combined with transcripts and search also facilitated the process of report generation and interrogation of summary reports. Finally, general reactions to the system from other NOC workers were positive - with requests to extend the system to technical engineers and to the wall of the NOC. The system was less successful however, in supporting message processing, where users complained about inaccuracies in the automatically generated transcripts.

Conclusions

We have presented fieldwork characterising a complex real-time team co-ordination problem, i.e. dealing with network trouble reports. That fieldwork suggested that current work practices and technology made individual work *invisible* to other team members. The nature of the voicemail messages, private handwritten notes and the practice of deleting voicemail messages meant that support engineers' activities were inaccessible to each other. On the basis of these observations, we designed and evaluated a system for addressing these co-ordination problems. The system visually represented the status of incoming messages, their details, and the notes taken by the person processing the message. Our system capitalised on prior work note-taking practices, but allowed such notes to be shared. This helped externalise individual work, making actions and decisions more visible. This in turn promoted greater collective awareness allowing engineers to co-ordinate and re-allocate work, and to take collective action where necessary. Our data also indicate that simpler systems that do not provide direct access to spoken data would have been less successful for this application.

While confirming prior observations about the utility of shared visual representations for team co-ordination, our findings contrast with other attempts to develop systems to support real-time co-ordination (Hughes et al., 1992, Sellen and Harper, 2002, Whittaker and Schwarz, 1999). In those studies users preferred existing paper-based practices to novel digital CSCW systems. How then can we explain the success of our system? One crucial feature of our system is that it requires access and co-ordination about *speech data*. In the NOC, existing work practices relied on taking (often poor quality) private notes and using the voicemail box to allocate work. These practices meant that neither the content nor the responsibility for different aspects of the work was visible. In contrast, our system capitalised on existing work practices in supporting note-taking, but critically provided lightweight access to message content and responsibility. This in turn allowed engineers to remain aware of others' work and to co-ordinate with them when necessary. These findings confirm and extend other research on audio groupware (Patterson et al., 1999) showing that novel CSCW systems can successfully support co-ordination when the primary work data is speech.

Furthermore, our approach may apply to a number of problems outside the NOC. A large number of companies have major operations to provide customer support. They often need to process customer reports and complaints that are delivered in voicemail. Many of the problems identified here seem to occur in those other support applications. For example, support teams need to co-ordinate their activity in dealing with sets of calls. The ability to make calls visible, along with supporting notes and reports would seem to be critical for this general type of task, suggesting our approach may be reasonably general.

Having said this, there are obvious places where our system can be improved. One problem is with the accuracy of the ASR transcripts. We have improved accuracy by 10% since our first installation, but clearly more work is needed to help with the difficult process of understanding and registering incoming calls. Another feature our users requested was the ability to edit transcripts directly, and we are working to provide this. We are also developing on a new forms-based user interface that will make it more straightforward for engineers to enter and view critical elements of the incoming message, such as caller name, number, problem and action taken. And in response to user requests we are also working on a large-scale display version of the interface, making it possible for everyone in the NOC to view the status of incoming trouble reports.

Finally our work underscores other research showing the importance of visual representations and awareness for co-ordination (Hutchins, 1995 Nardi et al., 1993, Hughes et al., 1992, Sellen and Harper, 2002, Whittaker and Schwarz, 1999). In contrast to voicemail, our new system made important aspects of work visible. Engineers could see at a glance who had processed which message, what that message was about and what action (if any) had been taken about it. That allowed them to co-ordinate their work with others. What was striking was how a relatively simple system was able to support these important co-ordination and reporting processes.

References

Heath, C., and Luff, P. (1992). Collaboration and control, *Computer Supported Cooperative Work*, 1, 65-80.

Hindus, D., Ackerman, M., Mainwaring, S., and Starr, B. (1996). Thunderwire: A Field Study of an Audio-Only Media Space. In *Proceedings of Conference on Computer Supported Cooperative Work*, NY: ACM Press.

Hughes, J., Randall, D. and Shapiro, D. (1992). Faltering from ethnography to design In *Proceedings of Conference on Computer Supported Cooperative Work*. NY: ACM Press, 115-122.

Hutchins, E. (1995). *Cognition in the Wild*. Cambridge, MA: MIT Press.

Malone, T., and Crowston, K. (1992). What is co-ordination theory and how can it help design cooperative work systems? In *Groupware and Computer Supported Cooperative Work*, ed., R. Baecker, CA: Morgan Kaufman, 375-388.

Nardi, B, Schwarz, H, Kuchinsky, A, Leichner, R, Whittaker, S., and Sclabassi, R. (1993). Turning away from talking heads: an analysis of "video-as-data". In *Proceedings of CHI' 93 Human Factorsri Computing Systems*, NY: ACM Press, 327-334.

Patterson, E., Watts-Perotti, J., and Woods. D. (1999) "Voice loops as coordination aids in space shuttle mission control." Computer Supported Cooperative Work, 8(4), 353-371.

Sellen A., and Harper, R. (2002). *The myth of the paperless office*. Cambridge, MA.: MIT Press.

Whittaker, S., Hirschberg, J., Amento, B., Stark, L., Bacchiani, M., Isenhour, P., Stead, L., Zamchick G., & Rosenberg, A. (2002) SCANMail: a voicemail interface that makes speech browsable, readable and searchable. In *Proceedings of CHI2002 Conference on Human Computer Interaction*, NY: ACM Press, 275-282.

Whittaker, S., and Schwarz, H. (1999) Meetings of the board: the impact of scheduling medium on long term coordination in software development. In *Computer Supported Cooperative Work*, 8,175-205.

K. Kuutti, E.H. Karsten, G. Fitzpatrick, P. Dourish and K. Schmidt (eds.), *ECSCW 2003: Proceedings of the Eighth European Conference on Computer Supported Cooperative Work, 14-18 September 2003, Helsinki, Finland*, pp. 239-258.

When Can I Expect an Email Response? A Study of Rhythms in Email Usage

Joshua R. Tyler, John C. Tang

Hewlett-Packard Labs, 1501 Page Mill Road, Palo Alto CA, 94304
Sun Microsystems Laboratories, 2600 Casey Avenue, Mountain View CA, 94043
joshua.tyler@hp.com, john.tang@sun.com

Abstract. A study of email responsiveness was conducted to understand how the timing of email responses conveys important information. Interviews and observations explored users' perceptions of how they responded to email and formed expectations of others' responses to them. We identified ways in which users maintain and cultivate a *responsiveness image* for projecting expectations about their email response. We also discuss other contextual cues people use to discover email responsiveness, which include using other tools such as the calendar and phone, accounting for the amount of work time overlap available, and establishing a pacing between email correspondents. These cues help users develop a sense of when to expect a response and when breakdown has occurred, requiring further action.

Anyone who uses email regularly has sent a message and wondered, "When will I get a response to this email?" Or, "How long should I wait for a response to this message before taking further action?" Beyond the content of email messages, the timing of when email is sent, when it is read, and when a response is received are all examples of rhythms of email activity that help users coordinate their email correspondence.

Previous work has demonstrated that people have rhythmic temporal patterns of activity in the workplace, and that these rhythms can help coordinate interaction (Begole et al., 2002). We wanted to extend this work by exploring what meaningful temporal patterns occur in the usage of email. Email is clearly a crucial and ubiquitous tool for office workers, and understanding the types of rhythms that govern its use will help identify design implications for improving the effectiveness of email services.

Specifically, we explored the following questions about email rhythms:

- How do individuals decide when to read and respond to a message?
- How do individuals form expectations about how long it will take others to respond to an email?
- How do these expectations affect email behaviors?

Email Background

While email usage has been studied since at least the 1980s, email usage has continued to evolve, suggesting an ongoing need to study and understand this evolution. Over the years, email has evolved into a multi-purpose tool used for more than just sending messages. Some people use email to track their work and manage their current responsibilities (Mackay, 1988), and some people have "overloaded" email with additional functionalities, such as managing an address book, task list, or conversation archive (Whittaker and Sidner, 1996).

People have also come to develop different, personally unique, and well-established strategies for dealing with the organization and storage of email (Bälter, 2000; Ducheneaut and Bellotti, 2001; Whittaker and Sidner, 1996). Similarly, one might expect individuals to have particular strategies for deciding when to respond to email messages, when to expect responses, and how to make those decisions. One recent study explored these differences by comparing the ability to check email continuously versus only three times a day, and found that checking email less often was actually more distracting (Patterson, 2000).

Context also plays a role in email rhythms. An early study of email (Sproull and Kiesler, 1986) found that the relative lack of social context cues in email had implications for what kind of information was exchanged and how that was percieved. Advanced communications systems have used contextual hints and information to better facilitate mutual understanding in work practice (Greenberg, 1996; Milewski and Smith, 2000; Tang et al., 2001). The PRIORITIES project uses classification learning algorithms to help assign the relative expected importance of incoming email messages, and incorporates this information into the user interface (Horvitz et al., 1999; Horvitz et al., 2002). In our research, we wanted to focus on the temporal patterns of email usage to see if they suggest tools to help users manage their email correspondence.

Study Methodology

We used interviews and qualitative observations to study rhythms in email usage. This study was conducted in two phases using semi-structured, observation-based interviews as a way to elicit users' perceptions and attitudes about email usage.

Phase I was an initial exploration that broadly surveyed e-mail rhythms and identified more focused issues on responsiveness to study in Phase II.

The subjects came primarily (37 out of 40 total individuals) from two large technology corporations (Sun Microsystems, Inc. and Hewlett-Packard). While both companies are headquartered in the San Francisco Bay area, they include tens of thousands of employees spread around the world. Hewlett-Packard (HP) had recently completed a merger with another company (Compaq), which sometimes came up in the interviews, as we noted differences in corporate culture regarding email practices. Three subjects were from the Stanford Graduate School of Business (GSB), and reflected email experiences from their prior work experience (4.5 years on average). Through the merger and through the business school students, we got a glimpse of email behaviors beyond the two main companies from which the subjects were drawn.

The subjects were regular email users and spanned a wide range of positions— research, development, sales, marketing, communications, administration, management, legal, etc. We note when our observations differ due to the organizational context of the subject's email use.

Interviews lasted from 40-60 minutes and were generally conducted in the subject's workspace. For most (31) of our subjects, the workspace was a typical office setting—in front of a computer, on a desk, in either an office or a cubicle. The three interviews with business students were conducted in a university computer lab, and six interviews with remote subjects were conducted over the phone with the subjects in their typical work environment.

While interviews are a good way to elicit users' perceptions on email usage, we were not able to verify to what extent these perceptions were substantiated by actual practice (i.e., we did not verify the user's responsiveness perceptions with actual time stamps on email messages). However, we believe these perceptions are valuable as they govern the users' email behavior.

A variety of email clients were represented, but most of the users primarily used Microsoft Outlook (20), CDE Mailer (9) or Netscape Messenger (8). While most of our observations concern features that are common to all email clients, we note cases in which users reacted to features specific to a client. The number of messages in the user's inbox ranged from zero to over 17,000, which reflected different strategies for managing email. Those with larger inbox sizes relied more on search rather than filing messages into folders. This wide range of inbox sizes was also found in previous studies (Mackay, 1988; Whittaker and Sidner, 1996).

Note that a significant proportion of email does not require a response. Many messages are broadcast or cc:'ed to users for informational purposes without requiring a response. However, such messages are usually dealt with quite easily. It is managing or tracking the messages that do require responses that demand user attention and cognitive effort. Our work focuses on these messages that elicit responses and how users manage the response process.

Phase I—Exploring Email Rhythms

Phase I was conducted with 16 subjects from Sun (7), HP (6), and the Stanford GSB (3). These interviews and observations were designed to broadly explore the concept of email rhythms—how users convey information through the timing of their email, and what they learn from the timing of email from their coworkers. We asked about:

- where, when, and how often email is checked
- how the handling of email is prioritized
- usage of advanced email features
- usage of other communication media, and how this interacts with email
- how absences or communication delays are handled
- perceptions of others' responsiveness, and how these are formed

Inbox Walkthrough

One technique we used was an "inbox walkthrough." With the subject's email client open, we would step through his or her inbox, asking him or her to describe the relationship with the sender of each message. In some cases this walkthrough was done on the email outbox or a mail folder.

At first, we conducted the walkthrough on a per-message basis. As we discovered that email rhythms are based much more on relationships than isolated messages, we began asking users to sort the inbox by sender (to see many or all messages from a particular sender). We then focused the interview on the relationships represented by the messages—it became more of a "relationship walkthrough."

Phase II—Focusing on Responsiveness Rhythms

In Phase II, we delved deeper into some of the topics identified in Phase I surrounding the rhythms of responding to messages. In particular, we focused on:

- how users decide when to reply to a particular message
- how long they expect the respondent to take to reply

To help explore these topics, we included people who work from home or at multiple locations, to see if they pay particular attention to email responsiveness. We also interviewed administrative assistants, because their role puts them in contact with a wide variety of people with different email behaviors. These subjects came from Sun (13) and HP (11) without any overlap with Phase I subjects.

Another modification we made to our walkthrough process was to ask the subject to choose relationships representing different levels of responsiveness (e.g., "very responsive" or "very unresponsive"). Finally, we constructed more focused questions on the topics identified in Phase I, which is why most of the quantitative data is only available for Phase II subjects.

Presentation of Quotes and Anecdotes

In both phases, interviews were audio-recorded and analyzed, along with our interview notes, to identify recurring issues. These issues are illustrated in this paper by representative anecdotes and quotes taken from both phases of the study. Where there was diversity in the responses, we offer multiple examples representing the various perspectives articulated. When possible, we also provide quantitative descriptions of our results, created by reviewing and coding our interview notes. The names used to refer to the subjects in this paper are fictitious, though we preserved gender with the substituted names.

Email Responsiveness and Rhythms

Our interviews showed that people had a clear sense of when to expect email responses from people based on how quickly they had responded in the past, and that they could form this expectation after just a few interactions. The time that users reported expecting an email response ranged from fifteen minutes to a few days. This varied depending on the urgency of the message, the correspondents involved, and the work culture. Expectations for quick responses (under an hour) reflected a high level of knowledge about the recipient's availability and behavior. In cases where little context about the recipient was known, the expectation was usually one day (mentioned by 16 out of 24 Phase II subjects).

> ... I would typically think it should be 24 hours. Even if they don't have the answer they should at least say, 'I got your email, it will require a little bit of research, and I'll get back to you by whenever.'

From our interviews, we identified seven main observations of email usage that we will discuss in this paper. We found that users:

- display typical patterns of response behaviors
- maintain a *responsiveness image*
- take advantage of contextual cues to explain responsiveness
- use email with other media
- use email *peri-synchronously* when quick replies are expected
- reciprocate the email behavior of others
- often experience apprehension when contacting a new email correspondent

Taken together, these observations demonstrate that, despite being considered an asynchronous communication medium, the use of email actually involves negotiation and coordination between senders and receivers. Current email clients do not support this negotiation that surrounds the use of email. By identifying and describing these observations in detail, we can begin to consider how to design email services that better support the email behaviors that have evolved in current use.

Response Behaviors

Most of our subjects (21 out of 24 in Phase II) check their email "constantly"—they have an email client open all day long (when at their computers), and are notified immediately of new email. One exception we found was Karen, an engineer who works from home, who turned off automatic fetching of new mail in her client:

> ... because it's too distracting... So I said, 'OK, forget it,' when I decide that I want to read email, I'll check it.

Some of the subjects who check email from home work in "offline" mode, where they explicitly download new email, rather than being automatically notified. This behavior is often the result of a technical limitation of not having an always-on Internet connection at home. But we also found that some people prefer to avoid the "distraction" of email when working outside the office:

> - I'm always on when I'm here... Constantly. Except when I'm at home... I'm in an offline mode... I'm going to deal with email very differently...

> - I don't want to be bothered by email, because the reason why I'm working at home is because I want to concentrate on something specific that should not have anything to do with email.

We initially expected individuals to exhibit different types of basal email rhythms (e.g. Alice is a "fast emailer" whereas Bob is "slow"). While those differences exist, we generally found more significant timing themes on a per-organization, per-relationship, and per-conversation basis. For example, our subjects typically responded more quickly to:

- messages from people within their workgroup (per-organization)
- messages from people with whom they have a history of quick communication (per-relationship)
- messages in a continuing conversation thread (per-conversation)

Responsiveness Image

In the course of our interviews, we found a family of behaviors that reflect a user's desire to project a specific image of the time between receiving and reading or replying to email. We call this projection the user's *responsiveness image*.

For example, we observed:

- users sending short messages signaling their intent to reply before they had read a message thoroughly
- users citing the perception of availability that they desired others to have of them as one of the most significant factors in prioritizing their responses
- a user who avoids opening read-receipt[1] marked messages until she has a reply prepared

---

[1] A "read-receipt" is a feature in some email clients that automatically notifies the sender of an email with a receipt when the message is read. The recipient typically is not aware that this receipt has been generated.

- users who became quite upset upon learning that read-receipts might be giving out information on their email reading habits of which they were not aware

These observations provide evidence of how individuals manage their responsiveness image. They evoke Goffman's (1959) notion of interaction as a performance, designed to leave specific impressions on its observers, consistent with the objective of the actor. In our interviews, we observed that people actively craft their image through the way they respond to email. People go to special lengths to project a certain type of responsiveness, in certain situations. While most "projecting" reflects an attempt to appear more responsive, there are also cases where people projected a less responsive image, as shown in the following examples from our interviews.

Bob, a lawyer, is meticulous about always acknowledging email messages immediately. If he does not have the time or resources to respond properly, he will at least send back a message signaling his receipt of the message, and intent to work on it soon. In this way, he projects a high level of responsiveness.

Carol, an administrative assistant for a high-level executive, will sometimes deliberately delay responding to an email to project a degree of inaccessibility. In response to requests of her manager that are low priority, she says:

> I don't want the people to think that they can get an immediate, I'll drop anything for you. ... people tend to think they can get Jerry [her manager] any time. I won't respond usually, not until the next day.

Diane is an office worker who typically responds very quickly to her email (usually within an hour). She had just begun an email relationship with her 11-year old niece where she was very deliberate about the pacing of her messages—she responds within a day.

> It's something I want to keep open, and so I may, on purpose, spread out my responses a little bit, so that she doesn't think it's a chore to respond to me, and then we can have more of an interaction, actually, than we've been able to have in the past.

People attempt to project an image in order to counteract assumptions that people might otherwise make about responsiveness. For example, Cindy, an engineer who works at home twice a week explained:

> I think I check mail more often when I'm at home. Because I feel I'm out of the group, say if they suddenly set up a meeting, I think I should know, I should keep checking.

Many of our interviewees (11 out of 13 at Sun) claimed to use a simple responsiveness-maintenance technique: If they are unable to respond in a "reasonable" amount of time (usually about 24 hours), they send a message saying they need more time. In this way, they are able to preserve a responsive image.

> I usually will get back to email or people the same day, ... even if it's just to say 'I need to look into that and I'll get back to you as soon as I can.' Because I kind of think it's rude if you ask someone for information and they just totally ignore you. It's one thing if they need time

to find out the answer, but it's nice to hear that, that they're in the office, that they received your message but just need some time to think about it.

Since users invest substantial effort to maintain a certain responsiveness image, they were frustrated to learn that their image could be undermined by features in their email client such as read-receipts. The default settings for Microsoft Outlook among the users we interviewed were that receivers were unaware that they were generating a read-receipt when they read e-mail messages. Thus, they did not realize that the senders could have more revealing information about when they read the messages than they were trying to project. This lack of control of what information others have of your activities can frustrate the maintenance of a responsiveness image and create privacy concerns.

We later learned of a related example (outside of our formal interviews) of a user who timed her email sending activity to manage when people could learn of her availability (an "availability image"). Rhonda, a high-level executive, likes to start her work early in the morning, in part to have undisturbed time before everyone else comes in to the office. Some of her work, however, involves collaborating with remote people who are in a time zone "ahead" of her. She discovered that if she sent email to those people when she first came in to work, she would often get incoming requests (by phone) since they realized that she was now available for contact. These requests disrupted her window of undisturbed work activity. Her solution was to compose responses as she went through her email at the beginning of the day, but to not send the messages until she was willing to be discovered as available.

Contextual Cues for Email Responsiveness

During the course of our interviews, we noticed that contextual cues were frequently used to help explain email responsiveness. These cues were often articulated when we asked why they thought people responded to email more slowly than expected:

> ... this week she happens to be in class. So she'll check her email on a break.

> My manager ... he's very busy, at meetings all day.

> I'm guessing, doesn't respond as quickly as I wish because, they're so busy they can't get to their email.

> I think it depends upon what he is doing when he gets the email.

Comments in the interviews helped identify what contextual cues were being used to help interpret email responsiveness. Many of these observations suggest ways it might be helpful to convey these cues through email or by integrating with other tools.

Contextual Cues From Within Email

Besides tracking people's historical response rates, other contextual cues for response rate were conveyed through email itself. An important resource is the use of "auto-reply" or "vacation" messages. This feature creates an automatic response to any email received with a message that usually explains that the user is absent and sets an expectation of when they will be able to respond to the message. The value of these messages is described by an administrative assistant who complained about people who failed to use them:

> You ask someone for information that they know, and you sit around waiting and waiting for them to get back to you, and you find out that they've been out of town.

In Phase II, we asked the subjects "How long of a work absence is required to cause you to use an auto-reply message?" The most common response was one day (8 out of 24), followed by two days (5) and one week (4). The other 7 respondents did not use an auto-reply mechanism.

One interesting use of the auto-reply feature was described by Ellen, a supply buyer. She typically takes a day to catch up on email after returning from an extended trip. During this time, she may be less responsive to new incoming mail. Her solution is to leave the "Out-of-office" auto-reply feature activated during this day after she returns (even though she is in her office), conveying to senders that they should not expect her typical responsiveness. We later learned of an example (outside of our interview study) of another user, Sam, who always leaves an auto-reply message on. The message explains that email is an unreliable way to reach him and his ability to respond to email is erratic, and directs people to contact him over the phone.

While auto-reply messages give an explicit explanation of why an email response might be delayed, these messages are only sent in response to receiving a message from someone. Thus, the sender would not know in advance about the delayed response, and might have composed the message differently if the delayed response could have been anticipated.

Another way context can be conveyed through email is through an email message itself. Several users mentioned that they would notify their work group via email when they expected to be out of the office (e.g., vacation, training). Others also mentioned that they could sometimes tell when an email correspondent was busy or in a rush through the writing style of the message. If the message had typographical errors, no capitalization or punctuation, incomplete sentences, or other indications of being hurried, that could convey that the email sender was busy, especially if that was not their usual writing style.

In a sense, a lack of an expected email response, if it becomes a recurring pattern, is also a contextual cue on email responsiveness. Many people (especially at Sun) were quick to suggest that they were not getting a response because their correspondent must be overwhelmed by email at the time. As the experience of struggling to manage email becomes more common, it becomes a more likely reason to project upon others to explain a lack of a timely response. By contrast, the subjects at HP were less likely to report feeling overwhelmed by email, demonstrating how the corporate culture of email usage provides context for expectations about email responses.

To the extent that our ability to keep up with email varies over time, it might be valuable to convey some indicator of the current size of the recipient's email backlog. This might be measured in terms of the number of unread messages in the user's inbox relative to what is typical for that user. Knowing if the user currently has a large email backlog may help prospective email senders consider the most effective way of contacting that person at the moment. For example, it may suggest a different way of crafting a message to get the attention needed, a different medium of contacting the person (e.g., using the phone instead of email), or waiting for a different time to send the message.

Contextual Cues From Outside Email

Besides cues from email itself, users cited a number of contextual cues from other sources that often helped explain delays in email response. Shared online calendars have been shown to be a valuable resource for coordinating group work (Palen, 1999), and several users mentioned them as a way of explaining email delays. Browsing someone else's calendar is one way of discovering that they are on vacation (especially if they do not use auto-reply vacation messages). At Sun, 9 of the 13 subjects described relationships and situations in which they expected a response within an hour, and sometimes within 15-20 minutes. Failure to receive a response within that time would prompt them to check the calendar of the correspondent. If her calendar showed that she had a meeting scheduled at that time, it would often explain the delay in responding, and suggest when she would return and have a chance to respond to the message.

Others mentioned that the knowledge of their correspondent's job role factored in to their expectation of response time. Certain jobs (e.g., programmers, administrative assistants) were typically associated with being at the desk most of the time, which would tend to indicate faster response times. Other jobs (e.g., managers) implied being in meetings a lot of the time and away from the desk (and thus unavailable for responding to email).

The recent emergence of using wirelessly connected laptops and mobile devices to read email during meetings represents another contextual cue that would modify the effect of meetings and other activities outside the office on email responsiveness. People who worked in the field were considered to be traveling or meeting with customers much of the time, thus limiting their access to email (and consequently their responsiveness).

The social context of email usage also provides cues about responsiveness. A few people mentioned reputations of email responsiveness that were shared among others:

I'm known by my bosses and by my employees to follow up through email probably, faster than anybody else around here.

… people would say, 'Send him email, he responds quickly.'

Thus, people not only formed expectations of when they would get email responses from those they corresponded with, they also shared their expectations with others to help form social reputations of email responsiveness.

Email behavior was also noted as a topic of social conversation that conveys expectations of response time. Two people, in particular, mentioned how others' complaints about "he's not responding to my email" would come up in conversation. In one case, however, the subject being interviewed was getting normal email responses from the person being complained about, reinforcing the observation that email response rates can differ for each pair-wise combination.

In another example, sharing among a team that no one was getting an email response from a particular person helped piece together a story that something was happening:

Once [our manager] was traveling … but we didn't hear from him for a day. And we thought, you know, something's going on. There must be some bad meetings, something bad must have happened. It was a day. None of us, we checked, none of us had heard from him.

Email users currently draw upon contextual cues from email, other tools such as a calendar, other people's experiences, and other knowledge to help interpret email responsiveness patterns. Understanding how these cues are used could help identify what cues would be useful to convey through an interface to someone who is preparing to compose an email message. Supporting this kind of awareness between sender and receiver builds on the notion of social translucence (Erickson and Kellogg, 2000) by providing cues that allow social negotiation of appropriate action.

Email with Other Media

Email is used in conjunction with other communication media, such as the telephone, instant messaging (IM), and face-to-face contact. A common tactic we observed when a message was important or urgent was to send a voicemail in conjunction with an email. Typically, the email contained detailed data or attached documents, and the voicemail signaled the urgency of the message. Of Phase II subjects, 10 out of the 11 at HP, and 4 of 11 at Sun claimed to use this tactic (at HP, voicemail is used more frequently than at Sun, where email is predominant). Typically, the email was sent as the "primary" message, and the voicemail served as a pointer to the email, but a few subjects mentioned the converse.

One subject even mentioned leaving voicemail at both office and cell phone numbers. Two more subjects reported combining an email with an electronic page to convey the message's urgency. This tactic appeared to address the concern that the recipient may not notice or have access to the email message quickly enough. However, using the phone or pager as an alert notification not only creates more work for the sender, but also adds to the load of messages (voice or page) that the receiver must deal with. This practice suggests the need for better ways of delivering or notifying recipients of urgent messages, perhaps through more integration with other communication media.

IM use was not common for our subjects. Only 4 of the 24 subjects in Phase II claimed to be current IM users. Two of them, however, described how they use IM in place of the telephone, not to replace email. They used IM in situations where they need an immediate answer (within a few minutes) or expect multiple rounds of dialogue, situations in which people have traditionally used the phone. Consistent with other studies of IM use (Nardi et al., 2000; Isaacs et al., 2002) our subjects preferred IM because it enables them to multitask—to continue with their other work in between dialogue exchanges, and to carry on multiple conversations at one time. For them, email is not as easily replaced by IM, since it is used for sending longer, detailed messages, file attachments, and messages with many recipients, which are difficult to accomplish over IM.

Asynchronous and Peri-synchronous Email

Email is often described as an asynchronous medium, and indeed, our subjects valued the ability communicate without actually having to catch the recipient at the moment. However, we also detected a distinct style of writing email *peri-synchronously*. By peri-synchronous, we mean sending messages nearly synchronously such that they are expected to receive a response shortly. Email correspondents who share a significant overlap of work time can exchange email peri-synchronously, allowing several exchanges to occur within a day. This style contrasts with completely asynchronous email usage, which might occur when emailing with international correspondents who are shifted in time by about seven hours or more. Such email will probably be read and acted upon while the sender is offline.

Most of the work-related email that our subjects talked about occurred within a peri-synchronous context. There was enough time overlap that correspondents could expect a response within a day, and would even afford iterations and discussion throughout the day. In this sense, any individual message could leave room for discussion or be incomplete, but the thread could resolve to a conclusion within a day.

However, email correspondents with international colleagues who were time shifted by seven hours or more exhibited a different pattern. Since they could not expect a response within a day, people talked about thinking more carefully about those messages and taking the time to be more clear, explicit, and complete. Gary, a California-based member of a field services team, commented on correspondence with people in Europe or Asia,

> You have to get everything that you need down in one shot, in order to get the turnaround time... So instead of saying 'I think it could be this, look here and tell me what that says,' I will list out four or five possibilities, 'Here's what I think it probably is, if it's not that it might be this and if it's not that it might be this other thing.'

Furthermore, international email correspondence was more likely to encounter cultural differences in styles of usage. Several of the American email users commented that messages to their colleagues in India or Asia did not prompt as quick or complete a response as they had hoped. They were quick to recognize that this might be due to a different work culture.

Also, personal email has a different asynchronous style associated with it. People often do not expect responses to personal email within a day. They do not seem to expect such a high priority in responding to personal email, and think of it more like traditional letter writing where a response could be more leisurely.

In this way, we found that the context of using email asynchronously or peri-synchronously affected the way they composed their messages. Peri-synchronous use did not require catching the recipient at the moment, like using IM or the phone, but did afford the flexibility of interaction and discussion through exchanges during the day. Being aware of this context and the underlying reason for it (e.g., different time zones, work culture, or relative priority) is another cue that people use to set expectations of when they might get a response (which in turn affects how they compose their messages).

Reciprocity in Email Behaviors

The influence of reciprocity in governing human behavior is the subject of much work in social and evolutionary psychology. For example, Trivers (1971) found that the reciprocation of seemingly insignificant favors and courtesies is crucial to the "social contract" fabric of human society, and others have described the biological and economic foundations of such actions (Sigmund et al., 2002). We found that there is also a notion of reciprocity between participants in an email conversation. This reciprocity appeared strongly in exchanges that evolved into IM-like exchanges of 1-2 line messages every few minutes, as well as in longer-term interactions—when one of the participants replied more slowly than the other, subsequent messages back and forth typically proceeded at the slower pace.

Kate, a business development leader, described a former manager who was very responsive—no matter where he was, he would send a clear, useful response to your message within 24 hours. This behavior inspired special efforts to reciprocate:

> His responsiveness made people very responsive to him... What I can tell you is what he did for the people who worked with him—incredible loyalty... You would work around the clock for this guy... You could not let him down. This was a problem. Because when you would ask him something, he would come back to you. So when he would ask you something ... you had to get back to him.

Kate also described a former peer who was "very unresponsive." He would rarely respond to email, instead requiring catching him on the phone. As a result, Kate "calibrated" her email relationship to his, becoming less responsive. Reciprocity is important to Kate: "People react to the way you treat them." If a peer is unresponsive, then "he's going to get the same deal."

> I've discovered that people do adjust their responsiveness… I've seen that happen. Because I try to be very responsive to people, and I expect that same responsiveness. So if they don't match up, then I'm going to change my responsiveness level. It's a real tit for tat kind of a mechanism.

Taking stock of how well you have reciprocated in responding to others can lead to a notion of watching out for a "responsiveness debt." For example, Patty, a solutions manager, will frequently scan the last week's worth of email in her inbox to assess whether or not she's maintained her responsiveness image on a per-person basis:

> I also take a look a lot at what's happened in the last seven days, and did I respond to everything that's been going on… I do it on a daily basis… In the last seven days, I've gotten three messages from Annie, seven messages from John, that kind of thing, what were those messages about, and am I still keeping up with all that.

We also noticed several instances of the same two people carrying on two or more overlapping conversations, each with distinct timing patterns. These observations suggest that reciprocity can be a per-*conversation* as well as a per-*relationship* phenomenon.

Another type of reciprocation we observed was the choice of media. Several subjects try to learn which medium their correspondents prefer, and will contact them in that way. Lois, a marketing manager, personally dislikes the phone and strongly prefers email or IM. However, she says:

> The first thing I ever find out about anybody I work with is how they communicate. That's just really important to me.

By adapting and reciprocating communication preferences in this way, she increases her chances of getting timely responses.

Anxiety in New Email Relationships

We found that when writing to a new email correspondent, the sender will often have anxiety about whether and when the email will be read, and if and when a reply can be expected. People typically develop these expectations over the course of an email relationship, but when there is no such foundation, they do not know what to expect. Even if the recipient is a personal acquaintance, there is a degree of anxiety because he or she is not an *email acquaintance*.

Conclusions

By treating email as an asynchronous communication medium, current email tools provide little opportunity for users to exchange cues about when to expect a response or when are good times to be reached by email. Yet, our observations demonstrate that there are subtle ways in which email is a mutually negotiated medium: People project responsiveness images to each other, they use email peri-synchronously, and they calibrate their email behaviors to mirror the rhythms of their correspondents. Finding ways to convey these contextual cues could provide better support for the mutual negotiation between senders and receivers, which would in turn enable the design of richer, more effective email services.

Mutually Setting Expectations

One perspective from which we can summarize our findings is in terms of the *recipient's burden.* Without any cues to negotiate between senders and recipients, much of the burden of managing email currently falls on the recipient. Recipients need to track whether or not they have responded to email messages in a timely way, and may also need to integrate notifications from email, voicemail, pagers, and other media. Without any mechanism for negotiating how much or what kind of email a recipient would like to handle, they are further saddled with the task of screening unwanted spam and managing incoming mail with filters, agents, tedious filing strategies, etc.

From the sender's perspective, our observations show that previous experiences in corresponding with a person enable the sender to formulate expectations about when a message he or she sends will be read, and more importantly, responded to (in cases where a response is desired). Distinct from this *response expectation* is a *breakdown perception*—when the sender believes that something has gone wrong, and will take further action. We observed a number of factors that influence these expectations.

We asked people about both expectations—when subjects expected an email response and how long they would wait before following up—and found that they expressed distinct time frames in their responses. For example, some expect a response within a half hour or an hour, but will wait a day until walking to the recipient's office to find him or her. Thus, they expected a response within an hour, but would wait until a day to consider it a breakdown that required follow-up. We saw a similar pattern in users who expected a response in fifteen minutes; after waiting for an hour with no response, they followed up with a telephone call or by checking the recipient's calendar to see if he or she was unavailable due to a meeting. Again, the response expectation (fifteen minutes) was distinct from the breakdown perception (one hour). Figure 1 shows a visualization of these expectations, and puts them on an abstract timeline.

254

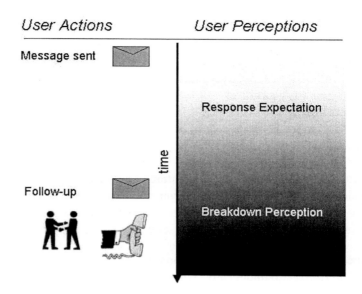

Figure 1. A visualization of the "expectation-to-breakdown timeline." When the breakdown perception is formed, the sender will initiate a follow-up action, such as a phone call, another email, checking their calendar, or a face-to-face visit.

This distinction between response perception and breakdown also governed how people maintained their responsiveness image. For example, most of our subjects said that they typically expect a response within 24 hours, and thus most people set auto-reply vacation messages if they were absent for a day. But some would only activate an out-of-office auto-reply message for absences of *two days* or more. This longer latency is calibrated to the breakdown perception, rather than the response expectation. In this case, they are not interested in maintaining a typical response time, but one that is just good enough to prevent the sender from worrying about not receiving a response. This distinction also governed when users will send an email alerting the sender that they need more time. This message is sent after the response expectation point (e.g., one day) has passed, but before the breakdown perception (e.g., two days).

Clearly, the expectation and breakdown points are not the same for every email, or even for every person. We observed the following influences on these expectations:

- The recipient—expectations of responsiveness vary from person to person
- Location of recipient—the time shift between sender and recipient may increase the time expected for a response
- Urgency of topic—people expect attention to be paid to urgent messages, which are often signaled with markers such as "URGENT:" in the subject field or priority flags

- Combination with voicemail—as described previously, important email messages are often accompanied by a voicemail, to convey the urgency of the request

If an email reaches the breakdown point without a response, the sender will either give up on the request or follow it up. The most common follow-up methods we observed were:

- contacting the recipient through different means, typically a telephone call or in-person visit (when possible)
- sending another email, with more urgency or adamancy in the subject line
- checking on the calendar or other context of the recipient, to see if there are explanations for the lack of responsiveness

The expectation-to-breakdown timeline is a useful framework for understanding how individuals track the progress of their incoming and outgoing email requests and correspondence.

Design Implications

Besides being a useful analytic framework, this timeline could also be a helpful design concept for future email services that help users manage their email responsiveness. Perhaps an *email responsiveness service* could analyze a variety of measures of email behavior and abstract a representation of this timeline for individual messages, and this timeline could be visualized in email clients. Such a timeline could remind recipients of messages that they have not yet responded to within their typical response times. The timeline could also alert senders of messages for which they have not received a response within their typical expectations.

Such a timeline representation should be designed so that it integrates these various measures of email behavior into a simple graphic that users can easily use as a basis for a responsiveness expectation (rather than having to examine many different metrics and sources to make that judgement themselves). The timeline portrayal should also appropriately reflect that these response expectations are inexact, so as not to mislead users into a false sense of precise predictions of when to expect a response. Furthermore, the service should be designed to aggregate and abstract the data in such a way as to protect the privacy of the users. A useful depiction of the timeline that gives users a sense of when to expect an email response does not need to reveal the detailed measures used to create that representation.

Many of the factors needed to create such a timeline representation for email messages could be drawn from observations about an individual's current email usage. Logs of how quickly people respond to particular email senders over time could be analyzed to develop a response time prediction for a message and identify a range after which breakdown has probably occurred. These predictions based on historical rhythms could also be modified by other inputs tracked by a dynamically updated awareness service. Just as current IM systems detect when users are logged on and how recently they have been active on their computer keyboard, this information could be tracked over time and used to develop a sense of how much opportunity a user has had to access and thus respond to email. That is, if an email recipient has been away from his keyboard more than usual, it might lengthen the time before a response should be expected without triggering an indication that a breakdown has occurred.

Another factor that could be tracked is the recipient's current backlog of email. If an email recipient currently has a larger than usual number of unread messages in her inbox, she may not be able to maintain her usual responsiveness. Aggregating and analyzing these and other existing data sources could provide a basis for constructing an expectation-to-breakdown timeline.

Taking current conditions into account to modify the expectation-to-breakdown timeline would be useful even to email correspondents that have expectations based on previous experience. For example, you may know someone to be a quick email responder, but if he is currently away from his keyboard and experiencing a large email backlog, the longer response expectation time depicted in the timeline would modify your default expectation. Thus, the timeline may suggest a different course of action (e.g., call instead of wait for an email reply or look for someone else to address the issue).

Another example application of such a timeline is in helping address the anxiety that many senders experience when emailing someone for the first time. Without any prior experience to establish an expectation, senders can face a dilemma of how long to wait for a response before deciding that follow-up actions are required. Appropriately conveying cues to set responsiveness expectations for someone to whom you are emailing for the first time could help smooth the initial contact through email. Of course, sharing cues about email responsiveness, especially with strangers who are emailing you for the first time, raises privacy issues. Users need to be aware of and maintain control of the responsiveness image that they present. More exploration is needed to understand the delicate balance between sharing useful contextual cues about email responsiveness and preserving users' control over their responsiveness image.

Our research identified some of the cues people use to form expectations of getting an email response. Faced with an impoverished communication medium such as email, people have developed many techniques for adding some of the richness of negotiation back to the medium through the use of timing and other responsiveness-related behaviors. Applying this understanding to the design of new email services that share the awareness of these behaviors among email correspondents, with proper respect to privacy concerns, could create a richer, more effectively negotiated communication channel.

Acknowledgements

We would like to thank Kyle Forster, Jason Heidema, and Randy Schwemmin for their involvement in this work, Jeanette Blomberg, Randy Trigg, and Pam Hinds for their guidance, Marie-Jo Fremont for calling in some favors, and all of our interview subject volunteers.

References

Bälter, O. (2000): 'Keystroke Level Analysis of Email Message Organization', in *Proceedings of CHI 2000*, ACM Press, 105-112.

Begole, J., Tang, J., Smith, R., and Yankelovich, N. (2002): 'Work Rhythms: Analyzing Visualizations of Awareness Histories of Distributed Groups', in Proceedings of CSCW 2002, New Orleans LA, November 2002, in press.

Ducheneaut, N. and Bellotti, V. (2001): 'Email as Habitat: An Exploration of Embedded Personal Information Management', in *Interactions,* 8 (5), (Sept/Oct 2001), 30-38.

Erickson, T. and Kellogg, W. (2000): 'Social Translucence: An Approach to Designing Systems that Mesh with Social Processes', in *Transactions on Computer-Human Interaction*, Vol. 7, No. 1, 2000, 59-83.

Goffman, E. (1959): *The Presentation of Self in Everyday Life*, Doubleday, Garden City NY, 1959.

Greenberg, S. (1996): 'Peepholes: Low Cost Awareness of One's Community', in *Companion Proceedings of CHI '96*, 138-145.

Horvitz, E., Jacobs, A., and Hovel, C. (1999): 'Attention-Sensitive Alerting', in *Proceedings of UAI '99, Conference on Uncertainty and Artificial Intelligence*, Stockholm, Sweden, July 1999, Morgan Kaufmann: San Francisco, 305-313.

Horvitz, E., Koch, P., Kadie, C., and Jacobs, A. (2002): 'Coordinate: Probabilistic Forecasting of Presence and Availability', in *Proceedings of the Eighteenth National Conference on Uncertainty and Artificial Intelligence*, Edmonton, Alberta, July 2002, AAAI Press, 224-233.

Isaacs, E., Walendowski, A., Whittaker, S., Schiano, D., and Kamm, C. (2002): 'The Character, Functions, and Styles of Instant Messaging in the Workplace', in *Proceedings of CSCW 2002*, New Orleans LA, November 2002, ACM Press, 11-20.

Mackay, W. (1988): 'More Than Just a Communication System: Diversity in the Use of Electronic Mail', in *Proceedings of CSCW '88,* Portland OR, Sep 26-29 1988, ACM Press, 344-353.

Milewski, Allen E., and Smith, Thomas M. (2000): 'Providing Presence Cues to Telephone Users', in *Proceedings of CSCW 2000*, Philadelphia PA, December 2000, ACM Press, 89-96.

Nardi, B., Whittaker, S., and Bradner, E. (2000): 'Interaction and Outeraction: Instant Messaging in Action', in *Proceedings of CSCW 2000*, Philadelphia PA, December 2000, ACM Press, 79-88.

Palen, L. (1999): 'Social, Individual and Technological Issues for Groupware Calendar Systems', in *Proceedings of the Conference on Computer Human Interaction (CHI) 1999*, Pittsburgh PA, May 1999, pp. 17-24.

Patterson, M. (2000): *Email in Daily Work*, draft available at (http://www.andrew.cmu.edu/user/mp72/email_in_daily_work.html).

Sigmund, K., Fehr, E., and Nowak, M. (2002): 'The Economics of Fair Play', in *Scientific American*, January 2002, 81-85.

Sproull, L., and Kiesler, S. (1986). 'Reducing Social Context Cues: Electronic Mail in Organizational Communication', in *Management Science*, 32, 1492- 1512.

Tang, J., Yankelovich, N., Begole, J., Van Kleek, M., Li, F., Bhalodia, J. (2001): 'ConNexus to Awarenex: Extending Awareness to Mobile Users', in *Proceedings of CHI '01*, ACM Press, 2001.

Trivers, R. (1971): 'The Evolution of Reciprocal Altruism', in *Quarterly Review of Biology*, 46, 35-37.

Whittaker, S., and Sidner, C. (1996): 'Email Overload: Exploring Personal Information Management of Email', in *Proceedings of CHI '96*, ACM Press, 276-283.

K. Kuutti, E.H. Karsten, G. Fitzpatrick, P. Dourish and K. Schmidt (eds.), *ECSCW 2003: Proceedings of the Eighth European Conference on Computer Supported Cooperative Work, 14-18 September 2003, Helsinki, Finland*, pp. 259-275.

Multi-team Facilitation of Very Large-scale Distributed Meetings

David R. Millen & Michael A. Fontaine

IBM, 1 Rogers Street, Cambridge, Massachusetts 02142 USA

{David_R_Millen,mfontain}@us.ibm.com

Abstract. Distributed work teams routinely use virtual meetings to support their collaborative work. In this paper, we present a case study of the facilitation that was provided for a *very large-scale distributed meeting*. Small teams of facilitators were recruited, trained, and assigned to each of six discussion forums of ManagerJam, a 48 hour meeting of over 8,000 managers in a large global technology company. Through examination of pre-Jam records, analysis of the Jam conversation archive, and post-event interviews with over 20 facilitators, we describe the planning and training efforts, and assess the impact of the facilitation teams on the meeting's effectiveness. Guidelines for effective team facilitation of very large-scale meetings are provided, and design implications for meeting support systems are described.

Introduction

Computer-supported meetings have been the focus of considerable research for some time. Early work on group support systems (GSS), used to augment face-to-face meetings, focused on productivity gains that arose from such systems (see, for example Dennis, Nunamaker, & Vogel, 1990; Grohowski, McGoff, Vogel, Martz & Nunamaker, 1990; Turoff, Hiltz, Bahgat, & Rana, 1993). Several researchers have identified the importance of facilitation in the effectiveness of a GSS (Bostrum, Anson, & Clawson, 1993; Clawson, Bostrom, 1993a; Kelley, & Bostrum, 1995; Limayen, Lee-Partiridge, Dickson, & DeSanctis 1993; Nunamaker, Applegate, Kosynski, 1987). For example, it has been shown that facilitation may be necessary to help participants with use of the tool as well as with assistance with the meeting's process (Fuller & Trower, 1994). Others have found that facilitation is important through encouragement of effective task behavior (Bostrum et al., 1993). Early work with GSS, concluded that "although the technology has matured to the point where it is very easy to use by almost anyone, our experience continues to confirm that the quality of the group session is predominantly dependent on the facilitator." McGoff and Ambrose (1991) identified several important characteristics of successful facilitators. First, they need excellent communication and group interaction skills. Second, they need to be skilled in the use of the GSS and in general group facilitation techniques.

Other GSS researchers have investigated the roles that facilitators take on during a meeting (Clawson & Bostrom, 1993b). Fuller and Trower (1994) identified eighteen roles for facilitators, including opinion seeker, elaborator, evaluator, compromiser, recorder, and standard setter. A second team of researchers identified over one thousand different characteristics of effective and ineffective behaviors of facilitators. These characteristics were grouped into 16 main role dimensions, including: appropriates, selects and prepares technology, creates comfort with and promotes understanding of the technology and technology outputs, actively builds rapport and relationships, and manages conflict and negative emotions constructively. Another team of researchers observed that various facilitation roles, such as technology facilitator and process/agenda facilitator emerge over time (Mark, Grudin, and Poltrock, 1999).

The facilitation of *distributed* group support systems has become increasingly important as economic and environmental concerns have motivated more and more virtual team interaction and collaboration. One recent empirical study reported that the facilitation challenges using a distributed GSS are different, and in some cases are greater than that of a face-to-face GSS (Romano, Nunamaker, Briggs, & Mittleman, 1999). For example, there were significant challenges with the technology, a greater need to establish and maintain focus on the meeting goals, and an increased difficulty attaining desired levels of participation.

Other research on *distributed facilitation* found that distance may increase necessary technology support due to heterogeneous technology infrastructures, and may pose additional challenges on planning activities for a remote leadership team Niederman, Beise, & Beranek (1993). The need for small groups of facilitators, or a hierarchy of facilitators was foreseen as the capacity of the distributed GSS increased.

One way to think about the challenges inherent in meeting facilitation is to consider various combinations of meeting *place* (same or different) and *number* of facilitators (individual or a team). In Figure 1, we show four quadrants of the resulting two by two matrix The upper left quadrant illustrates the traditional GSS environment; a single facilitator in a shared physical meeting room. The "distributed GSS" environment (members of the meeting are in different places) is shown in lower left quadrant. In the upper right cell, we find a multi-person facilitated GSS in which a team of facilitators (or instructors in the case of learning systems) interacts with a group of participants in as shared place. We believe that the final cell (lower right), multi-person facilitated distributed GSS, poses significant new challenges for effective facilitation of very large-scale meetings. Thus, as the scale of the meeting increases, quite often the number of facilitators also increases. This presents challenges for effective training and coordination of the group of facilitators.

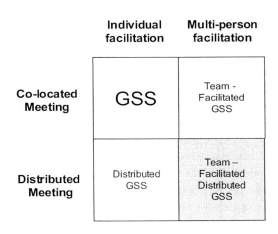

Figure 1: GSS meeting matrix

Very large-scale distributed meetings

It has become increasingly easy to host very large-scale distributed meetings to gather the collective ideas and decisions of a large group via a corporate intranet. One pioneering large-scale distributed meeting called WorldJam (also referred to as a *massively parallel conversation* (MPC) (Spira, Friedman, & Ebling, 2001) held in May 2001), brought together over 52,000 globally-dispersed employees to discuss a wide range of issues over 72 hours (Halverson, Newswanger, Erickson, Wolf, Kellog, Laff, & Malkin, 2002). While technology enabled large numbers of employees to debate and discuss topics in ten discussion forums, the facilitation teams who mediated, monitored and facilitated these global conversations were critical to meeting's success. These individuals—including experienced on-line facilitators, business executives, and novice communication brokers—helped foster the discussions by posing provocative questions, connecting discussion threads from different areas, helping employees make connections with colleagues halfway around the world, and mining the discussions for relevant practices and useful insights (Dorsett, Fontaine, & O'Driscoll, 2002; Fontaine, Burton, & Lesser, 2002).

In this paper, we present a case study of the facilitation of a similar large-scale distributed meeting, ManagerJam, and investigate the role and influence of multi-person facilitation teams. There are three characteristics of a meeting of this type. First, this is a meeting on a very large scale. Over 30,000 managers were invited to participate in ManagerJam. Second, a Jam runs nonstop for a bounded period of time. ManagerJam's forums were open continuously worldwide for 48 hours, which presented challenges to facilitators to keep the discussion interesting and lively across multiple time zones, geographies and cultures. The well defined start and stop times for the meeting provided focus and a sense of urgency for those interested in participating. Finally, the size of the meeting and its round-the clock duration necessitated the use of several multi-person, geographically-distributed facilitation teams. These teams were viewed as an important component in facilitating an event that was intended to be much more than an interactive discussion.

Through the following description and analysis of the facilitation activities that supported ManagerJam we will to answer two questions: (1) What are good facilitation practices that can serve as guidelines for future very large-scale distributed meetings? (2) What problems or difficulties did the facilitators encounter and what are the design implications for large-scale computer-supported meeting applications?

Note on method

The ManagerJam research team was comprised of researchers from the firm's various business units who focused on a variety of research topics: including facilitation, participant patterns and behaviors, and organizational effectiveness. Our understanding of the facilitation of ManagerJam was informed by observation of both the pre-meeting planning activities undertaken by the facilitation teams and the Jam event itself. We also performed content analysis on the archival records from the pre-Jam online collaborative workspace (TeamRoom Plus®)[1] as well as the conversation transcripts of the Jam event itself. Finally, we completed structured interviews with small groups of facilitators (2 to 7 per group) within three weeks after the completion of the ManagerJam event. In all, we interviewed 20 facilitators (out of a total of 48).

---

[1] TeamRoom Plus ®Notes Database

Preparing for the Jam

From its conception, ManagerJam was part of a larger human resources initiative to explore emerging issues for managers and to develop new management training and support programs. The mission of the larger project was to "successfully execute a Jam for senior managers and executives worldwide as part of the Manager Development program." ManagerJam was designed to be a six forum brainstorming session that would surface a good set of challenging management problems and a collection of creative, peer-vetted solutions—all of which could be widely shared and applied. It was expected that the output of the Jam would inform the other elements of the larger human resources program. (These six forum topics can be found in Table 1).

Table 1: Discussion topics for the six ManagerJam forums.

Forum	Forum Discussion Topics
1	**Translating Strategy into Results:** What do you do to help your people understand the company's business strategy, and use it to propel their own operational and personal success
2	**Building Careers:** How do you prepare employees to outgrow their current jobs?
3	**Fostering Innovation:** How do you encourage appropriate risk-taking, so that your department drives change and grows the business?
4	**Managing Performance:** What approaches have you found most effective at turning your team into a true meritocracy?
5	**The Human Face:** How do you use the resources at your disposal to make the company uniquely supportive for your employees
6	**The New Customer Landscape:** How do you help your people work actively with colleagues across the company to deliver what our customers need today?

Defining the role of moderators, facilitators, and participants

The moderators for each forum were expected to decide which postings were of sufficient interest and importance to be moved into a separate part of the discussion space for voting. In addition to reading and responding to participant postings, facilitators steered the dialogue, encouraged participation and deeper thinking, offered insight into the topic at hand and flagged comments containing ideas or solutions that had the potential for immediate implementation.

The most interesting and actionable ideas that emerged within each discussion fora were selected by facilitators and listed separately for participant voting. ManagerJam participants would be asked to rate ideas as:

1. *Ready now*: it can be implemented as is, and can help the business.
2. *Almost ready*: it needs some refinement…but not much.
3. *Not ready*: There may be something here, but it needs more work.

The best of these ideas would be offered to the Role of the Manager program for subsequent action.

The Jam's discussion and collaboration spaces

The discussion application supporting the Jam conformed to the design standards (look and feel) of the corporate intranet and was accessible from a standard browser. There was a separate *home* discussion page, where a menu displayed access links to each of the six forums. In an individual forum page (see Figure 2), a list of the most recently posted messages was presented with links provided to view earlier messages. A five-line summary of each topic message was provided. Also, a link was provided to drill down and see the complete message and the remaining message thread.

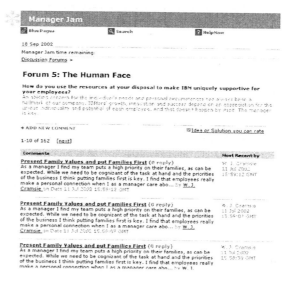

Figure 2: ManagerJam's discussion environment

The discussion forums were hosted on an NNTP (Network News Transport Protocol) server, while the message rating functions were supported by a DB2 server. JSP servlets were used to integrate the forums and the voting tasks.

An online collaborative workspace (TeamRoom Plus™) was also created for the globally-distributed project and facilitation teams, and the event preparation proceeded with a mixture of conference calls, email and chat messaging. Facilitators for the Jam were solicited from two organizations: corporate communications (event host) and organizational development (HR program sponsor). For each forum, there was a primary moderator supported by a group of six to eight facilitators.

Facilitator training and preparation

Since the Jam was to be held continuously for 48 hours, many of the teams had representation from different geographies to more easily provide time zone coverage. Teams were encouraged to meet in person (if possible) and remotely several times before the event to plan, prepare and strategize for their forum. Many of core topics required of more traditional GSS facilitators were covered (Yoong, 1995).

To prepare for the Jam and to navigate facilitating in an online environment, a one-day training workshop, a practice session (in the tool) and a short facilitation guide were provided to explain role responsibilities and online facilitation practices. Facilitators suggested that the mix of training methods not only provided their teams with the opportunity to become familiar with one another, but also created a foundation to work from.

In addition to training, facilitators were asked to prepare for the Jam by researching topic areas to better steer and support Jam dialogue. We found this to be quite useful for facilitators to get a general grasp of the topic, given that most were not subject matter experts. One facilitator commented on her experience:

> *I did a lot of the preparation work just looking on the web and looking through search engines on the topics of innovation and actually found some surprising resources out there that I didn't realize were available. What it did was help me get in the mindset of it. In answering or developing the threads, I found it was good context for helping push the threads in one direction or another.*

It is clear that this practice of topic preparation also assisted with facilitation teams' pre-Jam preparation. In future Jams, especially if they are time, resource or topic constrained, the use of subject matter experts trained in the art of e-facilitation may be appropriate.

The importance of schedule and communication strategy planning

As was revealed from the analysis of WorldJam (Fontaine et al., 2002), scheduling and communication are two key elements of Jam success. Facilitation teams who invest in both are better prepared to handle and address any situation that may arise. For ManagerJam, a strong emphasis was placed on operational planning for each of the forum teams. We found this to be extremely helpful in allowing facilitation teams to navigate potential obstacles and barriers. Not only was time zone coverage, methods of "passing the baton" and scheduling discussed, but also communication strategies and channels were decided beforehand. Teams pointed out that knowing who to turn to and what channel to communicate through greatly assisted in managing background support. One facilitator commented:

> ...So another area that we really was helpful was that we had to spend quite a lot of time trying to figure out our schedules—in terms of I'm working in AP [Asia Pacific], someone else is in the UK [United Kingdom], someone else is in the US [United States]—and how we are going to time ourselves and hand over process from one facilitator to the other.

Another facilitator suggested that scheduling along with a well-defined communication strategy helped his team stay connected. He stated:

> Well, first off we had a schedule and a protocol for exactly what you needed to do in terms of writing a summary of activity, sending that by email and then talking to the next person to facilitate—either by phone or by Sametime chat to confirm that they were on or to just touching base with them. That's pretty much we passed the baton.

Pre-Jam participant recruiting

Large-scale diffuse meetings of this sort need to use multiple methods to invite and encourage participation in the event. For ManagerJam, facilitators worked both personal networks and organization charts to recruit participants, and created a sense of awareness around forum topics pre-Jam. They also insured an evident online population as the Jam kicked off. The facilitators reported using existing email distribution lists, email directed at specific geographic areas, and special requests for senior managers to solicit meeting participation. Several of the facilitators said that personal quotas were assigned team members to ensure that a significant number of employees were personally invited to the meeting.

During the Jam

Communication among the facilitation teams

The descriptions of the Jam experience offered during our facilitation team interviews indicated that the pre-Jam preparation had paid off. Facilitators communicated frequently with other members of their team in predetermined communication channels (e.g., using the TeamRoom, email, or Sametime chat). Most of the facilitators said that they felt well prepared and found that they actually spent less time devoted to the facilitation task than they had estimated.

During the interviews, it surfaced that there were several different communication styles that developed among the teams. One facilitator described the team interaction during the Jam as follows:

> We set up periodic calls throughout the twenty-four hour period. We used somebody's 1-800 number, and we put those in place prior to the event because we hadn't really thought about keeping the Sametime chat window open during the entire period. So we thought one way to make sure that we kind of heard each other's voices and really were able to brainstorm was to kind of put that in play. It worked very well for the first half of the forum. But, by the end, the Sametime chat seemed to work so well we would opt not to have those calls.

A second facilitator described their team interaction in the following manner:

> There were certainly some facilitators who gravitated towards the TeamRoom. There were some who actually preferred a [conference] call. But, all preferred Sametime as a constant tool to use throughout the event because it was less obtrusive and actually it was a good way to capture previous conversations. So, you could kind of get up to speed if need be, and we actually used that much more collaboratively when it came to identifying comments for voting and even preparing summaries as opposed to email.

Given the difficulties coordinating the work within each forum, facilitators were assigned to a single team. In one case, to fill a coverage gap for hours covering the Asia Pacific geographies, one facilitator volunteered to help out on a second team. This resulted in an unplanned transfer of learning from one team to another. While helping Team 4, the facilitator noticed that an always-open group chat was an effective and easy way to keep the team informed about the work activities. She was able to transfer the idea to Team 6 on her next shift. The ability to easily share best facilitation practices across forums, as they emerge during the Jam would be a great benefit in cases where more than one team is facilitating a large event.

Facilitating the conversation

The biggest class of problems that arose during the Jam had to do with access or authentication issues. Since this was a restricted meeting, the prearranged list of invited employees was not complete. This is unfortunate, but not altogether surprising given the fact that over 30,000 employees were invited to ManagerJam. The facilitation teams followed the prescribed troubleshooting procedures, including telephoning a special support hotline. Most of these access problems were resolved quickly. There was no evidence of online *deviant* behavior, probably due in large part to the participant job role and the fact that the Jam participants were not anonymous.

One problem that surfaced early for the facilitators was primarily due to the interface design of the discussion tool. For each forum, the list view would only show about 10-12 top-level postings one at a time. During peak traffic times, for example, at the beginning of the Jam, messages would quickly become buried. One facilitator said:

> *It seemed like we had seventy-five postings right away and the audience was just coming to post their comment and go. So, you immediately had to navigate through four or five pages of comments. But, if there was a good thought buried on page four and you responded, you couldn't see the response and nobody would see that new comment.*

The difficulty navigating through multiple pages of postings resulted in several obvious problems. One facilitator commented:

> *We definitely had a lot of duplicate ideas. But to be honest, it was very difficult to scroll through and read the entire [postings]. It was a very big investment to read the whole forum before you posted.*

To help with these problems, facilitators often posted comments that linked similar discussion topics, encouraging the posters to comment more on each other's postings. This may not have been as effective as expected, since facilitator postings soon became buried in the discourse. Several of the facilitators indicated that it would be nice to have a section of the forum interface that would allow facilitator comments to be more visible.

Additionally, more than one facilitator mentioned that while they had done background research on the topic of their forum, it would have been helpful to have access to subject matter experts during the Jam. For example, one facilitator said:

> *We found some good stuff, but it would have been even better if we'd had somebody who really had a hook into that subject and could have brought to bare some survey work from outside the company. So we could say, "Okay, this obviously applies to the company, but we know that in 3M, Shell, BT or where ever, this or that actually happens". Bringing this to the Jam, would have been useful.*

During the Jam, only one facilitator proactively recruited a subject matter expert who was very knowledgeable in several of the topics that were developing in his forum.

Monitoring and measuring the effectiveness of facilitation teams

During the Jam, the facilitation team generally followed the planned process flow of reading new postings and selectively replying to some of the postings. The facilitators passed interesting postings off to moderators, who selected some postings for voting. An illustrative summary of the conversation activity for three of the forums has been provided in Figure 3.

It is noteworthy that the Jam sustained posting activity throughout the 48 period with a minimum of 41 postings during the quietest hour. There is a visible increase in the number of postings during the typical work hours in North America, which corresponds to the geographic distribution of potential Jam participants. The global make-up of the facilitation teams is evident by the heavy activity by Asian facilitators in Forum 2 during what would be night hours in North America (EST). In total, there were 4204 postings, including 496 postings from the facilitators during the Jam. The pattern of facilitator posting appears to lag behind the pattern of posting of the managers, which would make sense if the facilitators were essentially reacting to posted comments. Indeed, a correlation of number of postings by facilitators (delayed by four hours), with the number of posting from managers is relatively small but reliable ($r = .18$, p < .01).

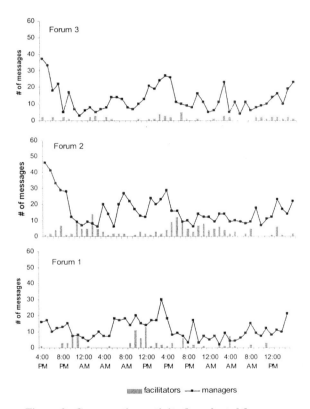

Figure 3. Conversation activity for selected forums.

One way to measure the effectiveness of the facilitation is to compare thread lengths (i.e. the number of messages posted to a single topic) for those threads that contained a facilitator posting with ones that do not. We would expect that if facilitators are supporting or stimulating conversation, then the facilitated threads will be longer on average. The average thread length for facilitated (vs. not facilitated) threads can be found in Table 2. It should be pointed out that facilitator's posting were *not* counted in the thread length in this analysis. The results show that when a facilitator is an active part of the conversation, the thread length is longer (3.9 postings) than when they are not active (2.4 posting).[2] The average thread length was also reliably greater in some forums[3], suggesting that some of the topics may have been of greater local interest or controversial.

Table 2: Mean thread length by forum.

Forum	Facilitator posting?		Mean
	Yes	No	
New Customer Landscape	2.4	2.0	2.2
Translating Strategy	3.2	1.8	2.5
Building Careers	3.4	2.2	2.8
Fostering Innovation	3.6	2.2	2.9
Managing Performance	5.3	3.1	4.2
The Human Face	5.7	3.2	4.4
Mean	**3.9**	**2.4**	

Some caution is warranted for the interpretation of these results. While there is clear evidence that conversation threads are longer when facilitators join in, it is possible that facilitators selectively choose to participate in already active threads or threads that showed significant promise. A controlled experiment would be necessary to confirm a *causal* link between facilitator postings and thread length.

A content analysis of each facilitator's posting was undertaken to determine whether the kind of posting was important in stimulating the online conversation. Postings were coded into one of six categories (adapted from Bales Interaction Process Analysis (Bales, 1950). The results can be seen in Table 3. There were reliable differences in the mean thread length as a function of the type of facilitator posting.[4] While it is reasonable to conclude that facilitation commentary of any kind promotes longer threads than no facilitation, further study is necessary to guide facilitators on exactly what kind of intervention is most effective.

---

[2] Main effect of facilitation (yes/no): [$F(1,1325) = 34.5, p < .001$].

[3] Main effect of forum: [$F(5,1325)=7.4, p < .001$].

[4] Main effect of posting type: [$F(5,1331)=8.54, p < .001$)

Table 3: Mean thread length by type of facilitator posting.

Facilitator posting type	Mean
No facilitation	2.4
Meta comment (about the forum)	2.8
Asked a question	3.1
Offered a comment	3.8
Mix (e.g., comment + question)	4.9
Affirmation (agreement, thanks)	5.4

The analyses of the thread lengths, taken together, provide reasonable evidence that the efforts of the facilitation teams were correlated with the length (and presumably richness) of the conversation threads. A more controlled field study of a future Jam event (planned for 2003) would be necessary to show precisely which facilitation actions can best result in stimulating specific participant behavior

While increasing online interaction is generally considered to be good, it does not guarantee that the quality of that interaction is high. One measure of the quality of the Jam interaction would be the number of postings that were generated, screened by the facilitation team and then rated for potential action or implementation in the larger manager development program. As can be seen in Table 4, 263 items were selected by the facilitation teams for rating and over 1500 votes were cast by Jam participants. The number of distinct ideas that were reviewed and voted actionable by more than ten participants ranged from three to nine in each of the forums. Together 39 ideas were identified as significant and ready for implementation.

Table 4: Summary results of forum voting.

Forum	Total Posts	Total items	#Votes cast	# Voted Actionable
Translating Strategy	703	49	206	3
Building Careers	1052	45	306	9
Fostering Innovation	721	45	203	8
Managing Performance	982	49	311	7
The Human Face	582	36	251	7
New Customer Landscape	504	39	250	5
Total	4544	263	1527	39

The Jam was undoubtedly successful in rapidly engaging a large group of practicing managers in discussing problems and brainstorming solutions for an important set of issues. At minimum, the Jam filled the funnel for subsequent action.

Assessing ManagerJam's success

By many accounts, the ManagerJam event was a success. Overall participation in the event was high, and almost one quarter of all participants visibly contributed to the conversation by posting a comment. A post-event survey of over 900 ManagerJam participants showed that 89% of the respondents would participate in ManagerJam again in the future, 68% said that Managerjam gave me ideas or solutions I can use in my work, 60% said that MJ could become a critical collaboration tool to help me perform my job, and 60% said that they intend to apply MJ best practices in their day-to-day work (Dorsett et al., 2002).

The long threads were carefully analyzed in an effort to create actionable steps for the new Manager Development program. As shown above, the facilitation teams were instrumental in sparking and shaping these discussion threads. The items that received high votes during the Jam were also carefully scrutinized and valuable ideas were handed off to the Manager Development program. Again, the facilitation teams played an important role in screening ideas during the Jam, and encouraging participants to vote. Analysis of the Jam transcripts has resulted in over 60 key ideas categorized by forums into *insights, best practices, and breakthrough thinking.*

Lesson Learned from ManagerJam

ManagerJam served as a cutting-edge example of the power of a very large-scale distributed meeting supported by teams of facilitators and moderators. We believe that the use of multi-person facilitation teams is a key element in holding and conducting meetings of this type, scope and scale.

However, to provide a rich experience for participants, Jams require facilitation teams with defined goals and a plan for stimulating the quality and degree of participation. Simply assigning personnel to support the transactional and operational aspects of these online environments would not be sufficient. Team facilitation in very large-scale distributed meetings should be structured, first and foremost, to facilitate connections among people and ideas, and thus help create rich social environments for participants (Fontaine et al., 2002).

To insure success and to facilitate these connections, Jam teams undertook certain activities that we feel deserve attention for future very large-scale distributed meetings. Several of the lessons learned from ManagerJam are relevant to future multi-member facilitation teams in very large-scale distributed meetings.

First, the *distributed facilitation teams require the same kinds of support that other kinds of distributed work teams require* (Maznevski & Chudoba, 2000). Feedback from the facilitator interviews suggests that a variety of collaboration tools are desirable for the planning part of the project. Most of the teams used conference calls and email to coordinate work tasks before the Jam. In addition, most teams shared background research and meeting minutes among themselves using the online workspace (i.e. TeamRoom). During a Jam, facilitation teams required different support. The team needed a private communication channel (Sametime chat), and some way to know which facilitators are "on duty." They also needed a mechanism to capture session summaries and communicate this information to the next shift. The team also required mechanisms to bring additional people in the facilitator's "space" to provide subject matter expertise or troubleshooting assistance. As the number of teams and team members increase and social norms develop within each team, explicit policies may need to be made about which channel is used for which kind of communication. The distributed facilitation team may require remote support for training sessions, as well as mechanisms to learn about the talents and expertise of other team members. In the case of ManagerJam, there was an explicit request for all facilitators to update a persona page in the corporate directory, which highlighted interests, projects, and skills.

Second, given the 48-hour, multi-time zone nature of the ManagerJam, *special attention to coordinating shift transitions is required.* In each ManagerJam team, there were shift schedules prepared, and agreements about how the transition process would occur. Different teams handled this differently and applied a wide range of techniques to manage both. Methods such as conference call updates, email summaries, and session status notes (posted into the shared TeamRoom), were all used. As mentioned above, some forum teams kept a chat window open for the duration of the Jam to provide a shared record of the team's decisions and activities.

A third lesson learned was *the importance of sharing information between facilitation teams.* With each team working frantically to keep their forum moving and on track, it is hard to take time to see if something is working better in another team. As teams find serendipitous solutions to problems, there should be lightweight mechanisms to share the learning with other teams. For example, if there is a problem with logon authentication in one forum, the solution may be also needed by others. It is also important for key ideas surfacing in the conversation in one forum to be made visible to facilitators in another. This would help facilitators direct participants to other forums where a related conversation is taking place.

Finally, for online meetings of this scale, *there is an incredible demand on browsing, navigating and monitoring discourse.* While this is generally true for other large meetings, the scale and temporal boundaries of ManagerJam make rapid understanding of the discourse even more challenging. In fact, many of the facilitators struggled to identify common threads and labored to connect participants who were discussing similar topics.

In sum, very large-scale meetings, like ManagerJam, will likely become increasingly popular. In fact, two large-scale Jams have already been held in the first half of 2003, one for the consultant community and one for Information Technology professionals. Work is underway to improve the team facilitation process and supporting tools for a new company-wide Jam to be launched in the second half of 2003. The lessons learned are relevant not only meetings that focus on internal corporate conversations, but also to large public discourse like those underway in various e-Democracy projects Ekelin, (2002) and in long distance, team-supported learning applications.

Acknowledgments

Many thanks to the members of the facilitation teams for the ManagerJam, for all that they shared about their Jam experience and insights. Thanks also to Mike Wing and James Newswanger, for comments and assistance at various parts of the project. And finally, thanks to three anonymous reviewers for their helpful comments and suggestions.

References

1. Bales, R. F. A Set of Categories for the Analysis of Small Group Interaction. *American Sociology Review,* 15, 1950, pp 257-263.
2. Bostrum, R.P., Anson, R., and Clawson, V.K. Group facilitation and group support systems. Jessup, L.M., & Valacich, J.S. (eds.) *Group Support Systems: New Perspectives.* New York: McMillan, 1993, 146-168.
3. Clawson, V.K. & Bostrom, R.P. Facilitation: The Human Side of GroupWare. *Proceedings of GroupWare '93,* 1993, pp 204-224.
4. Clawson, V.K. and Bostrom, R. P., The Facilitation Role in group Support Systems Environments. *Proceedings of the '93 Conference on Computer Personnel Research.* 1993, St. Louis, MO, pp 323-335.
5. Dennis, A.R., Nunamaker, J.F., Jr., and Vogel, D.R., A comparison of laboratory and field research in the study of electronic meeting systems. *Journal of Management Information Systems,* 7(3), 1990-91, 1070135.
6. Dorsett, L., Fontaine, M.A., & O'Driscoll, T. Redefining Manager Interaction at IBM: Leveraging massive conversations to exchange knowledge. *KM Review.* September/October 2002, pp 25-28.
7. Ekelin, A. Consulting the citizens. Relationship based interaction in e-government. *Proceedings of PDC 2002.* Malmo, Sweden, June 23-25, 2002, pp 295-300.

8. Fontaine, M. A., Burton, Y. C., & Lesser, E.L. WorldJam: Shaping Large-Scale Collaboration Through Human Intermediation. *KM Review* Volume 5, Issue 5, November/December 2002, pp. 6-7..

9. Fuller, M. A., & Trower, J. Facilitation, systems, and users: the complete socio-technical system. *Proceedings of the 27th Annual Hawaii International Conference on system Sciences.* January, 1994, 82-91.

10. Grohowski, R., McGoff, C., Vogell, D., Martz, W. & Nunamaker, J., Implementing electronic meeting systems at IBM: lessons learned and success factors. *Management Information Systems Quarterly,* 14(4), 1990, pp. 368-383.

11. Halverson, C. A., Newsranger, J. F., Erickson, T, Wolf, T., Kellogg, W., Laff, M., & Malkin, P. WorldJam: 50,000 + Online. Poster presented at ECSCW '01. September 16-20, 2001. Bonn, Germany.

12. Kelley, G. G., and Bostrum, R. P. Facilitating the socio-emotional dimension in group support systems environments. *Proceedings of the 1995 ACM SIGCPR conference on supporting teams, groups, and learning inside and outside the IS function reinventing IS.* 1995, Nashville, TN, pp 10-25.

13. Limayen, M., Lee-Partiridge, J.E., Dickson, G.W., and DeSanctis, G. Enhancing GDSS effectiveness: automated versus human facilitation. *Proceedings of the 26th Annual Hawaii International Conference on Systems Science,* January, 1993. pp. 95-101.

14. Mark, G., Grudin, J., and Poltrok, S. E., Meeting at the Desktop: An Empirical Study of Virtually Collocated Teams. *Proceedings of ECSCW'99, The 6th European Conference on Computer-Supported Cooperative Work.* September 12-16, 1999, Copenhagen, Denmark, pp. 159-178.

15. Maznevski, M.L., & Chudoba, K.M. Bridging Space Over Time: Global Virtual Team Dynamics and Effectiveness. Organization Science, Vol. 11, No. 5. September-October 2000, pp. 473-492.

16. McGoff, C.J., & Ambrose, L. Empirical Information from the Field: A Practitioners' View of Using GDSS in Business. *Proceedings of the 24th Annual Hawaii International Conference on System Science.* January, 1991., pp 805-811.

17. Niederman, F., Beise, C., & Beranek, P. M. Facilitation issues in distributed group support systems. *Proceedings of the '93 Conference on Computer Personnel Research.* 1993, St. Louis, MO, pp 299-312.

18. Nunamaker, J.F., Applegate, L.M., Konsynski, B.R. Facilitating Group Creativity: Experiences with a Group Decision Support System. *Journal of Management Information System,.* 3(4), 1987, pp 5-19.

19. Romano, N.C. Jr., Nunamaker, J.F., Briggs, R.O., & Mittleman, ,D. D. Distributed GSS facilitation and participation: field action research. *Proceedings of 32nd Annual Hawaii International conference on Systems Science.* January, 1999, 12 pp.

20. Spira, J., Friedman, S., and Ebling, S. IBM's WorldJam: How IBM created a new standard in intracompany communication. New York: Basex,, 2001.

21. Turoff, M., Hiltz, S. R., Bahgat, A, & Rana, A. Distributed group support systems. *Management Information Systems Quarterly,* 17(4), 1993. pp 399-416.

22. Yoong, P. Assessing Competency in GSS Skills: A Pilot Study in the Certefication of GSS Facilitators. In *Proceedings of SIGCPR, '95,* 1995, Nashville, Tennessee, USA.

K. Kuutti, E.H. Karsten, G. Fitzpatrick, P. Dourish and K. Schmidt (eds.), *ECSCW 2003: Proceedings of the Eighth European Conference on Computer Supported Cooperative Work, 14-18 September 2003, Helsinki, Finland*, pp. 277-293.

Proving Correctness of Transformation Functions in Real-Time Groupware

Abdessamad Imine, Pascal Molli, Gérald Oster
and Michaël Rusinowitch
ECOO and CASSIS Teams - LORIA France
{*imine,molli,oster,rusi*} @*loria.fr*

Abstract. Operational transformation is an approach which allows to build real-time groupware tools. This approach requires correct transformation functions. Proving the correction of these transformation functions is very complex and error prone. In this paper, we show how a theorem prover can address this serious bottleneck. To validate our approach, we have verified the correctness of state-of-art transformation functions defined on Strings with surprising results. Counter-examples provided by the theorem prover have helped us to define new correct transformation functions for Strings.

Introduction

Real-time groupware systems allow a group of users to manipulate the same object (*i.e.* a text, an image, a graphic, etc.) at the same time from physically dispersed sites that are interconnected by a supposed reliable network. In order to achieve good responsiveness and friendly collaboration, the shared objects are *replicated* at the local memory of each participating user. One of the most significant issues in building real-time groupware systems with replicated architecture is *consistency maintenance* of shared objects (Sun, Jia, Zhang, Yang & Chen, 1998).

Operational transformation is an approach (Ellis & Gibbs, 1989)(Sun & Chen, 2002) which allows to build real-time groupware like shared editors. Algorithms like aDOPTed (Ressel, Nitsche-Ruhland & Gunzenhauser, 1996), GOTO (Sun et al., 1998), SOCT 2,3,4 (Suleiman, Cart & Ferrié, 1998)(Vidot, Cart, Ferrié &

Suleiman, 2000) are used to maintain the consistency of shared data. However these algorithms rely on the definition of transformation functions. If these functions are not correct then these algorithms cannot ensure the consistency of shared data.

Proving the correctness of transformation functions even on a simple typed object like a String is a complex task. If we have more operations on more complex typed objects, the proof is almost impossible without a computer. This is a serious bottleneck for building more complex real-time groupware software.

We propose to assist development of transformation functions with SPIKE , an automated theorem prover which is suitable for reasoning about functions defined by conditional rewrite rules (Stratulat, 2001)(Imine, Molli, Oster & Rusinowitch, 2002). This approach requires specifying the transformation functions in first order logic. Then, SPIKE automatically determines the correctness of transformation functions. If correctness is violated, SPIKE returns counter-examples. Since the proofs are automatic, we can handle more (even complex) operations and develop quickly correct transformation functions.

This paper is organized as follows. The second section briefly presents the transformational approach. In the third section, we give the surprising results we have obtained when verifying the correctness of existing transformation functions about Strings. Thanks to counter-examples provided by SPIKE we define new *correct* transformation functions for Strings. The fourth section briefly overviews the features of SPIKE and describes how to specify transformation functions in this prover. Finally, we conclude with some remarks and with some perspectives for future works.

Transformational Approach

The model of transformational approach considers n sites. Each site has a copy of the shared objects. When an object is modified on one site, the operation is executed immediately and sent to the other sites to be executed again. So every operation is processed in four steps:

(1) generation on one site,

(2) broadcast to other sites,

(3) reception by other sites,

(4) execution on other sites.

The execution context of a received operation op_i may be different from the generation context of op_i. In this case, the integration of op_i by other sites may lead to inconsistencies between replicates. We illustrate this behavior in Figure 1. There are two sites working on a shared data of type $String$. We consider that a $String$ object can be modified with the operation $Ins(p, c)$ for inserting a character c at position p in the string. We suppose the position of the first character in the string is 1 (and not 0). The users 1 and 2 generate two concurrent operations: $op_1 = Ins(2, f)$ and $op_2 = Ins(6, s)$ respectively. When op_1 is received and executed on site 2, it produces the expected string "effects". But, when op_2 is received on site 1, it does not take into account that op_1 has been executed before it. So, we obtain a divergence between sites 1 and 2.

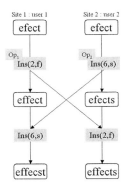

Figure 1. Incorrect integration.

In the operational transformation approach, received operations are transformed according to local concurrent operations and then executed. This transformation is done by calling transformation functions. A transformation function T takes two concurrent operations op_1 and op_2 defined on the same state and returns op_1' which is equivalent to op_1 but defined on a state where op_2 has been applied. We illustrate the effect of a transformation function in Figure 2. When op_2 is received on site 1, op_2 needs to be transformed according to op_1. The integration algorithm calls the transformation function as follows:

$$T((\overbrace{Ins(6, s)}^{op_2}, \overbrace{Ins(2, f)}^{op_1})) = \overbrace{Ins(7, s)}^{op_2'}$$

The insertion position of op_2 is incremented because op_1 has inserted the character "f" before "s" in state "efect". Next, op_2' is executed on site 1. In the same way, when op_1 is received on site 2, the transformation algorithm calls:

$$T(\overbrace{Ins(2, f)}^{op_1}, \overbrace{Ins(6, s)}^{op_2}) = \overbrace{Ins(2, f)}^{op_1'}$$

In this case the transformation function returns $op_1' = op_1$ because "f" is inserted before "s". Intuitively we can write the transformation function as follows:

$T(Ins(p_1, c_1), Ins(p_2, c_2)) :-$
   if $p_1 < p_2$ **return** $Ins(p_1, c_1)$
   else return $Ins(p_1 + 1, c_1)$

280

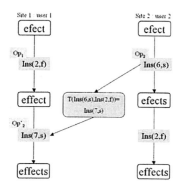

Figure 2. Integration with transformation.

This example makes it clear that the transformational approach consists of two main components: the integration algorithm and the transformation function. the integration algorithm is responsible of receiving, broadcasting and executing operations. It is independent of the type of shared data and it calls transformation function when needed. The transformation function is responsible for merging two concurrent operations defined on the same state. It is specific to the type of shared data (String in our example).

A lot of work has been devoted to defining a theoretical model (Sun et al., 1998)(Suleiman et al., 1998)(Sun & Chen, 2002, Sun, 2002). Basically, transformational approach defines a new consistency criteria for replicates. To be correct, an algorithm has to ensure three general properties:

Convergence. When the system is idle (no operation in pipes), all copies are identical.

Causality. If on one site, an operation op_2 has been executed after op_1, then op_2 must be executed after op_1 in all sites.

Intention preservation. If an operation op_i has to be transformed into op'_i, then the effects of op'_i have to be equivalent to op_i.

To ensure these properties, it has been proved (Sun et al., 1998)(Suleiman et al., 1998) that the underlying transformation functions must satisfy two conditions:

- The condition C_1 defines a *state equivalence*. The state generated by the execution op_1 followed by $T(op_2, op_1)$ must be the same than the state generated by op_2 followed by $T(op_1, op_2)$:

$$C_1 : op_1 \circ T(op_2, op_1) \equiv op_2 \circ T(op_1, op_2)$$

- The condition C_2 ensures that the transformation of an operation according to a sequence of concurrent operations does not depend of the order in which operations of the sequence are transformed:

$$C_2 : T(op_3, op_1 \circ T(op_2, op_1)) = T(op_3, op_2 \circ T(op_1, cp_2))$$

It is important to note that although many algorithms have been designed, only few sets of transformation functions have been delivered to the community (Palmer & Cormack, 1998)(Davis, Sun & Lu, 2002)(Molli, Skaf-Molli, Oster & Jourdain, 2002). Proving C_1 and C_2 on transformation functions is very hard and error prone even on a simple string object. For example, there are 123 different cases to explore when trying to prove C_2 on a String object. Each time the specification of transformation functions is changed, it is necessary to redo the proof.

Without a correct set of transformation functions, the integration algorithm cannot ensure consistency and the resulting groupware tools would not be reliable. Consequently, to be able to develop the transformational approach with simple or more complex objects, proving conditions on transformation functions must be automatic.

Verifying Transformation Functions

In this section, we return to existing transformation functions defined on String objects, where a String is considered as an array of characters starting at range 1 (and not 0). We have formalized them using SPIKE and checked their correctness. We show in the fourth section how to specify these functions in SPIKE . Two operations are defined on String:

- $Ins(p, c)$: Inserts a character c at position p.

- $Del(p)$: Deletes the character located at position p.

Ellis's Transformation Functions

Ellis and Gibbs (Ellis & Gibbs, 1989) are the pioneers of the operational transformation. They have defined the transformation functions shown below. Operations Ins and Del are extended with a new parameter pr representing the priority. Priorities are based on the site identifier where operations have been generated [1]. $Id()$ is the Identity operation, which does not affect state.

$T_{ii}($ Ins $(p_1 ,c_1 ,pr_1$), Ins $(p_2 ,c_2 ,pr_2$)) :−
  if $p_1 < p_2$ **return** Ins $(p_1 ,c_1 ,pr_1$)
  else **if** $p_1 > p_2$ **return** Ins $(p_1 + 1 , c_1 ,pr_1$)
      else **if** $c_1 == c_2$ **return** **Id**$()$
         else **if** $pr_1 > pr_2$ **return** Ins $(p_1 + 1 ,c_1 ,pr_1$)
            else **return** Ins $(p_1 ,c_1 ,pr_1$)

---

[1] This priority becomes even more complex since it is also used like a list.

$T_{id}(\text{Ins}(p_1, c_1, pr_1), \text{Del}(p_2, pr_2)) :-$
  if $p_1 < p_2$ **return** $\text{Ins}(p_1, c_1, pr_1)$
  else return $\text{Ins}(p_1 - 1, c_1, pr_1)$

$T_{di}(\text{Del}(p_1, pr_1), \text{Ins}(p_2, c_2, pr_2)) :-$
  if $p_1 < p_2$ **return** $\text{Del}(p_1, pr_1)$
  else return $\text{Del}(p_1 + 1, pr_1)$

$T_{dd}(\text{Del}(p_1, pr_1), \text{Del}(p_2, pr_2)) :-$
  if $p_1 < p_2$ **return** $\text{Del}(p_1, pr_1)$
  else if $p_1 > p_2$ **return** $\text{Del}(p_1 - 1, pr_1)$
    else return Id$()$

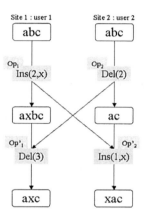

Figure 3. Counter-example violating condition C_1.

It is well known that these transformation functions are not correct (Sun et al., 1998)(Suleiman et al., 1998)(Ressel et al., 1996). Nevertheless, they were submitted to SPIKE in order to verify if the problem can be automatically detected. SPIKE found the counter-example depicted in figure 3 in a few seconds. SPIKE detected that condition C_1 is violated.

The counter-example is simple:

(1) $user_1$ inserts x in position 2 (op_1) while $user_2$ concurrently deletes the character at the same position (op_2).

(2) When op_2 is received by site 1, op_2 must be transformed according to op_1. So $T_{di}(Del(2), Ins(2, x))$ is called and $Del(3)$ is returned.

(3) In the same way, op_1 is received on site 2 and must be transformed according to op_2. $T(Ins(2, x), Del(2))$ is called and return $Ins(1, x)$. Condition C_1 is violated. Accordingly, the final results on both sites are different.

The error comes from the definition of T_{id}. The condition $p_1 < p_2$ should be rewritten $p_1 \leq p_2$. But if we re-submit this version to the theorem prover, it is still not correct with the counter-example detailed in the next section.

This gives a typical example of working with SPIKE . In some way, we use this prover like a compiler. We express transformation functions using the SPIKE syntax and SPIKE checks conditions in few seconds or few minutes depending of the number of different cases induced by the specification.

Ressel's Transformation Functions

Matthias Ressel (Ressel et al., 1996) have modified Ellis's transformation functions in order to satisfy C_1 and C_2. Priorities are replaced by the parameter $u_i \in 1, 2, ..., n$. This parameter represents the user who generates the operation. M. Ressel wrote that T_{id} and T_{di} are exactly the same as those of Ellis. In this case, the set of transformation functions does not satisfy C_1 as in the counter-example of Figure 3. We assume M. Ressel refers to a corrected version of Ellis where T_{id} is redefined with $p_1 \leq p_2$. On the other hand, Ressel modified the definition of T_{ii} as follows: when two insert operations have the same position p, the character produced by the site with the lower range is inserted at p.

$T_{ii}(\text{Ins}(p_1 ,c_1 ,u_1), \text{Ins}(p_2 ,c_2 ,u_2)) :-$
    if $p_1 < p_2$ or $(p_1 = p_2$ and $u_1 < u_2)$ **return** $\text{Ins}(p_1 ,c_1 ,u_1)$
    else return $\text{Ins}(p_1 +1, c_1 ,u_1)$

$T_{dd}(\text{Del}(p_1 ,u_1), \text{Del}(p_2 ,u_2)) :-$
    if $p_1 < p_2$ **return** $\text{Del}(p_1 ,u_1)$
    else if $p_1 > p_2$ **return** $\text{Del}(p_1 - 1, u_1)$
        else return $\text{Id}()$

$T_{id}(\text{Ins}(p_1 ,c_1 ,u_1), \text{Del}(p_2 ,u_2)) :-$
    if $p_1 \leq p_2$ **return** $\text{Ins}(p_1 ,c_1 ,u_1)$
    else return $\text{Ins}(p_1 - 1 ,c_1 ,u_1)$

$T_{di}(\text{Del}(p_1 ,u_1), \text{Ins}(p_2 ,c_2 ,u_2)) :-$
    if $p_1 < p_2$ **return** $\text{Del}(p_1 ,u_1)$
    else return $\text{Del}(p_1 + 1 ,u_1)$

This strategy seems to work but SPIKE found the counter-example given in figure 4. This counter-example requires three users where operations $op_1 = Ins(2, x)$, $op_2 = Del(2)$ and $op_3 = Ins(3, y)$ are concurrent:

(1) First of all, op_2 is integrated on $user_3$'s site. So, we apply $T(Del(2), Ins(3, y))$ which returns $op'_2 = Del(2)$.

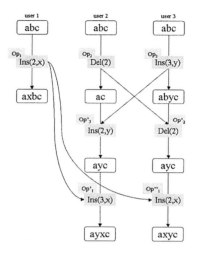

Figure 4. Counter example violating condition C_2.

(2) When integrating op_3 on site 2, we apply $T(Ins(3, y), Del(2))$ which returns $op'_3 = Ins(2, y)$.

(3) Next, op_1 is integrated on site 2 as follows: op_1 must be transformed according to op_2 and the result of this transformation must be transformed according to op'_3. $T(op_1 = Ins(2, x), op_2 = Del(2))$ which returns a new operation $Ins(2, x)$. This operation must be transformed again according to op'_3:

$$T(Ins(2, x), \overbrace{Ins(2, y)}^{op'_3}) = \overbrace{Ins(3, x)}^{op'_1}$$

(4) op_1 is integrating on site 3 in the same way. So we calculate the result of:

$$\overbrace{Ins(2, x)}^{op''_1} = T(T(Ins(2, x), \overbrace{Ins(3, y)}^{op_3}), \overbrace{Del(2)}^{op'_2})$$

Copies on site 2 and 3 do not converge. Consequently, transformation functions of Ressel do not verify C_2.

Sun's Transformation Functions

Chengzheng Sun (Sun et al., 1998) has derived the set of transformation functions below. The signature of operations Ins and Del are slightly different. Indeed, Ins may be used to insert either a character or a string at position p.

T(Ins (p_1, s_1, l_1), Ins (p_2, s_2, l_2)) :−
  if $p_1 < p_2$ **return** Ins (p_1, s_1, l_1)
  else return Ins $(p_1 + l_2, s_1, l_1)$

T(Ins(p_1,s_1,l_1), Del(p_2,l_2)) :−
  if $p_1 \leq p_2$ **return** Ins(p_1,s_1,l_1)
  else if $p_1 > (p_2 + l_2)$ **return** Ins$(p_1 - l_2,s_1,l_1)$
      else return Ins(p_2,s_1,l_1)

T(Del(p_1,l_1), Ins(p_2,s_2,l_2)) :−
  if $p_2 \geq p_1$ **return** Del(p_1,l_1)
  else if $p_1 \geq p_2$ **return** Del$(p_1 + l_2,l_1)$
      else return [Del$(p_1,p_2 - p_1)$; Del$(p_2 + l_2,l_1 - (p_2 - p_1))$]

T(Del(p_1,l_1), Del(p_2,l_2)) :−
  if $p_2 \geq p_1 + l_1$ **return** Del(p_1,l_1)
  else if $p_1 \geq p_2 + l_2$ **return** Del$(p_1 - l_2,l_1)$
  else if $p_2 \leq p_1$ and $p_1 + l_1 \leq p_2 + l_2$ **return** Del$(p_1,0)$
  else if $p_2 \leq p_1$ and $p_1 + l_1 > p_2 + l_2$ **return** Del$(p_2, (p_1 + l_1) - (p_2 + l_2))$
  else if $p_2 > p_1$ and $p_2 + l_2 \geq p_1 + l_1$ **return** Del$(p_1, p_2 - p_1)$
  else return Del$(p_1, l_1 - l_2)$

For a better comparison with others set of transformation functions, we have rewritten Sun's transformations functions for characters. The result is given below.

T(Ins(p_1,c_1), Ins(p_2,c_2)) :−
  if $p_1 < p_2$ **return** Ins(p_1, c_1)
  else return Ins$(p_1 + 1, c_1)$

T(Ins(p_1,c_1), Del(p_2)) :−
  if $p_1 \leq p_2$ **return** Ins(p_1,c_1)
  else return Ins$(p_1 - 1,c_1)$

T(Del(p_1), Ins(p_2,c_2)) :−
  if $p_1 < p_2$ **return** Del(p_1)
  else return Del$(p_1 + 1)$

T(Del(p_1), Del(p_2)) :−
  if $p_1 < p_2$ **return** Del(p_1)
  else if $p_1 > p_2$ **return** Del$(p_1 - 1)$
      else return Id$()$

SPIKE has found that this set of transformation functions violates C_2 with the counter-example presented in Figure 5. Let us consider the following three concurrent operations $op_1 = Ins(2, y)$, $op_2 = Del(2)$ and $op_3 = Ins(3, y)$.

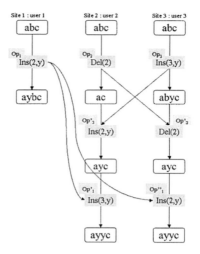

Figure 5. Counter example scenario which violates condition C_2.

(1) Site 3 integrates op_2:

$$\overbrace{Del(2)}^{op'_2} = T(\overbrace{Del(2)}^{op_2}, \overbrace{Ins(3,y)}^{op_3})$$

(2) Then, Site 2 integrates op_3:

$$\overbrace{Ins(2,y)}^{op'_3} = T(\overbrace{Ins(3,y)}^{op_3}, \overbrace{Del(2)}^{op_2})$$

(3) Next, Site 2 integrates op_1:

$$\overbrace{Ins(3,y)}^{op'_1} = T(T(\overbrace{Ins(2,y)}^{op_1}, \overbrace{Del(2)}^{op_2}), \overbrace{Ins(2,y)}^{op'_3})$$

(4) Finally, Site 3 integrates op_1:

$$\overbrace{Ins(2,y)}^{op''_1} = T(T(\overbrace{Ins(2,y)}^{op_1}, \overbrace{Ins(3,y)}^{op_3}), \overbrace{Del(2)}^{op'_2})$$

The final result is the same as in site 2 and 3, but C_2 is not satisfied. In fact:

$$\overbrace{Ins(3,y)}^{op'_1} = T(op_1, op_2 \circ T(op_3, op_2)) \neq \overbrace{Ins(2,y)}^{op''_1} = T(op_1, op_3 \circ T(op_2, op_3))$$

Note that if we use $op_1 = Ins(2,x)$ instead of $op_1 = Ins(2,y)$, then the result will diverge on site 2 and 3 as in the counter-example of Figure 4.

Suleiman's Transformation Functions

Suleiman (Suleiman, Cart & Ferrié, 1997) proposes a different set of transformation functions. He adds two new parameters to function Ins which is defined as follows: $Ins(p_i, c_i, b_i, a_i)$ where b_i (a_i respectively) is the set of concurrent operations to this insertion operation and that have deleted a character before (after respectively) the position p_i. Hence, for two concurrent operations $Ins(p_1, c_1, b_1, a_1)$ and $Ins(p_2, c_2, b_2, a_2)$ defined on the same state, the following cases are given:

- if $(b_1 \cap a_2) \neq \emptyset$ then c_2 was inserted before c_1,

- if $(a_1 \cap b_2) \neq \emptyset$ then c_2 was inserted after c_1,

- if $(b_1 \cap a_2) = (a_1 \cap b_2) = \emptyset$ then c_1 and c_2 were inserted at same position. Hence, we can use the *code* of character $code(c_i)$ to determine which character we have to insert at this position.

$T(Ins(p_1, c_1, b_1, a_1), Ins(p_2, c_2, b_2, a_2)) :-$
  if $p_1 < p_2$ **return** $Ins(p_1, c_1, b_1, a_1)$
  else if $p_1 > p_2$ **return** $Ins(p_1 + 1, c_1, b_1, a_1)$
    else $// p_1 == p_2$
  if $(b_1 \cap a_2) \neq \emptyset$ **return** $Ins(p_1 + 1, c_1, b_1, a_1)$
  else if $(a_1 \cap b_2) \neq \emptyset$ **return** $Ins(p_1, c_1, b_1, a_1)$
    else if $code(c_1) > code(c_2)$ **return** $Ins(p_1, c_1, b_1, a_1)$
      else if $code(c_1) < code(c_2)$ **return** $Ins(p_1 + 1, c_1, b_1, a_1)$
        else return $\mathbf{Id}()$

$T(Ins(p_1, c_1, b_1, a_1), Del(p_2)) :-$
  if $p_1 > p_2$ **return** $Ins(p_1 - 1, c_1, b_1 + Del(p_2), a_1)$
  else return $Ins(p_1, c_1, b_1, a_1 + Del(p_2))$

$T(Del(p_1), Del(p_2)) :-$
  if $p_1 < p_2$ **return** $Del(p_1)$
  else if $p_1 > p_2$ **return** $Del(p_1 - 1)$
    else return $\mathbf{Id}()$

$T(Del(p_1, pr_1), Ins(x_2, p_2, b_2, a_2)) :-$
  if $p_1 < p_2$ **return** $Del(p_1)$
  else return $Del(p_1 + 1)$

SPIKE has proved that this set of transformation functions is correct. The only problem is the management of the sets a_i and b_i associated with each Ins operation. The implementation is more difficult and transferring the Ins operation is not efficient.

Proposed Transformation Functions

We propose a new set of correct transformation functions which is simpler than the ones by Suleiman. In fact, Suleiman's transformation functions are over-specified. Managing the set of operations before and after each Ins operation is not necessary. By studying the counter-examples given by SPIKE, we have noted that the problem came from the conflict between the insertion operations which have the same position. To solve this problem we need to know the exact insertion positions at the generation of each of the two operations. Then two cases are possible: either the two users had effectively inserted the characters in the same position or they had inserted them into different positions and other users concurrently erased the characters located between these two positions.

Accordingly, we propose to add a new parameter ip_i to every Ins operation. This parameter represents the *initial position* of character c_i. Suppose the user insert a character x at position 3, then an operation $Ins(3, 3, x)$ is generated. If this operation is transformed, only the position will change. The initial position parameter is not affected.

T(Ins(p_1, ip_1, c_1), Ins(p_2, ip_2, c_2)) :−
  if $(p_1 < p_2)$ **return** Ins(p_1, ip_1, c_1)
  else if $(p_1 > p_2)$ Ins(p_1+1, ip_1, c_1)
      else // $p_1 == p_2$
      if $(ip_1 < ip_2)$ **return** Ins(p_1, ip_1, c_1)
      else if $(ip_1 > ip_2)$ **return** Ins(p_1+1, ip_1, c_1)
         else // $ip_1 == ip_2$
         if $(\text{code}(c_1) < \text{code}(c_2))$ **return** Ins(p_1, ip_1, c_1)
         else if $(\text{code}(c_1) > \text{code}(c_2))$ **return** Ins(p_1+1, ip_1, c_1)
            else // $c_1 == c_2$
            return Id()

T(Ins(p_1, ip_1, c_1), Del(p_2)) :−
  if $(p_1 > p_2)$ **return** Ins$(p_1 - 1, ip_1, c_1)$
  else return Ins(p_1, ip_1, c_1)

T(Del(p_1), Del(p_2)) :−
  if $(p_1 < p_2)$ **return** Del(p_1)
  else if $(p_1 > p_2)$ **return** Del$(p_1 - 1)$
      else return Id()

T(Del(p_1, pr_1), Ins(p_2, ip_2, c_2)) :−
  if $(p_1 < p_2)$ **return** Del(p_1)
  else return Del$(p_1 + 1)$

This set of transformation functions is correct, *w.r.t.* C_1 and C_2. This kind of result shows an important aspect of our approach. By studying counter-examples of Ellis and Ressel, we were sure that the priority systems are unsafe. After proving that Suleiman's functions were safe, we tried to simplify them. With the theorem prover, it was easy for us to try different kind of simplifications and finally converge towards these transformation functions. One serious bottleneck for verifying transformation functions is the number of possible cases to be considered. With our approach, we delegate this task to the theorem prover. Hence we can try a lot of different solutions in a short time. By this way, we have a process to develop quickly correct transformation functions.

Formalization of Transformation Functions

In this section, we describe the principles of SPIKE prover and then we explain how to specify transformation functions and convergence conditions (C_1 and C_2).

The Theorem Prover: SPIKE

Theorem provers have been applied to the formal development of software. They are based on logic-based specification languages and they provide support to the proof of correctness properties, expressed as logical formulas. Theorem provers can be roughly classified in two categories: (i) the *proof assistants* need many interactions even sometimes for simple proof steps; (ii) the *automatic provers* are working in a push-button mode. Tools from the second category are especially useful for handling problems with numerous but relatively simple proof obligations.

For the analysis of collaborative editing systems we have employed the SPIKE induction prover, which belongs to the second category and seems particularly adapted to the task.

SPIKE induction prover has been designed to verify quantifier-free formulas in theories built with first-order conditional rules. SPIKE proof method is based on the so-called *cover set induction*: Given a theory SPIKE computes in a first step induction variables where to apply induction and induction terms which basically represent all possible values that can be taken by the induction variables. Typically for a nonnegative integer variable, the induction terms are 0 and $x + 1$, where x is a variable.

Given a conjecture to be checked, the prover selects induction variables according to the previous computation step, and substitutes them in all possible way by induction terms. This operation generates several instances of the conjecture that are then *simplified* by rules, lemmas, and induction hypotheses.

Note that if the conjecture is false, then it is guaranteed that the prover will exhibit a counter-example. This is very important for our approach.

Formal Specification

For modelling the structure and the manipulation of data in programs, *abstract data types* (ADTs) are frequently used (Wirsing, 1990). Indeed, the *structure* of data is reflected by so called *constructors* (*e.g.*, zero 0 and successor $s(x)$, meaning $x + 1$, may construct the ADT *nat* of natural numbers). Moreover, all (potential) data are covered by the set of *constructors terms*, exclusively built by constructors. An ADT may have different *sorts*, each characterized by a separate set of constructors. Furthermore, the *manipulation* of data is reflected by *function symbols* (*e.g.*, *plus* and *minus* on *nat*). The value computed by such functions are specified by *axioms*, usually written in equational logic. An *algebraic specification* is a description of one or more such abstract data types (Wirsing, 1990).

Specification of Functions

More formally a real-time groupware system can be considered as a structure of the form $G =< S, O, Tr >$ where:

- S is the structure of the shared object (*i.e.*, a string, an XML document, a CAD object),

- O is the set of operations applied to the shared object,

- Tr is the transformation function.

In our approach, we construct an algebraic specification from a real-time groupware system . Indeed, the shared object structure is transformed in ADT specification $State$. We define a sort Opn for the operation set O, where each operation serves as a constructor of this sort. For instance, a collaborative editing text has a character string as shared object structure, and $O = \{O_1, O_2\}$ where:

- $O_1 = Ins(p, c)$ inserts character c at position p,

- $O_2 = Del(p)$ deletes the character at position p.

For the character string we may specify it with the list ADT; its constructors are $\langle \rangle$ and $l \bullet x$ (*i.e.*, an empty list and a list composed by an element x added to the end of the list l respectively). Because all operations are applied to the object structure in order to modify it, we give the following function:

$$\odot : State \times Opn \rightarrow State$$

All appropriate axioms of the function $\odot$ describe the transition between the object states when applying an operation. For example, the operation $Del(p)$ changes the character string as follows:

$$l \odot Del(p) = \begin{cases} \langle \rangle & \text{if } l = \langle \rangle \\ l & \text{if } l = l' \bullet c \text{ and } p \geq |l| \\ l' & \text{if } l = l' \bullet c \text{ and } p = |l| - 1 \\ (l' \odot Del(p)) \bullet c & \text{if } l = l' \bullet c \text{ and } p < |l| - 1 \end{cases}$$

where $|l|$ returns the length of the list l.

To overcome the user-intention violation problem, a transformation function is used in order to adjust the parameters of one operation according to the effects of other operations executed independently. Writing the specification of a transformation function in first-order logic is straightforward. For this we define the following function:

$$T : Opn \times Opn \rightarrow Opn$$

which takes two arguments, namely remote and local operations and produces another operation. The axioms concerning this function show how the considered real-time groupware transforms its operations when they are broadcasted. For example, the following transformation:

$T(\text{Del}(p_1), \text{Ins}(p_2, c_2)) :-$
    if $p_1 > p_2$ **return** $\text{Del}(p_1 + 1)$
    else return $\text{Del}(p_1)$

---

is defined by two conditional equations:

$p_1 > p_2 \implies T(\text{Del}(p_1), \text{Ins}(p_2, c_2)) = \text{Del}(p_1 + 1)$
$p_1 \not> p_2 \implies T(\text{Del}(p_1), \text{Ins}(p_2, c_2)) = \text{Del}(p_1)$

This example illustrates how it is easy to translate transformation function into the formalism of SPIKE . This task is straightforward and can be done automatically. The cost of formalisation is not expensive.

Specification of Conditions C_1 and C_2

We now express the convergence conditions as theorems to be proved in our algebraic setting. For this purpose, we use a predicate $Enabled : Opn \times State \rightarrow Bool$ expressing the condition under which an operation can be executed on a given state. Adding this predicate allows to avoid the generation of unreachable executions which violate conditions C_1 and C_2 (Imine et al., 2002).

The first condition, C_1, expresses a *semantic equivalence* between two sequences. Each sequence consists of two operations. Given two operations op_1 and op_2, the execution of the sequence of op_1 followed by $T(op_2, op_1)$ must produce the same state as the execution of the sequence of op_2 followed by $T(op_1, op_2)$.

Theorem 1 (Condition C_1).

$$\forall op_i, op_j \in Opn \text{ and } \forall st \in State :$$
$$Enabled(op_i, st) \wedge Enabled(op_j, st) \implies$$
$$(st \odot op_i) \odot T(op_j, op_i) = (st \odot op_j) \odot T(op_i, op_j)$$

The second condition C_2 stipulates a *syntactic equivalence* between two sequences, where every sequence is composed of three operations. Given three operations op_1, op_2 and op_3, the transformation of op_3 with regards to the sequence formed by op_2 followed by $T(op_1, op_2)$ must give the same operation as the transformation of op_3 with regards to the sequence formed by op_1 followed by $T(op_2, op_1)$.

Theorem 2 (Condition C_2).

$$\forall op_i, op_j, op_k \in Opn \ and \ \forall st \in State :$$
$$Enabled(op_i, st) \wedge Enabled(op_j, st) \wedge Enabled(op_k, st) \implies$$
$$T(T(op_k, op_i), T(op_j, op_i)) = T(T(op_k, op_j), T(op_i, op_j))$$

Conclusion and Perspectives

We have demonstrated in this paper the difficulty of building correct transformation functions. Even on a simple String object, all existing transformation functions are incorrect or over-specified. The difficulty stems from the complexity of correctness proof for transformations functions. On a simple String object, each time a function definition changes, you have to explore 123 different cases carefully. We are convinced that this task cannot be done properly without assistance of a computer. Our approach is very valuable:

- The result is a set of safe transformation functions.

- During the development, the guidance of the theorem prover gives a high value feedback. Indeed, the theorem prover quickly produces counter-examples.

- Formalization is easy.

We are convinced that this approach allows the transformational approach to be applied on more complex typed objects (Imine et al., 2002). We are working in several directions now:

- As we can prove C_1 and C_2 on large number of operations, we are currently developing correct transformation functions for a file system, XML files, blocks of text, etc. We are working not only on new sets of safe transformation functions but also on correctness of composition of these sets.

- We are currently modifying the SPIKE theorem prover in order to build an integrated development environment for transformation functions. Within this environment a user will enter functions like in this paper and will call the theorem prover on them like a compiler. If errors are reported then the environment gives counter-examples immediately. We believe that this kind of environment can greatly improve the process of deriving transformation functions.

Acknowledgments

Many thanks for Fethi A. Rabhi, Senior lecturer at University of New South Wales of Sydney and Hala Molli, Associate Professor at University of Nancy, for their reviewing of this paper.

References

Davis, A. H., Sun, C. & Lu, J. (2002): 'Generalizing Operational Transformation to the Standard General Markup Language', *in Proceedings of the 2002 ACM conference on Computer supported cooperative work*, ACM Press, pp. 58–67.

Ellis, C. A. & Gibbs, S. J. (1989): 'Concurrency Control in Groupware Systems', *in SIGMOD Conference*, Vol. 18, pp. 399–407.

Imine, A., Molli, P., Oster, G. & Rusinowitch, M. (2002): 'Development of Transformation Functions Assisted by a Theorem Prover', *in Fourth International Workshop on Collaborative Editing*, New Orleans, Louisiana, USA.

Molli, P., Skaf-Molli, H., Oster, G. & Jourdain, S. (2002): 'SAMS: Synchronous, Asynchronous, Multi-synchronous Environments', *in The Seventh International Conference on CSCW in Design*, Rio de Janeiro, Brazil.

Palmer, C. R. & Cormack, G. V. (1998): 'Operation Transforms for a Distributed Shared Spreadsheet', *in Proceedings of the 1998 ACM Conference on Computer Supported Cooperative Work*, ACM Press, pp. 69–78.

Ressel, M., Nitsche-Ruhland, D. & Gunzenhauser, R. (1996): 'An Integrating, Transformation-oriented Approach to Concurrency Control and Undo in Group Editors', *in Proceedings of the ACM Conference on Computer Supported Cooperative Work (CSCW'96)*, Boston, Massachusetts, USA, pp. 288–297.

Stratulat, S. (2001): 'A General Framework to Build Contextual Cover Set Induction Provers', *Journal of Symbolic Computation* **32**(4), 403–445.

Suleiman, M., Cart, M. & Ferrié, J. (1997): 'Serialization of Concurrent Operations in a Distributed Collaborative Environment', *in Proceedings of the International ACM SIGGROUP Conference on Supporting Group Work : The Integration Challenge (GROUP'97)*, ACM Press, pp. 435–445.

Suleiman, M., Cart, M. & Ferrié, J. (1998): 'Concurrent Operations in a Distributed and Mobile Collaborative Environment', *in Proceedings of the Fourteenth International Conference on Data Engineering (ICDE'98)*, IEEE Computer Society, Orlando, Florida, USA, pp. 36–45.

Sun, C. (2002): 'Undo as Concurrent Inverse in Group Editors', *ACM Transactions on Computer-Human Interaction (TOCHI)* **9**(4), 309–361.

Sun, C. & Chen, D. (2002): 'Consistency Maintenance in Real-Time Collaborative Graphics Editing Systems', *ACM Transactions on Computer-Human Interaction (TOCHI)* **9**(1), 1–41.

Sun, C., Jia, X., Zhang, Y., Yang, Y. & Chen, D. (1998): 'Achieving Convergence, Causality-preservation and Intention-preservation in Real-Time Cooperative Editing Systems', *ACM Transactions on Computer-Human Interaction (TOCHI)* **5**(1), 63–108.

Vidot, N., Cart, M., Ferrié, J. & Suleiman, M. (2000): 'Copies Convergence in a Distributed Real-Time Collaborative Environment', *in Proceedings of the ACM Conference on Computer Supported Cooperative Work (CSCW'00)*, Philadelphia, Pennsylvania, USA.

Wirsing, M. (1990): 'Algebraic specification', *Handbook of Theoretical Computer Science (vol. B): formal models and semantics* pp. 675–788.

K. Kuutti, E.H. Karsten, G. Fitzpatrick, P. Dourish and K. Schmidt (eds.), *ECSCW 2003: Proceedings of the Eighth European Conference on Computer Supported Cooperative Work, 14-18 September 2003, Helsinki, Finland*, pp. 295-314.

Awareness in Context:
A Light-Weight Approach

Tom Gross, Wolfgang Prinz
Fraunhofer Institute for Applied IT
{tom.gross, wolfgang.prinz}@fit.fraunhofer.de

Abstract. Users who work together require adequate information about their environment—group awareness. In the CSCW literature several models and systems for group awareness have been presented. They basically capture information from the environment, process it, and present it to the users. In general, only the information *per se* is captured without capturing information about its context of origin. Furthermore, the information is then often presented to the users regardless of their current context of work. In this paper we present a light-weight approach for modelling awareness contexts. We describe the concept, report on its examination, and discuss implications for the modelling of contexts and the design of group awareness support.

Introduction

In the CSCW literature it has been emphasised for years that efficient and effective cooperation requires that the cooperating individuals are well informed about their partners activities (Dourish and Bellotti, 1992) (Schmidt, 2002). They require information about the other persons they are cooperating with, about their actions, about shared artefacts, and so forth. This information is often referred to as awareness (sometimes with prepositions such as *group* awareness (Begole et al., 1999) (Erickson et al., 1999) or *workspace* awareness (Gutwin and Greenberg, 1998).

In situations where the cooperating individuals are at the same place this information is often perceived automatically (Heath and Luff, 1991). In other situations where individuals, who are at different places, have to cooperate as a group, technological support for the cooperation process as well as the perception of cooperative activities is essential. This technological support ranges from workflow management systems to shared workspace systems and other groupware systems. Typically, these systems provide users with information about the members of the group, the shared artefacts, and the process of the group activities. However, most of the approaches and systems only provide this information within the borders of the respective applications.

We have designed and developed an infrastructure that provides group awareness across applications called ENI (Event and Notification Infrastructure). ENI is an event-based awareness environment, which includes various sensors for the capturing of events and various indicators for their presentation. Interviews with application partners and discussions with colleagues who have been using ENI showed that they have the impression that they are better informed than before using ENI. However, several users pointed out that the information was not always provided in the situation when it was of utmost use and that on some occasions the information was to coarse and on other occasions it was to detailed. On a whole the feedback of the users can be summarised to three major requirements for the support of group awareness:

- First, awareness environments should provide awareness information in a way that is adequate for the current situation of the user. The individual user requires personalised information that is adapted to the situation. Besides personal preferences the type of information and its presentation largely depend on the context in which a user is. The context itself depends on parameters like the current task, the current type of cooperation, the artefacts and tools used, and so forth.
- Secondly, awareness environments should not only provide the pure awareness information, but also information about the context of origin of the awareness information. The context in which an event occurs vastly determines its meaning.
- Thirdly, awareness environments should allow users to share awareness contexts. Users with shared interests should be able to share and exchange their awareness profiles.

For the provision of awareness within a closed application such as PoliAwaC (Sohlenkamp et al., 2000) these requirements can be satisfied in an application-specific way. However, for a generic awareness infrastructure a more open concept is required. In this paper we will present such a concept and the implementation of awareness contexts in a generic infrastructure reflecting these requirements. We will shortly introduce the ENI awareness environments, which served as a basis for the realisation of awareness contexts. We will then detail awareness contexts and specify their structure. We will describe how these awareness contexts were integrated into ENI and report on an examination of their quality in terms of effectively identifying actual work contexts. Related work and a summary will conclude this paper.

Event and Notification Infrastructure

The ENI event and notification infrastructure is a generic extendible awareness environment, which includes simple but powerful and lightweight mechanisms for the generation and user configurable presentation of awareness information at the standard desktop interface (Prinz, 1999). The concept of ENI is based on sensors, events, and indicators. Figure 1 shows the architecture of ENI.

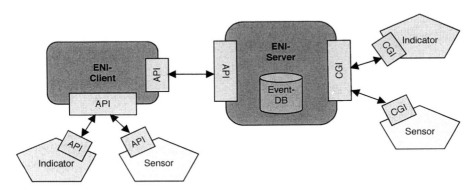

Figure 1. The notification architecture.

Sensors are associated with actors, shared material, or any other object constituting or influencing a cooperative environment and generate events related to them. Sensors can capture actions that take place in the electronic space (e.g., changes in documents, presence of people at virtual places) and actions in the physical space (e.g., movement or noise in a room). Some examples of sensors we have realised so far are presence sensors checking for the presence of users; web presence sensors checking the visits of users on Web sites; a web content watcher checking updates to specific Web pages (e.g., newspapers on the Web); sensors integrated in office documents, and a shared workspace system.

The generated *events* are sent to the ENI server—either via the application-programming interface (API) of the ENI client or via a common gateway interface (CGI). They are described as attribute-value tuples. The ENI server stores the events in an event database. This database is realized as a semi-structured database (Abiteboul et al., 1999) using XML formatted tuples as the storage format. This decision was made to allow for a flexible handling of different event types, which would not be possible in a relational database. The communication protocol between the server and client application is http and the data exchange is XML-based.

Users can use the ENI clients to subscribe to events at the ENI server and to specify indicators for the presentation of the awareness information. Subscriptions have the form of event patterns. The client registers these patterns at the server via the API. When the server receives an event that matches the pattern, the event is forwarded to the respective client. Additionally, users can specify how they want to be informed about the event; that is, which indicators should be used for the presentation.

Indicators are offered in various shapes ranging from pop-up windows, to applets in Web pages, to ticker tapes (Fitzpatrick et al., 1998), to 3D graphical presentations in a multi-user environment. Cadiz et al.,(2002) present numerous examples for the integration of indicators into the windows desktop environment.

On a whole ENI is a flexible tool for the application-independent support of group awareness. A disadvantage that was discovered in everyday use is the immediate notification of the users who have specified interest for a certain event. In many cases users are notified regardless of their current context of work. In order to provide users with the right information at the right time in an adequate quality and quantity, we introduce awareness contexts.

Awareness Contexts

In the Merriam-Webster a context is defined as "1: the parts of a discourse that surround a word or passage and can throw light on its meaning; 2: the interrelated conditions in which something exists or occurs". In this paper we see contexts in the second meaning: in this paper a context can be defined as the interrelated (i.e., some kind of continuity in the broadest sense) conditions (i.e., circumstances such as time and location) in which something (e.g., a user, a group, an artefact) exists (e.g., presence of a user) or occurs (e.g., an action performed by a human or machine).

Awareness contexts can emerge in various dimensions: geographical contexts and locations such as buildings, floors, offices; organisational contexts such as departments or projects, but also clubs, where people are members of; personal and social contexts like family, close friends; technological contexts such as users of specific technologies (e.g., ICQ); action or task contexts such as users who perform similar actions or tasks with similar tools; and so forth.

In order to make context descriptions computable and interpretable by a computing system we decided to represent a context using the following set of attributes (cf. Table I).

These attributes allow the matching of events to contexts of origin and the detection of the current work context of the user. They are described subsequently:

- Each awareness context has a unique *name*.
- The *administrator* of a context is the person who created and manages the context.
- *Members* of a context are all users who work in a context and who consequently produce events through their actions.
- *Locations*, at which events can be produced, are either electronic (e.g., a shared workspace) or physical areas (e.g., a meeting room).
- The *artefacts* of a context are all objects on which users can operate.

- Each context is associated with various single-use and cooperative *applications* (e.g., text editors, programming environments, groupware applications).
- *Events* that are produced in a context are described by their types.
- An *access control list* for an awareness context comprises a list with all the rights that exist for each context; each member of an awareness context may have the right to produce events, to subscribe to events or event types, and to decide how she wants the events to be presented. Context-specific ACLs guarantee that the members of a context are informed about the events within the context, but that privacy is kept concerning users who are not members of the context. For each context, context members can define their own privacy policy. This can be seen as an extension of the pure reciprocity that is often claimed. In some contexts members can agree upon reciprocity in others they can define other models.
- Each awareness context has various connections to its *environment* and to other contexts (e.g., two projects with one awareness context respectively, which have overlapping membership). Big contexts consisting of many members, many shared artefacts might be spread over several locations and might be organised in sub-contexts (Agostini et al., 1996).

Attribute	Description
context-name	Name of the context
context-admin	Human or non-human actor who created the context
context-member	Human members of a context
context-location	Physical locations related to a context
context-artefact	Artefacts of a context
context-app	Applications related to a context
context-event	Events relevant to a context
context-acl	Access control list of a context
context-env	Related contexts

Table I. Awareness context attributes.

It is important to note that the context description does not require the specification of all attributes. For instance, a context can be created and some attributes like locations or applications are specified only later on; or a context could have no locations or no applications at all. Nevertheless, the more details are available for a context, the better events can be matched to the context. In many cases the attributes of a context can be generated automatically. For instance, if a context consists of a shared workspace the list of members and artefacts of the context can be dynamically gained from information about the shared workspace. Furthermore, it is possible to use pattern or predicates over a set of possible attribute values to specify an attribute value.

Applying Awareness Contexts

For the provision of awareness information it is important that event notifications are presented in the appropriate situation; that is in the situation in which the information is most relevant to the user.

For those systems in which the awareness information is presented in the context of the origin (e.g., a document), often awareness widgets (Sohlenkamp et al., 2000) (Gutwin et al., 1996) are used that overlay the presentation of a document. Thus, whenever users open the document they immediately see the awareness information attached to the document.

In other cases this problem cannot be solved that straightforward, for example when awareness information is not directly coupled to a document or when information shall be presented independent of a document access. In these latter cases the context of origin of an event and the context of work of a user who receives a notification are distinct, which entails the following requirements for context processing:

1. the system has to know the *context of origin* of an event or deduce the context of origin;
2. the system has to know the current *context of work* of the users who need to be informed; and
3. the user has to be able to specify in which *situation* she wants to be informed about events from a specific context in a specific format.

Figure 2 illustrates the processing of events according to these requirements. The left side illustrates the association of an event with a context. The right side illustrates the association of a user with a context of work based on his/her current activities. We will describe the three processing steps subsequently.

Identifying the Context of Origin (1)

Events can either be mapped to a context when they are produced or when they reach the server. Events can only be mapped to a context at the time of creation, if either the sensor has information about the context specification (from the Context-DB describing the contexts of origin) or if the sensor is used for only one context. In these cases the sensor can immediately add a context attribute to the produced event. However, often this is not the case and therefore we describe an alternative method for the association of a context at the server later in this paper.

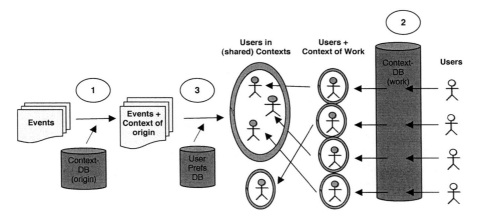

Figure 2. 3 Steps to bring user in context.

Identifying the Users' Context of Work (2)

Once the computed context attribute is added to the respective event the system needs to detect the current context of a user. For this purpose, the interaction of the user with the physical and electronic world is captured and analysed. Fine-grained activities such as typing on the keyboard or passing light barriers have to be aggregated and matched to contexts. That is, the attributes of the events produced by the user are compared to the attributes of the known contexts (from the Context-DB describing the work contexts of users). The result is the selection of a single context or a list of contexts from the context descriptions that matches best with the current activities.

Checking the Users' Preferences (3)

The users can specify in which context of work, i.e., in which situation they want to be informed about an event from a specific context of origin. Furthermore, they can specify the format of the presentation of the event information and the schedule for the presentation. For instance, a user can specify that whenever she is in the work context 'Project A' she wants to receive information related to "Project A' and 'Project B' in a tickertape with a 15 Minute rhythm.

As a result the system knows what is happening in the environment on a whole and in which part the user is involved. The system can them put the user in a context. Users with similar activities are informed about each other—and are put in a shared context. After we have presented these general concepts of awareness contexts and their processing, we will now show how awareness context are applied in ENI.

Awareness Contexts in ENI

In order to support awareness contexts in ENI we added two main extensions: at the ENI server we added a context module and at the ENI client we added a situation module. Figure 3 shows the extended ENI architecture.

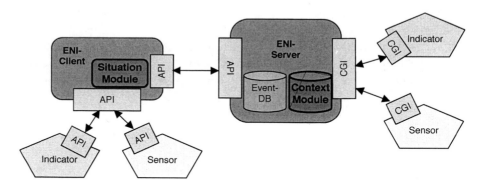

Figure 3. The extended ENI architecture.

The context module maps incoming events to a context of origin. It compares attributes of the incoming events with the attributes stored in the context database. Table II shows the mapping of event attributes to context attributes (see also Figure 4 for an example event).

Event attributes	Context attributes
sensor	context-app
event-originator	context-member, context-location
artefact	context-artefact
event-attributes	context-event

Table II. Mapping of event attributes to context attributes.

The *sensor* attribute of the event indicates the application, by which the user activity was performed. It is therefore matched with the *context-app* attribute of the context description. The *event-originator* is compared with the people listed as *context members*, i.e., it verifies if the user is a member of one of the registered contexts. If a location-based service submits the event (indicated by a special sensor type) it is compared with possible *context-locations* to determine the context based on the location where the activity took place. The *artefact* attribute identifies the object on which the user action took place (e.g., a document or file). In addition, further *event-attributes* are evaluated if the context description contains a specification of additional *context-event* attributes. Examples for such attributes are the operation performed by the event-originator, the folder in which the artefact is stored, or the date and time at which the event was submitted. The latter is useful if the context is valid only during a certain time interval.

The result of the comparison between the event attributes and the context description is a list of one or more contexts that match with the event attributes, combined with a weight indicating the strength of the match. The weight depends on the number and importance of the matching attributes. The importance of each context attribute is described as part of the attribute specification. This result is attached to the event by a context attribute (*event-context*).

Users can take this attribute for the specification of their interest profiles in the ENI client. Thus, the specification of the interest cannot only be based on discrete events, but users can also specify a general interest on events of a specific context. This guarantees that a user is informed about future events of a context. There is no need to explicitly describe new event patterns for new events. This addresses a drawback that is often criticized with event based notification systems (Sandor et al., 1997).

With an additional element of the interest profile users can specify the situation in which they prefer to be informed about an event. Table III shows the options for the timing of the presentation of the awareness information. If users want to be informed immediately, no scheduling has to be done by the Context Module in the ENI-Server; if users want other timing of their notifications, a scheduling component of the context module has to make sure that the users are informed according to their preferences.

Time	Description
immediately	an event is presented immediately
in the same context	an event is presented if the interested user is in the context in which the event was generated
specific context	an event is presented when the user is in a specific context
date	an event is presented at a defined date and time (e.g., at lunch time)
age	an event is presented after some time—if it has not been presented because of one of the above rules

Table III. Schedule of notifications and description of situations.

These situations are not exclusive—that is, the users can combine different schedules. For instance, a user could decide to see events of a specific context any time she is working in that context and additionally at a certain time (e.g., at login).

In order to analyse the current context of work of a user, a situation module is added to the ENI client. This component monitors the current activities of a user and tries to match them to a context. For this purpose, the module uses information from the operating system about running applications and processed objects. This information, as well as the events that are generated by the actions of the user, is also compared to the descriptions of the working contexts. This is done in analogy to the above mapping of events to contexts of origin. And, similarly, the result can contain an ambiguous match with more than one context with different weights. In this case the attributed *context-env* of the attribute description is evaluated. If the contexts are connected, the system assumes that the user is in one of the contexts and the respective events are presented. If no match can be found, a sequence of actions of a user is monitored and the system tries again to match them to a context. When a context of work is found with a probability that exceeds the threshold defined by the user, then the respective events are presented.

Application and Examination of the Model

In this section we will first describe how we applied this context modelling and processing approach to a shared workspace system, and then we will describe some results from a study of its use.

Context Support for Shared Workspaces

Cooperative work is often organised with the help of shared workspaces (Pankoke-Babatz and Syri, 1997). These shared workspaces specify lists of members and contain shared objects as well as shared applications. If the workspaces of a project are considered as a context, many attributes of a context can be gained from the workspace. Thus, actions of the members of shared workspaces can be mapped to contexts likewise. Therefore, we have chosen such an application to validate the applicability of the proposed model. We describe experiences and consequences of the application of our model for a specific Web-based shared workspace system, the BSCW system (Appelt, 1999). Although this is a specific example, we believe that the results are of general nature, since the considered data is common to almost all shared workspace systems.

We first describe the event information that is provided from the system on each user activity, and then the context descriptions for the mapping of events to specific project contexts. These descriptions are used as a test case for an examination of the proposed context model. We use a data set of approx. 16.000 events gathered over period of 18 month to discuss the suitability of our mapping.

The BSCW server generates for each user action an event that is forwarded to the ENI server via http in XML-based format. For this purpose a special BSCW sensor has been realized in the BSCW server. Figure 4 presents an example for a BSCW event.

The *sensor* attribute denotes the application that submitted the event. The *event-originator* attribute contains the user-id of the user who performed the *operation* on a document (*artefact*) in a *folder* (i.e., the containing folder). The complementary *bscw-object-id* and *bscw-folder-id* attributes contain a unique system identifier. The *bscw-class* and *bscw-content*-attributes specify the document (mime)-type. The *acl* attribute lists the user-ids of all users who have access to the artefact. This list is constructed from the list of members who have access to the folder that contains the accessed object. The ENI-server uses this list as access control list for the validation of access operations on the event. Therefore, only users who have access to an object in BSCW can read the corresponding events. *Date* contains the date/time of the user action and *expires* the expiration time of the event.

```
<EVENT>
   <ATTRIBUTE type="sensor" value="BSCW"/>
   <ATTRIBUTE type="event-originator" value="Uta.Pankoke"/>
   <ATTRIBUTE type="operation" value="ReadEvent"/>
   <ATTRIBUTE type="artefact" value="weiser_cacm.pdf"/>
   <ATTRIBUTE type="bscw-object-id" value="135578"/>
   <ATTRIBUTE type="folder" value="Related Work"/>
   <ATTRIBUTE type="bscw-folder-id" value="132978"/>
   <ATTRIBUTE type="bscw-class" value="Document"/>
   <ATTRIBUTE type="bscw-content"value="application/pdf"/>
   <ATTRIBUTE type="acl" value="tom.gross, karl-heinz.klein,
                     uta.pankoke, wolfgang.prinz"/>
   <ATTRIBUTE type="date" value="2003-02-03 09:09:45"/>
   <ATTRIBUTE type="expires" value="2003-02-04 09:09:45"/>
</EVENT>
```

Figure 4: An example event produced by a user operation in BSCW.

In order to describe a possible mapping of events to a context we now explain the understanding of a context for this shared workspace application. It is common that a user is member of many different workspaces, whereas each workspace is associated with a project, a task, or an organizational unit. For the following, we consider this use and intention of a workspace as the context of this workspace. Often workspaces contain a large number of folders or subfolders, each containing a number of documents of different types. Thus, we interpret all user actions on these objects as actions that happen in the context of this workspace.

However, we can see from the example in Figure 4, that the events themselves do not contain an indication of the workspace itself. That is, the event does not indicate the context to which it belongs. This is due to the fact that BSCW system itself has no notion of a context since this is an external user- or group-specific interpretation of a shared folder. It is therefore necessary that the association of a context to an event is computed external to the application.

Figure 6 shows a screenshot of a BSCW workspace of a project on 'Mobile and Ubiquitous Cooperation Support'. In this example workspace we have 4 folders (which contain respectively 4, 9, 1, and 9 documents) and 3 documents. Figure 7 shows a screenshot of the members of this BSCW workspace. This example workspace only has 4 members.

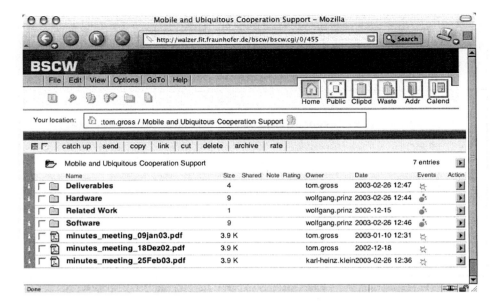

Figure 6. Screenshot of a BSCW workspace (including folders and documents).

Figure 7. Screenshot of the members of this BSCW workspace.

When a new workspace is created, the BSCW server send corresponding information to the context module of the ENI-server. The context module of the ENI-server then creates a context description and starts to periodically (in general, in a 24 hour interval) to query the BSCW server for information of all workspaces it knows (the folders and documents, the members, etc.). The BSCW server sends back for each workspace a list of properties of the respective workspace in XML. Figure 8 shows an excerpt of this list (for simplification we only include part of the folder and document list as well as the user list).

```
<Mobile and Ubiquitous Cooperation Support>
  <ATTRIBUTE type="bscw-folder-id" value="455"/>
  <ATTRIBUTE type="date" value="2003-02-03 09:09:45"/>
  ...
  <ATTRIBUTE type="artefacts" value="Deliverables, D1.1.doc,
                    D1.2.doc, D2.doc, D3.doc, Hardware,
                ...
                    minutes_meeting_25Feb03.pdf"/>
  <ATTRIBUTE type="members" value="tom.gross,
                    karl-heinz.klein, uta.pankoke,
                    wolfgang.prinz"/>
  ...
</EVENT>
```

Figure 8: Workspace property list from BSCW server (excerpt).

The context module of the ENI-server then updates its context descriptions accordingly.

Examination of the Model

In order to find an expressive description for the event-context mapping, we have analysed events that were produced by user operations over a period of 18 months. For a specific (real) user whom we have selected as a test user, the ENI server contained 15.800 events, to which the user had access (i.e., in which the user-id was contained in the ACL attribute of the event). From our experiences with the BSCW-usage and a comparison of the user's workspaces with that of others, we can consider this user as a representative user.

Each event has the structure of the example event shown in Figure 4. The user uses the BSCW server to support cooperation processes in 11 different projects or tasks. The workspaces contained between 25 and approx. 1200 different objects, but most contained more than 100 objects. The number of members for a workspace ranged between 8 to 12 (for 75% of all workspaces) and 30 (seminar group at the university). In the following, we describe our approach for the specification of a context mapping by which each event is associated with one of the 11 different contexts.

The previously presented context model requires the specification of the following parameters (see Table II): context-app, context-member or context-location, context-event, or context-artefact. In all cases of our specific application, the context-app is equal to "BSCW", the context-location does not apply since we do not consider real-world locations. Thus, the following mappings remain for comparison, which will be discussed subsequently:

- event-originator attribute to context-member
- artefact attribute to context-artefact
- event-attributes to context-event

The *event-originator attribute to the context-member* mapping allows a selection of a context based on the membership of the event-originator in a certain team or community that is described as the group of people that constitute a context. For a project, this would be the project-members. Analysing the data set, we found, that for our particular user 7 out of 11 contexts contain similar membership list (i.e., the list of members differed only in 2 or 3 members). These typically were users from outside the local organisation, whereas the overlapping set contained colleagues from the local organisation. This shows that the event-originator attribute is not sufficient for a context selection. Since the distribution of events is almost equal over all event-originators, an unambiguous mapping can be made only for less than 20% of all events. This is the percentage of members who are member in just one context.

A more reliable mapping is accomplished by a comparison of the *acl* attribute of an event with the *context-member* attribute of a context. Due to the complete enumeration of the workspace members in this event attribute and the complete listing of the context members in the context-member attribute, a reliable selection of a context is possible. However, this requires that the context-member list is always kept up-to-date with the membership list of the shared workspace. Although automatic update procedures can guarantee this consistency, this approach still has a drawback. Our data shows that 3 out of the 11 contexts contain the same members. Two of the three contexts a related to each other, thus this ambiguity might not be very problematic from the user's viewpoint. However, the third context covers a different topic than the others. Thus, we need to consider additional criteria for the context selection.

The *artefact attribute* to *context-artefact* comparison enables an unambiguous mapping, but it requires that the context artefact attribute enumerates all artefacts that constitute the context. Consequently, the context database mirrors almost the complete context data. To avoid this duplication we need to find properties that classify or aggregate artefacts of a context. In our application scenario the *folder,* respectively the *bscw-folder-id* attributes provide such an aggregation. Since the number of folders is much lower than the number of objects (in our case only 13% of the number of objects), this reduces the number of duplicates by a significant factor.

However, compared to the membership list investigated above, the folders that constitute a context are more dynamic. Therefore, automatic update mechanisms must ensure that the context database is consistent with the actual context data. Since the context module is informed about the creation of a new subfolder by an event, this update mechanism is realised as a simple learning process. Whenever a new folder is created as a subfolder of a folder that is already listed in a context description, this new subfolder is automatically added to the context description. This ensures that the context description is always consistent.

Some lessons learned

This examination of the contextualisation approach for notification systems illustrates that the context description as well as the contextualisation of event information requires a careful investigation of the application data. In the presented case different properties of the event information as well as the context description were considered to find a suitable mapping.

In the easiest case, the context is hardwired in the event by the application, such that each event contains an attribute that identifies the context unanimously. However, this would result in an inflexible solution. The definition of a new context or the modification of an existing context would require an adaptation of all involved applications. Furthermore, such an approach makes it difficult to realise a user specific mapping, in which the same event is mapped to different contexts, because of different user- or group-preferences. For example, one user group might decide that all events, which originate from a workspace containing organisational material (e.g., forms, organisational statistics, etc.) belongs to the context "organisational stuff", while the user group that produces this information regards this as the project context "corporate identity".

Thus, the presented approach of a centralised context module that provides a flexible and lightweight approach to model awareness contexts in a user specific way provides more flexibility. Nevertheless, we have learned that the event to context matching requires a very detailed and specific context description. This result is important for the development of future context based systems since it implies that all activity representation must be as detailed as possible and that successful matching algorithms must rely on very detailed context description. However, a very detailed context description is problematic for dynamically changing context data, since it requires continuously updated context description. The solution for this problem is twofold. First, it is important to find categories and aggregations of context data to avoid the necessity to enumerate and thus duplicate workspace information in the context description. The folder-id serves this purpose for the shared workspace application. Second, a simple learning mechanism that automatically updates the context description by interpreting incoming events that contain update information is useful.

Context sharing

Shared workspaces can also be used for sharing context descriptions. The creator of an awareness context uses a shared workspace for the storage and administration of the descriptions. In a shared workspace, the administrator can then specify the members of the context and grant them access to the context description. So, all members of the awareness context can update the context description. For instance, they can add new applications or event types.

As mentioned above user can specify preferences that describe in which situation a user wants to be informed about which context, in which format and by which media the events should be presented, and when they should be presented. Similar to the sharing of context descriptions, shared workspaces can also be used for sharing user preferences. So, the members of a context cannot only share context descriptions, but also their preferences. This is a means for context members to be uniformly informed.

We expect that this kind of support for awareness contexts will allow users to establish conventions — which we call 'Context-iquette'. Members of an awareness context can establish conventions for the kind of information that is monitored and also conventions for the presentation of this information. This is a major step towards the protection of privacy — in each context users can find a context-specific solution to this challenge. In one context users might want to have reciprocity; in another context users might want to accept asymmetry.

Related Work

The AREA system offers similar group awareness support to our system. Situations are described as relationships among objects. Objects are single persons, artefacts, or aggregations such as groups of people. Users can specify which events and artefacts they are interested in and when and in which intensity they want to be informed (Fuchs, 1999) (Sohlenkamp et al., 2000).

As opposed to the ENI system the AREA system is based on an object-relationship model that is application specific and requires detailed specifications. The modelling of contexts with attribute-value pairs in ENI allows a simple and easy adaptation. Furthermore, any number of new attributes can be added. Therefore, one event can be matched with any number of contexts. In AREA events are caused by actions within the relationship model. In ENI situations relate to actions of users — that is, the system analyses the actions of users and tries to identify the context in which a user is in, instead of requiring a pre-specification of object and event relations.

The Atmosphere model (Rittenbruch, 1999) describes contexts as 'spheres'. Users classify their actions on artefacts by means of 'contextors' and map them to specific contexts. When an action is performed a pre-defined contextor has to be selected. Consequently, the model offers a better quality of event information (e.g., write report, instead of simply open report), but requires the users to explicitly specify the respective contextor. As opposed to ENI Atmosphere is based on a detailed and static description of relationships among artefacts, objects, and actions.

Besides the above-mentioned event-based models, spatial models have been presented. In spatial models awareness between objects — persons or artefacts — is calculated by means of the distance between them in a medium. Objects are surrounded by the aura, which can be seen as an area in which objects can be perceived. At the same time all objects have a focus; that is, an area which they can capture. Mutual overlaps between auras and foci determine mutual awareness of objects (Benford and Fahlén, 1993) and can be seen as spatial context. Spatial models are, in general, only used for synchronous group awareness, because presence of several users at the same time is necessary. The group awareness is mainly calculated based on the distance between objects and does not respect individual interests of users.

The AETHER model can be seen as an extension of the spatial model; the concepts of aura, focus and medium are also used, although in a slightly modified manner. The AETHER model defines the relations between objects with a semantical network (Sandor et al., 1997). The Model of Modulated Awareness (MoMA) is based on a reaction-diffusion metaphor. This metaphor is based on the idea that whenever two or more entities have contact their state is modified in some way. Group awareness is produced and consumed through fields (Simone and Bandini, 2002). Both models, AETHER and MoMA are rather sophisticated, but have the disadvantage that their setup is complicated and that adaptation is hardly possible.

ELVIN (Fitzpatrick et al., 1999) and NSTP (Patterson et al., 1996) are event notification systems similar to our prior version of ENI—that is, they are client/server infrastructures that capture events and present events regardless of the context of origin and the users' context of work.

In the area of knowledge management complex ontologies are used to model the contexts of information seekers in order to improve search results. Whereas these ontologies provide very detailed and adequate models, they are hard to adapt and, therefore, too rigid for the support of dynamic group processes (Gross and Klemke, 2002).

Conclusions

In this paper we contributed a model, an implementation and an examination for the contextualisation of awareness information. We believe that—as it has been said in the area of global information systems like the WWW—in future it will not only be important that information can be provided at all. Rather, one of the big challenges will lie in the selection of the relevant information. In our opinion, awareness contexts are an interesting step towards this direction.

The evaluation of the context model for the contextualisation of events from a shared workspace system demonstrated the applicability of the model. But, it also indicated that contextualisation requires a careful investigation of the application to identify properties that permit a unique mapping of events to a context. In cases where such properties cannot be identified, the presented approach allows a graded mapping of events to a context.

Some future challenges are questions of the evolution of contexts. Questions like: who will model awareness contexts; how will the evolution of these models be supported; who will be allowed to change the model are very important for the success of awareness contexts.

Further future challenges lie in the presentation of awareness information. Because users are members of several awareness contexts and want to be informed about several awareness contexts at the same time, we need mechanisms for merging information from different awareness contexts and displaying it. This leads also to a problem of prioritising awareness contexts; that is, it has to be constantly decided which kind of information from which awareness context is to be displayed immediately and which kind of information of which awareness context can be displayed after a delay. Algorithms could calculate the current actuality of an awareness context form information like the number of present users (in absolute figures and relatively to the whole number of members of an awareness context), the fluctuation of an awareness context, the frequency of changes to documents in an awareness context (either with equally important documents or with a hierarchy of importance of documents). Furthermore, the current awareness context a user is in, will vastly influence the type of information to be displayed and also the means of presentation.

Finally, we believe that contexts play a vital role for proper understanding of any kind of information (cf. the above-mentioned first definition of context above). This cannot only support persons who already share an awareness context, but also newcomers because the awareness context can be used as guidance of the new users.

Acknowledgements

The research presented here was carried out by the IST-10846 project TOWER, partly funded by the EC. We would like to thank all our colleagues from the TOWER team. In particular with thank our colleague Karl-Heinz Klein for the implementation of the concepts presented in this paper and many useful discussions on the applicability and usefulness of concept itself.

References

Abiteboul, Serge, Peter Bunemann, and Dan Suciu (1999): Data on the Web - From Relational to Semistructured Data and XMLMorgan Kaufmann.

Agostini, A., G. de Michelis, M. Grasso, W. Prinz, and A. Syri (1996): Contexts, Work Processes, and Workspaces. Computer Supported Cooperative Work: The Journal of Collaborative Computing, vol. 5, no. 2-3, pp. 223-250.

Appelt, Wolfgang (1999). WWW Based Collaboration with the BSCW System SOFSEM'99, Milovy, Czech Republic. Springer Lecture Notes in Computer Science 1725, pp. 66-78.

Begole, J., M.B. Rosson, and C.A. Shaffer (1999): Flexible Collaboration Transparency: Supporting Worker Independence in Replicated Application-Sharing Systems. ACM Transactions on Computer-Human Interaction (TOCHI), vol. 6, no. 6, pp. 95-132.

Benford, Steve and Lennart Fahlén (1993). A Spatial Model of Interaction in Large Virtual Environments In G. d. Michelis, C. Simone, and K. Schmidt (eds.): Third European Conference on Computer Supported Cooperative Work - ECSCW ´93, Milan. Kluwer, pp. 109-124.

Cadiz, Jonathan, Gina Venolia, Gavin Jancke, and Anoop Gupta (2002). Designing and Deploying an Information Awareness Interface Conference on Computer Supported Cooperative Work, CSCW 2002, New Orleans. ACM Press.

Dourish, Paul and V. Bellotti (1992). Awareness and Coordination in Shared Workspaces In J. Turner and R. Kraut (eds.): CSCW ´92 - Sharing Perspectives, Toronto, Canada. ACM Press, pp. 107-114.

Erickson, T., D.N. Smith, W.A. Kellogg, M. Laff, and J.T. Richards (1999). Socially Translucent Systems: Social Proxies, Persistent Conversation, and the Design of Babble. Proceedings of the Conference on Human Factors in Computing Systems - CHI'99, Philadelphia, PE. ACM press, pp. 72 -79.

Fitzpatrick, Geraldine, Tim Mansfield, Simon Kaplan, David Arnold, Ted Phelps, and Bill Segall (1999). Augmenting the Workaday World with Elvin In S. Bødker, M. Kyng, and K. Schmidt (eds.): ECSCW'99: Sixth Conference on Computer Cooperative Work, Copenhagen. Kluwer Academic Publishers, pp. 431-450.

Fitzpatrick, Geraldine, Sara Parsowith, Bill Segall, and Simon Kaplan (1998). Tickertape: Awareness in a Single Line CHI'98: ACM SIGCHI Conference on Human Factors in Computing, Los Angeles, CA. ACM Press.

Fuchs, Ludwin (1999). AREA: A cross-application notification service for groupware In S. Bødker, M. Kyng, and K. Schmidt (eds.): ECSCW'99: Sixth Conference on Computer Supported Cooperative Work, Copenhagen. Kluwer Academic Publishers, pp. 61-80.

Gross, Tom and Roland Klemke (2002). Context Modelling for Information Retrieval - Requirements and Approaches In P. Isaias (ed.): Proceedings of the IADIS International Conference - WWW/Internet 2002, Lisbon, Portugal. IADIS Press, pp. 247-254.

Gutwin, Carl and Saul Greenberg (1998). Design for Individuals, Design for Groups: Tradeoffs between Power and Workspace Awareness In S. Poltrock and J. Grudin (eds.): CSCW '98 Computer Supported Cooperative Work, Seattle, WA. ACM Press NY, pp. 207-216.

Gutwin, Carl, Mark Roseman, and Saul Greenberg (1996). A Usability Study of Awareness Widgets in a Shared Workspace Groupware System In M. S. Ackermann (ed.): CSCW'96: Conference on Computer Supported Cooperative Work, Boston, MA. ACM Press, pp. 258-267.

Heath, C. and P. Luff (1991). Collaborative Activity and Technological Design: Task Coordination in London Underground Control Rooms In L. Bannon, M. Robinson, and K. Schmidt (eds.): Third European Conference on Computer Supported Cooperative Work, Amsterdam. Kluwer, pp. 65-80.

Pankoke-Babatz, Uta and Anja Syri (1997). Collaborative Workspaces for Time Deferred Electronic Cooperation In S. Hayne and W. Prinz (eds.): GROUP'97: International ACM SIGGROUP Conference on Supporting Group Work, Phoenix, AZ. ACM Press, pp. 187-196.

Patterson, John F., Mark Day, and Jakov Kucan (1996). Notification Servers for Synchronous Groupware In M. S. Ackermann (ed.): Conference on Computer Supported Cooperative Work (CSCW'96), Boston, MA. ACM Press, pp. 122-129.

Prinz, Wolfgang (1999). NESSIE: An Awareness Environment for Cooperative Settings In S. Bødker, M. Kyng, and K. Schmidt (eds.): ECSCW'99: Sixth Conference on Computer Supported Cooperative Work, Copenhagen. Kluwer Academic Publishers, pp. 391-410.

Rittenbruch, M. (1999). Atmosphere: Towards Context-Selective Awareness Mechanisms Human-Computer Interaction: Communication, Cooperation and Application Design - HCI'1999, Munich, Germany. Lawrence Erlbaum, Hillsdale, NJ.

Sandor, Ovidiu, Christian Bogdan, and John Bowers (1997). Aether: An Awareness Engine for CSCW In H. Hughes, W. Prinz, T. Rodden, and K. Schmidt (eds.): ECSCW'97: Fifth European Conference on Computer Supported Cooperative Work, Lancaster, UK. Kluwer Academic Publishers, pp. 221-236.

Schmidt, Kjeld (2002): The Problem with Awareness: Introductory Remarks on Awareness in CSCW. Computer Supported Cooperative Work: The Journal of Collaborative Computing (Kluwer Academic Publ., Dordrecht), vol. 11, no. 3-4, pp. 285-298.

Simone, Carla and Stefania Bandini (2002): Integrating Awareness in Cooperative Applications through the Reaction-Diffusion Metaphor. Computer Supported Cooperative Work: The Journal of Collaborative Computing (Kluwer Academic Publ., Dordrecht), vol. 11, no. 3-4, pp. 495-530.

Sohlenkamp, Markus, Wolfgang Prinz, and Ludwin Fuchs (2000): PoliAwac - Design and Evaluation of an Awareness Enhanced Groupware Client. AI and Society - Special Issue on CSCW, vol. 14, no. 1, pp. 31-47.

K. Kuutti, E.H. Karsten, G. Fitzpatrick, P. Dourish and K. Schmidt (eds.), *ECSCW 2003: Proceedings of the Eighth European Conference on Computer Supported Cooperative Work, 14-18 September 2003, Helsinki, Finland*, pp. 315-334.

Customizable Collaborative Editor Relying on treeOPT Algorithm

Claudia-Lavinia Ignat and Moira C. Norrie
ETH Zurich, Switzerland
ignat@inf.ethz.ch, norrie@inf.ethz.ch

Abstract. Research in collaborative editing tends to have been undertaken in isolation rather than as part of a general information or application infrastructure. Our goal is to develop a universal information platform that can support collaboration in a range of application domains. Since not all user groups have the same conventions and not all tasks have the same requirements, this implies that it should be possible to customize the collaborative editor at the level of both communities and individual tasks. One of the keys to customization is to use a structured rather than linear representation of documents that can be applied to both textual and graphical editors. In this paper, we propose the treeOPT (tree OPerational Transformation) algorithm that, relying on a tree representation of documents, applies the operational transformation mechanism recursively over the different document levels. Applications using this algorithm achieve better efficiency, the possibility of working at different granularity levels and improvements in the semantic consistency.

Introduction

Within the CSCW field, collaborative editing systems have been developed to support a group of people editing a document collaboratively over a computer network. These systems can be used in a wide range of advanced computing application areas, including collaborative writing, collaborative CAD (Computer Aided Design) and CASE (Computer Aided Software Engineering). The major benefits of collaborative editing include reduced task completion time and distributed collaboration. On the other hand, the challenges that it raises are many, ranging from the technical challenges of maintaining consistency coupled with good performance to the social challenges of supporting group activities and conventions across many different communities.

Within the existing collaborative-editors' community, research tends to have been undertaken in isolation rather than as part of a general information or application infrastructure. Also, most of the research tends to be theoretical with limited implementation and studies of use in practice. Where applications have been considered, i.e. collaborative editing for a particular task such as writing scientific articles or music, the solutions often assume particular characteristics of both the users and the documents that they are editing. We consider that it is important to take into account all aspects of collaborative editing together, inclusive of theoretical foundations, technical aspects of implementation and issues of user interaction. Further, it is important to integrate it within a general information and application infrastructure so that it can support collaboration for a range of communities and activities within these communities. Since not all user groups have the same conventions and not all tasks have the same requirements, this implies that it should be possible to customize the collaborative editor at the level of both communities and individual tasks.

Most existing collaborative editors deal either with textual or graphical editing, using quite different document representations. In the case of textual editors, a linear representation is usually used. Our goal is to develop general textual and graphical collaborative editors that have a more structured representation that enables us to deal with consistency maintenance efficiently in both forms of editing, while offering the flexibility of customization of collaborative access.

In this paper, we propose the treeOPT (tree OPerational Transformation) algorithm that relies on a tree representation of the document. Our algorithm relies on the same principles for consistency maintenance as the GOT (Sun et al., 1998), and GOTO (Sun and Ellis, 1998) algorithms, but applies the same basic mechanisms recursively over the tree. Applications using this algorithm achieve better efficiency, the possibility of working at different granularity levels and improvements in the semantic consistency relative to other existing operational transformation algorithms.

We begin in the next section by motivating our choice of the operational transformation approach and giving a short overview of the consistency model on which our algorithm is based. We then present our algorithm in the following section, highlighting its advantages over other existing algorithms which rely on a linear structure representation. Next, we present some problems encountered when integrating the algorithm into the collaborative editor and the solutions we have adopted. Features of the customizable collaborative editor are presented in a separate section and this is followed by a section dedicated to a discussion of related work. Concluding remarks and the main directions of our future work are presented in the last section.

Principles of consistency underlying the algorithm

Real-time operation is an important aspect to be considered in the design of collaborative editing systems as users should be able to see the effects of their own actions immediately and those of other users as soon as possible. To ensure high responsiveness, a replicated architecture where users work on copies of the shared document and instructions are exchanged by message passing is necessary. High concurrency is also an essential requirement of real-time collaborative editing systems, i.e. any number of users should be able to concurrently edit any part of the shared document.

Approaches such as *turn-taking* protocols, *locking* or *serialization-based* protocols fail to meet at least one of these requirements. Turn-taking protocols (Greenberg, 1991) allow only one active participant at a time, the one who "has the floor"; this approach is equivalent to document locking and lacks concurrency. Locking (Greenberg and Marwood, 1994) guarantees that users access objects in the shared workspace one at a time. Concurrent editing is allowed only if users are locking and editing different objects. Non-optimistic locking introduces delays for acquiring the lock. Optimistic locking avoids the delays, but it is not clear what to do when locks are denied and the object optimistically manipulated by the user must be restored to its original state. In the case of serialization-based protocols, operations are executed in the same total order at all sites. Non-optimistic serialization delays the execution of an operation until all totally preceding operations have been executed (Lamport, 1977). Optimistic serialization executes the operations upon their arrival, but uses undo/redo techniques to repair the out-of-order execution effect (Karsenty and Beaudouin-Lafon, 1993).

The *operational transformation* approach has been identified as an appropriate approach for maintaining consistency of the copies of the shared document in real-time collaborative editing systems. It allows local operations to be executed immediately after their generation and remote operations need to be transformed against the other operations. The transformations are performed in such a manner that the intentions of the users are preserved and, at the end, the copies of the documents converge. Various operational transformation algorithms have been proposed: dOPT (Ellis and Gibbs, 1989), adOPTed (Ressel et al., 1996), GOT (Sun et al., 1998), GOTO (Sun and Ellis, 1998), SOCT2 (Suleiman et al., 1997; Suleiman et al., 1998), SOCT3 and SOCT4 (Vidot et al., 2000). Although these algorithms are generic operational transformation algorithms, they can be applied only for applications that use a linear representation of the document. The real-time collaborative text editors relying on these algorithms represent the document as a sequence of characters.

We therefore base our work on the operational transformation approach. Specifically, our algorithm follows the same principles for consistency maintenance as presented in Sun et al. (1998). In the remainder of this section, we give a brief overview of the consistency model underlying our algorithm.

We start by defining the notions of causal ordering relations and dependent and independent operations.

Causal ordering relation "→": Given two operations O_a and O_b generated at sites i and j respectively then O_a is causally ordered before O_b, denoted $O_a \rightarrow O_b$ iff: (1) $i=j$ and the generation of O_a happened before the generation of O_b; or (2) $i \neq j$ and the execution of O_a at site j happened before the generation of O_b; or (3) there exists an operation O_x such that $O_a \rightarrow O_x$ and $O_x \rightarrow O_b$.

Dependent and independent operations: Given any two operations O_a and O_b, (1) O_b is *dependent* on O_a iff $O_a \rightarrow O_b$; (2) O_a and O_b are said to be independent or concurrent iff neither $O_a \rightarrow O_b$, nor $O_b \rightarrow O_a$. This is denoted $O_a \| O_b$.

The consistency model satisfies the following consistency properties:

- The *convergence* property requires that all copies of the same document are identical after executing the same collection of operations.
- The *causality preservation* property requires that, for any pair of operations O_a and O_b, if $O_a \rightarrow O_b$, then O_a is executed before O_b at all sites.
- The *intention preservation* property requires that, for any operation O, the effects of executing O at all sites are the same as the intention of O and the effect of executing O does not change the effects of independent operations.

To satisfy the above consistency properties different algorithms follow different approaches.

To achieve *causality preservation*, most operational transformation algorithms (dOPT, adOPTed, GOT(O), SOCT2) use a timestamping scheme based on a data structure called a State Vector (Ellis and Gibbs, 1989). With the aid of this vector, the conditions for execution of an operation at a certain site (causally-ready operation) are defined.

To achieve *intention preservation*, a causally ready operation has to be transformed before its execution in order to cope with the modifications performed by other executed operations. In the GOT algorithm two types of transformations are defined: inclusion transformations and exclusion transformations. An *inclusion transformation* of an operation O_a against an independent operation O_b, denoted $IT(O_a, O_b)$, transforms O_a such that the impact of O_b is included in O_a. An *exclusion transformation* of an operation O_a against a causally-preceding operation O_b, denoted $ET(O_a, O_b)$, transforms O_a such that the impact of O_b is excluded from O_a. Additionally, in the GOTO algorithm, a *transpose* function is defined to change the execution order of two operations while respecting the user intentions. The dOPT algorithm uses *dOPT transformation*, the equivalent of inclusion transformation. To achieve intention preservation, the adOPTed algorithm uses an N-dimensional interaction model graph and the *L-transformation* based on the same principle as inclusion transformation. SOCT2 and SOCT3 algorithms use *forward transposition* (the equivalent of inclusion transformation) and *backward transposition* with the same underlying ideas as the transpose operation.

To achieve *convergence* most of the algorithms (adOPTed, GOTO, SOCT2) require that two conditions C1 and C2 be satisfied by the transformation functions. Condition C1 guarantees that the operation resulting from the transformation operation of two concurrent operations will not depend on the order in which they are serialized. Condition C2 aims at making the transformation of an operation with a sequence of operations independent of the order of the operations in the sequence. The dOPT algorithm uses only C1, but it fails to ensure the convergence of copies in all cases. GOT imposes neither of these conditions, but requires a total ordering relation "$\Rightarrow$" between operations and an undo/do/redo scheme. SOCT3 and SOCT4 require only C1 and replace C2 by a continuous global order of execution of operations.

The treeOPT algorithm

Most real-time collaborative editors relying on existing operational transformation algorithms for consistency maintenance use a linear representation for the document, such as a sequence of characters in case of text documents. This way of representing documents has several crucial disadvantages, which we present below.

All existing operational transformation algorithms keep a single history of operations already executed in order to compute the proper execution form of new operations. When a new remote operation is received, the whole history needs to be scanned and transformations need to be performed, even though different users might work on completely different sections of the document and do not interfere with each other. Keeping the history of all operations in a single buffer decreases the efficiency. The existing algorithms for integrating a new causally ready operation into the history have a complexity of order n^2, where n is the size of the examined history buffer (for example GOT, SOCT2, SOCT3). Exceptionally, the dOPT algorithm has a complexity of order n, but convergence of copies is not always achieved. Consequently, a long history results in a higher complexity. This complexity negatively affects the response time, i.e. the time necessary for the operations of one user to be propagated to the other users, which is a factor of critical importance in real-time editing systems.

Dourish (1996) classifies conflicts as either syntactic or semantic. Syntactic conflicts occur at the system infrastructure level, while semantic conflicts are inconsistencies from the perspective of the application domain. Therefore, in the case of a multi-user text editor, consistency from the users' perspective is often not the same as consistency from the system's. Although the existing algorithms solve the syntactic inconsistency problems, they do not enforce semantic consistency. Let us consider that a shared document contains the text: "*The child go alone to school.".* Assume that a user adds the letters *"e"* and *"s"* at the end of the word *"go"* intending to obtain: *"The child goes alone to school.".* At the same time, another user, deletes *"go"* and inserts *"went"* aiming to obtain: *"The child went alone to school.".* Unfortunately, there is no automatic way to execute these conflicting operations and obtain a semantically consistent result. The best that the algorithms such as GOT(O) can obtain is the following: *"The child wentes alone to school.".* The same kind of inconsistencies happen if operations insert or delete not letters as previously described, but whole words. Consider again the previous example. First user, would then delete the word *"go"* and insert the word *"goes"* in order to obtain: *"The child goes alone to school.".* Suppose now that, simultaneously, the second user inserts the word *"can"*, changing the text into: *"The child can go alone to school.".* Unfortunately, after each user receives the operations performed by the other one, the result is: *"The child can goes alone to school.".* As we can see, even though all operations were operations involving whole words, semantic consistency could not be enforced. The conclusion we can draw is that working at any level of granularity can result in semantic inconsistencies, but working at a higher level usually translates into a more semantically consistent final result. However, semantic consistency remains an open issue that should also be tackled by operational transformation algorithms.

We propose a new algorithm overcoming the disadvantages presented above. The algorithm relies on operational transformation and on modelling the document using a hierarchical rather than linear structure. We present the algorithm applied to a text document, but it can be easily adapted for any other document that uses a hierarchical structure. In the case of text documents, we model the document as consisting of paragraphs, each paragraph consisting of sentences, each sentence consisting of words and each word consisting of letters. Therefore, the tree structure has the following levels of granularity together with their assigned numeric values: document (0), paragraph (1), sentence (2), word (3) and character (4), corresponding to the common syntactic elements used in natural language.

We are now in a position to formally present our algorithm and we begin by defining the basic notions of node and composite operation.

Definition *Node*

A node N is a structure of the form N=<*level, children, length, history, content*>, where

- *level* is a granularity level, *level* $\in \{0,1,2,3,4\}$, corresponding to the element type represented by node (i.e. document, paragraph, sentence, word or character)

- *children* is an ordered list of nodes $\{child_1,...,child_n\}$,

　　level($child_i$)=*level*+1, for all i$\in \{1,...,n\}$

- *length* is the length of the node,

$$length= \begin{cases} 1, & \text{if } level = 4 \\ \displaystyle\sum_{i=1}^{n} length(child_i), & \text{otherwise} \end{cases}$$

- *history* is an ordered list of already executed *operations* on children nodes
- *content* is the content of the node, defined only for leaf nodes

$$content= \begin{cases} \text{undefined}, & \text{if } level < 4 \\ aCharacter, & \text{if } level = 4 \end{cases}$$

Note that *operations* are equivalent to those defined by the model used in the GOT(O) algorithm.

Definition *Composite Operation*

A composite operation is a structure of the form
cOp=<*level, type, position, content, stateVector, initiator*>, where:
- *level* is a granularity level, *level*∈ {1,2,3,4}
- *type* is the type of the operation, *type*∈ {*Insertion, Deletion*}
- *position* is a vector of positions
    position[i]= position for the ith granularity level, i∈ {1,...,*level*}
- *content* is a node representing the content of the operation
- *stateVector* is the state vector of the generating site
- *initiator* is the initiator site identifier

The *level* of a composite operation can be equal to 1, 2, 3 or 4, but not 0 (deleting the whole document or inserting a whole new document are not permitted). The vector *position* specifies the positions for the levels corresponding to a coarser or equal granularity than that of the operation. For example, if we have an insertion operation of word level (3), we have to specify the paragraph and the sentence in which the word is located, as well as the position of the word within the sentence. The *content* of a composite insertion operation specifies the node to be inserted in the position given by the *position* vector. The attributes *stateVector* and *initiator* have the same meaning as in the case of the operations used by the GOT(O) algorithm.

For the sake of simplicity, in future examples, we will denote operations by specifying only their *type, level, position* and the text conversion of *content*, ignoring the other attributes. For example, *InsertWord(3,1,2,"ECSCW")* denotes a composite operation of *type Insertion*, having the *level* word, in paragraph 3, sentence 1, at word position 2 inside the sentence, and having as *content* a node of type *word* which stands for the text "*ECSCW*".

In what follows we will give an intuitive explanation of the algorithm, and afterwards describe it formally.

Each site stores locally a copy of the *hierarchical structure* of the shared document. The root node of the tree will be the document node, having as children paragraph nodes. Each paragraph node, in its turn, will have as children sentence nodes, and so on. The leaf nodes will be character nodes. For a leaf node, the content of the node is explicitly specified in the *content* field. For nodes situated higher in the hierarchy, the *content* field will remain unspecified, but the actual content of each node will be the concatenation of the contents of its children. Each node (excluding leaf nodes) will keep a history of *insertion* or *deletion* operations associated with its *children nodes*. An example showing the structure of a document is illustrated in Figure 1: the document contains three paragraphs; paragraph 3 contains two sentences; sentence 1 of paragraph 3 contains three words; 2nd word of sentence 1 in paragraph 3 is *"ECSCW"*.

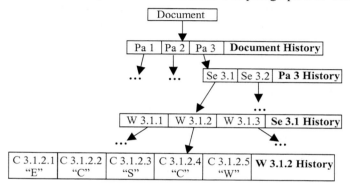

Figure 1. Example of structure of a document

The algorithm follows the same principles as those of the GOT(O) algorithm. Each site can generate composite operations, representing insertions or deletions of subtrees in the document tree. Note that each node of a subtree to be inserted has an *empty* history buffer. The site generating a composite operation executes it immediately. The operation is also recorded in the history buffer associated to the parent node of the inserted or deleted subtree. Finally, the new operation is broadcast to all other sites, being timestamped using a state vector. Upon receiving a remote operation, the receiving site will test it for causal readiness. If the composite operation is not causally ready it will be queued, otherwise it will be transformed and then executed. Transforming the operation is somewhat more difficult (but also much more efficient) than in the case of the GOT(O) algorithm. We will illustrate the way transformations are performed using an example.

Consider a site receiving the following remote composite operation: *InsertWord(3,1,2,"ECSCW")*. It is an operation intending to insert the word *"ECSCW"* in paragraph 3, sentence 1, as the 2nd word. The newly received operation must be transformed against the previous operations, as described below.

First of all, we consider the paragraph number specified by the composite operation, which in this case is equal to 3. We do not know for sure that paragraph number 3 of this site's local copy of the document is the same paragraph as that referred to by the original operation. Suppose a concurrent operation inserts a whole new paragraph before paragraph 3. Then, in this case, we should insert the word *"ECSCW"* not in paragraph 3, but in paragraph 4. Therefore, we must first transform the new operation against previous operations involving whole paragraphs, which are kept in the *document history* buffer. Note that this could be done using any existing operational transformation algorithm working on linear structures such as the GOT(O) algorithm. After performing these transformations, we obtain the position of the paragraph in which the operation has to be performed, paragraph number 4 in our example. Consequently, the new composite operation will become *InsertWord(4,1,2,"ECSCW")*. Here it is important to note that previous concurrent operations of finer granularity are not taken into account by these transformations, because the *document history* buffer contains only operations at the paragraph level. Indeed, we are not interested in whether another user has just modified another paragraph, because this fact does not affect the number of the paragraph where the word *"ECSCW"* has to be inserted.

The next step obtains the correct number of the sentence where the word has to be inserted. Therefore, the new operation is transformed against the operations belonging to *Pa4 history*. *Pa4 history* only contains insertions and deletions of sentences that are children of paragraph 4. We again apply an existing operational transformation algorithm, and obtain the correct sentence position (for example sentence 2), transforming the operation into *InsertWord(4,2,2,"ECSCW")*. The algorithm continues by obtaining the correct word position in the same manner.

Finally, the operation can be executed and recorded in the history. Because it is an operation of word level, it must be recorded in the history associated with the parent sentence.

As we can see, the algorithm achieves consistency by repeatedly applying an existing concurrency control algorithm on small portions of the entire history of operations, which, rather than being kept in a single linear structure, is distributed throughout the tree.

We now present the general form of the treeOPT algorithm.

Algorithm *treeOPT(cOp, rootNode, noLevels)* {

Given a new causally ready composite operation, *cOp*, the root node of the hierarchical representation of the local copy of the document, *rootNode*, and the number of levels in the hierarchical structure of the document, *noLevels*, the execution form of *cOp* is returned.

$currentNode = rootNode$;

for $(l = 1; l <= noLevels; l++)$

$o_{new} = Composite2Simple(cOp, l)$;

$eo_{new} = Transform(o_{new}, history(currentNode))$;

$position(cOp)[l] = position(eo_{new})$;

$$\text{if } (level(cOp) = l)$$
$$\quad \text{return } cOp;$$
$$currentNode = child_i(currentNode), \text{ where } i=position(eo_{new});$$
}

In the case of the text editor *noLevels*=4 and *rootNode*=document.

As we have seen in the previous examples, determining the execution form of a composite operation requires finding the elements of the *position* vector corresponding to a coarser or equal granularity level than that of the composite operation. For each level of granularity *l* (starting with paragraph level and ending with the level of the composite operation), an existing operational transformation algorithm is applied to find the execution form of the corresponding regular operation. Traditional algorithms do not perform transformations on composite operations, but rather on regular ones. Therefore, we had to define the function *Composite2Simple*, that takes as arguments a composite operation, together with the granularity level at which we are currently transforming the operation, and returns the corresponding regular operation. The operational transformation algorithm is applied on the history of the *currentNode* whose granularity level is *l*-1 (recall that, for example, to find the corresponding paragraph position, transformations need to be performed against the operations kept in the document history). The lth element in the *position* vector will be equal to the *position* of the execution form of the regular operation. If the current granularity level *l* is equal to the level of the composite operation, the algorithm returns the execution form of the composite operation. Otherwise, the processing continues with the next finer granularity level, with *currentNode* being updated accordingly.

By *Transform(op, history)* we denote any existing concurrency control algorithm, that, taking as parameters a causally-ready regular operation *op* and a history buffer *history*, returns the execution form of *op*. The implementation of the *Transform* method depends on the chosen consistency maintenance algorithm working on a linear structure of the document. We tested the operation of our algorithm when combined with the GOT algorithm and adapted to the undo/do/redo scheme of this algorithm. A detailed implementation of the *treeOPT-GOT* algorithm as well as of the *Composite2Simple* function can be found in (Ignat and Norrie, 2002). Combining our algorithm with dOPT can be easily performed. The transform function should be replaced with the part of dOPT algorithm for executing a causally ready operation (Ellis and Gibbs, 1989). When combined with SOCT2, the algorithm has to be adapted to the mechanism of integrating an operation into the history by performing forward and backward transpositions (Suleiman et al., 1998).

The *treeOPT* algorithm is a general algorithm in that it can be applied to any document having a hierarchical structure. A trivial application would be the case of a book modelled as being composed of chapters, with each chapter consisting of sections, each section of paragraphs, each paragraph of sentences and so on. Another application is the case of XML documents. If we consider an XML document as being composed of elements without attributes, the algorithm is straightforward. In the case of elements with attributes, the treeOPT algorithm is still applicable, but an underlying algorithm for a linear structure dealing, not only with concurrent operations of insert and delete, but also with operations for modifying attributes needs to be implemented.

An important advantage of the algorithm is related to its improved efficiency. In our representation of the document, the history of operations is not kept in a single buffer, but rather distributed throughout the whole tree, and, when a new operation is transformed, only the history distributed on a single path of the tree will be spanned. This will turn out to be a very important increase in speed, especially given the fact that the complexity of the concurrency control algorithms for a linear structure is usually of $O((spanned\_history)^2)$. Moreover, when working on medium or large documents, operations will be localized in the areas currently modified by each individual user and these may often be non-overlapping. In these cases, almost no transformations are needed, and therefore the response times and notification times are very good (recall the fact that in the case of algorithms working on linear structures, every operation interferes with any other, independently of the distance between the positions specified in the operations).

Another important advantage is the possibility of performing, not only operations on characters, but also on other semantic units – words, sentences and paragraphs. The transformation functions used in the operational transformation mechanism are kept simple as in the case of character-wise transformations, not having the complexity of string-wise transformations. An insertion or a deletion of a whole paragraph can be done in a single operation. Therefore, the efficiency is further increased, because there are fewer operations to be transformed, and fewer to be transformed against. Moreover, the data is sent using larger chunks, thus the network communication is more efficient. Our approach also adds flexibility in using the editor, the users being able to select the level of granularity they prefer to work on.

Last, but not least, our algorithm can help users in enforcing the semantic consistency of the documents, because working at a coarser granularity is allowed.

Adapting the algorithm to the collaborative editor

In this section we want to report on some problems we had when adapting the treeOPT-GOT algorithm for the text collaborative editor application and the solutions we have adopted to overcome these problems.

Even though the algorithm works very well with insert and delete primitives at different levels of the hierarchy, in practice these two primitives are not sufficient

326

to perform all possible operations. Actually this happens due to the introduction of the different hierarchic levels. Let us consider the following example. Suppose the second paragraph of a document consists of the following sentence: *"Nobody influences her like her brother."* as shown in the Figure 2 (a). Suppose we want to split this sentence into two other sentences: *"Nobody influences her. She likes her brother."* How can we perform this operation by using only insert and delete primitives? One alternative would be to first delete the words *"like"*, *"her"* and *"brother"*, from the first sentence, and then to insert the whole sentence: *"like her brother."*. As a result of performing these operations, the new structure of Paragraph 2 will be the one illustrated in Figure 2(b).

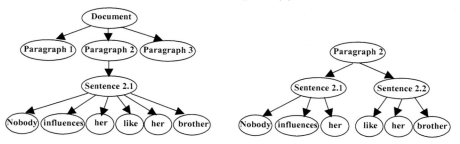

Figure 2. (a) Initial structure of the document; (b)Structure of the Paragraph 2 after splitting the Sentence 2

Unfortunately this approach does not work. Suppose that concurrently with the split operation of the sentence, another user, noticing the poor English, tries to insert the word *"does"* at the end of the sentence, in order to obtain *"Nobody influences her like her brother does."* The operation sequence is illustrated in Figure 3(a). As we can see, by the time operation *InsertWord(2, 1, 7,"does")* is received at Site1, the words *"like"*, *"her"* and *"brother"* are already deleted from the paragraph 2, sentence 1, and these operations of word deletion are kept in the history of Sentence 2.1. Applying the algorithm, the operation *InsertWord(2, 1, 7, "does")* will be transformed into *InsertWord(2, 1, 4,"does")*. The resulting structure of the paragraph, shown in Figure 3 (b), is not what the user at Site2 intended.

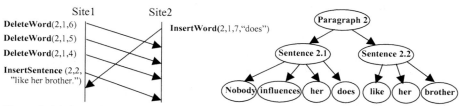

Figure 3. (a) Operation sequence (b) Erroneous result due to emulating split by using insertions and deletions

An unexpected result would be also obtained if the user at Site2 intends to change the word *"brother"* into *"brothers"*. The operation is performed on the Sentence 2.1, but the word *"brother"* has been already deleted from this sentence.

As we can see, splitting a sentence (or a word, or a paragraph) is not as simple as it seems at first sight. Some other possible ways of simulating the split operation using only insertions and deletions exist, but none of them is feasible. The reason is that a structural element might appear different on two hosts at the same time, and the two structures converge only because the history of operations on that element is kept at both sites. When an element is split into two parts, its history must be also split. Using only elementary insert/delete operations cannot detect the case when the history needs to be split or not. The same problem is encountered in the case of joining two elements. For example, if we delete a sentence separator, the two adjacent sentences will be joined into a single one implying the joining of the histories of the two sentences.

An alternative solution would be to introduce two other primitives: *split* and *join*, and to modify the algorithm by implementing operational transformation functions for these primitives as well. By means of an example, we show that this solution also does not work. Suppose that initially we have the sentence S_1 = *"He really enjoyed the movie."* in both the local copies of users at Site1 and Site2 and the operation sequence is shown in Figure 4.

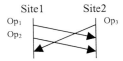

Figure 4. Counterexample for split and join primitives

Operation Op_1 initiated by the user at Site1 splits sentence S_1 in two sentences S_{11} = *"He really enjoyed."* and S_{12} = *"the movie.".* Operation Op_2 deletes only sentence S_{12}. However, when operation Op_2 arrives at Site 2, it cannot be directly executed, because it is independent of the operation Op_3 (whatever Op_3 is), and consequently must include the effect of Op_3. But before accomplishing this, Op_2 has to have the same initial context as Op_3. That is why we need an exclusion transformation of Op_2 against Op_1. If we exclude the effect of Op_1, that splits S_1 into S_{11} and S_{12}, deleting the sentence *"the movie."* will have to be transformed into two different operations, which are not of the same granularity: *DeleteWord("the")*, *DeleteWord("movie")*. This is not an acceptable solution because the idea of the treeOPT algorithm is to transform operations against other operations of the same level of granularity, the result being also an operation of the same level of granularity.

The most appropriate solution we have so far found, although somehow disappointing, is not to split or join elements in the tree structure. For example, given the text *"god father"* composed of two words, deleting the space between the two words, will still have as a result the two words, even though not separated by anything. The same approach can be adopted in the case of splits. If we insert a sentence separator, for instance a dot, or even a paragraph separator, for instance new line, inside a sentence, the text will be kept as a single sentence. Embracing this approach will however lead to degenerated elements. For example, the text *"Life is beautiful. So are you."* might be a single large degenerated word, and the text *"deep"* can be stored in three degenerated sentences: *"d"*, *"ee"*, and *"p"*. Obviously, the hierarchical structure resulting in the case of degenerated elements is different from the one obtained by parsing the text and by delimiting the elements using their natural separators.

Even with this drawback, the algorithm works well. We afford degenerated elements because, when issuing an operation, the positions of the elements of different granularity levels (paragraph, sentence and word) are computed by taking into account the length of the previous elements. Consequently, the fact that the elements are degenerated does not matter. The efficiency of the algorithm remains unaffected by the degenerated elements, because the structure of the document will remain hierarchical, and operations will be transformed locally, spanning only a small part of the whole history of operations. Unfortunately, semantic consistency will be more difficult to maintain. It is harder to combine the algorithm with locking on a specific level of granularity. For example, trying to lock a word might result in locking a whole paragraph which is stored into a degenerated word. However, the problem is not as severe as it seems, because the reparsing of the whole document will be performed every time a new user begins the editing of the same document, or when the document is reloaded. Reparsing restores the semantic consistency of elements, only non-degenerated elements being generated. Reparsing the document should be enforced as often as possible. But, parsing the document implies having the same copy of the document at all sites. This means that reparsing can be performed only in moments of quiescence. Either the system can detect the moments of quiescence and initiate reparsing on copies of the document at all sites, or quiescence could be enforced by the system from time to time.

Analyzing the situation, the algorithm still keeps the anticipated efficiency boost, and also enhances the semantic consistency, even though not as well as expected.

We believe that the other approaches that apply operational transformation mechanisms for maintaining consistency in the case of a tree structure (Davis and Sun, 2002; Molli et al., 2002b) are also faced with the same problem of splitting or joining elements. However, nothing related to this problem is mentioned in their publications. Let us consider the example of an XML document modeling information about articles. Part of such a document is given below:

```
<article>
    ...
    <author> Grady Booch </author>
    <author> Ivar Jacobson </author>
</article>
```

If a user realizes that only first *author* is the author of the article and the second author is one of the authors of another article, then the article element may need to be split as follows:

```
<article>
    ...
    <author> Grady Booch </author>
</article>
<article>
    ...
    <author> Ivar Jacobson </author>
</article>
```

From the example presented above, we can see that the problem of splitting XML elements is a similar problem to that of splitting elements of different granularity levels in our approach.

Customizable Collaborative Editor

It is desirable to have a collaborative editor that is customizable for not only application domains, but also activities and upon user request.

We have implemented a multi-document collaborative text editor relying on the treeOPT-GOT algorithm (Nedevschi, 2002). Users can join or leave the editing of any document or of the whole session whenever they want. Users can be made aware of the modifications done by other users, through the use of different colours and the application can provide a legend with the users editing the same document and the associated colours. Users are also informed by means of messages that appear on the lower part of the editor about the ongoing activity of the group, such as the joining of new users. Users can select the level of granularity they prefer to work on. Some users prefer to wait until writing a whole paragraph and, only then, to send an insert operation containing this paragraph. Others prefer to send operations character by character, in order to enable the other users to visualize the modifications as soon as possible.

In what follows we present some other functionality that we want to offer to the editor.

Optional locking as a complementary technique to operational transformation (Sun, 2002) can be used for maintaining the semantic consistency. Group undo (Sun, 2000) (global versus local, single step, chronological or selective) should be provided for error-recovery or alternative exploration. Members of a team might wish to work independently in parallel, "insulated" in their private workspaces for some period of time (Molli et al., 2002a; Dourish, 1995). For example, when writing an entire new paragraph, some users might prefer to make it visible only after completing the work, or, in the case of an architectural design, it seems natural that an architect does not want to publish very sketchy initial drafts of their plans.

Social aspects such as audio communication or chat systems between users are also very important for avoiding or resolving conflict between users. Even though our system automatically resolves conflicting operations generated by different users, the conflicts can also be solved more easily by mutual agreements among users. A great feature of our application is that conflicts are always solved, but they should be avoided to begin with. Messages like *"I'm now working on the Introduction section."* prevent other users from modifying the same part of the document. Even in the case of conflicts, after an automatic solution has been generated and perhaps produced something unexpected, the users involved in the conflict can communicate with each other, finding out the intentions of the others and agreeing on a solution. Different activities of users can be tracked (Chalmers, 2002). For example, for avoiding conflicts, it might be useful to have information about the frequency of modifications on different parts of the document performed in the last period of time. The scroller can change the intensity of its colour according to the number of modifications performed on that part of the document. Also, for each user, a chronological list of operations performed can be kept. Although almost all of the aspects mentioned above were researched into in isolation, open questions exist and we feel it is important to integrate and study many of these in the context of a single system.

Collaborative applications can offer a real improvement in the users' working activities if the underlying architecture of the implementation platform is able to provide required functionality already integrated at a lower-level, so that applications do not have to deal with aspects such as metadata handling, persistence, distribution and multi-user support. We therefore plan to integrate the collaborative editors into the Universal Information Platform (UIP) (Rivera, 2001), an object-oriented, multi-user, distributed, persistent information management system. For example, the collaborative editor application can easily be enhanced with access rights and roles associated to users and groups of users, as these features are already integrated into the core of the project.

Related work

Starting with the dOPT algorithm of Ellis and Gibbs (1989), various algorithms using operational transformation for maintaining consistency in collaborative systems have been proposed: adOPTed (Ressel, 1996), GOT(Sun et al., 1998), GOTO (Sun and Ellis, 1998), SOCT2 (Suleiman et al., 1997), SOCT3 and SOCT4 (Vidot et al., 2000). As mentioned previously, all of these algorithms are based on a linear representation of the document whereas our algorithm uses a tree representation of the document and applies the same basic mechanisms as these algorithms recursively over the different document levels.

Other recent research has also looked at tree representations of documents. The dARB (Ionescu and Marsic, 2000) algorithm also uses a tree model for document representation, however it is not able to automatically resolve all concurrent accesses to documents and, in some cases, must resort to asking the users to manually resolve inconsistencies. Their approach is similar to the dependency detection approach for concurrency control in multi-user systems where operation timestamps are used to detect conflicting operations and the conflict is then resolved through human intervention (Stefik et al., 1987). The dARB algorithm may also use special arbitration procedures to automatically resolve inconsistencies; for example, using priorities to discard certain operations, thereby preserving the intentions of only one user. In our approach, we preserve the intentions of all users, even if, in some cases, the result is a strange combination of all intentions. However, the use of different colours provides awareness of concurrent changes made by other users and the main thing is that no changes are lost. Moreover, because operations (delete, insert) are defined only at the character level in this algorithm, i.e. sending only one character at a time, the number of communications through the network increases greatly. Further, there are cases when one site wins the arbitration and it needs to send, not only the state of the vertex itself, but maybe also the state of the parent or grandparent of the vertex. Sending whole paragraphs or even the whole document in the case that a winning site has performed a split of a sentence or a paragraph, respectively, is not a desirable option. In our approach, we tried to reduce the number of communications and transformations as much as possible, thereby reducing the notification time, which is a very important factor in groupware. For this purpose, our algorithm is not a character-wise algorithm, but an element-wise one, i.e. it performs insertions/deletions of different granularity levels (paragraphs, sentences, words and characters). Moreover, we do not need retransmissions of whole sentences, paragraphs or of the whole document in order to maintain the same tree structure of the document at all sites.

Some very recent publications have used operational transformation applied to documents written in dialects of SGML (Standard General Markup Language) such as XML and HTML (Davis and Sun, 2002; Molli et al., 2002b) or to CRC cards (Molli et al., 2002b). These are particular cases where a tree model of the document is required. These works were performed in parallel to our implementation of the editor relying on the treeOPT algorithm. However, their motivation for developing the algorithms differs from ours. They wanted to adapt operational transformation to XML-like structured documents and this required the transformation functions (Sun et al., 1998; Vidot et al., 2000) to be extended to allow concurrent operations of insertion/deletion of elements and modification of the attributes of the elements in the XML structure. Our goal is to find a general and efficient algorithm for maintaining consistency applicable to all kinds of documents: raw, XML, graphical, etc. The hierarchical model seems a suitable model for a set of application domain documents. Therefore the treeOPT algorithm was designed and then implemented as the basis of a collaborative text editor where the hierarchical structure is not so obvious.

The existing collaborative graphical editors are based on one of three basic approaches to consistency maintenance, namely, locking - e.g. Aspects (von Biel, 1991), Ensemble (Newman-Wolfe et al., 1992), GroupDraw (Greenberg et al., 1992), serialization - e.g. GroupDesign (Karsenty and Beaudouin-Lafon, 1993), LICRA (Kanwati, 1992) or multi-version techniques - e.g. Tivoli (Moran et al., 1995), GRACE (Sun and Chen, 2002). The only work investigating a tree model for the graphical documents is (Ionescu and Marsic, 2000), but their approach, as previously mentioned, has the main disadvantage of not resolving inconsistencies automatically.

Conclusions and future work

In this paper, we have presented a consistency maintenance algorithm relying on a tree representation of documents. The hierarchical representation of a document is a generalisation of the linear representation and, in this way, our algorithm can be seen as extending the existing operational transformation algorithms. The algorithm applies the same basic mechanisms as existing operational transformation algorithms recursively over the different document levels and it can use any of the operational transformation algorithms relying on linear representation. When used by applications that rely on a hierarchical structure of the document, it achieves better efficiency, the possibility of working at different granularity levels and improvements in the semantic consistency. We have presented the algorithm focusing on its functionality for text documents, but it can also be applied for any kind of document relying on a hierarchical representation. We highlighted some key features of the customizable editor relying on the treeOPT algorithm and also discussed our plans to integrate the editor into the universal information platform UIP which provides a complete and rich API that could be used for the development of collaborative space for general document management.

In the future, we plan to investigate the possibility of introducing locking at different granularity levels (paragraph, sentence, word). We anticipate a set of challenges due to split and join operations as described in the paper and to the distributed locking conflict resolution protocol because of the peer-to-peer architecture of our application. Also, we want to develop a consistency maintenance algorithm for the case of a collaborative graphical editor relying on some of the main concepts that were used for the text editor, such as the tree representation of the document. We also plan to perform some benchmarking and to evaluate the performance of the treeOPT algorithm in comparison with other existing algorithms.

References

Chalmers, M. (2002): 'Awareness, Representation and Interpretation', in *J. CSCW*, vol. 11, 2002, pp. 389-409.

Davis, A.H. and Sun, C. (2002): 'Generalizing Operational Transformation to the Standard general Markup Language', *Proceedings of Conference on Computer Supported Cooperative Work*, 2002, pp. 58-67.

Dourish, P. (1995): 'The Parting of the Ways: Divergence, Data Management and Collaborative Work', *Proc. Fourth European Conference on Computer-Supported Cooperative Work ECSCW'95*, Stockholm, Sweden, September 1995.

Dourish, P. (1996): 'Consistency Guarantees: Exploiting Application Semantics for Consistency Management in a Collaboration Toolkit', *Proc. ACM Conference on Computer-Supported Cooperative Work CSCW'96* , 1996, pp. 268-277..

Ellis, C.A., and Gibbs, S.J. (1989): 'Concurrency control in groupware systems', *Proceedings of the ACM SIGMOD Conference on Management of Data*, May 1989, pp. 399-407.

Greenberg, S. (1991): 'Personalizable groupware: Accomodating individual roles and group differences', *Proceedings of the European Conference on Computer Supported Cooperative Work*, Amsterdam, September 1991, pp.17-32.

Greenberg, S., Roseman, M., Webster, D. and Bohnet, R. (1992): 'Issues and experiences designing and implementing two group drawing tools', *Proceedings of the 25th Annual Hawaii International Conference on the System Science*, 1992, pp. 138-150.

Greenberg, S. and Marwood, D. (1994): 'Real time groupware as a distributed system: Concurrency control and its effect on the interface', *Proceedings of the ACM Conference on Computer Supported Cooperative Work*, North Carolina, October 1994, pp. 207-218.

Ignat, C.L. and Norrie, M.C. (2002): 'Tree-based Model Algorithm for Maintaining Consistency in Real-Time Collaborative Editing Systems', *The Fourth International Workshop on Collaborative Editing Systems, CSCW 2002*, New Orleans, USA, November 2002.

Ionescu, M. and Marsic, I. (2000): 'An Arbitration Scheme for Concurrency Control in Distributed Groupware', *The Second International Workshop on Collaborative Editing Systems, CSCW 2000*, December 2000.

Kanwati, R. (1992) 'LICRA: a replicated-data management algorithm for distributed synchronous groupware application', in *Parallel Computing* 22, 1992, pp. 1733-1746.

Karsenty, A., and Beaudouin-Lafon, M. (1993): 'An algorithm for distributed groupware applications', *Proceedings of the 13th International Conference on Distributed Computing Systems*, May 1993, pp.195-202.

Lamport, L. (1977): 'Time, clocks, and the ordering of events in a distributed system', in *Communication of the ACM*, vol. 21, no. 7, July 1977, pp.558-565.

Molli, P., Skaf-Molli, H. and Oster, G. (2002a): 'Divergence Awareness for Virtual Team through the Web', in *Integrated Design and Process Technology, IDPT-2002*, Pasadena, CA, USA. Society for Design and Process Science, June 2002.

Molli, P., Skaf-Molli, H., Oster,G. and Jourdain, S. (2002b): SAMS: 'Synchronous, asynchronous, multi-synchronous environments', *Proceedings of the Seventh International Conference on CSCW in Design*, Rio de Janeiro, Brazil, September 2002.

Moran, T., McCall, K., van Melle, B., Pedersen, E. and Halasz, F. (1995): 'Some design principles for sharing in tivoli, a whiteboard meeting-support tool', in *Groupware for Real-Time Drawings: A designer's Guide*, S. Greenberg, Ed. McGraw-Hill International(UK), 1995, pp. 24-36.

Nedevschi, S. (2002): 'Concurrency control in real-time collaborative editing systems', *Diploma Thesis*, ETH Zurich, 2002.

Newman-Wolfe, R.E., Webb M., and Montes, M. (1992): 'Implicit locking in the Ensemble concurrent object-oriented graphics editor', *Proc. of the ACM Conference on Computer Supported Cooperative Work (CSCW'92)*, New York, 1992, pp. 265-272.

Ressel, M., Nitsche-Ruhland, D. and Gunzenbauser, R. (1996): 'An integrating, transformation-oriented approach to concurrency control and undo in group editors', *Proc. of ACM Conference on Computer Supported Cooperative Work*, November 1996, pp. 288-297.

Rivera, G. (2001): 'From File Pathnames to File Objects: An approach to extending File System Functionality integrating Object-Oriented Database Concepts', *Doctoral Thesis* No. 14377, ETH Zurich, September 2001.

Suleiman, M., Cart, M. and Ferrié, J. (1997): 'Serialization of Concurrent Operations in Distributed Collaborative Environment', *Proc. ACM Int. Conf. on Supporting Group Work (GROUP'97)*, Phoenix, November 1997, pp. 435-445.

Suleiman M., Cart M. and Ferrié J. (1998): 'Concurrent Operations in a Distributed and Mobile Collaborative Environment', *Proc.14th IEEE Int. Conf. on Data Engineering IEEE/ ICDE'98*, Orlando, February 1998, pp. 36-45.

Sun, C. (2000): 'Undo any operation at any time in group editors', *Proceedings of ACM Conference on CSCW*, Philadelphia, USA, December 2000, pp. 191-200.

Sun, C. (2002): 'Optional and Responsive Fine-grain Locking in Internet-based Collaborative Systems', in *IEEE Transactions on Parallel and Distributed Systems*, vol. 13, no. 9, September 2002, pp.994-1008.

Sun, C. and Chen, D. (2002): 'Consistency Maintenance in Real-Time Collaborative Graphics Editing Systems', in *ACM Transactions on Computer-Human Interaction*, vol.9, no.1, March 2002, pp. 1-41.

Sun, C. and Ellis, C. (1998): 'Operational Transformation in Real-Time Group Editors: Issues, Algorithms, and Achievements', *Proc. ACM Int. Conf. On Computer Supported Cooperative Work (CSCW'98)*, Seattle, November 1998, pp. 59-68.

Sun, C., Jia, X., Zhang, Y., Yang, Y. and Chen, D. (1998): 'Achieving Convergence, Causality-preservation, and Intention-preservation in Real-time Cooperative Editing Systems', in *ACM. Trans. on Computer-Human Interaction*, vol. 5, no. 1, March 1998, pp.63-108.

Stefik, M., Foster, G., Bobrow, D.G., Kahn, K., Lanning, S. and Suchman, L. (1987): 'Beyond the chalkboard: Computer support for collaboration and problem solving in meetings', *Communications of the ACM*, vol. 30, no.1, January 1987, pp.32-47.

Vidot, N., Cart, M., Ferrié, J., and Suleiman M. (2000): 'Copies convergence in a distributed real-time collaborative environment', *Proceedings of the ACM Conference on Computer Supported Cooperative Work*, Philadelphia, USA, December 2000, pp.171-180.

von Biel, V. (1991): 'Groupware Grows Up', in *MacUser*, June 1991, pp. 207-211.

K. Kuutti, E.H. Karsten, G. Fitzpatrick, P. Dourish and K. Schmidt (eds.), *ECSCW 2003: Proceedings of the Eighth European Conference on Computer Supported Cooperative Work, 14-18 September 2003, Helsinki, Finland*, pp. 335-354.

Tourism and mobile technology

Barry Brown and Matthew Chalmers

Computing Science, University of Glasgow, Glasgow, G12 8QQ, United Kingdom

barry@dcs.gla.ac.uk, matthew@dcs.gla.ac.uk

Abstract. While tourism presents considerable potential for the use of new mobile technologies, we currently have little understanding of how tourists organise their activities or of the problems they face. This paper presents an ethnographic study of city tourists' practices that draws out a number of implications for designing tourist technology. We describe how tourists work together in groups, collaborate around maps and guidebooks, and both 'pre-' and 'post-visit' places. Implications are drawn for three types of tourist technology: systems that explicitly support how tourists co-ordinate, electronic guidebooks and maps, and electronic tour guide applications. We discuss applications of these findings, including the *Travelblog*, which supports building travel–based web pages while on holiday.

Introduction

In recent years, interest in CSCW has expanded to include the use of technology in non-work settings, for example, the organisation of households (Hughes et al., 2000), teenagers' use of mobile phones (Grinter and Eldridge, 2001) and music listening (Brown et al., 2001). These studies have shown both the applicability of CSCW methods to these new contexts, and the relevance of findings from these contexts to core CSCW issues.

In this paper we discuss a study of *city tourists*, examining the problems they encounter as they move between and visit new places. Tourism has been a popular area for mobile information systems, in particular the Lancaster GUIDE system (Cheverst et al., 2000), and other PDA based systems (Abowd et al., 1997; Fesenmaier et al., 2000; Woodruff et al., 2001). Indeed, as mobile phones and other portable devices becoming more advanced, tourism is one obvious application area. However, commercial technologies in this area have had only limited success. There has also been little work that has studied tourism and drawn implications specifically for the design of these mobile technologies.

Here we present an ethnographic study of tourists' practices, based on a wide range of data, including observations of tourists, 'video diaries' of days out with tourists, and video recordings of tourists in public. We draw from this a number of design implications for how we could build better tourist technology. In particular, we focus on the *collaborative* nature of the tourist experience—the ways in which tourism is a richly social activity. The paper starts by discussing how tourists work together in groups, negotiating and arranging their activities, and co-ordinating their locations when separated. We then discuss how tourists collaborate around maps and guidebooks, focusing on the problems that tourists have in 'putting the guidebook in its place' i.e. moving from printed publications to specific attractions. Lastly, we look at how tourists both 'pre-visit' and 'post-visit' places. Tourists spend considerable time planning their activities, both before they visit and on the visit itself. However, tourists deliberately make plans that are not highly structured and specific, so that they can take advantage of changing circumstances.

We argue that systems need to better support this collaborative nature of tourism, even if this support is as simple as better links with paper maps which allow tourists to interact around a wider surface than a PDA's small screen. We also suggest how technologies could help tourists to move between the guidebook and planning their activity, such as maps that show some of the 'social structure' of cities, and guides that better support the flexible nature of tourists' plans. We are currently applying these recommendations within the City project and the Equator collaboration (www.equator.ac.uk), as we develop experimental tourist systems, extend a system to support 'co–visiting' between local and remote visitors to a museum (Brown *et al.*, 2003), and explore theoretical issues such as the interdependence of new and old media in city life (Chalmers 2003).

Tourism in the literature

Tourism is an activity of great importance both economically and in terms of the pleasure it gives to holidaymakers worldwide. Nearly all individuals in the western world take some sort of holiday away from home every year, although the number of days differs across and within different countries. Tourism is also an activity that can divide rich and poor, through a negative or parasitical effect that damages places: 'touristification' (Apostolopoulos et al., 1996). As one would expect, there is a large body of literature that explores these issues from economic, cultural, environmental and other perspectives (Pearce, 1995; Urry, 1995; Tribe, 1999). Given this large body of existing work, one obvious question is what could CSCW offer to studying tourists.

Previous tourism studies have noted that insufficient attention has been paid to the experience and practices of the tourist. Instead, most work has focused on the *effects* of tourism. Fodness and Murray comment that "detailed knowledge of the basis of actual tourist behaviour [is] lacking" (Fodness and Murry, 1997), and Aramberri argues that much tourism research "does not help to explain the nature of modern mass tourism" (Aramberri, 2001). The work that has looked in most detail at tourist practice has been the "tourist information seeking" literature (Snepenger et al., 1990; Moore et al., 1995). This literature has tended to avoid detailed qualitative description, focusing more on broad categorisations of tourist practice and questionnaire–based studies (Riley and Love, 1999).

This lack of detailed observations presents a number of problems for the design of technologies. Specifically, there is a lack of understanding of the methods tourists use to choose and arrange their various activities. This motivated our choice of ethnographic methods to look in depth at how tourists arrange their activities, rather than concentrating on the effects of tourism, as is more traditional. In doing this, our approach is similar to recent studies of museum visitors (vom Lehn et al., 2001), interactions between local people and tourists (Lee and Watson, 1993; Munro, 1998), and tourist information centres (Crabtree, 1999). In these cases a focus on the 'how' of ordinary activities, such as looking at a shared museum exhibit, can lead to findings useful for the design of technologies. Looking at tourism also presents an opportunity to explore leisure activities within CSCW and the particularly the sociality of leisure. As the growth in online gaming shows, many leisure technologies take on a new life when designed for group or social interaction. This presents opportunities for CSCW research, not least in understanding how technology can support existing rich social bonds.

Studying tourism

In this study, we combined video with conventional ethnographic observational work. We used small cameras to videotape activities in which we were participants and observers. We collected four main pieces of qualitative data. Five days were spent studying tourists in Edinburgh and Glasgow, combining observation with videoing their activities. A focus of this work was the documents that tourists used, such as maps, guidebooks, train timetables and so on. Our observations were conducted around major tourist areas: the main train stations, hostels, luxury hotels, Glasgow's main city square, and an historic street in Edinburgh called the Royal Mile. We combined these with five 'video diaries', made by accompanying tourists while sightseeing on a day in the city. We recruited groups of visitors to the city from friends and family of our university's staff. We then followed these visitors around for a day, videoing them as they chose what to do, arranged their visit and navigated their way around the city. We supplemented these observations with twelve interviews with tourists, which were tape recorded and later transcribed. Lastly, we conducted a five day ethnography in the Glasgow tourist information centre, collecting data from the activities of both staff and tourists asking for information[1].

The data collected was diverse, but it allowed us to think about and explore what tourists do in a number of different ways, while remaining close to what tourists do. In analysing this diverse range of data we aimed to produce an *ethnographic* understanding of tourism; that is to say one that reflected the pressures, viewpoints and feelings of tourists as much as cataloguing their activities. In describing our analysis, we have therefore attempted to communicate our understandings of the tourist predicament, as much as describing specific fieldwork incidents.

The cities that we studied, Edinburgh and Glasgow, are the second and third most popular cities for tourists to visit in the U.K., after London (Star-UK, 2000). Summer is a particularly busy time of the year for both cities, with the Edinburgh Festival (as well as the better weather) a major tourist attraction. This influenced the type of tourists that we found. The tourists that we spoke to and studied were predominantly independent travellers, who had mostly arranged their own travel although some used the assistance of a travel agency. While the package tour market is obviously a very important part of tourism (31% in the case of leisure visitors to the US), we focus more on tourists who arrange their activities themselves, since this group suffers more acutely from problems of organisation. While a major proportion of independent travellers are 'backpackers', young people travelling for a prolonged period of time before entering paid employment (Loker-Murphy and Pearce, 1995), independent travellers are a diverse group with a wide age range. In our case it encompassed older travellers (so called 'Peter Pan' travellers), those on short city breaks, and travellers with a specific sporting interest—most prominently hill-walking and golf.

In thinking about what tourists do, we found it useful to consider tourist 'problems' and 'solutions'. One example from the fieldwork is that tourists often need to use public transport to get between places. To do this they need to solve a number of practical problems, such as finding where bus stops are, finding out which bus to get, and so on. Discussing tourist activity in this way gave us a focus on practical activities: the most important part of tourism for the purposes of designing new tourism systems. This emphasises the decisions that tourists make and the information they use to make these decisions. However, we must be careful not to become too focused on utility, as tourists' problems are not like work problems. Solving these problems is actually part of the enjoyment of being

---

[1] One additional source of data was our own experiences as tourists during the time we conducted the study. While we did not collect this data as systematically as the other sources, field notes were taken during four tourist trips by the authors.

a tourist. In deciding what to do and how to do it, a tourist learns about the place they are visiting. As the old saying goes: "getting there is half the fun".

We discuss our fieldwork and its implications in three sections. First is a general discussion of the problems which tourists face, and the decisions that tourists have to make. Second, we look at the solutions tourists use and in particular the resources that they bring to bear on these problems. This includes working with others, guidebooks, maps and plans. Lastly, we discuss the possibilities for the design of new tourist technologies, and outline two prototype systems informed by our studies and currently under development.

Tourist problems

We start by outlining the problems which tourists face on their holidays. Although these observations come from our fieldwork, we will refrain from discussing the fieldwork in depth until the next section. The first, seemingly straightforward, problem which tourists face in an unfamiliar place is *what to do*. Unlike work, where tasks are often determined (in part) by an overall goal or by other people's plans, tourism is much more open-ended. Tourism encompasses a broad range of activities such as sightseeing, relaxing, shopping, visiting friends and visiting family. Indeed, since tourism can be part of business travel, the boundary between work and leisure is often blurred. Yet whatever tourists do, they must at least make some sort of decision about what to do, often in advance. This decision must take into account the time it takes to get to different places, as well as balancing the attraction of different sites. Even when one arrives at a tourist 'attraction' this problem reappears at a different scale, e,g. which parts of a large museum to visit?

Along with the question of what to do, tourists need to work out *how* they are going to do these different activities. When one reaches a tourist site one has to be careful about how one acts, since behavioural norms can be different in different countries. Ignorance about local customs is an oft mocked feature of tourists. Even straightforward activities such as buying goods can be organised differently in different countries, compounded with the problems of working with a new currency, and avoiding being exploited, or just 'looking stupid'.

Along with what and how, tourists have to manage *when* they do different activities. Tourism is usually constrained in time, because of the need to return home. Time is also a problem in that tourists work with organisations that provide services: opening times must be co-ordinated with the times of public transport, such as trains or buses. This is compounded by the 'pre–booking problem'. Many facilities require pre–booking, so decisions need to be made before one has been to a place.

These two problems in turn interact with our third tourist problem: finding *where* things are. In visiting a city many of the attractions are distributed around the city. There is therefore a need to avoid spending too much time travelling between places, understand what one might see and do along the way, and group together attractions which are close together. In doing so tourists must also navigate public transport, often with limited information, or unfamiliar road systems.

Lastly, an important part of a holiday is sharing that holiday with others who are at home. Although the tourist fascination with taking photos or videos has been often criticised (Bourdieu, 1990), it displays how visitors are not isolated individuals but are part of a social group. Tourists record and represent experiences in the form of photos and stories, to remind themselves of the visit and to share with others after they return home. This is a valuable part of tourism. The most successful tourist technology is the camera, specifically designed for this 'taking the visit back home'. The popularity of Internet cafés for tourists also suggests that email sent back home is becoming a significant part of the tourist experience.

Tourist solutions

We emphasise again that these 'problems' are not a negative part of tourism. Travelling and finding out where to go is part of the very enjoyment of tourism. Tourism transforms what might seem mundane activities into something enjoyable or even romantic. Train journeys, for example, are a common resource for the travel writer, and bus and underground travel can have their own pleasures (such as the smell of the train's tires in the Parisian metro, or the electronic sounds of the Tokyo subway). Particularly in city visits, walking between places is an important part of being in a place, with 'street life' being one of the easiest ways to access the natural life of locals (chapter vii, De Certeau, 1984). These pleasures are a whimsical yet crucial part of the enjoyment of tourism.

So, in solving these problems tourists are not simply looking for some optimal solution. Instead, solving these problems is part of the enjoyment of the experience; finding a nice café or reading a map, for example, is enjoyable in itself. Accordingly, the solutions that tourists have to these problems are often finely tuned to both the problem and the enjoyment of working through the problem.

Sharing the visit with others

One method that tourists use to solve their problems is sharing the visit with other tourists. Tourism is very much a social activity. A tourist generally travels with others, e.g. as part of a family group, and statistics from the US show that 79% of leisure visits involve groups of two or more (USDTI, 1999). Since leisure travel is predominantly group-based, there is considerable intra-group interaction and collaboration. For example, Figure 1 shows some frames taken from a video of two tourists who have just arrived at Edinburgh's main train station. The first tourist holds an "A to Z" street guide to Edinburgh, and is looking through it. While the second tourist glances around the railway station, the first tourist finds the correct page of the map. Then the second tourist takes out her glasses to look

at the map, glances at the map and then points at an exit sign in the train station that names the street to which the exit leads. They then give the street guide a last look, pick up their bags and leave the station.

Figure 1: Tourists at a train station

Even in this simple excerpt one can see a division of labour between the two tourists. The second tourist looks around the station to find the exit, while the first tourist tries to find the correct page on the map. She holds the map so as to make both the map and her progress in using it available to her companion. On finding the station, she describes the location of the station to her friend, and the friend adds the name of the street reached via the exit. With these two items of information, they now know where they are on the map, where the exit will take them and how to proceed to their destination. Reading the map is done here in such a way that it can be 'checked' by the first tourist's companion. If she makes a mistake (which is easy to do), or if they later find themselves lost, the companion can intervene. The job of remembering the route is thus shared by the two tourists. Together they use the environment to move between the map and a course of activity. The sign in the station is used to link the map with where the station exit leads.

Along with these collaborative advantages of working together, visiting with others is not without its own overheads. With the collaborative 'working out' in this clip there is also an implicit negotiation going on. The two tourists are deciding *what* they are going to do as well as how. Visiting with others involves considerable co-ordination in this way. The desire to visit different attractions, or simply to see different museum exhibits, means that tourist groups often split up and then need to co-ordinate getting back together. This can present considerable challenges since tourists are highly mobile. It is in these situations that mobile phones become a useful tool, in that calls can be made between individuals or sub-groups[2]. A more local form of this co-ordination problem also takes place in particular sites where individuals go to different rooms, or different exhibits, and they need to locate their travelling companions. This is particularly the case for tourists with children, since children sometimes run off, and must be carefully watched to see that they come to no harm. In the incidents we observed, mothers spent considerable time shepherding children around museums, in particular, collecting all the children together before leaving the museum. For these parents a large part of their holiday was 'managing' the group and making sure that nobody got lost.

A second way in which visits are shared is through meeting other tourists (Loker-Murphy et al., 1995). The standard jokes about holiday romances displays something of the way that meeting other people is an integral part of many tourist experiences. In part, these opportunities come from the lowered barriers to social contact. Individuals are 'on holiday' from many of their home commitments. The facilities that tourists use, such as hostels, trains and buses, also can also afford social contact. One reason behind these social contacts, and certainly a common conversation topic, is the exchange of stories and advice on where to go and what to visit. In our interviews this advice was given great value, greater even than information given by guidebooks or tourist information staff. This 'word of mouth' sharing allows tourists to exchange information on sites that have changed, as well as informal information about different places and facilities, such as their friendliness. However, these meetings and conversations are not just forums for the exchange of information. They provide a 'ticket to talk' (Sacks, 1992) with other tourists: an excuse and a basis for more general conversation. The social contact that these conversations initiate may be of more value than the exchange of information—they are as much platforms for establishing other (possibly temporary) social bonds, or simply enjoying the company of new people.

---

2 With many mobile phone charging systems these are the most expensive calls possible with the cost as high as two international calls to connect a call between two foreign mobile-phones in the same country.

Putting guidebooks in their place

A second way tourists solve their problems is the use of published information. The two most quintessential tourist publications are the guidebook and the map. These are often used in combination when tourists navigate and find out about what to do in different places and how to get between them. While both have been subject to computerisation, this has had only limited success. For example, we did not observe any use of digital maps or guidebooks in our observations. In part, this limited success can be put down to a lack of knowledge about how maps and guidebooks are actually used by tourists. Studying the use of these conventional paper publications can reveal to us some of the advantages of paper publications and how to better design their digital equivalents.

Guidebooks come in many different forms, from free handouts to Michelin and Baedeker guides. One reason why guidebooks are so useful to tourists is that they catalogue, in a structured and relatively standardised form, relevant aspects of the places that tourists visit. They list accommodation (with phone numbers), attractions (with opening times), recommended bars and restaurants, and so on. This standardisation can make strange places feel considerably safer to tourists by reducing their uncertainty.

Guidebooks also offer short 'guides to action', highlighting differences in everyday activities that might cause embarrassment. In use, however, this information needs considerable interpretation—guidebooks need to be 'put in their place'. What the guidebook says has to be combined with other information, in particular information on maps, or advice from locals. We frequently found tourists holding a map and a guidebook, and using these in combination. In particular, guidebooks were collaborative artefacts, conversation would take place around the guidebook with tourists pointing at the guidebook, and then pointing either at a map or in a direction, so as to link together the establishments being discussed with their position.

Indeed, finding something from a guidebook can be a challenge even when it is very close by. In the following extract (figure 2), a group of tourists are looking for a particular historic house. The confusion of the tourists here is apparent, and the volunteered assistance of the researcher (B) is only partially helpful. The conversation takes place here around a map contained in a guidebook and a page of text describing different attractions. The tourists talk about an old house they are looking for, point at its location on a map in the guidebook and then attempt to find that location on the street. As can be seen from this extract the guidebook is a rich collaborative artefact—it supports a group working around the book, pointing at different items and solving their problems together. Yet even though they are only a few metres from the house, navigating with the map and the guidebook together causes some confusion. A GPS positioning system here would have been of little help; the tourists' problem is in moving from the guidebook to the street they are on. Although they find the house on a map, its street name ("Lawnmarket") is not enough for them to find the house without some work. The street they are on is labelled "Lawnmarket", it is often simply called "the High Street" by locals since it is a continuation of that street. Confusingly, "Castle Hill Street" is very close by too:

```
A: Maybe it's down there it could be down there Fran
B: Are you looking for a street? *1*
A: Nooo it's a (.5) a very old house is it Gladstone
or Livingstone. (.5) Very old place. I think it's to
the left of Deacon Brodie's ehh
C: Gladstones Land? ↑Gladstones Land?↓ (walks over) *2*

A: Uhh I think


C: Gladstones land is number *3* six. *4*
A: Wheres six?
C: Six is (.5) fifteen. Five. Six. Castle hill
(1.5) hill street
B: Castle hill is [just there]
C:                [iddsh] well it has a
description lets see what it says *5*
C: it's a six story home and look at the year
1620
B: its on the lawn market
A: Yeah
C: Where does it say, oh lawn market Oh.  He said it
was on the high street
A: Maybe they've got it .. ok
B: Lawnmarket's just here
C: ↑Oh↓ ohhh whats this street called is this Lawnmarket too?
B: This is Lawnmarket.  [It becomes High Street] ermm
A:                       [This is Lawnmarket]
C: Ohhhh
A: So 477.
C: So where does it become High Street (1.0)
C: oohhh it's across the street right over there.  It's probably
the old one, lets go and look
```

Figure 2: Tourist using a guidebook to find a historic house

The tourists go through a number of descriptions of where the house is and what it is like to help them find it ("to the left of Deacon Brodies", "very old", "six story", "477") with eventually the *age* helping them to find the house "its probably the old one" (on this sort of activity see (Schlegoff, 1972)). These descriptions help the tourists to find the house, along with informing them about what they are visiting. Even with a map, a guidebook, and the assistance of a local, the tourists need to work the guidebook to 'place' the old house on the street they are actually on, and overcome some of the confusions of streets which change name, the difference between how a street is named on a map and a name that locals use. In this way, tourists take the information held in guidebooks and combine this with information they find from particular places, such as street

Figure 3: A tourist reads a guidebook but keeps his finger on another page, so that he can quickly go back.

Figure 4: Multiple publications are laid out on the counter of the Tourist Information Centre

names or train timetables in a railway station. This is how guidebooks are 'put in their place'.

In designing technologies for tourism we should also pay attention to a second aspect of guidebooks: their physical form. The photographs attached to the last extract, and Figures 3 and 4, all show how the physical form of the guidebook plays a role in its use. Pages in guidebooks can be easily bookmarked by placing one's fingers into the pages at multiple points in the book, and opening the book on a particular page (Figure 3). While this might seem a trivial operation, it supports jumping between different pages quickly so as to compare and combine information, with the fingers acting as bookmarks. This is important, since much of the work of tourists is this very comparison and combination—as in combining information on maps with descriptions. Different publications can also be arranged so that they are in the visual field at the same time. Conversations over accommodation at the TIC would often take place with the guides laid across the serving desk, with staff helping visitors through the guides to show where different sorts of accommodation in the city were (Figure 4). In this way, the format of the paper guide allowed both staff and visitor to interact around the guide (see also (Sellen and Harper, 2001)).

Moving with maps

The second popular tourist publication that we saw widely used in our observations was the map. Maps have of course been a well–researched artefact in fields as widespread as cognitive psychology and cultural studies. The specific topic of way-finding has been explored in depth (MacEachren, 1995; Hunt and Waller, 1999). One finding from these studies is that map users are significantly better at tasks that involve configuration information (such as how far one landmark is from another) than those without maps, sometimes better even than local people with years of knowledge of a place (Lloyd, 1989).

However, perhaps surprisingly, there is little work that has examined the in–situ, non–experimental use of maps. As Cornell and Heth argue, there is a need for work which studies "humans navigating real world routes" (Cornell and Heth, 2000) since little work has looked at the 'naturalistic' use of maps: how they are used *in situ* without an experimental task[3].

Looking at our data on map use shows many different uses of maps, which differs from the notion of maps as a straightforward tool for planning a route between points A and B. We observed tourists using maps in situations where they did not know exactly where they are going, but only had an idea of a particular area that they were heading towards. This was usually because they believed that they would find something interesting in that area, although they had no specific attraction in mind. Alternatively, tourists used maps to go towards a specific type of attraction, such as a café, but with no *specific* café in mind—they would head towards a street where they thought there would be cafés.

Tourists also often only had a rough idea of where they were, and would use a map to locate or orient themselves so as to head in a 'roughly correct' direction, rather than along a specific route. So, in using a map, tourists might not know where they were, might have little idea about their orientation, might not know where they were going, and might even be unsure about what they were looking for. So, map use is often less about explicit route planning and more about wandering a city in a 'roughly correct' manner. The routes that tourists used were more directional than specific, with tourists frequently stopping en route, using the map to find the direction to walk in, and then setting off again.

A second feature of map use is their combination with guidebooks. A key aspect of this is how tourists combine characteristics and geography in an attempt to simultaneously solve the problems of where things are and what things there are. One way of doing this that we observed exploits the 'social zoning' of cities. As any frequent traveller will know, one of the most effective ways to find a restaurant in an unfamiliar city is to simply wander around a central area. Although by no means a perfect way of finding particular amenities, walking around exploits the tendency of certain facilities (such as bars and restaurants) to be clustered in particular area[4]. In this way, one can also judge establishments by their appearance and menu, as one walks past.

These 'clusters' are exploited in tourists' use of maps. When choosing where to go to, it is often safer to pick an *area* with more than one potential facility. We observed tourists heading towards a 'restaurant zone' of a city, often with one restaurant in mind, but with the flexibility to go elsewhere should that restaurant prove to be busy or unsuitable. By combining maps and guidebooks, tourists can look for 'clusters' of facilities in particular areas and go towards these particular areas rather than (or in addition to) heading towards a specific establishment.

This is not to say that maps are never used for working out how to get to specific places or attractions, but our observations showed some of the problems

---

[3] Alternatively, in CSCW, maps have also been discussed as resources for guiding activity (Schmidt, 1997).

[4] Although this is a tendency of smaller or denser cities: Manhattan rather than Los Angeles.

that tourists had in doing this. Following a route on a map involves considerable interpretation as one moves around a city (Smith, 1996). A tourist has to link between the map and what they see of streets and landmarks. Our observations showed many tourists pointing or turning their bodies towards different places to help them work out where to go (Figures 5 and 6).

Figure 5: tourists point at a place and   Figure 6: two tourists turn around to
a map to link them together   orientate themselves

Even though the places that these tourists were going to were not visible, they turned so as to see where they were going. This is our *embodied* sense of position and location (Jonsson, 2002), how we see and understand where things are in and beyond our visual field. Indeed, when staff in the tourist information centre gave directions, they combined two different methods. One set of directions was given by drawing a line on a map—a portable and abstract version that can be used by a tourist to find their destination. Staff combined this with 'showing' in physical space where the destination was and how to get there: saying "it's behind us on Argyle Street" while using an arm movement to point in a specific direction.

A last point about maps' use concerns how they are frequently read in advance of getting to the place the map describes. This was a common use of maps we observed. Indeed, this pointed us towards a much–neglected aspect of using maps: their educational function. A major aim of using a map is to learn about a place sufficiently that one can get around *without* using a map, *learning* about a place by looking at where the streets go, the names of the streets and potential landmarks. We observed one tourist who spent over twenty minutes at a Glasgow train station reading a map of a popular mountain walk. In looking at the map, this tourist was learning about his walk. While not explicitly finding his way, he was learning about things that would help him when on the walk, such as the distances between places and what landmarks and sights there are around the area. When we use maps *in situ* by the process of travelling around, we are also learning about sites and streets in such a way that if we return we will have more idea of our location and how to get around. If, technologically, we just support wayfinding then we will neglect this crucial function. Maps provide an overview and allow us to fit our observations and our travelling together.

Pre- and Post-visiting

The last solution we will discuss concerns how tourists use 'pre-visiting' and 'post-visiting' of places to manage their holiday. While our focus so far has been on the visit, considerable work is done by tourists before they travel, in gathering information and planning what to do. Tourists pre-visit a place by reading about it before they go there. Through arranging information and reading about a place before travelling, a tourist can do some of the organising activity for the holiday before the holiday. As with many of the other solutions outlined above, pre-visiting is not only practical; it is enjoyable. It extends the excitement of the holiday and builds anticipation as well as giving the visitor some sort of idea of what they are visiting before they get there.

Pre-visiting also happens while on the holiday itself, with tourists gathering information about places and planning what they are going to do. One important aspect of tourist planning is that it is 'satisficing' (Simon, 1955), in that plans are 'good enough' rather than detailed plans of activity. Indeed, tourists' plans are often *deliberately* ambiguous so that they can take into account future contingencies. As Suchman argues, plans often do not determine behaviour but rather are used flexibly in deciding what to do (Suchman, 1987). This acknowledges that decisions are often easier to make when one is actually in a particular place. For example, when planning a route, planning the complete route in advance using a map is often quite difficult. An alternative approach is to plan an *ambiguous* route in advance, and then picking specific roads by using road signs when one is driving.

In this way, tourist plans are often deliberately designed to be only as specific as necessary. A number of the tourists we interviewed talked about allocating days to particular places before they travelled. This sort of planning leaves a lot unspecified: when each day is, and what activities are done in each place, for example. Yet this sort of planning acknowledges that these sort of details are better kept flexible until closer to the time, as they will be dependent on local transport details, and can be adjusted in the face of other local contingencies, such as changing weather. Indeed, a stereotypical bad holiday is one that is excessively planned, in that changing circumstances are not be taken into account.

A second interesting aspect of tourist plans is how they follow or copy plans provided by others. A popular example of this is the package holiday, but even on package holidays not all of one's time is structured: many activities (such as choosing a restaurant) still involve some planning during the visit. For the tourists we followed, bus tours were frequently used to help structure the visit in this way. One group we followed took the tour bus on the first day they visited the city, so as to obtain an 'overview' of the city that they used on later days to organise the rest of their visit. While on the bus, one passenger drew a line on his map as the bus travelled around the city, letting him record where he had been for later recollection, and helping him to link the different sights together. In this way these bus tours had a role as an 'organising device' for a city visit, providing information about the key streets and attractions and allowing one to visit these again at leisure. The tours thus provided information and structure about the city, as much as being a strict plans or activity to follow in themselves.

If *pre*-visiting is about planning, then *post*-visiting is about reminiscing and sharing. Tourists often get together in groups to talk through their holidays, or to talk about their holidays to others who were not there (Frohlich et al., 2002). Photographs are very important for this activity in that they provide a framework around which stories can be told and experiences shared. Talking through the visit with photographs can take place both with those who were present on holiday and those who were not; in one form it is reminiscence, in another it allows the holiday to be shared. The combination of talk and interaction around pictures supports both these activities.

Post-visiting is thus a powerful way of extending the enjoyment of a tourist visit out beyond the visit itself. It also acts as a recommendation mechanism for different places – it allowing us to see 'what places are like' through our friends, and outside the commercially produced views of brochures and television (Crang, 1999). Indeed, some tourists who are on longer holidays go to the point of creating rich travelogues of their holiday, involving photographs, videos and text that are brought together to tell the story of their holiday. These travelogues usually exist in the form of photo albums, although a number of travelogues do exist on the Internet. However, there are considerable barriers to creating travelogues online — crafting web pages can take considerable time, and access to a PC and the Internet can be difficult while on holiday.

Leisure and pleasure

While we have described the experiences of tourists in terms of their 'problems' and 'solutions', we must not lose sight of the pleasurable nature of tourism, and how much of tourism involves activities that are not goal–oriented. That is to say, tourism is often nebulous with only tentative arrangements — we were struck by how the tourist experience was often not about finding the *best* restaurant, attraction or hotel, but in finding *suitable* attractions that allowed enjoyable experiences with travelling companions. These enjoyable experiences can range from the aesthetic (seeing a beautiful building), to the mundane (getting confused in a shop), to the social (spending time with a friend or family member whom one seldom sees). Tourism can thus be characterised as hedonic and emotional (Goosens, 2000), an experience typified by "wandering", where we attempt to enjoy the city environment and chance upon things of interest, rather than "optimising".

Learning how to design for these sorts of activities is one future challenge for CSCW, as interest extends from worksites to other environments. Interfaces may succeed as much for their playful nature as their usability. The popularity of games like 'geo-caching' even suggests opportunities for threading games into the tourist experience. CSCW may have much to learn from games, in particular online games (Dyck et al., 2003) and games that interact with travellers' changing environments (Runnberg and Juhlin, 2003).

Designing technologies for tourists

Although tourism presents a number of barriers to introducing new technology - in particular the need for devices to be sufficiently mobile - tourists have already adopted many new technologies, e.g. the web, mobile phones and digital cameras. This suggests that there are opportunities for new tourist systems that fit tourist practice. We now move on to discussing the implications from our study for designing better tourist technologies.

Sharing the visit

As emphasised above, an important part of tourism is sharing the visit with others. One problem that tourists face is co-ordinating their activities while they are separated—in particular getting groups back together again. One application that would assist this is a handheld or phone–based system that allowed tourists to communicate their locations to each other. So, if a group splits into two, they could choose to 'tie' their locations together so that each subgroup would be able to see where the other was. 'Tying' in this way could support synchronous awareness without running into difficult privacy problems. In addition, technology could support tourists showing the routes they took and things they did when they meet up again. This could allow them to make recommendations to their companions and also to other tourists whom they meet.

A second aspect of sharing visits is collaboration between tourists who do not know each other. One recommendation here is for technology to support sharing comments and reviews on different tourist attractions. However, it is important here to make this an interactive experience between tourists; as we discussed above, exchange of information is as much about meeting other tourists as it is exchanging information. This could be supported by using public machines or message walls where tourists can meet as they exchange information, or by enhancing existing sights where tourists meet, such as on city tours.

Electronic guides and maps

As discussed above, electronic guidebooks and maps have been a popular application area for mobile technology, with existing system generally following a similar format to paper guidebooks, augmented with GPS (for example TomTom CityMaps). Our fieldwork implies a number of limitations with this design. One innovation that electronic guidebooks could support is in making connections between *where* attractions are and *what* they are. Electronic guidebooks should explicitly support the comparison of information, allowing users to quickly move between related pieces of information. Partly due to the limited screen size, mobile systems seldom offer this feature. Pocket Internet Explorer, for example, only allows the user to load one web page at a time. One solution to this could be paper maps and electronic guidebooks that are designed to be used together. This would remove some of the disadvantages of the small screen by allowing users to juxtapose the PDA and the map in their visual field. More direct coupling is also feasible, e.g. through the PDA's sensing of printed glyphs and barcodes.

Mapping systems could also support more of the 'wandering' behaviour of tourists; for example, showing at a glance whether a tourist is going in the right direction rather than simply supporting a pre-determined route. Indicators could show nearby attractions, cafés, areas or main streets to support serendipitous discovery. This sort of representation moves beyond supporting wayfinding to supporting the broader range of tasks that tourists undertake when navigating. So, such a representation would support going between one shopping district and another, while looking for a café. In cases like this it is not the exact route that is important, although walking in the right direction is important, but a more general sense of learning about the city as one wanders around. Maps themselves could also show more of the 'social zoning' of different places, such as what areas are good for shopping, going out, or eating.

Supporting pre and post- visiting

Distinct from guidebooks, electronic *tour guide* systems attempt to offer information about a visitor's current location, and suggestions of where they might want to go next. These systems, such as the Lancaster GUIDE system, and more recently the EU funded "m-toGuide" system (http://www.mtoguide.org/), have generally been based around a 'walk-up pop-up' model where information (voice and text) is pushed at users based on their current location. Our observations suggest some limitations with this model. We observed that tourists frequently used maps and guides *before* visiting a place—an activity we call 'pre–visiting'. Presenting information to tourists while they are actually at an attraction may have limited utility, since at that point the environment is likely to contain richer sources of information than can be provided by a PDA. Our fieldwork also showed that tourists often do not follow tours in a straightforward way. Tours instead act as structures through which tourists can learn about the place being visited, and can use to build their own, more *ad hoc* plans. Systems should therefore present tours and attractions to tourists in such a way as to allow them to browse and learn from the tours rather than strictly following them, and to be aware of 'official' tourist attractions without being restricted to them. Viewing tours in advance would allow tourists to 'pre-visit' and judge different places and make their own plans about what to do rather than only following an official tour.

Lastly, our fieldwork emphasised the importance of post-visiting for tourists, allowing them to communicate and discuss their visit when they got home. We have been experimenting with support for this with the 'travelblog' system. This system allows tourists to build web–based travelogues describing their travels. These entries consist of pictures, videos and text captured on a Nokia 7650 camera-phone. These entries are then emailed from the phone to a server that automatically builds a web log combining the images and text. While some travelblogs are already on the Internet, created through increasingly popular web-logging software, our system also supports users replying to entries and having these messages forwarded via SMS to the tourist. Although this mechanism is very simple, it supports travellers updating their travelblog from anywhere in the world and extends the value of weblogs to the travelling tourist.

Conclusion: Building technologies for leisure

In this paper we have explored some important aspects of tourism, presenting an ethnographic study and design implications for tourist technologies. Using the metaphor of 'tourist problems' we explored the solutions that tourists use to arrange their visits. These solutions covered how tourists worked with other, used maps and guidebooks, and both pre- and post-visited places. We drew implications from this fieldwork for new technologies for tourists such as systems for remote co–visiting, and electronic guides and maps.

Designing technologies for tourists presents a number of specific challenges. Good tourist technologies are not only those that make tourists more efficient, but that also make tourism more enjoyable. As we discussed above, much of what is enjoyable about leisure is that it provides an opportunity to spend time with friends or family. In some senses, the leisure activity itself is less important than the fact that time is spent with significant others. Technologies that are woven into this sociality are likely to be used in preference to those that are not. Yet supporting sociality, sharing time and experiences together as part of friendships, may involve different technologies than those that support collaboration. One example of a system that does this is the *Sotto Voce* system, which allows visitors to an historic house to share a spoken commentary (Woodruff et al., 2001). The City project's system also addresses this, with support for co-visiting between groups of tourists and their friends at home.

In closing we would argue that support for leisure is both a new area of interest for CSCW and an area that is amenable to the methods and approaches developed in CSCW. As attention extends beyond the realm of work, and beyond technologies that support collaboration, it is the social aspect of leisure that may be the most important yet most challenging to support.

Acknowledgements

We would like to thank Areti Galani and Eric Laurier for conversations around the issues discussed here. Ian MacColl helped build the travelblog system, and Jon Hindmarsh and Carl Gutwin gave useful comments on earlier drafts. We would also like to thank the very patient tourists who suffered our investigations, and to acknowledge our funding by the UK Engineering and Physical Sciences Research Council.

References

Abowd, G. D., *et al.* (1997): 'Cyberguide: A mobile context-aware tour guide', *ACM Wireless Networks*, vol. 3, no. 3, pp. 421-433.

Apostolopoulos, Y., *et al.*, Eds. (1996): *The sociology of tourism: theoretical and empirical investigations*, Routledge.

Aramberri, J. (2001): 'The host should get lost: paradigms in tourism theory', *Annals of Tourism Research*, vol. 28, no. 3, pp. 738-761.

Bourdieu, P. (1990): *Photography: a middlebrow art*, Polity Press, London.

Brown, B., *et al.* (2001): 'Music sharing as a computer supported collaborative application', in W. Prinz (Ed.) *Proceedings of ECSCW 2001*. Bonn, Kluwer, pp. 179-198.

Brown, B., et al. (2003): 'Lessons from the Lighthouse: Collaboration in a shared mixed reality system', in *Proceedings of CHI 2003*. Fort Lauderdale, ACM Press, pp. 577–584.

Chalmers, M. (2003): 'Awareness, representation and interpretation', *J. CSCW*, vol. 11, no. 3–4, pp. 389–409.

Cheverst, K., *et al.* (2000): 'Developing a Context-aware Electronic Tourist Guide: Some Issues and Experiences', in *Proceedings of CHI 2000*. The Hague, ACM Press, pp. 17-24.

Cornell, E. H. and C. D. Heth (2000): 'Route learning and navigation', in R. Kitchin and S. Freundschuh (Eds.): *Cognitive mapping: past, present and future*. Routledge, pp. 66-83.

Crabtree, A. (1999): The tourist information centre study: eSCAPE Deliverable 4.2, The Tourist Physical Electronic Landscape Demonstrator: 3-12. http://www.mrl.nott.ac.uk/~axc/PDF/eSCAPE%20D4.2.pdf.

Crang, M. (1999): 'Knowing, tourism and the practices of vision', in D. Crouch (Ed.) *Leisure/tourism geographies: practices and geographical knowledge*. London, Routledge, pp. 238-256.

De Certeau, M. (1984): *The practice of everyday life*, University of California Press, Berkeley.

Dyck, J., *et al.* (2003): 'Learning from Games: HCI Design Innovations in Entertainment Software'. To appear in *Proceedings of Graphics Interface 2003*.

Fesenmaier, D., *et al.*, Eds. (2000): *Information and communication technologies in tourism*, Springer.

Fodness, D. and B. Murry (1997): 'Tourist information search', *Annals of Tourism Research*, vol. 24, no. 3, pp. 503-523.

Frohlich, D. M., *et al.* (2002): 'Requirements for photoware', in *Proceedings of CSCW '02*. New York, ACM Press.

Goosens, C. (2000): 'Tourist information and pleasure motivation', *Annals of Tourism Research*, vol. 27, no. 3, pp. 301-321.

Grinter, R. E. and M. Eldridge (2001): 'y do tngrs luv 2 txt msg?', *Proceedings of ECSCW 2001*. Bonn, Kluwer, pp. 219-238.

Hughes, J., *et al.* (2000): 'Patterns of Home Life: Informing Design For Domestic Environments', *Personal Technologies (Handheld and Ubiquitous Computing)*, vol. 4, no. 3, pp. 11-39.

Hunt, E. and D. Waller (1999): Orientation and wayfinding: A review, ONR technical report N00014-96-0380. Arlington, VA, Office of Naval Research.

Jonsson, E. (2002): *Inner Navigation*, Scribner.

Lee, J. R. E. and D. R. Watson (1993): Final Report to the Plan Urbain: Public Space as an Interactional Order. Manchester, Department of Sociology, University of Manchester.

Lloyd, R. (1989): 'Cognitive maps: encoding and decoding information', *Annals of the Association of American Geographers*, vol. 79, no. 3, pp. 101-124.

Loker-Murphy, L. and P. L. Pearce (1995): 'Young budget travellers: backpackers in Australia', *Annals of Tourism Research*, vol. 22, no. 3, pp. 819-843.

MacEachren, A. M. (1995): *How maps work*, Guilford Press, New York.

Moore, K., *et al.* (1995): 'Behavioural conceptualization of tourism and leisure', *Annals of Tourism Research*, vol. 22, no. 3, pp. 67-85.

Munro, A. (1998): Fringe benefits: an ethnographic study of social navigation at the Edinburgh Festival. Stockholm, Sweden, SICS, Persona deliverable 2.1.1.

Pearce, D. (1995): *Tourism today: a geographical analysis*, Longman Scientific & Technical, Harlow.

Riley, R. and L. Love (1999): 'The state of qualitative tourism research', *Annals of Tourism Research*, vol. 27, no. 3, pp. 164-187.

Runnberg, L. and O. Juhlin (2003): 'Movement and Spatiality in a Gaming Situation - Boosting Mobile Computer Games with the Highway Experience'. To appear in: *Proceedings of Interact 2003*.

Sacks, H. (1992): *Lectures on conversation*, Basil Blackwell, Oxford.

Schlegoff, E. (1972): 'Notes on a conversational practice: Formulating place', in D. Sudnow (Ed.) *Studies in Social Interaction*. New York, Free Press, pp. 75-119.

Schmidt, K. (1997): 'Of maps and scripts: The status of formal constructs in cooperative work', in *Proceedings of Group'97*. Phoenix, ACM Press, pp. 138–147.

Sellen, A. and R. Harper (2001): *The myth of the paperless office*, MIT Press.

Simon, H. A. (1955): 'A Behavioural Model of Rational Choice', *Quarterly Journal of Economics*, vol. 69, no. 3, pp. 99-118.

Smith, D. E. (1996): 'Telling the truth after postmodernism', *Symbolic Interaction*, vol. 19, no. 3, pp. 171-202.

Snepenger, D. J., *et al.* (1990): 'Information search strategies by destination-naive tourists', *Journal of Travel Research*, vol. 29, no. 3, pp. 13-16.

Star-UK (2000): United Kingdom Tourism Survey. London, UK, Star UK - statistics on tourism and research. http://www.staruk.org.uk//default.asp?ID=468&parentid=469.

Suchman, L. (1987): *Plans and situated actions: The problem of human-machine communication*, Cambridge University Press, Cambridge.

Tribe, J. (1999): *Economics of Leisure and Tourism*, Butterworth-Heinemann, London.

Urry, J. (1995): *Consuming Places*, Routledge, London.

USDTI (1999): Survey of international air travelers: Profile of Overseas Travellers to the U.S, US department for Tourism Industries. http://www.tinet.ita.doc.gov/view/f-1999-07-001/.

vom Lehn, D., *et al.* (2001): 'Exhibiting Interaction: Conduct and Collaboration in Museums and Galleries', *Symbolic Interaction*, vol. 24, no. 3, pp. 189-216.

Woodruff, A., *et al.* (2001): 'Electronic Guidebooks and Visitor Attention' in *Proc. 6th Int'l Cultural Heritage Informatics Meeting*. Archives and Museum Informatics, pp. 437-454.

K. Kuutti, E.H. Karsten, G. Fitzpatrick, P. Dourish and K. Schmidt (eds.), *ECSCW 2003: Proceedings of the Eighth European Conference on Computer Supported Cooperative Work, 14-18 September 2003, Helsinki, Finland,* pp. 355-374.

Moving to get aHead: Local Mobility and Collaborative Work

Jakob E. Bardram[1] and Claus Bossen[2]
1: Computer Science Department; 2: Information and Media Science
University of Aarhus, Denmark
{bardram,bossen}@daimi.au.dk

Abstract: Local mobility is a central aspect of collaborative work that is in need of close analysis. Between the face-to-face interaction of offices or control rooms and long-distance interaction facilitated through e.g. telephones, e-mail, the www or teleconferences lie a number of work-settings in which actors move about continuously in order to accomplish their work. They do so because they need to get access to knowledge, resources, persons and/or places. We analyze the integral nature of mobility to this kind of work practice from the ethnographic description of a hospital department, and the challenges that actors have to face to accomplish their work. Based on this ethnographic case, we propose a set of concepts for understanding local mobility as an intermediate field of distributed cooperation between centres of coordination and remote collaboration. Finally, we introduce the concept of 'mobility work' as complementary to the concept of 'articulation work'.

Introduction

In this paper, we look at *local mobility*. Local mobility as we understand it occupies the intermediate space between working together over distance on the one hand and working face-to-face in an office or a control room on the other. As such local mobility takes place in cooperative work settings where actors constantly are on the move to get ahead with their work: maybe because they need the knowledge inside a head of an expert, or because they need special equipment, a certain person or access to a particular room.

In recent years, there has been an emergent literature on local mobility, which has argued that despite the technological achievements of computers and their ability to communicate over distances, their effect has been to make work ever-more static since they all focus on the desktop computer and fix the actors to their desks (Bellotti and Bly 1996; Luff and Heath 1998). Recent developments in cell phones, tablet computers and wireless networks promise to bridge this ambiguous situation of being able to link across vast distances and yet still be fixed to the desktop. If however, these promises are to be realized, we think that a more thorough understanding of local mobility is needed. Local mobility needs special attention and its problems are not just solved by introducing technology that enables remote collaboration into a setting of local mobility.

We argue our case in the following way. In section one, we look at the existing literature, and go on, in section two, to present our case of local mobility: the description of mobility in a hospital department based on ethnographic fieldwork. In section three, we propose, in the spirit of 'grounded theory' (Glaser and Strauss 1967) to look at local mobility as a result of attempts by actors to achieve the right configuration of people, places, resources and knowledge and we discuss the challenges involved in such a pursuit. Finally, we look beyond the hospital department and discuss local mobility more broadly, and propose the concept of 'mobility work' as complementary to that of 'articulation work' (Strauss 1985).

Background – Local Mobility

The term 'local mobility' within the CSCW literature gained its present currency through Bellotti and Bly (1996) and Heath and Luff (1998). A critical review of these shows, however, that local mobility tends to get out their central focus.

Belotti and Bly argued that local mobility enhances local collaboration while at the same penalizing remote collaboration severely, since it takes actors away from their desks where their phones and emails are found (Bellotti and Bly 1996:p209). They found that previous research had focused on 'desktop collaboration' only and aimed to show that "…mobility may be critical to many work settings that have been traditionally considered non-mobile and that its existence and purpose must be accommodated by CSCW design" (Bellotti and Bly 1996:p209). In their case of a consulting firm of product designers with a remotely located sub-branch, local mobility arose as a result of a pursuit of resources and other people and supports local collaboration because it enabled the sharing of resources, face-to-face communication, and shared awareness between collaborators (Bellotti and Bly 1996:p210-1). At the same time, however, local mobility took people away from the desktops upon which the resources that enabled communication and collaboration over vast distances (e.g. phones or e-mail) were found. Their design efforts were accordingly directed towards a re-production of the advantages that local mobility provided for remote collaboration, and towards reducing the penalties for being away from the desktop – i.e. the penalties for remote collaboration. Thus, while they focus on getting away from the desktop, they direct their attention towards linking local and remote collaboration rather on local mobility and collaboration itself.

Luff and Heath (1998) similarly lament the fact that new technologies that promise to provide new spaces and environments for collaboration are only "…available on devices which are static and tied to the desk" (Luff and Heath 1998:p305). The static nature of then present technologies entailed the risk of "…undermining an important resource in collaboration, namely, and individual's ability to reconfigure him or herself with regard to ongoing demands of the activity in which he or she is engaged" (Luff and Heath 1998:p306). A point which is well illustrated by Kristoffersen and Rodden (1996) who argue that the introduction of a video consultation between bankers and customers tied the former to their desks and hence restricted their opportunities to consult with colleagues for advice and managers for decisions as well as looking into archives. Luff and Heath (1998) found a lack of studies devoted to mobility and provided three cases in which the importance of mobility was analyzed: a medical practice, construction sites, and stations in London Underground. The central problem in the two former instances however, is that of micro-mobility: the ability of paper to be "…handlable, manipulable, portable, dismantlable and can easily be reordered and reassembled…" (Luff and Heath 1998:307). Under the label 'micro-mobility', they describe the face-to-face interaction between physician and patient at a medical practice and focus on the 'ecological dexterity', i.e. the handability of paper. Likewise, in the case of a construction site under the label 'remote mobility' they argue that the provision of an electronic allocation sheet used for coordination and status making by the foreman, failed in part because the computer did not support the sharing between the foreman and the local workers like its paper-version did. Its micro-mobility was too limited (Luff and Heath 1998:p308).

Only in the London Underground case, labelled 'remote and local mobility', is local mobility a central concern in the analysis of movement around stations which often consist of a central operation room and several platforms, passageways, entrances etc. In the ensuing analysis of what we think is a good case of local mobility, Luff & Heath give good empirical examples of the challenges that technological support has to meet and argue for a "heterogeneous combination of technologies" (Luff and Heath 1998:p311. See also Nielsen and Søndergaard 2000). In the end however, micro-mobility - the "…local and detailed uses of objects-in-interaction…" (Luff and Heath 1998:313) - becomes the central concern rather than local mobility as such.

Another study of local mobility is provided by Bødker & Bertelsen (2001) who describe collaboration on a wastewater plant. The wastewater plant does not have a control room as such and instead the people working there gather information as they move around and inspect the various parts of the plant.

> "They retrieve information as they move about, and their information needs depend on where they are, who they are, as well as on what they are doing. They do not need access to the entire information space independent of location and purpose, on the contrary. This is what we have called zooming with the feet." (Bertelsen and Bødker 2001:p6)

The need to be mobile derives from the fact that the workers have to access things locally: the smell and colour of the water, reading meters, and judging the viscosity of polymer. Workers do cooperate and coordinate but mainly locally when they move about through ad hoc face-to-face meetings on the plant and during coffee-breaks. This dominance of decentralised, ad hoc coordination in daily routine is probably possible because of the slow processes at the plant where exact, prompt information is not needed with regards to the fermentation processes. The insights derived from this analysis of local mobility are directed towards the concept of common information spaces, and Bertelsen and Bødker label the wastewater plant a 'massively distributed information space'

There are other studies which have taken up the issue of mobility: Fagrell et al (1999) focus on knowledge management and give a case where a laptop is driven around while being connected to the internet and a GPS system, while Bergqvist et al (1999) focus on support for informal meetings.

We acknowledge these contributions, but want to pay closer attention to local mobility itself. However, we do not think that the challenge is to understand local mobility through its consequences for remote collaboration or through the importance of micro-mobility. Local mobility is not only about what happens when people leave their desktop computer, but also about understanding what goes on if collaborators do not have their own desktop at all, why people constantly move about and how they accomplish their work in such circumstances. We will attempt to achieve this through the case of a hospital department, which we think is a case of local mobility par excellence. From this case, a set of concepts emerge that we suggest as a starting point for developing an understanding of local mobility and which might lead to a comprehensive framework for the analysis of local mobility.

Mobility in Hospital Work

For many people working at hospitals, mobility is an ever-present aspect of their work. Not just page boys and hospital orderlies move around all the time, but so do nurses, physicians and patients. At a trivial level, this is necessary because bed rooms, conference rooms, meeting rooms, and offices are distributed in space, and hence force people at the hospital to cover a lot of physical space with their feet.

At another level, the need for moving around is caused by the ongoing process of specialization that has characterized the development of hospitals since the beginning of the last century and which seems to continue into the future (Vallgårda 1992). The expansion of knowledge about human body, deceases, medicine and care has entailed an accompanying contraction of the field in which individual clinicians can have expertise. Another kind of specialization has occurred through the development of technologies of introspection and intervention into the human body and for analyzing human tissue. These technologies are mostly concentrated in specific places. Either because of the room they require, the special kind of environment they need or because of the cost of construction, maintaining and using them. MR-scanners (magnetic resonance), CT-scanners (computer tomography) and PET-scanners (positron emission tomography) are all recent example of this process in which laboratories, operation room etc. are older ones. A consequence of this specialization of knowledge and technology is the continuous subdivision of hospitals into dedicated departments, which entails a need for moving about between people, things and places in order to get ahead with work. Strauss et al. (1985) point out, a special feature of medical specialization and technological innovation is that the two are simultaneously parallel and interactive, creating an impetus to further technological innovation and specialization.

Research Site and Methods

In the following, we describe collaborative work at haematology department (labelled department B) at a large Danish metropolitan hospital. The case is based on an ongoing research project which has lasted 2 years and includes 2 periods of ethnographic field work, each lasting 2 months, and including 12 open-ended interviews. Furthermore, 11 workshops have been conducted, which have focused on technological support for hospital work and in which nurses, physicians, an anthropologist and computer scientists participated. Finally, 10 hours of video-recording of specific episodes, like medical conferences, and the following personnel around a whole day have been made. Field notes were transcribed and videotapes logged.

Department B treats blood related diseases of which the most severe are various forms of cancer including leukaemia. The department presently consists of two bed wards, an outpatients' ward, an ambulatory, a laboratory, an admittance office with two adjacent consultancy rooms, and a section with rooms for the secretaries, physicians, teaching and meetings. The main part of the haematology department is situated in a three storey building: the floor level consists of the admittance office, conference rooms and auditoriums, and offices for physicians, while the two bed wards comprise the first and second levels. The two bed wards are identical in terms of staff and number of patients. The ambulatory and the outpatients' ward are located in another part of the hospital 5 minutes walk away. The department can have 46 hospitalized patients at a time and treats approxi-

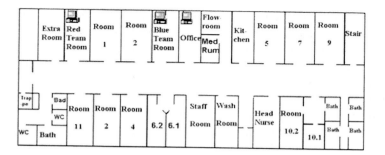

Figure 1: The physical layout of a ward at department B.

mately 11.000 patients a year in the outpatient clinic. The department employs about 167 physicians, nurses, clinical assistances, laboratory workers, etc. The ground plan for one of the bed wards is illustrated in figure 1 and figure 4 shows a picture from the ward.

A Physician's Typical Day at Department B

To illustrate the degree of mobility covered by clinicians, figure 2 shows the movements between 5 different places by one physician followed around at a typical day. The physicians meet at 8 am for the morning conference at the ground floor where they are briefed on the night's events by the physician who was on night shift. After the conference, they take the staircase to the bed ward where they meet with the nurses in the team room. Here, the nurses' team leader reports on the patients associated with the team, emphasising the last days' events and the nurses' assessment of the situation. Later, when the team conference is over, the physicians walk down to the radiology department located in the centre of the hospital, where they meet for the radiology conference. All physicians at department B (not just the ones working at the ward) meet at the radiology conference to hear the radiologist's assessment of the X-ray and CT images made the day before. Going back to the bed wards, four physicians commence making their ward rounds in collaboration with the team leader by moving from patient to patient in their bedrooms, bringing the often voluminous records along on a trolley (see figure 5). The cooperation between the physician and the nurse during the ward round pivots around the physician having the knowledge and authority to make diagnosis and prescribe treatment, whereas it is the team leading nurse who has an overview of the patients and updated knowledge upon their state. At noon, the physicians meet again in department B's conference room to discuss special patient cases upon which a physicians would like to consult the collective knowledge of his colleagues and the expertise of the leading physician. If the physician has finished the round which occasionally lasts until 2.30 pm, the afternoon is spent doing paperwork in his office or attending meetings.

Place	Time in min.																			Sum	%
Conference room, physicians	11																		24	35	13%
Team room		32		2							7			3						44	17%
Radiology conference room			15																	15	6%
At the trolley - the aisle					3	6	8	4	7	7	5	13	2	5	9					69	27%
At the patient						10	10	6	11	14		16	6		10	2				85	33%
Transportation		2	5	4													1			12	5%
																				260	100%

Figure 2: The location of a physician over the duration of a ward round. Transportation covers the physician walking between locations and he is in this period of time physically located in corridors, staircases, hallways, lifts, etc.

Local Mobility

In the following, we will frame our findings about mobility as an essential and integral aspect of cooperative work at hospitals in four categories (see figure 3): the need for mobility caused by the need for being at different *physical places*; the need for mobility to access *general (medical) knowledge*; the need for mobility to access or use different *shared resources*; and the need for mobility to get in contact with *specific persons*.

Places

Places are often specialized in the sense that they have a purpose or that certain types of activities can take place in there. For example, the radiology conference takes place in a conference room equipped with light displays that can hold the large amount of images to be analyzed. As a consequence the physicians have to move to the radiology conference room.

Looking closer at the spatial layout of a ward (figure 1), it is on the one hand obviously subdivided into a number of rooms for patients to ensure some degree of quietness and privacy for these. On the other hand, the staff has its own rooms for their work. Secretaries need a room to receive and guide relatives to admitted patients, and to receive and distribute incoming mail, phone calls and fax. They also take care of sending records around the department. Their place thus centralises communication and traffic in and out of the ward. Nurses and physicians each have their own rooms for coordinating work and for discussing treatment and care of patients. They need special places for the common reasons of having a place to meet and talk undisturbed, to ensure confidentiality of information upon patients and in order to enable clinicians to discuss patients freely: patients rarely want to listen to discussions about prospects for recovery, pro and cons about the suitability of particular chemotherapies, etc. There are, however, also places that are special because of their intrinsic qualities of which hygiene is one of the most perti-

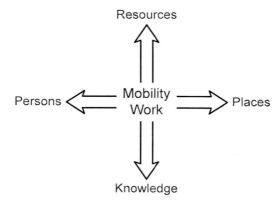

Figure 3: Four aspects of Mobility Work – Resources, Places, Knowledge, and Persons.

nent: a special room for cleaning patients' urine bottles, wash bowls etc; rooms for showering and special patient's rooms for those who have undergone a bone marrow transplant, or whose immune system has to recover after chemotherapy.

Mobility at the ward in the perspective of place arises from the need for quietness, privacy, different hygiene regimes and to ensure close cooperation between different groups.

Knowledge

Medical diagnosis and care is an intellectually complex task, which is a product of a complex social process involving individuals who vary in status and area of expertise (Cicourel 1990). The idea of socially distributed cognition (Hutchins 1995) refers to the observation that participants in collaborative working relationships are likely to vary in the expertise they posses and must therefore engage each other in dialogues that allow them to pool resources and negotiate their differences to accomplish their tasks. Because of the specialized nature of organizing work in modern hospitals, such cooperative solution of problems is made by a decentralized and loosely coupled collection of knowledge sources located in different medical specialities. Hence, 'problem solving' becomes distributed in terms of both knowledge (mentally in different 'heads') and space (physically in different 'locations'), which in many instances implies that there is a need to move to get together and engage in cooperative problems solving – the need for mobility to 'get a head'.

The pooling of knowledge and hands takes place routinely at Department B. The team conference, for example, is a central source of knowledge sharing and coordination of the treatment and care of the patient, because it is an event where physicians, nurses, SHAs, physiotherapists, and other experts involved in the care of patients meet. To assemble the collective knowledge of the department, all these experts move physically to combine the mentally distributed expertise. Similarly, the medical conference at noon is a central source of knowledge sharing and development. In these conference situations, clinicians do not move in order to access specific knowledge, but participate in these conferences in order to acquire and contribute to a more general knowledge sharing. Often in these conferences a question is raised by one physician and is discussed by several people at the conference, each contributing with central knowledge and information. This knowledge is not only medical knowledge, but also more mundane things like knowledge about the family background of the patient, his mental wellness, and whether he has been travelling. In addition to the routinely held conferences, there are a host of ad hoc pooling of knowledge, as, for example, when a physician requests another specialized doctor (e.g. a surgeon or a dentist) to have a look at a patient. Patients often have complicated sets of more or less inter-related deceases that need to be attended to by different experts. Hence, the mobility caused by the need for meeting expertise works both ways – moving to get to the expertise, and the expertise moving as such.

The perception of a patient's condition and state of treatment is thus contingent on several sources of distributed expertise which assembles to cooperatively produce an accumulative knowledge base. A fundamental premise for this accumulation to take place is the local mobility of the physicians, nurses and other professions at the hospital. While it is possible to enable such pooling by phone, e-mail or videoconferences, face-to-face meetings are yet still the most efficient means of achieving this.

Resources

Modern hospitals employ a wide range of different resources – especially medical equipment and machinery – which are essential to patient diagnosis, treatment, and care. At the very core of medical work is the need for moving the patient to a medical device. Central to the treatment of haematological patients is the monitoring of the degree of deterioration of the skeleton and they are therefore frequently taken to the radiology department where there is a subsequently need for moving patient in and out of the X-ray machine. Similarly, there is often a need for more advanced types of radiology images – e.g. MR, PET, and CT scanning - which are located in other hospitals in the city and hence require the patient to be transported by ambulance or car. On the other hand, there are several types of mobile equipment within a hospital that need to be moved (by someone) to the patient. For example, intravenous chemotherapeutical cures are often infused by pumps, which are taken to the patient's bedside..

In addition to these medium sized and large artefacts, there are a host of smaller artefacts which are constantly moved around such as equipment for measuring basic physiological data like weight, pulse, blood-pressure, and temperature. On the medical ward, the different records, medicine schemas and work schedules

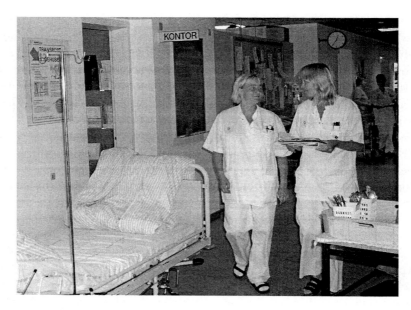

Figure 4: Two nurses in a conversation while moving around at the ward. Notice that they are carrying a lot of stuff, both in their hands and in their pockets. Furthermore, notice the 'mess' in the hallway – it illustrates how a lot of things constantly are moved around within a hospital, like beds, tables, food, medical records, etc.

are central for coordination and documentation of patient treatment and care, and physicians and nurses have difficulties (and legal problems) if they treat a patient without having the proper documentation. At present these records and plans are paper-based and the mere work of locating and getting hold of these documents is a source of much mobility at the ward. Nurses, for example, constantly walk between the trolley and the medicine room in order to locate and get their hands on the medicine schema, which at the same time is needed by the physician making the round and by the nurses for administrating medicine. Evaluation of treatment by the physician takes place either at the trolley in the hallway in front of the patient's room or at the patient's bedside, whereas the preparation of medicine takes place in the medicine room. Sometimes nurses take the medicine plan from the round trolley to the medicine cabinet and the round team then has to locate and get hold of it when attending that particular patient. The mobility of artefacts creates mobility of persons, and vice versa.

Persons

In the example above, the physicians attended the radiology conference to consult an expert on radiology – not to meet a specific radiologist. In contrast to this, another source of mobility arise due to the need to access persons as *specific individuals* and not as keepers of roles such as being the radiologist on duty.

The need for getting hold of a specific person arises when this person is the central source of information or authority. It is, for example, sometimes important to get in contact with the physicians who made an entry in the medical record, in order to get more details of the exact reasoning behind a decision. Similarly, there is a need for getting hold of the person(s) who have the latest information 'in their head' because it has not yet been documented and distributed, such as the images described at today's radiology conference. Finally, the need for a specific person may arise when the highest expertise and authority upon a question is personalised in one individual.

Another specific person of central importance is clearly the *patient*. Because of the individual nature of diagnosis, treatment and care, *the* patient is the central source of information. Patients are distributed to different departments within the hospital according to their main diagnosis and again within the haematology department according to a mix of criteria: according to hygiene regime; the attempt to ensure single-sex rooms; the attempt to ensure care by the same team of nurses and physicians to achieve continuity in their trajectory (Strauss, Fagerhaugh et al. 1985); the attempt to ensure that newly diagnosed patients are not put next to terminally ill patients with the same diagnosis, and with respect to the respective personality of the different patients. Since patients are continuously admitted and discharged, their distribution between the different rooms on the ward has to be reordered quite often. Patients are often mobilized locally at the ward for the exercise of it, and to go for examination or treatment at other wards. Critically ill patients are moved to the intensive care unit, which is situated in another building. For these reasons, patients are distributed and moved around, and locating them in order to make diagnoses, examinations, give treatment or provide care is not a trivial issue.

All in all, local mobility from the perspective of persons arises from the fact that patients, who are a central source of information and essential of subject of work, are distributed within the department and even, at times, within the hospital and move about; and when specific persons are carries of information that has not yet been distributed.

Mobility and its Challenges

Above, we have described how local mobility arises because clinicians' tasks are accomplished by the presence of a combination of people, places, resources and knowledge, whose configuration changes from task to task. Clinicians move from patient to patient, from place to place, from one piece of technology to another, and from one source of information to another to *make the right configuration of people, places, resources and knowledge emerge.*

Achieving this configuration entails then again several challenges as to move and locate any of the four "corners" in figure 3 – e.g., how to move and locate relevant knowledge. This is basically a coordination problem, but the mobility of persons and things within a hospital puts further stress on the challenge of coordinating the work done. As put by one of the physicians, when explaining what was going on after the morning conference: *"Now everybody [the physicians] is literary spread out all over the hospital. Most of us will not meet again before the conference at noon"*. He was referring to the fact that ad hoc coordination and social awareness of the work of other colleagues is very difficult because they are on the move constantly. Strategies for meeting this challenge of coordinating while moving is to meet on a regular basis for conferences, as shown in figure 2. These regular morning and noon conferences are very efficient means through which to coordinate, and the overhead of arranging them is minimal since they are done routinely.

Complementary to this kind of institutionalized coordination work, there is a need for constant informal coordination during a shift. In these cases, there is a substantial challenge in getting the work of mobile clinicians synchronized. Asynchronous communication can be done by writing post-its, email, sending a fax, or leaving a message with a secretary. But some issues need to be handled in dialogue – urgent matters and in situations, where authorization is required. This however creates a contradiction between the need for being contacted and being able to do one's job. Clinicians do not carry cell phones or pagers because they have a reasonable fear of being interrupted constantly if this was the case. Phones are only found in the secretaries and team rooms and hence people can be called to the phone, but also have the option of fitting the call into their own schedule and call back later. This might be a major obstacle to the one calling since she might not be able to go on with her job before having spoken with the other person. There is hence a constant negotiation of the balance between acknowledging the necessity of interrupting and ensuring a smooth flow of work, between being accessible and being able to plan one's work.

Let us consider how clinicians (and patients) at department B deal with the challenges associated with moving and locating places, people, resources, and knowledge.

Moving Resources, Persons, and Knowledge

As simple as it might sound, there are often challenges associated with the sheer movement of things and persons. As described above, somebody and something has to move and move on in hospital work. Physicians, nurses and other staff at the hospital move themselves around and while it may take some time to learn the geography of a hospital and people occasionally get lost, the movement itself poses no problems to these except of course for sore feet. If we look at patients and medical records the picture is different.

Figure 5: The trolley used to move records around during the ward round.

While some patients are capable of walking around internally at the ward or inside the hospital, quite a lot have to be moved around while they are in their beds or in a wheelchair. The transport itself is taken care of by the hospital orderly who have an impressive knowledge about 'getting around'. While banal, it is not always trivial to ensure that the right patient arrives at the right place at the right time, and it happens in some occasions that a patient waits in the corridor for hours at the wrong examination room.

Looking at moving artefacts, the paper-based medical record is a nice example. The medical record needs to be present when treating a patient. Hence, there is a need for physically moving the record around as the patient is transferred to and from other departments and hospitals, and in and out of the archive when the patient is discharged and admitted. A record cannot be copied, because the existence of several copies could create doubt as to which copy was updated most recently and whether it contained all information. The information in the record would not have the authoritative and authentic status that is needed for proper diagnosis, treatment and care. The secretaries organize the movement between the archive, the wards and the teams and try to keep updated files upon their present location. The actual movement of the record between departments and files is primarily accomplished by a page girl or an orderly. The movement around the ward during e.g. a wards round is done by having all the records on a mobile trolley, shown in figure 5. This trolley is use to move the often voluminous records around, because they are too bulky and heavy to carry.

However, knowledge cannot always be carried around as written documentation in medical records. First of all, it is impossible for clinicians to carry with them all the records and documents for the different patients they are treating. Second, due to the typical delay between oral and written information, most recent information is provided orally and stored mentally. X-ray physicians, for example, give their assessment of the images in the morning orally to the physicians, but it takes to the afternoon or even next morning before these are available in writing. Similarly, the decisions made by the physician making the round during the day may not be written before the next morning by the secretaries. Hence, we learned that clinicians seem to have a remarkably good memory. Due to the mobility of the work, much information simply needs to be in the head of the clinicians.

Locating Resources, Persons, and Knowledge

In a mobile environment where people and things move about locating these becomes a major challenge. Important artefacts for locating people are the whiteboards. They list, for example, to which patients a nurse is associated. Thus, it is reasonable to look for her in one of her patient's rooms. They furthermore list the order in which the round will take the patients and ideally the round would check off patients as the go along, in which case the round can be located by looking at the bed number of the next patient. Often, however, the list is not updated and since the round brings the trolley into the rooms finding it may be difficult. Therefore, the round has a written sign that is hung highly visible outside the room into which the round has gone. Also by the help of the whiteboard, nurses may locate patients since it lists their bed numbers and, in addition, the major examinations of a patient. Hence, nurses can see that a patient has gone for X-ray, MR or CT for example.

This, however, is only approximations of the whereabouts of people. Since clinicians, patients, records etc. are constantly on the move, the exact whereabouts of these have to be assessed by moving around and finding them. Hence, mobile persons create more mobility (Bellotti and Bly, 1996). But mobile artefacts as well create more mobility, as the following excerpt from our field notes shows.

> While following a nurse around on the ward, the team leader comes running around the corner. "Where is the medicine plan?" she exclaims. She is doing the morning round with the physician and they have come to a patient whose medicine plan is not with all the other plans which they have brought along on the trolley. She runs into the cabinet rooms where the medicine plan ought to be, then into the room for intravenous medicine and out again. It turns out that the medicine plan is with patient's associated nurse, who, however, has taken the medicine plan with her to another room where she was needed.

Turning to the location of knowledge, we have already seen how the medical record and the care record exist in one copy only. Taking their mobile nature into account, locating and getting access to them is a constant challenge. In some instances, however, information can be replicated and distributed. This applies for a patients name, bed and room number, primary diagnosis and associated nurse which are all listed on large whiteboards in the team rooms and in the secretaries rooms and updated during the day by nurses as patients are moved. In addition this information is also found on the nurses' work schedule which covers a day and also lists all major actions to be taken with regards to individual patients and the status of these tasks. Via these whiteboards and the work schedule information is distributed within the bed ward.

As we have argued above, information is mobile because the artefacts (documents) that contain information are often moved around. A common strategy at the ward for increasing the probability of locating and accessing information is to make social agreement about the 'right place' for things. For example, the medicine schema is usually found in the medicine room, and records on the trolley. When things are not at their 'right place' a second strategy can be applied, which is to decipher the temporal rhythms of the department and ward (Zerubavel 1979; Bossen 2002; Reddy and Dourish 2002). If you know when a physician makes his round, when blood-test results arrive, or when nurses pour medicine, then you know where and when to find records, examination results and medicine schemas. Yet another strategy is to use the division of work to find the most update information. For example, the nurse and physician has the most recent information about the treatment of a patient, the secretaries knows the latest about the transportation and whereabouts of patients, and a patient's primary nurse knows about the social background and family-relations of the patient. In these circumstances, clinicians need to seek out and locate persons that have the latest information 'in the head'.

Mobility Work

In this paper we have analyzed mobility work at a hospital, and we have analyzed how local mobility is caused by the need for bringing together people, places, resources, and/or knowledge – as illustrated in figure 3. Mobility work is the work that needs to be done in order to make *the right configuration* of people, places, resources and knowledge emerge. We also analyzed the number of challenges that mobility work implies with regards to moving and locating people, places, resources and knowledge.

Based on our analysis we argue that each of the four aspects of mobility work shown in figure 3 can be further subdivided into two aspects, as illustrated in figure 6. People are different to the degree in which they are needed because of the role they have (e.g. physician on round; team leading nurse) or because of their specificity (patients, carriers of non-distributable information). Places are different as to whether they have inherent qualities (sterile environment) or ordinary character (meeting room), while resources differ as to whether they are mobile or stationary. And knowledge differs as to whether is can be distributed (patients' bed number) or has to be authentic (singular records, expert judgement).

The specific configuration of the 'corners' in figure 6 emerge as a response to carrying out a specific work task. But the configuration is also premised by the given order of things and people – an order, which is the result of a social, political and cultural process (Tellioglu and Wagner 2001; Prior 1988). Looking at de-

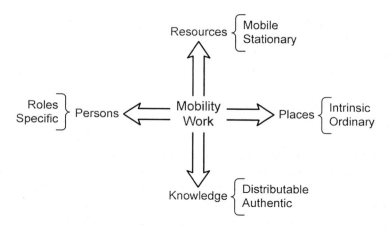

Figure 6: Aspects of Mobility Work.

partment B, changes in e.g. the division of work, available technology, established routines, cultural norms or specific requirements have changed the specific pattern of local mobility. With respect to the division of work, for example, nurses were previously not allowed to give chemotherapy, which instead was done by physicians which imposed a lot of mobility on these because they normally are further away from the patients. Giving chemotherapy was then handed over to nurses on the provision that they had passed a special course, alleviating physicians to move to the ward for setting up chemotherapy. As for technology, the introduction of an electronic patient record (EPR) in some Danish hospitals has made the record more stationary, because the EPR is only accessible through desktop PCs. While the EPR has enabled updated information to be available at multiple places at the same time and thus has distributed the records, it has simultaneously meant that these records are more fixed to desktops. The clinicians can no longer bring the records to the patients, and they either have to read the records in an office before seeing the patient and subsequently oscillate between that office and the patient's bed if questions arise, or give up making a round and instead bring the patients to a consultancy room. With respect to cultural norms, confidentiality of personal information requires nurses and doctors not to discuss a patient in the presence of other patients, just as considerations to the individual patient requires that the internal discussions between clinicians of a patient's case is not done in the presence of that particular patient.

Looking into the future, one can envision technology that would change the need for mobility: video-conferences could replace face-to-face discussions with experts; smaller, mobile CT- and MR-scanners could bring the examination equipment to the patient instead of vice versa; efficient bacteria- and virus annihilators in the whole department could do away with places for special hygiene requirement, etc. However, even if the attempts to achieve a certain configuration of persons, places, resources and knowledge are configured by a historical process, it is exceedingly difficult to envision a state in which local mobility would disappear: experts often have to look at the patients themselves; EPRs tie the records to desktops and to particular rooms, mobile CT-scanners still require the interpretation of data by collaborating staff; etc. Whatever new organisation of work comes up or whatever new technology is introduced, some kind of local mobility will prevail.

The contingent character of local mobility becomes even more evident when it is realised that its specific pattern is also premised on the balancing of sets of *contradictory* concerns which may be changed by reorganisation of the work and/or through the introduction of new technology. As described, there is balance to be kept between *availability and seclusion* for clinicians. For example, a technological solution that tries to reduce the penalties for remote collaborators, who try to communicate by suggesting portable computers or video-based awareness systems (Bellotti and Bly 1996) would imply severe penalties for the work of clinicians. If they became constantly available to other, they would be interrupted constantly. On the other hand, total seclusion is not an option either since they very often carry authentic information in the sense that they have expertise upon a certain disease, carry oral information not yet distributed, or posses the latest information about a certain issue. Another balance to be considered exists between *mobility and localisation*: the more mobile people and things are the more difficult they are to locate. Hospital work inherently necessitates mobility and in order to accomplish their work, clinicians rely on the mobility of e.g. the records and patients, but which at the same time demands orderly registration of their movement in order to be able to locate them. Finally, a balance has to be achieved between *orderliness and flexibility* of work processes: ordering is highly efficient for coordination in a mobile work setting, but the cost of a rigid order is a system that cannot absorb unforeseen events and the cost of ordering into too much detail is a great overhead on articulation work. As described, order in the form of procedures, routines, coordination mechanisms is central to hospital work right down to detailed documentation of the status of giving of e.g. blood. At the same time, however, there is no formal planning of when two nurses have to assemble to give blood since such scheduling would lock their multi-tasking and constant re-planning because of unforeseen events into a rigid scheme (See e.g. Bowers, Button et al. 1995).

Discussion and Outlook

Even though we suggest the above set of concept in the spirit of 'grounded theory' and have pointed to the contingent nature of the specific pattern of local mobility at the haematology department, we believe that our analysis reaches beyond the specific case. The application of the concepts on the cases of local mobility described initially is rather straightforward. In the case of the wastewater plant (Bertelsen and Bødker 2001), workers were 'zooming with their feet' because they had to look at intrinsic qualities found only at specific places (e.g. the smell and colour of water), to exchange knowledge and coordinate with other workers (ad hoc meetings around the plant), pool knowledge (the coffee break) or access resources (polymer, machinery). Similarly, in the case of the construction site (Luff and Heath 1998) a major concern of the foreman was to roam around to monitor problems as they occurred, check on the status of tasks and get information from gangers and colleagues, which in turn relied in their work on him to passed by frequently. Here people, places and knowledge figures centrally, while the main resource was an allocation sheet that was brought along. In contrast, resources posed a central problem in the case of London Underground, since the necessity to become mobile took personnel away from the control room where most means of communication and surveillance was found. Thus, whenever employees had to move to specific places, e.g. in order to monitor platforms in times of congestion or cases of 'suspect packages', they lost access to central resources.

The concepts we have introduced might even be used to look at mobility in general, which raises the question to which extent they apply specifically to *local* mobility. There are two ways of addressing this question. One is to look more closely into the defining characteristics of local mobility and the developed set of concepts presented above. Another, possibly complementary option would be to first look more generally at mobility and then return to more specific instances. Here we think that it might be fruitful to introduce the concept of '*mobility work*' in parallel to the concept of 'articulation work' (Strauss 1985). 'Articulation work' refers to the fact that collaborative action requires a lot of working-out in terms of coordination and reaching common understanding, and can only at a superficial level be understood through a rational means-end scheme (Strauss 1993:p20). In CSCW this has lead to a focus on coordination (Bardram 2000, Schmidt & Simone 1996), which has a temporal as well as a spatial dimension – the latter of which is often overlooked. As Strauss (1993), amongst many other authors, points out, actors not only have minds but also bodies and feet and have to move around in space in order to act and interact. This entails gaining the right view, placing oneself in the right position with regards to place, things and other actors – in short *mobility work*. Action is intrinsically not only temporal but also spatial.

To sum up, we have looked at local mobility, which occupies the intermediate space between centres of coordination (e.g. control rooms) and remote collaboration and communication (using e.g. mobile phones or video conferencing). We have analysed local mobility at a hospital ward, proposed that local mobility can be understood as an attempt to make the right configuration of person, places, knowledge, and resources emerge, and pointed to the challenges that such attempts face. Finally, we have introduced the concept of 'mobility work' as worthy of further investigation.

Acknowledgments

Our warmest thanks the physicians and nurses at Department B. This research was funded by the Danish National Centre for IT-Research (CIT), grant #211.

References

Bardram, J. (2000): 'Temporal Coordination. On Time and Coordination of Collaborative Activities at a Surgical Department.', *Computer Supported Cooperative Work*, vol. 9, pp157-87.

Bellotti, V. and S. Bly (1996): 'Walking away from the Desktop Computer: Distributed Collaboration and Mobility in a Product Design Team.', in M. S. Ackerman (ed.): *Proceeding of the Conference on Computer Supported Cooperative Work 1996*, pp209-18.

Bergqvist, J., P. Dahlberg, F. Ljungberg, and S. Kristoffersen (1999): 'Moving out of the Meeting Room', in S. Bødker, M. Kyng and K. Schmidt (eds.): *Proceedings of the Sixth European Conference on Computer-Supported Cooperative Work*, Netherlands, Kluwer Academic Publishers, pp81-98.

Bertelsen, O. W. and S. Bødker (2001): 'Cooperation in massively distributed Information Spaces', in W. Prinz, M. Jarke, Y. Rogers, K. Schmidt and V. Wulf (eds.): *Proceedings of the Seventh European Conference on Computer-Supported Cooperative Work*, Netherlands, Klüver Academic Publishers, pp1-17.

Bossen, C. (2002): 'The Parameters of Common Information Spaces: the Heterogeneity of Cooperative Work at a Hospital Ward', in *Proceedings of the Conference on Computer-Supported Cooperative Work 2002*, New Orleans, ACM, pp176-86.

Bowers, J., G. Button, and W. Sharrock (1995): 'Workflow from Within and Without: Technology and Cooperative Work on the Print Industry Shopfloor', in H. Marmolin, Y. Sundblad and K. Schmidt (eds.): *Proceedings of the Fourth European Conference on Computer-Supported Cooperative Work*, Dordrecht, Kluwer Academic Publishers, pp51-66.

Cicourel, A. V. (1990): 'The Integration of Distributed Knowledge in Collaborative Medical Diagnosis', in J. Galegher, E. Kraut and C. Egido (eds.): *Intellectual Teamwork,* Hillsdale, NJ, Lawrence Earlbaum, pp221-42.

Fagrell, H., F. Ljungberg, and S. Kristoffersen (1999): 'Exploring Support for Knowledge Management in Mobile Work', in S. Bødker, M. Kyng and K. Schmidt (eds.): *Proceedings of the Sixth European Conference on Computer-Supported Cooperative Work*, Netherlands, Kluwer Academic Publishers, pp259-75.

Glaser, B. G. and A. Strauss (1967): *The Discovery of Grounded Theory: Strategies for Qualitative Research*, Chicago, Aldine.

Hutchins, E. (1995): *Cognition in the Wild*, Cambridge Mass. & London, MIT Press.

Kristofferson, S. and T. Rodden (1996): 'Working by Walking Around. Requirements of flexible Interaction Management in Video-supported Collaborative Work' in B. Spence and R. Winder (eds.): *Proceedings of Human Computer Interaction*, Springer Verlag, pp315-29.

Luff, P. and C. Heath (1998): 'Mobility in Collaboration', in *Proceeding of the ACM 1998 Conference on Computer Supported Cooperative Work*, pp305-14.

374

Nielsen, C. and A. Søndergaard (2000): 'Designing for Mobility - an integration approach supporting multiple technologies', in *Proceedings of the 1ˢᵗ Nordic Conference on Human-Computer
Interaction* (CD-rom). Available at http://www.daimi.au.dk/~sorsha

Prior, L. (1988): 'The Architecture of the Hospital: a Study of Spatial Organization and Medical
Knowledge', *British Journal of Sociology*, vol. 39, issue 1, pp 85-113.

Reddy, M. and P. Dourish (2002): 'A Finger on the Pulse: Temporal Rhythms and Information
Seeking in Medical Work', in *Proceedings of the Conference on Computer-Supported Cooperative Work 2002*, New Orleans, ACM Press, pp344-53.

Schmidt, K. and L. Bannon (1992): 'Taking CSCW seriously: supporting Articulation Work', *Computer Supported Cooperative Work*, vol. 1, issue 1, pp7-40.

Schmidt, K. and C. Simone (1996): 'Coordination Mechanisms: towards a Conceptual Foundation
of CSCW Systems Design', *Computer Supported Cooperative Work*, vol. 5, pp155-200.

Strauss, A., S. Fagerhaugh, B. Suszek, and C. Weiner (1985): *Social Organization of Medical
Work*, Chicago & London, University of Chicago Press.

Tellioglu, H. and I. Wagner (2001): 'Work Practices Surrounding PACS: the Politics of Space in
Hospitals', *Computer Supported Cooperative Work*, vol. 10, issue 2, pp163-88.

Vallgårda, S. (1992): *Sygehuse og sygehuspolitik i Danmark. Et bidrag til det specialiserede sy-
gehusvæsens historie 1930-1987*, København, Jurist- og Økonomforbundets Forlag.

Zerubavel, E. (1979): *Patterns of Time in Hospital Life: a Sociological Perspective*, Chicago, University of Chicago Press.

K. Kuutti, E.H. Karsten, G. Fitzpatrick, P. Dourish and K. Schmidt (eds.), *ECSCW 2003: Proceedings of the Eighth European Conference on Computer Supported Cooperative Work, 14-18 September 2003, Helsinki, Finland*, pp. 375-394.

'Repairing' the Machine: A Case Study of the Evaluation of Computer-Aided Detection Tools in Breast Screening

Mark Hartswood[1], Rob Procter[1], Mark Rouncefield[2], Roger Slack[1], James Soutter[1] and Alex Voss[1]

[1]Social Informatics Cluster, School of Informatics, University of Edinburgh
[2]Department of Computing, Lancaster University
sic@inf.ed.ac.uk

Abstract. In this paper, we consider the problems of introducing computer-based tools into collaborative processes, arguing that such an introduction must attend to the sociality of work if it is not to impact negatively upon the work that they are intended to support. To ground our arguments, we present findings from an ethnomethologically-informed ethnographic study carried out in the context of the clinical trial of a computer-based aid in medical work. Our findings highlight the problematic nature of traditional clinical trials for evaluating healthcare technologies, precisely because such trials fail to grasp the situated, social and collaborative dimensions of medical work.

Introduction

Our research is focused on investigating and understanding the relationships between work practices and technologies. One of the work settings in which we have a longstanding interest is healthcare. In this paper we present some findings from an ethnographic study carried out in the context of clinical trial of a computer-aided detection (CADe) tool that is intended to support the work of radiologists working in breast screening.

The aims of this study are twofold. First, we are interested in understanding the impact of CADe tools on the situated, collaborative practical actions of reading mammograms – actions that we argue constitute radiologists' *professional vision*, i.e., "socially organized ways of seeing and understanding events that are answerable to the distinctive interests of a particular social group" (Goodwin, 1994:606). Elsewhere, we have argued for the importance of professional vision for the maintenance of radiologists' decision-making performance, and documented the various ways in which they act to sustain professional vision through the organisation of reading and the artefacts used for reporting this work (Hartswood, Procter, Rouncefield and Slack, 2002). One of the issues that we wish to examine in this paper is how the adoption of CADe tools might – or might not – mesh with these practices.

Second, by bringing the situated and practical actions of reading work to the fore, we aim to question the value of the 'gold standard' for medical technology evaluations: the quantitative, randomised, control clinical trial. In particular, we would stress the importance of complementing the clinical trial's quantitative emphasis with qualitative investigations of the impact of technological interventions on the everyday working and mundane interactional practices of medical workers.

Breast screening in the UK

Breast cancer is the most common non-skin related malignancy and accounts for one-fifth of deaths among women from all forms of cancer in the UK, and is the second leading cause of cancer death among women in the US and Europe. A screening programme, based upon mammography, has been in operation in the UK for more than 10 years. The initial screening test is by mammography, where one or more X-ray films (mammograms) are taken of each breast by a radiographer. The usual types of mammogram taken are mediolateral oblique (Oblique) and craniocaudal (CC). Each mammogram is examined for evidence of abnormality by at least one trained reader[1]. Types of feature that are indicators of malignancy include: micro-calcification clusters are small deposits of calcium visible as tiny bright specks; ill-defined lesions are areas of radiographically-dense tissue appearing as a bright patch that might indicate a developing tumour; stellate lesions are visible as a radiating structure with ill-defined borders. Architectural distortion may be visible when tissue around the site of a developing tumour contracts; asymmetry between left and right mammograms may be the only visible sign of some features.

---

[1] Most, but not all, readers are qualified radiologists. For the sake of simplicity, we will use the more general term of reader.

The practice of breast screening calls for readers to exercise a combination of perceptual skills to find what may be faint and small features in a complex visual environment, and interpretative skills to classify them appropriately – i.e., as benign or suspicious. Two reader performance parameters are particularly important: specificity and sensitivity. A high specificity (high true positive rate) means that few women will be recalled for further tests unnecessarily; a high sensitivity (low false negative rate) means that few cancers will be missed. Achieving high specificity *and* high sensitivity is difficult.

The goal of screening is to achieve a high, reliable and controlled cancer detection rate. Current UK breast screening practice is that each mammogram should be 'double read', i.e., assessed independently by two readers (Blanks, Wallis and Moss, 1998). Superficially, this suggests that each reading of a mammogram is the work of the individual reader. Our earlier studies reveal, however, that reading mammograms is a thoroughgoingly social enterprise that is achieved in, and through, the making available of features that are relevant to the community of readers (Hartswood, Procter, Rouncefield and Slack, 2002). This involves a number of formal and informal collaborative practices. As an example of the latter, through the use of annotations on the screening reporting form, readers contrive to use double reading in order to make their work observable-reportable as they read, thereby enabling them to intersubjectively calibrate their performance without sacrificing their independence as decision-makers.

Because of the growing shortage of trained readers, there is interest in the UK breast screening programme in using CADe tools to replace double reading with a single reader using a CADe tool. The principle of CADe is to apply image analysis algorithms to identify target features in each mammogram and draw these to the reader's attention through the use of prompts. The prompts act as an attention cue, and so counteract the effects of variability in concentration and, more generally, make the visual search pattern more systematic and complete. A number of CADe tools have now been developed, but the practical realisation of their potential benefits is not easy (Hartswood, Procter and Williams, 1998). As Warren-Burhenne et al. (2000) comment, while CADe tools appear useful "we must also realize the possible drawbacks and fully understand the proper use of such a device".

The implications of CADe for readers' work practices is one of the issues that we focus on in this paper. In particular, as we will show, the proposed reconfiguration of readers' work is problematic by virtue of the very manner in which the CADe tool under trial works.

Ethnomethodologically-informed ethnography and the evaluation of healthcare technologies

While this paper is primarily concerned with presenting an empirical study of a technology in use, it also necessarily problematises some of the issues involved in the evaluation of healthcare technologies in general. It thereby documents some of the real difficulties of any evaluative exercise, addressing the concern raised by Bannon (1996) that "evaluations are important yes, but it is also important to be aware of the quality of the evaluation, and of what can legitimately be learned from any particular study". Bannon (1996) goes on to suggest:

> "a careful systematic account of what happens in particular settings when a prototype or system is installed, and how the system is viewed by the people on the ground, can provide useful information for 'evaluating' the system and the fitness for the purpose for which it was designed." (Bannon, 1996:427)

The gold standard for evaluation of healthcare technologies is the randomised control clinical trial. The method is increasingly seen as problematic for evaluating computer-based systems, however, since while these may perform well under trial conditions, they are nevertheless often are found wanting in use (e.g., Hartland, 1993).

> "By insisting on evidence from randomised control trials we waste precious resources on evaluation work that is methodologically flawed and impractical and at best provides results that are difficult or impossible to generalise." (Heathfield and Buchan, 1996:1008)

Following Heathfield and Wyatt (1993) and Heathfield and Buchan (1996), we argue that while the traditional clinical trial methodology may provide useful measures of *efficacy*, as measure of *effectiveness* it is entirely inappropriate. The problem is that, for the sake of statistical repeatability, the randomised, control trial glosses the way in which the work that the technology is intended to support is actually done and so fails to get to grips with understanding (and evaluating) technologies in their social and organisational circumstance of use.

As an attempt to address this problem, we have sought to complement the clinical trial methodology with ethnomethodologically-informed ethnographic investigative and evaluative techniques (Hughes et al., 1994). The main virtue of ethnography lies in its ability to make visible the real-world sociality of a setting and efforts to incorporate ethnography into IT systems development processes stem from the realisation that the success of design has much to do with the social context into which systems are placed. Ethnography argues for understanding the situatedness of individual activities and of the wider work setting, highlighting the interdependencies between activities, and stressing the 'practical participation' of individuals in the collaborative achievement of work. As Suchman argues:

> "… ethnographies provide both general frameworks and specific analyses of relations among work, technology and organization. Workplace ethnographies have identified new orientations

for design: for example, the creation and use of shared artifacts and the structuring of communicative practices." (Suchman, 1995: 61)

The advantage of applying ethnographic methods lies in the 'sensitising' they promote to the real-world character of activities in context and, consequently, in the opportunity to help ensure that the design of technologies resonates with the circumstances of use. As a method of evaluation, ethnography attends to the haecceities[2] of the setting, showing in this study, for example, how practical actions such as mammogram arrangement, gesturing and pointing to features on mammograms, manipulating mammograms, and annotations are all components of the lived work of doing reading.

The CADe machine was evaluated using the conventional clinical trial methodology in order to quantify its differential impact on reader performance, i.e., on their sensitivity and specificity. This quantitative evaluation was complemented by ethnographic studies of its use under trial conditions with the aim of contextualising and explaining the performance data.

Evaluating the machine

The CADe machine consists of two components, a digitising and image analysis unit and an optical mammogram viewer with two built in computer screens to display any prompts generated by the analysis (see Figure 1). Up to twenty cases (sets of mammograms for an individual woman; typically four mammograms per case, i.e., Oblique and CC views of each breast) can be digitised in a single 'session', although the machine can store up to 1000 cases. When the mammograms have been digitised, analysed and loaded onto the viewer, moving on to the next set of mammograms automatically triggers the display of the appropriate prompts.

Once digitised, analysed and loaded, the mammograms are arranged in the following order: Right-Oblique Left-Oblique; Right-CC Left-CC – mirroring the way the prompts appear on the computer displays. Mammograms on the viewer are scrolled up and down. When the button used to scroll the next set of mammograms into view is pressed then the prompts screens are 'switched off' and a further button needs to be pressed to see the prompts. In this way readers are encouraged to examine the mammograms prior to looking at the prompts.

---

[2] By this we mean that it is important to attend to the 'just this-ness' of the setting, just what it is, here and now with these members and this assemblage of technologies and so forth. See Garfinkel and Wieder (1992) for more on this topic.

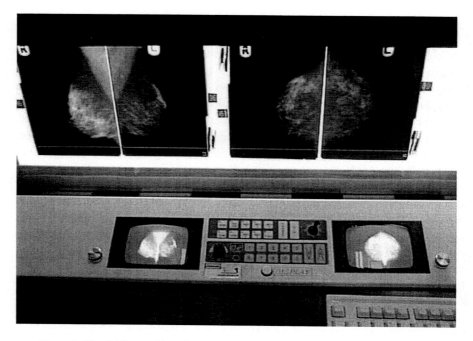

Figure 1: The CADe machine showing the mammogram viewer and prompt displays.

The CADe machine targets ill-defined and speculated lesions and micro-calcifications. Calcification clusters are marked by a shaded triangle. Ill-defined lesions are marked with an asterix and a circle is drawn around either prompt type if the machine's confidence is high. The machine does not perform a comparison between left and right views (i.e., for asymmetry). The machine's image analysis algorithms cause it both to prompt features that are not cancer as well miss some obvious cancers. As an example of the former, normal features in the breast such as calcified arteries or crossing linear tissues can be prompted as micro-calcifications, while other normal features such as ducts and tissue radiating from the nipple or inadvertent crossing of parenchymal tissue can produce a prompt for a cancerous mass. As an example of the latter, the machine will miss masses that may be obviously cancers because they are either under 10mm or over 20mm in size, the machine's preset range for mass detection.

Following conventional clinical trial design, three sets of 60 prompted and unprompted (control) cases were prepared using historical mammograms. During the trial, readers were shown the appropriate mammogram – CCs and Obliques, but not previous mammograms (or any notes) – and asked to indicate areas of concern and to make a decision as to whether the case should be recalled for further investigation using a four point decision scale: 1. Recall; 2. Discuss but probably recall; 3. Discuss but probably no recall; 4. No Recall – with decisions 1 and 2 treated as recall decisions for the purpose of analysis. Before the trial was run, each reader was given a brief explanation of how the machine worked, emphasising that the machine was merely for detection, not diagnosis. Readers were told that the machine 'spotted' masses and calcifications and about the appropriate prompts. They were also advised that the threshold of sensitivity of the machine had been set such that there would inevitably be many false prompts; and warned that since this was a trial set there would be more cancers than in a 'normal' reading session.

Trial observations

As part of the ethnographic evaluation, readers were observed doing the various test sets and then asked about their experiences of using the CADe machine. The readers were also taken back to cases identified in the test sets where they had appeared to have had difficulty or spent a long time making their decision, and asked to talk through any problems or issues to do with the prompts and their decisions. Although there were variations in how readers approached a reading and the test, the fieldwork extract below gives some idea of the process observed:

Simplified fieldwork extract 1:

Case 1: Gets blank film to mask area of the film ("so I can concentrate on it" ... these are set up differently from the way I usually look at them ... so I have to train my eye each time."). Using magnifying glass. Marking on booklet. Looking from booklet to scan. Homing in on an area – "I'd say it's benign"

Case 2: Using blank film. Takes film off roller and realigns. Magnifying glass. Looking from booklet to film. "I'd not recall ... what the computer has picked up is benign ... it may even be talcum powder."

Case 10: Looking at film – using blank film to mask area. Magnifying glass. Looking at booklet prompts – looking back at film. "This is a case where without the prompt I'd probably let it go ... but seeing the prompt I'll probably recall ... it doesn't look like a mass but she's got quite difficult dense breasts ... I'd probably recall." Marks decision.

Case 15: Looking at film – aligns on roller – gets blank film to mask – gets magnifying glass. Looking at booklet prompts - looking at film – back to booklet - looking at film. "There's quite a suspicious mass on the CC – I'm surprised it didn't pick it up on the oblique." Marking booklet – makes decision.

It was observed that, as with 'everyday' reading, readers used a repertoire of manipulations to make certain features 'more visible'. A magnifying glass may be used to assess the shape, texture and arrangement of calcifications or, where the breast is dense, the mammogram may be removed and taken to a separate light box. Where a reader wished to attend to a particular segment of the mammogram, a blank film was used to blank off a part of the mammogram (see Figure 2).

In cases where a suspicious feature was seen on one view, readers used their fingers or an object such as a pen for measurement and calculation so as to check for the feature's appearance in the other view. As we discuss later, these repertoires of manipulations are an integral part of the embodied practice of reading mammograms (see Figures 3 and 4).

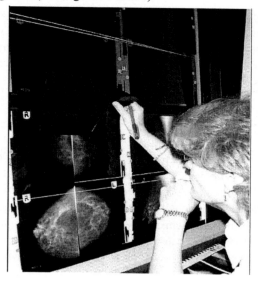

Figure 2: Using an opaque film to block off areas of a mammogram.

Figure 4: Using fingers for measuring and comparing.

Figure 3: Using a magnifying glass.

The main strengths of the CADe machine in supporting this kind of work seemed to lay in picking up subtle signs – signs that some readers felt they might have missed – and stimulating interaction between reader and the available technology by prompting them to re-examine the mammogram. As one reader said:

> "Those micros that the computer picked up … I might have missed it if I was reading in a hurry … I'd certainly missed them on the oblique … This one here the computer certainly made me look again at the area. I thought they were very useful, they make me look more closely at the films … I make my own judgment … but if the prompt is pointing things out I will go and look at it again but I make my own judgment … it might bring up abnormalities that I haven't seen whether they're benign or … nothing but its still nice to have a prompt so that I can look again."

There was also a perception that the CADe machine was more consistent than readers might be:

> "… it's just the fact that its more consistent than you are … because it's a machine."

Readers frequently express the opinion that they are better at 'spotting' some cancers – as having skills or deficiencies in noticing particular types of object within films. This was another area where the CADe machine prompts were seen as useful, as both compensating in some (consistent) way for any individual weaknesses of the reader and as a reminder of 'good practice':

> "My approach tends to be to look for things that I know I'm not so good at … there are certain things that you do have to prompt yourself to look at, one of them being the danger areas."

> "I'd made up my mind about where the cancer was … but I was looking at all these other areas … because one has to look at the other breast from experience because one has to look for the second cancer that maybe difficult to see … and also you're looking for multi-focal cancer."

Amongst the weaknesses identified by readers was the distracting effects of too many prompts:

> "This is quite distracting … there's an obvious cancer there (pointing) but the computer's picked up a lot of other things … there's so many prompts … especially benign calcifications … you've already looked and seen there are lots of benign calcs."

The machine was also seen to prompt the 'wrong' things – benign features or artefacts of the mammogram production process:

> "… what the computer has picked up is benign … it may even be talcum powder … I'm having trouble seeing the calc its picked up there … (pointing). I can only think it's an artefact on the film (a thin line at the edge of the film)."

At the same time, the machine was seen to be missing obvious prompts that raised wider issues to do with trusting and 'understanding' the machine:

> "That's quite a suspicious mass on the CC … I'm surprised it didn't pick it up on the oblique. (Points to area) I'm surprised the computer didn't spot it … it's so spiky … I'd definitely call that back."

> "I'm surprised the computer didn't pick that up … my eye went to it straight away."

In documenting the reactions to the prompts above, it is interesting that the need to *account for* the prompt – even if it is dismissed – distracts the reader. Evidently, the machine does not appear to be capable of reciprocating the perspective of the skilled practitioner. In other words, its 'docile' prompts call attention to features that the readers have decided are not important enough to merit attention. Nevertheless, for readers, the fact that the machine prompts for features other than candidate cancers is still in need of account.

Reading work: 'worldly interpretations' and 'professional vision'

We have noted elsewhere (Hartswood, Procter, Rouncefield and Slack, 2002) how readers make use of 'worldly interpretations' (Driessen, 1997) of the significance of the object – through ideas about 'territories of normal appearance' and 'incongruity procedures' (Sacks, 1972). Just as Sacks explicates how police officers spot criminals attempting to 'pass' as normal persons, readers are able to spot abnormalities within mammograms: what is normal is contingent on its presence in a particular site and time. Just as there are people who do not belong in a certain part of the city, there are objects which do not belong in a 'normal' (i.e., non-recallable) mammogram. A reader faced with a set of mammograms where the pectoral muscle is not seen equally on both mammograms will be able to marshal a candidate version of why this is the case – they will be able to suggest, for example, that the woman was difficult to position and then seek confirmatory sources within the ensemble of evidence at their disposal (equally, they might find no such reason and hold the staff responsible for making the mammograms accountable).

Thus, the positioning of an object in a particular area of the breast renders it more suspicious than if it had been elsewhere. At the same time, certain areas within the mammogram are regarded as more difficult than others to interpet and readers particularly orient to them in their reading. As one reader noted:

"I do ... I have areas where I know I'm weak at seeing ... you know ones that you've missed ... one is over the muscle there ... its just because the muscle is there ... if you don't make a conscious effort to look there you tend not to see that bit of breast and the other area is right down in the chest wall – breast and chest wall area ... because in older women the cancers tend to be in the upper outer quadrant so I look in that area very carefully ... it depends on the type of breast really ... with some breasts they're very fatty and you can just look and not see something but in other breasts ... so I try to look at the whole film, because I know if I just glance at it and don't make that conscious effort I don't look ... and also these rather big breasts where all the breast tissue gets scrunched up ... that's sometimes difficult."

Readers are sensitive towards the set of criteria for correctness and what is required for the satisfaction of the maxims that constitute it:

"My approach tends to be to look (positively?) for things that I know I'm not so good at ... there are certain things that you do have to prompt yourself to look at, one of them being the danger areas."

Readers are also aware of the work that they have done over the course of a day and the reasonableness of their finding or not finding recallable objects therein:

"Paranoia can set in if I have a large number of films that have passed as normal – might think 'what have I missed?'"

"If you get to the end of a session, the end of a pile of reporting and you haven't recalled anything, then you think 'this is ... maybe I've missed something' then in the next bunch you find that you will recall every other one. So, it averages out."

We would also stress the self-reflective nature of readers' behaviour. Readers know about their own strengths and weaknesses (in one centre a reader is referred to as 'the calcium king' because of his ability to detect calcifications; a member of another centre is referred to as 'Mrs Blobby' because of her ability to detect lesions in dense areas).

As so far described, the work of reading mammograms has the appearance of an individualised task. However, our earlier studies have shown that it has significant collaborative dimensions that are important for its reliable performance (Hartswood, Procter, Rouncefield and Slack, 2002). Reading mammograms is a thoroughgoingly social enterprise and is achieved in, and through, the making available of features that are relevant to the community of readers. It is for this reason that we turn to the work of Goodwin and, in particular, his notion of 'professional vision' (1994), to explicate the social, intersubjectively available nature of reading work. Goodwin suggests that professional vision might be thought of as follows:

"Discursive practices are used by members of a profession to shape events in the domains subject to their professional scrutiny. The shaping process creates the objects of knowledge that become the insignia of a profession's craft: the theories, artifacts, and bodies of expertise that distinguish it from other professions. Analysis of the methods used by members of a community to build and contest the events that structure their lifeworld contributes to the development of a practice-based theory of knowledge and action." (1994, p. 606).

Goodwin's analysis is based on an ethnographic study of field archaeologists and shows how, in what is a complex 'semiotic field' (Goodwin, 2000a; 2000b), archaeologists are able to find and make observable-reportable features such as post holes through their action on and scrutiny of a piece of ground. How one "establishes a figure in what is quite literally a very amorphous ground" (Goodwin, 1994:610) requires that features in that ground are made visible and accountable, in the case of archeology, by circling the surrounding dirt with a trowel. "It is in this way that the perceptual field provided by the dirt is enhanced in a work-relevant way by human action on it" (op cit:611). As Goodwin notes, it is through coding, highlighting and "producing and articulating material representations" that participants build professional vision. Professional vision is a way of seeing, a technique for making work relevant features available, making them stand out from the rest of the field and accounting for just what they are in and as a part of this or that domain of scrutiny.

As with archaeology, so with mammography: a reader has to learn how to interpret the features on the mammogram and what they mean, as well as how to find them. We have described how readers employ a number of techniques for making features visible: these 'repertoires of manipulation' make the area one on which to perform an analysis of the feature and come to a formulation of what it is or might be. Methods for doing this include using the magnifying glass; adopting particular search patterns:

> "Start at top at armpit … come down … look at strip of tissue in front of armpit … then look at bottom ... then behind each nipple ... the middle of the breast."

As we saw in the summary of the trial observations, readers also attempt to 'get at' a lesion by measuring with rulers, pens or hands from the nipple in order to find a feature in the arc; comparing in the opposite view; aligning scans; looking 'behind' the scans; 'undressing lesions' by tracing strands of fibrous tissues into and out of the lesion area and so on. Such features are not work arounds, but an integral part of the ecology of practice built up in and as a part of doing reading mammograms. That is to say, such practices are constitutive of the discipline. We should keep in mind Garfinkel et al's notion of the 'potters object' here: it is the 'intertwining of worldly objects and embodied practices' (Garfinkel et al., 1981:165) that realises – literally makes real for all practical purposes – the accountable decisions of the reader. In and of itself, the mammogram is not enough – it is a start, but it is only realised as an 'increasingly definite thing' (*idem*) through the practical actions undertaken. That is to say, it is "real in and as of inquiry's hands on occasions." (*idem*).

Such manipulations should not be thought of as 'private' – merely there to facilitate the single reader's interpretation of the case at hand – but rather, and also, they are the means that readers routinely use to make features within, and interpretations of, the mammogram available and accountable to others. This is what we mean when we say that they are 'constitutive of the discipline' – they are significant in particular ways that are readily intelligible to other film readers in and through their common socialization as readers. Similarly, and as we noted above, readers use annotations as a means of communication with each other through the work of double reading. That a first reader can make an economic mark such as 'calc?' on the reporting form to suggest that a feature has been seen as an example of a calcification, whilst, at the same time, signaling the first reader's uncertainty and prompting the second reader to examine the region, demonstrates the richness and power of these manipulations given readers' professional vision.

Finding order in the machine

It is important to note that the CADe machine should not be taken to make things less uncertain – decisions still have to be made and these fall to the readers. The prompts are docile in that their character is simply to prompt as opposed to say what should be done. In the trial observations we see that readers attempt to ascertain what a prompted feature is. That a prompt occurs is a meaningful thing, but what to do about it is still a readers' matter. There is still a deal of sense-making to be done in order to account for what the machine is showing as accountably this or that feature, warranting this or that decision. In other words, the machine still requires the professional vision of the reader to remedy prompts as what they accountably are. The following extracts of readers' commentaries give some indication of this concept:

"I'm having trouble seeing the calc it's picked up there (pointing). I can only think its an artifact on the film (a thin line at the edge of the film)."

"... just making sure there's nothing the other side (using fingers) and there is ... a bit of chalk but it's harmless.

(aligns scans) (using fingers) "so what I thought was an asymmetry is probably completely OK."

In each case, we find that the reader makes what is seen or prompted accountable in and through the embodied practices of professional vision. That a mammogram feature or a prompt is there is not, of itself, constitutive of a lesion or other accountable thing, it must be worked up through these embodied practices and ratified in the professional domain of scrutiny. The machine knows nothing of what it is to be a competent, professional reader and what it is to look for features in a mammogram beyond its algorithms – that is self evident – and the reader must 'repair' what the machine shows, making it accountable in and through their professional vision. Readers' professional vision turns on their being a competent practitioner, their ability to distinguish between 'normal' and 'abnormal' features of a mammogram. This is, as we have shown, a thoroughgoingly social procedure and as such something that the machine cannot be a part of.

Beyond its algorithms, the machine cannot account for what it has and has not prompted, it cannot be queried as colleagues (informally or formally) routinely are in normal screening work. It is here, then, that the machine runs into problems – its docile prompts render it a 'dumb colleague'. Put simply, when the machine draws attention to something, what it has prompted for may be clear, but the basis for saying what it has drawn attention to is different: the machine is limited to its algorithms, while readers can make sense of the 'prompt' of a colleague through their intersubjectively constituted professional vision. The machine is impoverished in terms of what it can do *qua* colleague – it is not just that a colleague can be interrogated, but that the manner in which they came to their reading can be ascertained, for example, through the repertoires of manipulations. The point is that a colleague's reading is artfully accomplished and accountably artful in character whereas the machine is limited to its algorithms. Added to this is the notion that colleagues have an idea of the artful practices of finding features in mammograms, whereas the machine's findings are relatively opaque precisely because they rely upon algorithms.

The fact that the CADe machine did not always behave as readers expected, directs us to try to understand how readers made sense of its actions. We found a variety of responses. Readers were sometimes baffled by false prompts, others they were able to rationalise by devising explanations of the machine's behaviour that were grounded in the properties of the mammogram image – e.g., that it was talcum powder, or an artefact of the developing process. In yet other cases, readers came up with explanations of the machine's behaviour that were grounded in incorrect notions of its capabilities. As we have argued elsewhere, how readers make sense of the CADe machine's behaviour influences how they use its prompts to inform their decision-making (Hartswood and Procter, 2000) and may have implications for its dependable use. This, in turn, points to general issues concerning trust – users' perception of the reliability of the evidence generated by decision aids – and how trust is influenced by users' capacity for making sense of how the decision aid behaves.

CADe tools draw attention to features on the mammogram by use of a prompt. The aim is then for the reader to examine the prompted region to see if the prompt indicates something they may have overlooked. The reader should use her own judgment (and was instructed to do so as part of the trial protocol) as to whether the prompted region contains a feature and whether that feature is benign or malignant. For a CADe tool to be used in this way, two conditions must hold. First, readers should not use the machine to inform their judgment as to whether a feature exists or is benign or malignant. Second, the reader should take the given prompts seriously enough to warrant examining the prompted regions. It would appear that this account encompasses a straightforward type of trust in relation to the machine, however, in practice we find that the situation is more complex. If we unpack the work involved in trusting the machine there are various ways in which the prompts are made accountable. First, there is the machine's biography – readers' accumulated experience of how the machine responds to different sorts of objects within the image – and second, there is what readers might reasonably expect the machine to prompt if they were to be given some understanding of how the machine works. Relying solely on either of these ways of accounting can lead to mistaken views about how prompts should be interpreted.

The question, of course, is how *do* readers construct, achieve or *make* sense of the machine? Following Schutz, we might argue that readers render mammograms intelligible using a mosaic of 'recipe knowledge': "a kind of organisation by habits, rules and principles which we regularly apply with success." (Schutz, 1964:73). While the common experiences and rules embodied in the 'mosaic' are always open to potential revision they are, nevertheless, generally relied upon for all practical purposes as furnishing criterion by which adequate sense may be assembled and practical activities – reading the mammogram – realised. Of course, in everyday interaction with colleagues any breakdown in sense is rapidly repaired and 'what is going on' readily understood.

But when the other participant in the interaction is a computer, difficulties can arise as readers (in this case) characteristically rush to premature and often mistaken conclusions about what has happened, what is happening, what the machine 'meant', what the machine 'is thinking', and so on. The problem is, of course, that the machine provides no such account of its actions. As Dourish (2001) writes:

"In just the same way as they approach all other activities, they (users) need to be able to decide what to do in order to get things done. In everyday interaction ... accountability is the key feature that enables them to do this. The way that activities are organised makes their nature available to others; they can be seen and inspected, observed and reported. But this feature – the way that actions are organized – is exactly what is hidden by software abstractions. Not by accident either but by design ... the information that is hidden is information about how the system is doing what it does, how the perceived action is organised." (Dourish, 2001: 83)

"It requires a technical approach that provides three primary features. First we need to find a way to ensure that the account that is offered of the system's behaviour – a representation of that behaviour – is strongly connected to the behaviour that it describes ... Second, we need to find a way to allow this representation to be tied to the action in such a way that the account emerges along with the action rather than separately from it ... Third, we need to ensure that the account that is offered is an account of the current specific behaviour of the system." (Dourish, 2001:85)

While it might be desirable to make a CADe machine 'self-accounting', or 'technomethodological' (Dourish and Button, 1998), in practice this may be the more complex route. While it is certainly possible to conceive of richer representations of the machine's behaviour than the bare prompts it currently furnishes, it is an open question as to whether such representations could be sufficiently contexted in the manner that would enable readers to use them in any meaningful sense. It seems to us that such representations are not accounts in themselves but *resources* for the realisation of accounts by society members. We argue that even a series of representations from which readers could choose may not provide sufficient detail to answer 'why that now?' types of question. At the very least, the provision of such accounts must be complemented by the engagement of readers and CADe developers with the machine over time – where a formulation of what has happened and how things came to this at this time is provided.

In this trial, readers were given only a brief explanantion of the image analysis algorithms used in the machine and, arguably, a more detailed explanation would have been beneficial. It is common for such algorithms to consist of a number of stages where the outputs of one feed into the inputs of the next. An ill-defined lesion detection algorithm, for example, might look for 'blobs' in an image and then decide on some other criteria to actually prompt. Clearly, a negative decision by the machine may be due to the failure of either of these stages. So, if a reader has identified a feature that they are then unsure about recalling and then make a decision on the basis of the absence of the prompt, then the weight that could be given to machine's 'decision' in this respect could depend on whether the candidate blob was discarded at stage 1 or 2. In other words, the 'evidence' that a reader presumes they are making use of may be more or less strong in a particular instance. A case may be made for providing readers with additional information about, e.g., how a ill-defined lesion prompts are arrived at – perhaps by making available to the readers details about which features in the mammogram were detected as blobs, so the reader might be able to disambiguate the above situation in specific circumstances. This does not mean that machine would be providing an account for prompts as one might expect an algorithm designer to do – but rather furnishing the resources for a reader to be able to realise an account for themselves for all practical purposes.

Conclusions

Our ethnographic study of the use of the CADe machine in the context of a clinical trial has raised significant questions as to their impact on screening work and, therefore, as to how healthcare technologies should be evaluated. In particular, the artificial character of the clinical trial, divorced from the lived reality of everyday medical work and the various affordances of the workplace casts some doubt on its value for determining the value of healthcare technologies in a (very different) real world setting.

In our study, we find there a number of threads to this argument. First, in everyday practice, readers use more than the mammograms provided on the viewer. They will consult previous mammograms and various documents in the patient's record. Thus, it makes sense to regard the decision as being achieved through the coherent marshalling of ensembles of evidence. That is to say, reading takes place within a familiar, 'known in common' territory of appearances – not just normal appearances, but appearances that will come to this or that, occasioning a recall or no recall decision. There are territories of known appearance which readers encounter during their training and their everyday work: further, these are known about in terms of their implications, but also in terms of the circumstances of their production. Readers are skilled in marshalling these ensembles over time, they know and use information within the corpus and know how it came to be produced: it is precisely because of this diachronically achieved familiarity that they can rely on the information.

Second, when we look at the nature of reading work, we see that it is profoundly social in character: readers interact and come to a collaboratively realised diagnosis of the feature. Readers formulate the essential reasonableness of their work and reflect upon its achievement as a part of the day's work. Calculations of this type – formulating 'where we are' and 'what we have done' – are members' judgments, and we might ask how the CAD machine impacts on this. The CAD machine is engaged in its own algorithm based calculation, but that this is of a very different order to the calculation work readers are engaged in – the machine cannot 'know' that it is prompting too many features and cannot be socialised as a new reader can into 'how we do things around here'. In an attempt to cope with this, readers develop biographies for the machine, suggesting what features it might be good and bad at prompting for: that is to say, readers use their professional vision to account for the machine's strengths and weaknesses by assembling preliminary accounts based on their interactions with the machine over time. It is through practices such as this that the machine might be integrated into the workplace – although how far this can happen in the limited time of clinical trials is a moot point.

Third, the docile nature of the prompts has the consequence of a reader having to make two readings – their own and one of just what the machine might have intended by that which it has prompted. Just as importantly, there is the need to provide an account for what the machine has missed and why. Readers cannot know of the machine's reasons for this as, of course, it has none: the machine is not accountable like human colleagues are and readers need to render it accountable, in and through their own practices of looking at what has been prompted and what this has come to. The work of the CADe machine is stubbornly opaque and in need of remedy to decide what it amounts to for the diagnosis.

Fourth, when considering how trust might be achieved between reader and machine, it is instructive to consider how readers trust one another. Readers are trusted to act in a professionally adequately way, and as part of that their recall decisions are credited as having value and are taken seriously. Thus, when a reader recommends recall, this is taken seriously – and other readers will treat this in a professionally proper way as having the status as a potentially recallable patient. This does not mean to say that the decision would not be contested – but that any contestation would have to be accountable – reasons would have to be furnished that both accord with readers' professional vision in such a way that signal that the candidate diagnosis has been taken seriously. That is: a candidate decision made by a colleague cannot be lightly dismissed in the same way as it might be for a novice. Within readers' professional vision there is space for versions to be contested in a way that does not challenge a reader's status as an adequately competent practitioner. Trust here is not a binary value, but rather it is fine grained. It is not just that decisions by other readers are taken seriously, but that this is done in light of a reader's biography – what it is known that a reader is more or less competent at detecting ('blobby' people, good at calcs etc). Similarly, readers show an awareness of their own strengths and weaknesses and place trust in their own ability accordingly. Trust in other readers is not something that is a given, but rather, it is an ongoing social achievement and is established afresh in and as a part of doing the work of reading. This is not to say that a reader is only treated as good as their last decision (slips and lapses are accountable, but not necessary fatal to judgments that a reader is adequately competent as performance is accepted as being for all practical purposes), but rather in order to be treated as competent, a reader has to continuously demonstrate their competence.

Fifth, there is an important sense in which the readers use the prompts in a way that turns on a biographical familiarity with the machine that has yet to be achieved. What a prompt might mean, what it might come to in certain circumstances is an achievement of knowing the biography of the machine – something that can only be done diachronically. Practically speaking, CADe tool developers must appreciate how it is used in practice, while readers must understand the ways that the machine works to produce the prompts such that they can say 'ah yes, it is doing that because of that reason', for all practical purposes. There is no need for the readers to know in full technical detail the algorithms but, conversely, descriptions of the character 'it just does that' are not satisfactory either. The descriptions of the machine's behaviour might arise in dialogue between developers and readers around the situated uses of the machine. Given that readers develop some understanding of the machine, we may also need to consider and understand how use of machine changes over time. Reader training programmes for CADe tools may need to be designed to provide not only a resource for initial familiarisation, but also to support continued learning and evolving of practices. The issue of change over time also raises some wider issues of evaluation in that many of the benefits of CADe technology are unlikely to be evident for a substantial time after its introduction and adaptation to the particular circumstances of use. Yet, as a part of their 'grammar', clinical trials are set up to investigate evidence of *immediate* benefits.

Sixth, perhaps the most fundamental way that the clinical trials paradigm is divorced from the reality of screening practice is that no account is taken of the routine ways in which readers intersubjectively 'calibrate' decision-making within the clinic, through, *inter alia*, annotations made on the screening reporting form. The impact of this cannot be overstated; it is the intersubjective character of things such as annotations that achieves the practical work of doing mammography. It is precisely here that the CADe machine cannot take part by its very nature; that is to say it cannot collaborate with a reader except in the manner that a signpost collaborates with a traveler in pointing the way. Important questions then are how replacing double reading with CADe assisted single reading will effect the diachronic maintenance of performance previously achieved in large by the informal collaboration between the first and second reader, and what alternative strategies might be employed to facilitate maintenance of professional vision in this scenario?

Finally, our findings raise questions as to whether practice changes new technologies are intended to support are actually achievable. Related to this is the wider issue of how such machines should be designed and implemented (Berg,

1997). As IT systems and artefacts become ubiquitous, and as design becomes more entwined with the complexities of organisational working, so the challenges facing systems designers correspondingly increase. The 'design problem' becomes not so much concerned with the simple creation of new computer tools as it is with the effective integration of IT systems with existing and developing localised work practices. Such 'socio-technical' systems are mutually constituting and adaptive. This effectively takes the 'design problem' beyond the design phase to implementation and deployment, where users must try and apply any new system to their work practice (Hartswood, Procter, Rouncefield and Sharpe 2000).

Acknowledgements

We would like to thank the readers who participated in this study for their time and patience. This work was supported by the UK Engineering and Physical Sciences Research Council under grant number GR/R24517/01 and the ESRC/EPSRC Dependability Interdisciplinary Research Initiative.

References

Bannon, L. (1996): 'Use, design and evaluation: Steps towards an integration', in D. Shapiro, M. Tauber and R. Traunmüller (eds.): *The Design of Computer Supported Cooperative Work and Groupware Systems*, North-Holland, pp 423-444.

Berg, M. (1997): *Rationalising Medical Work: Decision Support techniques and Medical Practices*, Cambridge: MIT Press.

Blanks, R., Wallis, M. and Moss, S. (1998): 'A comparison of cancer detection rates achieved by breast cancer screening programmes by number of readers, for one and two view mammography: results from the UK National Health Service breast screening programme', *Journal of Medical Screening*, vol. 5, no. 4, pp. 195-201.

Dourish, P. and Button, G. (1998): 'On "Technomethodology": Foundational relationships between Ethnomethodology and System Design', *Human-Computer Interaction* vol. 13, no. 4, pp. 395-432.

Dourish, P. (2001): *Where The Action Is: The Foundations of Embodied Interaction*, MIT Press, Cambridge Mass.

Driessen, J. (1997): 'Worldly Interpretations of a Suspicious Story', *Ethnographic Studies*, vol. 1, no. 2.

Garfinkel, H, Lynch, M. and Livingston, E. (1981): 'The Work of a Discovering Science Construed with Materials from the Optically Discovered Pulsar', *Philosophy of the Social Sciences*, vol. 11, pp. 131-158.

Garfinkel, H. and Wieder, L. (1992): 'Two Incommensurable, Asymmetrically Alternate Technologies of Social Analysis', in Watson, G. and Seiler, S.M (eds.): *Text in Context: Contributions to Ethnomethodology*, New York: Sage, pp. 175-206.

Goodwin, C. (1994): 'Professional Vision', *American Anthropologist*, vol. 96, pp. 606-633.

Goodwin, C. (2000a): 'Action and Embodiment within Situated Human Interaction', *Journal of Pragmatics*, vol. 31, pp. 1489-1522.

Goodwin, C. (2000b): 'Practices of Seeing: Visual Analysis: An Ethnomethodological Approach', in T. van Leeuwen and C. Jewitt (eds.): *Handbook of Visual Analysis*, London: Sage, pp. 157-82.

Hartland, J. (1993): 'The Use of Intelligent Machines for Electrocardiograph Interpretation', in G. Button, (ed.): *Technology in Working Order*, London: Routledge.

Hartswood, M., Procter, R. and Williams, L. (1998): 'Prompting in practice: How can we ensure radiologists make best use of Computer-Aided Detection Systems?', in Karssemeijer, N. et al. (eds.): *Proceedings of the Fourth International Workshop on Digital Mammography*, Nijmegen, Netherlands, June 7th-10th. Kluwer Academic Publishers.

Hartswood, M., Procter, R., (2000): 'Computer-aided Mammography: A Case Study of Error Management in a Skilled Decision-Making Task', *Topics in Health Information Management*, vol. 20, no. 4, pp. 38-54.

Hartswood, M., Procter, R., Rouncefield, M. and Sharpe, M. (2000): 'Being There and Doing IT in the Workplace: A Case Study of a Co-Development Approach in Healthcare', in T. Cherkasky, J. Greenbaum, J. and P. Mambery (eds.): *Proceedings of the CPSR/IFIP WG 9.1 Participatory Design Conference,* New York, November 28th-December 1st, pp. 96-105.

Hartswood, M., Procter, R., Rouncefield, M. and Slack, R. (2002): 'Performance Management in Breast Screening: A Case Study of Professional Vision and Ecologies of Practice', *Journal of Cognition, Technology and Work*, vol. 4, no. 2, pp. 91-100.

Heathfield, H. and Wyatt, J. (1993): 'Philosophies for the design and development of clinical decision support systems', *Methods of Information in Medicine*, vol. 32, no. 1, pp. 1-8.

Heathfield, H. and Buchan I. (1996): 'Letters: Current evaluations of information technology in health care are often inadequate', *BMJ* 1996, vol. 313, pp. 1008.

Hughes, J., King, V., Rodden, T. and Anderson, R. (1994): 'Moving Out from the Control Room: Ethnography and Systems Design', in *Proceedings of the ACM Conference on Computer-Supported Cooperative Work*, ACM Press, pp. 429-439.

Sacks, H. (1972): 'Notes on the Police Assessment of Moral Character', in D. Sudnow (ed.): *Studies in Social Interaction*, NewYork:Free Press, pp. 280-93.

Schütz, A. (1964): 'The Problem of Rationality in the Social World', in *Collected Papers, Volume Two, Studies in Social Theory*, Den Haag: Martinus Nijhoff.

Suchman, L. (1995): 'Making Work Visible', *Communications of the ACM*, vol. 38, no. 9, pp. 56-64.

Warren-Burhenne, L., Wood, S. and D'Orsi, C. (2000): 'Potential contribution of computer-aided detection to the sensitivity of screening mammography', *Radiology*, vol. 215, pp. 554-62.

Index of Authors